# Globalization in Question

## THIRD EDITION

Paul Hirst, Grahame Thompson and
Simon Bromley

polity

First published in 2009 by Polity Press
Reprinted 2009, 2010, 2012 (twice), 2013, 2015, 2016

Polity Press
65 Bridge Street
Cambridge CB2 1UR, UK

Polity Press
350 Main Street
Malden, MA 02148, USA

ISBN-13: 978-0-7456-4151-5
ISBN-13: 978-0-7456-4152-2(pb)

A catalogue record for this book is available from the British Library.
Typeset in 10 on 11.5 pt Times Ten
by SNP Best-set Typesetter Ltd, Hong Kong
Printed and bound in the United States by RR Donnelley

For further information on Polity, visit our website: www.politybooks.com

# Contents

# Figures

# Tables

# Preface

When Paul Hirst and I embarked upon the first edition of *Globalization in Question* in the mid-1990s we had firmly in our sights the then emerging debate about the 'end of the national state'. Globalization, it was suggested, had fatally undermined the possibility of sensibly deploying the category of the nation-state, since national frontiers were no longer a reality that made sense. Unconstrained market forces and transnational political movements were imposing their own logic on the global system, sweeping away the constraints of national politics and creating a new political and economic order beyond the control of traditional nation-state-centred actors.

As the third edition is published thirteen years later, it is perhaps surprising that this fundamental issue still remains at the heart of the debate over globalization. Paul Hirst and I were designated 'sceptics' in this debate: we wanted to reassert the possibility of continued domestically based regulatory initiatives that could have an impact, and the possibilities of managing the international order that placed the nation-state at the centre of such a multilateral governance system. At its heart, this argument still forms the central one of this new edition, though newly nuanced and updated to take account of events that have often shaken the world since. And this restatement of the argument has been aided by my new writing colleague Simon Bromley, who now becomes the third co-author with this edition. When Paul Hirst died suddenly in June 2003, he and I were then actively planning a third edition. His death interrupted that project and it was put on hold for several years. Needless to say, I was delighted when my work colleague Simon Bromley agreed to become a co-author as the thought of finally generating the third edition re-emerged in early 2007. In our conversations Paul had always been a great champion of Simon: he recognized his sharp intellect and incisive analytical skills. Broadly speaking Simon has concentrated on redrafting the more 'political' chapters dealing with the state capacities and governance issues, while I have concentrated on the historical and more 'economic' ones. This more or less mirrored the original division of labour between Paul and myself.

But we both take collective responsibility for the final product. All chapters have been closely scrutinized for necessary changes and consistency. Most of them have been extensively revised or entirely rewritten, though some more so than others. Chapter 1 lays out the broad thesis of the book and characterizes various senses of globalization that have appeared in the debate. In addition, we have responded to the criticism that our characterization of strong globalization represents a 'straw man' and we have redrafted the contents section. Chapter 2 has been extensively updated and extended. Chapter 3 has been widely pruned, but what remains is more or less as before, though updated. Chapter 4 has been completely revamped and updated. Chapter 5 has been effectively rewritten as a new chapter, while chapter 6 is a completely new addition. Chapter 7 is also a substantially new chapter and chapter 8 has been extensively rewritten to take account of current debates. At the end of chapter 1 the substantive concerns of these chapters are outlined in more detail.

All in all, we think this represents a substantial update of the argument and introduces extensive new empirical material that backs up that argument. The book has always been centrally concerned with providing *evidence* for its arguments, not just assertions of them, and this approach has been adopted again. Too often wild claims are made about the processes and effects of globalization without these being grounded in adequate empirical justification. Of course, empirical evidence is never neutral and always requires judgement and interpretation, but as a minimum careful generation and scrutiny of evidence is absolutely vital.

This edition was being prepared during a time of some important changes and events in the international system. We are perhaps seeing several developments that are straining against the conception of a stable and truly globalized system. There has been a growth of populist left movements in Latin America that threaten a withdrawal from the full extent of globalization's programmatic embrace. In addition, Russia has begun to reassert its independence from 'global forces' as it takes advantage of high energy prices and increased demand. The idea that China and India are going to bow down and roll over before the full rigours of the global, liberal marketplace is hardly credible. And the USA is taking an increasingly unilateral line on many aspects of global relationship and governance. As far as trade policy is concerned, the apparent collapse of the Doha Round of negotiations puts in doubt the centrality of the WTO and further trade liberalization as an end in itself (rather than as a means to an end).

All this has developed over the past few years alongside a serious disruption of the international financial system with the 2007 'credit crunch'. This saw essentially national regulatory systems reasserting their traditional roles as guardians of the 'lender-of-last-resort' function to shore up their domestic economies. The credit crunch may also have begun the erosion of exotic financial engineering developments associated with hedge funds, private equity and 'structured investment vehicles'. All of these were argued to have emerged from the liberalized and 'global' financial markets of the 1990s and early 2000s. In their place is developing the next problem for the international financial system: sovereign wealth funds. But these also speak to a potential new phase of investment intentions based upon national interest and state control.

None of this should lead us to expect any sudden undoing of the international system, however. But these developments may delay any further genuine globalization. The 'global system' – such that it is – has always been at heart an *international* one. That, anyway, is the argument of this book. Nevertheless, and given this, the underlying sentiment the book expresses is summed up in a slogan that it would do well for all to heed as far as the international system is concerned: 'always expect the unexpected'. Never think that what has gone on in the past, or what seem to be well-entrenched trends and directions of the present, will necessarily extend into the future. This is a basic sceptical and pragmatic lesson which, it is hoped, will be reinforced with the publication of this third edition.

*Grahame F. Thompson*
September 2008

# Abbreviations

| | |
|---|---|
| AB | Appellate Body (of the WTO) |
| APEC | Asia-Pacific Economic Cooperation |
| ASEAN | Association of South-East Asian Nations |
| B2B | business to business |
| B2C | business to consumers |
| BIS | Bank for International Settlements |
| BWS | Bretton Woods system |
| CIS | Commonwealth of Independent States |
| DM | Deutschmark |
| EEC | European Economic Community |
| EMS | European Monetary System |
| EMU | European Monetary Union |
| EU | European Union |
| FDI | foreign direct investment |
| FTA | free trade agreement |
| FTAA | Free Trade Area of the Americas |
| GATT | General Agreement of Tariffs and Trade |
| GCC | global commodity chain |
| GDP | gross domestic product |
| GPC | global production chain |
| GVC | global value chain |
| HDD | hard disk drive |
| ICT | information and communication technology |
| ILE | interlinked economy |
| ILO | International Labour Organization |
| IMF | International Monetary Fund |
| IOSCO | International Organization of Securities Commissions |

| | |
|---|---|
| LDC | less developed country |
| M&A | merger and acquisition |
| MDC | more developed country |
| MENA | Middle East and North Africa |
| MNC | multinational corporation |
| NAFTA | North American Free Trade Agreement |
| NATO | North Atlantic Treaty Organization |
| NGO | non-governmental organization |
| NIC | newly industrializing country |
| NIE | newly industrializing economy |
| OECD | Organization for Economic Cooperation and Development |
| OTC | over-the-counter |
| R&D | research and development |
| RULC | relative unit labour cost |
| S&A | subsidiary and affiliate |
| SWF | sovereign wealth fund |
| TFP | total factor productivity |
| TNC | transnational corporation |
| UNCTAD | United Nations Conference on Trade and Development |
| WSA | World Systems Analysis |
| WTO | World Trade Organization |

# Acknowledgments

The publisher would like to acknowledge permission to reproduce the following copyright material:

Page 29, 'Journal of Economic Literature', Maddison 1987, table A-21, p. 694; 31 & 32, *An Atlas of International Migration* by Aaron Segal, (London: Hans Zell Publishers, 1993, pp. 21 & 23). Reproduced with the permission of Hans Zell Publishers, on behalf of the estate of Aaron Segal. Copyright © The estate of Aaron Segal; 33, A.M. Taylor and J.G. Williamson, 'Convergence in the age of mass migration', *European Review of Economic History* Volume 1(01): pp27–63, (1997), Cambridge University Press; 33, *The World Economy: A Millennial Perspective*, A. Maddison, 2001. OECD, Paris; 51, BIS 1996–7, table V.1, p. 79, www.bis.org; 51, table 10, p 33, *An assessment of financial reform in OECD countries*, Edey and Hviding, OECD Economics Department, Working Paper 154, 1995, OECD, Paris; 52, table 1, [Title], [Page], [Book Title], [Author], 1998, OECD, Paris; 53, IMF, *International Financial Statistics Yearbook*, 186 and 1997; 55, *Financial Market Trends* (OECD), no. 55 (June 1993); no. 58 (June 1994); no. 69 (Feb. 1988), p. 49; 56, *Financial Market Trends* (OECD), no. 55 (June 1993), table 3, p. 26; BIS 1998, table VIII.5, p. 155; 57, European Union 1997a, chart 18, p. 15; 72, UNCTAD World Investment Report 2005, UNCTAD. Geneva and New York, Figure I.1, p. 3; 73, OECD Economic Globalization Indicators, OECD 2005, Figure A.8.1, p. 30; 80, Alan M. Rugman, *The Regional Multinationals, MNEs and 'Global' Strategic Management*, 2005, Cambridge University Press, Cambridge; 87, Nikolaos Karagiannis & Michael Witter eds., *The Caribbean Economies in an Era of Free Trade*, 2004, Ashgate; 92, OECD Employment Outlook 2007, Figure 3.3, p. 112; 96, Louis W. Pauly and Simon Reich, 'National Structures and Multinational Corporate Behavior: Enduring Differences in the Age of Globalization', International Organization, 51:1 (Winter 1997) © 1997 by the IO Foundation and the Massachusetts Institute of Technology; 117, J. Fagerberg, 'Technology and Competitiveness', *Oxford Review of Economic Policy*, Autumn 1996, page 41, by permission of Oxford University Press; 132, Winters and Yusuf, 2006, table 1.1, World Bank and World Development Report 2006, World Bank; 132, Winters and Yusuf, 2006, table 1.3, World Bank; 148, Based on data from Bourguignon, F. and Morrisson, C., 'Inequality Among World citizens: 1820–1992', in The American Economic Review, vol.92, no.4, September 2002, pp.727–744; 150, Sala-i-Martin, X., The Disturbing 'Rise' of global Income Inequality, New York: Columbia university Press, Fig 12; 162, Derived from Princeton Institute for International and Regional Studies (2006) *Data and Selected Images from the GKG Project*: Princeton, NJ; 164, WTO International Trade Statistics 2005, derived from table III.3, p. 40; 164, adapted from Heathcote and Perri (2002), table 6, p. 7; 168, Cai, F. & Warnock, F.E. (2004), International Diversification at Home and Abroad, International Finance Discussion Papers 2004–793, Figures 1 & 2; 169, Derived from: Sassen (2006) table 5.4, p. 258; World Federation of Exchanges Annual Report 2006, table 1.3, p. 68; table 1.5, p. 71; table 2.2, p. 89; table 2.1, p. 88 and table 2.5, p. 92; 172, Eichengreen, B. & Luengnaruemilchai, P. (2006), 'Bond markets as conduits of capital flows: How does Asia compare?', table 2, p. 27, IMF Working Paper wp/09/238, IMF, Washington; 185 & 186, Adapted from Levy Yeyati, 'Liquidity Insurance in a Financially Dollarized Economy', NEBR Working Paper 12345, June 2006, p. 31 and p. 25, table 1; 186, calculated from Levy Yeyati (2006), table 2, p. 73.

# 1

# Introduction: The Contours of Globalization

All old-established national industries have been destroyed or are daily being destroyed. They are dislodged by new industries, whose introduction becomes a life and death question for all civilized nations, by industries that no longer work up indigenous raw material, but raw material drawn from the remotest zones; industries whose products are consumed, not only at home, but in every quarter of the globe. In place of the old wants, satisfied by the productions of the country, we find new wants, requiring for their satisfaction the products of distant lands and climes. In place of old local and national seclusion and self-sufficiency, we have intercourse in every direction, universal inter-dependency of nations.

(K. Marx and F. Engels, *The Communist Manifesto*, 1850, repr. in *Marx and Engels Selected Works*, London: Lawrence & Wishart, 1968, p. 39.)

The inhabitant of London could order by telephone, sipping his morning coffee in bed, the various products of the whole earth, in such quantity as he might see fit, and reasonably expect their early delivery upon his doorstep; he could at the same moment and by the same means adventure his wealth in the natural resources and new enterprises in any quarter of the world, and share, without exertion or even trouble, in their prospective fruits and advantages; or he could decide to couple the security of his fortunes with the good faith of the townspeople of any substantial municipality in any continent that fancy or information might recommend. He could secure forthwith, if he wished it, cheap and comfortable means of transit to any country or climate without passport or other formality.

(J. M. Keynes, *The Economic Consequences of the Peace*. London: Macmillan, 1919, pp. 6–7)

## The basic argument

Globalization has become a fashionable concept in the social sciences, a core dictum in the prescriptions of management gurus, and a catch-phrase for journalists and politicians of every stripe. It is widely asserted that we live in an era in which the greater part of social life is determined by global processes, in which national cultures, national economies, national borders and national territories are dissolving. Central to this perception is the notion of a rapid and recent process of economic globalization. A truly global economy is claimed to have emerged or to be in the process of emerging, in which distinct national economies and, therefore, domestic strategies of national economic management are increasingly irrelevant. The world economy has globalized in its basic dynamics, it is dominated by uncontrollable market forces, and it has as its principal economic actors and major agents of change truly transnational corporations that owe allegiance to no nation-state and locate wherever on the globe market advantage dictates.

This image is so powerful that it has mesmerized analysts and captured political imaginations. But is it the case? This book is written with a mixture of scepticism about global economic and political processes and optimism about the possibilities of control of the international economy and about the continued viability of national political strategies. One key effect of the concept of globalization has been to paralyse radical reforming national strategies, to see them as unfeasible in the face of the judgement and sanction of global markets. If, however, we face economic changes that are more complex and more equivocal than the extreme globalists argue, then the possibility remains of political strategy and action for national and international control of market economies in order to promote social goals.

We began this investigation, originally in the early 1990s, with an attitude of moderate scepticism. It was clear that much had changed since the 1960s, but we were cautious about the more extreme claims of the most enthusiastic globalization theorists. In particular it was obvious that radical expansionary and redistributive strategies of national economic management were no longer possible in the face of a variety of domestic and international constraints. However, the closer we looked, the shallower and more unfounded became the claims of the more radical advocates of economic globalization. In particular we began to be disturbed by three facts. First, the absence of a commonly accepted model of the new global economy and how it differs from previous states of the international economy. Second, in the absence of a clear model against which to measure trends, the tendency casually to cite examples of the internationalization of sectors and processes as if they were evidence of the growth of an economy dominated by autonomous global market forces. Third, the lack of historical depth and the tendency to portray current changes as unique, without precedent and firmly set to persist long into the future.

To anticipate, as we proceeded, our scepticism deepened until we became convinced that globalization, as conceived by the more extreme globalizers, is largely unfounded. Thus we argue that:

1   the present highly internationalized economy is not unprecedented: it is one of a number of distinct conjunctures or states of the international economy that have existed since an economy based on modern industrial technology began to be generalized from the 1860s. In some respects, the current international economy has only recently become as open and integrated as the regime that prevailed from 1870 to 1914.

2   genuinely transnational companies appear to be relatively rare. Most companies are based nationally and trade regionally or multinationally on the strength of a major national location of assets, production and sales, and there seems to be no major tendency towards the growth of truly global companies.

3   capital mobility has only recently begun shifting investment and employment from the advanced to the developing countries, and here it is just a very few of the emerging economies that are benefiting. Foreign direct investment (FDI) is still highly concentrated among the advanced industrial economies, and the Third World remains marginal in both investment and trade, a small minority of newly industrializing countries apart. As we show below, however, the emergence of India and particularly China represents a disruption to this imagery, though as yet it has not significantly shifted the centre of gravity from the already advanced countries.

4   as some of the extreme advocates of globalization recognize, the world economy is far from being genuinely 'global'. Rather trade, investment and financial flows are concentrated in the Triad of Europe, Japan/East Asia and North America, and this dominance seems set to continue. In fact, the growth of supranational regionalization is a trend that is possibly stronger than that of globalization as normally understood.

5   these major economic powers, centred on the G8 with China and India, thus have the capacity, especially if they coordinate policy, to exert powerful governance pressures over financial markets and other economic tendencies. Global markets are thus by no means beyond regulation and control, even though the current scope and objectives of economic governance are limited by the divergent interests of the great powers and the economic doctrines prevalent among their elites.

These and other more detailed points challenging the globalization thesis will be developed in later chapters. We should emphasize that this book challenges the strong version of the thesis of economic globalization, because we believe that, without the notion of a truly globalized economy, many of the other consequences adduced in the domains of culture and politics would either cease to be sustainable or become less threatening. Hence most of the discussion here is centred on the international economy and the evidence for and against the process of globalization. However, the book is written to emphasize the possibilities of national and international governance, and as it proceeds issues of the future of the nation-state and the role of international agencies, regimes and structures of governance are given increasing prominence. But in addition, given one of the intriguing (but also infuriating) aspects of the globalization debate is that the term 'globalization' seems to have an almost infinite capacity to inflate – so that more and more aspects of the modern condition are increasingly drawn under its conceptual umbrella – we have taken the opportunity in this introduction to expand our discussion a little beyond the book's central focus on economic globalization and governance. Globalization is now a term with such a wide embrace that it seems incumbent upon us at least to comment on some of these matters. This we do below, but mainly only in so far as it serves to clarify what this particular book is *not* about.

## Challenges and responses

The third edition of this book is very much a product of the previous two editions. While its basic thesis remains substantially the same – that is, there is an exaggeration of both the extent and the significance of 'globalization' – things have moved on from the previous two editions. In this edition we have tried to capture many of these developments without undermining the basic thesis, to which, as will become clear below, we still hold. Of course, if this volume were being entirely written afresh in early 2008 we would no doubt recast it somewhat differently, and in the rest of this introduction we allude to these recastings. But it seriously concerns us that the strong 'globalization' thesis is now largely and uncritically accepted as the mainstream, whether it be by the public authorities or our academic colleagues. Thus it seems worthwhile – to us at least – to re-emphasize and reinforce the original thesis in the light of the more or less total acquiescence to a strong globalization imagery by all shades of opinion.

For an example of the attitudes of the public authorities one need look no further than the UK Treasury's thinking on 'globalization'. Gordon Brown (the chancellor when the reports alluded to in a moment were written but who subsequently became the prime minister), and the New Labour government more generally, has completely fallen under the spell of the full globalization story. Among a number of reports from the Treasury in the mid-2000s about globalization and the UK economy can be found one titled *Long-Term Global Economic Challenges and Opportunities for the UK* (HM Treasury 2004). This document buys completely into a conventional and uncritical globalization story, for the UK economy and the international economy beyond. It is a great shame that no one from the Treasury seems to have read any critical books and papers produced over the past five years or so that have challenged the full globalization thesis, though admittedly these are few and far between. If, however, they had done so, then the Treasury might have been much better informed of the options facing the UK economy in its relationship with the EU and, indeed, the rest of the world. Instead we have had other documents which just repeat the mantra, and this time directed at telling 'Europe' how it should reform to meet the same undifferentiated global challenges: *Global Europe: Full Employment Europe* (HM Treasury 2005a) and *Responding to Global Economic Challenges: UK and China* (HM Treasury 2005b).

Of course, the academic literature is another matter, but even here a largely acquiescent position is to be found. It is one thing to be sceptical about various uses of the concept of globalization, it is another to explain the widespread development and academic reception of the concept since the 1970s. But the literature on globalization is vast and varied. Although we have deliberately chosen not to rewrite this book so as to summarize and criticize this literature, in part because, given the scale and rate of publication on the topic, that would be a never-ending enterprise, it is perhaps incumbent upon the third edition to address this in part, and to respond to some of the more cogent critics. We begin with the positions and move on to the criticisms and our responses later.

### Alternative globalizations

As pointed out above, it is not our intention to review all the positions in respect to globalization. The following discussion picks on the most notable and forceful of these. By and large these positions take globalization as an accomplished fact, though they all hedge about this in various ways and with various degrees of reservation. And, as will become clear, these alternative positions are not totally exclusive of one another: rather they overlap and merge into one another. We outline these positions here, beginning with those that are furthest from the immediate concerns of this book, gradually moving closer towards those that are nearest to our own perceptions and analytical stance on the globalization debate – which, it should be emphasized, is concerned mainly with its political economy and governance aspects.

1) The first proposition on globalization is one that is furthest from our concerns. In fact, it is one that actually challenges it from what is termed a 'post-colonial perspective'. Often based around avant-garde anthropological and post-structuralist intellectual tendencies, this position works with a number of complex concepts, stressing such aspects as different spatial levels

in the global arena and their imbrications, which involve multiple connections, and relationships, flexibilities, flows, etc. (Ong and Collier 2004; Tsing 2005). These 'assemblages' are argued to be continually dissolving and evolving, producing new and surprising terrains of activity. In this case globalization is treated as an accomplished fact – the consequence of these multiple flows and connections – and one that now needs to be transcended. One of the most forceful of the terms within this perspective is 'planetarity'. This is designed to describe a possible world 'above' the North–South divide, 'beyond' the colonial and the Other, 'outside' of the national and the global (Spivak 2003, chap. 3). The project associated with 'planetarity' involves the development of a certain kind of new analytical language and discourse to express this possible world that lies 'beyond globalization'.

Although it is not directly aligned with the post-colonial discourses, there is a closely associated conception that perceives the global as a series of 'camps' – zones of indistinction and the suspension of the rule of law – that infect the rest of the social order (e.g. Agamben 1998, 2005). One rather pessimistic consequence of this conception is that such zones of indistinction embody the final expression of a degenerate modernity. It can lead to a rather hopeless and disarming response: the global is beyond control, management or regulation.

2) A second characterization is one that does not offer a critique of globalization as such but rather a critique of a particular political appropriation of it. In this case current globalization is expressed as the emergence of a new empire based upon the hegemony of the USA. The USA is considered the only truly global power, and it is using this status, aligned with neo-conservative ideology, to construct a world order in its own image. In doing so it has thrown off the mantle of proceeding through multilateral agreements and compromises with its partners. Instead it has adopted a new strategy of unilateral action, building under its leadership transient 'coalitions of the willing' that vary in composition depending upon the objective at hand. In the section immediately following this one we assess this claim in the context of the idea of imperialism, seen as a possible mode of contemporary global governance.

Somewhat aligned to this position, we would suggest, is one that sees the global arena as made up of a 'clash of civilizations' or as a 'clash of fundamentalisms' (e.g. Huntingdon 1996). The USA is seen as the central defender of Western civilization, thus it is in the forefront of constructing a coalition to reinforce its hegemonic leadership in this respect. But in this case the global is fatally fractured, something we allude to in the comments on the cosmopolitan position discussed below. But this is in no way meant to endorse this position. There may be clashes in the international arena, but for us these are not clashes between such large aggregations as civilizations or fundamentalisms. The problem is whether civilizations or fundamentalisms exist in any seriously homogeneous way such that there could be an organized clash between them. Rather, there would seem to be as many clashes within civilizations (whatever these may be) as between them, and fundamentalisms do not exist as unitary entities either, but are already always riven with rivalries, disputes and indeed armed clashes (as in the case of religious fundamentalist-driven insurgencies in many Middle East contexts). But fundamentalisms are not just religious based; there are also secular fundamentalisms such as extreme neo-liberal market fundamentalism and some animal rights activism (Thompson 2007).

3) A third position on globalization would stress the emergence of a new international cosmopolitanism in the wake of the complex interdependency and integration that characterizes what is seen as the break-up of the Westphalian international system. In this case, new political responses are required to address the deterritorialization of authority in the global system. Very much developed in the shadow of Kant's pamphlet *Perpetual Peace* (Kant [1919] 1990) – which itself was a call to arms for a new world order – this position stresses the role of transnational civil society actors in the formation of global democratic accountability and political responsibility. The most incisive and insistent advocate of this position has been David Held and his co-authors (e.g. Held and McGrew 2002, chap. 9; Held 2004). It is particularly embodied in his call for a 'new global covenant' among the 'democratic peoples' of the globe designed to address the growing democratic deficit he sees as resulting from the leaking of power from sovereign states towards what is at present a highly problematic and unsatisfactorily ungoverned but coordinated international market order.

Again, there is a nuanced and elaborated defence to be made of this position, but we would stress that it is underpinned (at least implicitly) by an acceptance of the full globalization story, otherwise why is there a need for such a radical and new political order? But if – as we would argue is demonstrated by our analysis in the chapters below – there is no complete globalization of the international system, then the 'global' of globalization does not (yet?) exist in this form: there is no single 'cosmos' for cosmopolitanism to address. Against this we would argue that we are still caught in a 'pluriverse' rather than in a 'universe' (e.g. Latour 2004): there remains a set of heavily competing voices in the international system that do not necessarily address one another in a 'common language', and without such a universal language for all to lock into these voices will continue to a large extent to speak past one another (as in the case of fundamentalism briefly mentioned above). Thus we are not in a position to forge such an ambitious global covenant or a global cosmopolitanism. Rather we will have to continue to learn to live with – and within – a certain *disorder* (as outlined later in this introduction), where the best that can be hoped for is ad hoc and limited governance responses to emergent problems combined with fire-fighting 'crises' as they arise, and the installation of prudential regulation in their wake.

4) A fourth take on globalization is to see this as involving the development of networks of cross-cutting relationships in various domains that straddle national borders (Castells 2000). In part this conceives of the system in the light of issues about the role of ICTs in stimulating locational disengagement, and the move towards global standard-setting discussed below. Global standard-setting involves not only the traditional public bodies of international governance but also increasingly fully private or quasi-private actors that both claim and exercise a public power in this respect (Cutler et al. 1999; Cutler 2003). An added aspect to this development is the way 'international governance' is increasingly being rendered into various networked legal forms, something stressed (and celebrated) by Slaughter (2004), but also involving the progressive juridicalization and constitutionalization of the international sphere without a clear single sovereign presence or legitimating authority to sanction these (e.g. Gerber 1994; Jayasuriya 2001; Joerges et al. 2004).

Additionally, we would align this position loosely with one that is tied in with the global conceived in the image of a Luhmannesque-type system and subsystem (non-)integration (Albert et al. 2001; Albert and Hilkermeier 2004). For Niklas Luhmann – the spiritual father of this position – the social order is made up of a series of autonomous spheres of meaning, displaying different 'logics of observation'. These may be economic, political or legal systems, organizational entities or even individuals, each of which orients itself according to its own distinctions, its own constructions of reality and its own observational codes. Here the global system is characterized by overlapping relatively enclosed systems which pose the problem of their macro-level coordination and governance. But the constitutive differentiation of society into (sub)systems means that they all operate according to their own distinctions, thereby continually reproducing new differences as they abut and collide with one another. The best that can be expected from this is loose couplings between different subsystems. This frustrates any attempt at overall coordination or governance by a competent authority. All that is possible is 'self-governance', driven by the enclosed inner logic of each (sub)system. One consequence is that new perturbations, differentiations, irritations, provocations and unexpected events continually arise in the world. This enables Gunther Teubner – a related and leading figure in this style of analysis – to align it with an understanding of the global as a radically differentiated 'polycontextual' space, where territories and national sovereignties are broken apart as contingent events produce a 'global law without a state': a transnational legal order for global markets that has developed outside of national and international law strictly speaking. In turn, this connects to the question of the surrogate juridicalization and constitutionalization of the international sphere as mentioned immediately above (Teubner 1997).

5) Another, and fifth, characterization of the global system places this in the longer historical tradition of Marxist and quasi-Marxist 'World Systems Analysis' (WSA) theories. Originally associated with the names of André Gunder Frank (Frank and Gills 1996), Immanuel Wallerstein (2004) and Giovanni Arrighi (Arrighi and Silver 1999), this position has advanced along several related trajectories, some of which no longer pay particular heed or explicit homage to their historical tradition. The first of these, and the one that continues to pay most respect to its intellectual lineage, is the 'global cities' approach (Sassen 2002; Knox and Taylor 1995; Taylor 2003). Here the global is seen as a continuation of a structured 'centre–periphery' set of exploitative relations involving the emergence of a network of global cities that becomes the new 'centre' of the international system. This network of cities in turn exploits the hinterlands of their locations, which become the new 'semi-peripheries'. And in turn there is a periphery of non-global cities that are also structured into these relationships as the ultimate source of surpluses appropriated by their more powerful neighbours or cousins.

Another variation of this logic, though one that has now somewhat lost its connection to the original WSA approach, is 'global value chain' analysis (GVC). In fact there are a number of alternative formulations of this basic position that address the global economy, including 'global commodity chain' (GCC) and 'global production chain' (GPC) analysis. For those involved in this type of analysis these differences are highly relevant (Gibbon et al. 2008), but for our purposes they can all be treated similarly. Within this perspective, the global is conceived as a series of linked stages in various discrete chains of production and distribution. These chains involve production units, wholesalers, markets, shipping companies, retailers, consumers, etc., all of which serve to link several remote stages into a global production network. This particular position is concerned with how such chains are organized and governed (by producers or retailers in the main) and how this establishes who gets what in the chain of value distribution.

6) The sixth development discussed here would stress the emergence of supra-state regional economic and social configurations or blocs. Typical examples of these would be the EU, NAFTA, Mercosur or the proposed Andean trading bloc, ASEAN or the Asian Free Trade Area, etc. We define and discuss this position in more detail in chapter 6. It involves both *de facto* and *de jure* aspects, which do not necessarily advance at the same pace or in coordination with one another. Thus for our purposes supranational regionalism involves the development of geographically contiguous areas composed of the territories of those nation-states that have either combined in an integrative economic or monetary union or whose economies have evolved into a closely interdependent entity through normal market-based trade and investment integration.

7) The final position is perhaps the most conventional one. It stresses the continuation of multilateral interdependency and integration between essentially independent national economies or societies. This involves dealing with flows of resources across space and time. As will become clear later in the book, we partly endorse this position, but would emphasize the limits to the process, and perhaps the exhaustion of its possibilities under current conditions (chapter 6). Thus while our account is compatible with growing and deepening international connectedness in trade and investment – with an open world economy of interlinked trading nations – it is also sceptical of the continued pertinence of this imagery. So those who see extreme globalizers as one pole of the debate and people who deny globalization as the other, putting themselves conveniently in the sensible middle ground, are thus doing us and the issue a disservice. The issue for us is to 'trouble' both of these conceptions.

These last two positions represent the main ones in contention in current economic debates about globalization, and they raise important questions about their compatibility and governance. Broadly speaking, the point is whether the development of these trading and investment blocs is complementary to the 'multilateralism' of the global system (as embodied in the final position just described), or whether these two processes are in some sense in competition with one another (de Lombaerde 2007; Cooper et al. 2008). Such competition could manifest itself in the trade diversionary aspects of these blocs as opposed to the trade creation aspects, in terms of alternative and discriminatory regulatory initiatives, and in terms of their potential political rivalry. We reserve our own position on this dispute until after the analysis of chapter 6.

What, then, emerges from this description of various positions in the globalization debate, and from our emphasis on the latter two positions in particular? We would suggest that there are now four fairly separate (though connected) senses in which the term 'economic globalization' is commonly used in the academic globalization literature that connects to these positions:

1   to refer to the growth of interdependency and integration by way of the movement or flows of economic resources and activity across distance, space and borders. This is the traditional usage, concentrating upon international trade, investment and migration patterns.
2   to refer to an increase in the sensitivity of movements of key economic variables in any given place to those in another place. The movements of prices of goods, services and assets, rates of change of real variables such as output and employment, and factors such as preferences and technologies may become increasingly aligned across territorially distinct economic spaces.

3   to refer to the growth of processes without a fixed territorial location
    or with little regard to distance. Here it is the emergence of information
    and communication technologies (ICTs) that is focused upon, particu-
    larly the world wide web and internet, but also involving such things as
    telephone traffic or broadcasting.
4   to refer to the growth of interdependency and integration by way of the
    adoption or harmonization of common standards. Clearly, in this case,
    globalization does not need to involve the flow of resources across
    borders since, if all agents adopt a common global standard and operate
    within it, globalization has emerged surreptitiously, so to speak, from
    behind our backs without anyone necessarily noticing it.

It is fair to say that in the current phase of globalization, as issues around
global standard-setting have come to the fore, and as questions of trade
and investment integration recede into the background, the emphasis in
many analyses has shifted from the first of these to the fourth. We examine
in more detail these senses of globalization as the main chapters of the book
unfold. But our overall position is to problematize these conventional
aspects and show how, in the present phase of globalization, none of them
can be taken for granted or accepted as a necessarily accurate characterization of the international system.

## General governance possibilities

Given these brief descriptions of current claims on globalization, how can
we deal with the general issues of the governance of any emergent global
order that they might imply? This issue we tackle in this section, beginning
with the bold claim that the international is now to be understood as governed through the means of a new imperial power.

Clearly, it is possible to run an international system as an *imperial
project*. But this is only one of the 'logics' by which the international arena
can be organized. Such a logic of an imperial system is typified by several
emblematic features: the use of coercive power on the part of the imperialist, its deployment of direct administrative action in the imperial territories,
and the mobilization of local elites as allies in those locations as crucial
supports for the imperial effort. At issue is whether the USA does – or,
indeed, could ever – resort to these features in the modern world. Two
obvious major constraints on any return to imperial rule are the rise of
'nationalism' on the one hand and 'democracy' on the other. Both of these
political ideologies and movements effectively destroyed the imperialisms
of the nineteenth and early twentieth centuries, condemning them as failed
political movements of a past age. Unless these ideologies can be
completely displaced under present circumstances it is very unlikely
that 'imperialism' could return. In addition, the USA has been unable

seriously to mobilize local supporters for its efforts at direct rule in any but a very few parts of the world, notably in the Middle East, and even here such support is weak and highly unstable. Thus, on this account at least, it is impossible for the USA to be described as a new imperialist or for it to become one. Thus might it be wise quickly to forget all those many books and articles that combine 'imperialism' with 'the USA' in their titles?

So what is the nature of the emerging international governance system if not an imperial one? Three other possible formations or logics present themselves.

The first of these is as a *hegemonic project*. Under this formulation the hegemon provides 'leadership' but does not coercively rule directly. The hegemon organizes 'consent' through negotiation and compromise with the other parties in the system, and must also compromise itself as a result. In so doing it often finds itself providing the major 'public goods' for that system – such as a security and defence umbrella, or the main international currency for trade and investment. Clearly, historically, this form of organizing the international system has proved very expensive for the hegemon (as well as for any imperial power, of course). It more or less bankrupted the USA in the post-war period up until the mid-1970s (before the next system kicked in, which is described in a moment). Inasmuch as a hegemonic project in the military sense exists at present, it is probably best described as the formation of 'coalitions of the willing'. But, as the USA has found, these are difficult to stabilize under present circumstances, backed as they are by its insistence on a basically unilateralist military stance.

A second possible logic is provided in the form of a *multilateralism*. This involves the formal equality of partners in any arrangement (if not always their actual equality, of course). These partners then negotiate and bargain between themselves to generate collective agreement or consensus as outcomes. It often involves self-policing by the partners to secure and monitor the implementation of these outcomes. Despite its somewhat discredited nature among current US neo-conservatives, this system has the great advantage that it is cheap to run. Because of this – and despite the neo-conservative distaste for it – countries will not give up their commitment to multilateralism easily, including, one suspects, the USA itself in the longer run.

Along with *imperialism* then, *hegemonic projects* and *multilateralism* amount to the three conventional approaches to running an international system that are recognized by contemporary scholarship. While we have emphasized their different 'logics' above, they, of course, overlap in the actual conduct of international organization and rule.

But there is a third contender to *imperialism* per se, which we would argue is possible as at least a semi-permanent logic of running an international system, and that is as a *durable disorder*. This involves a patchwork of overlapping, often competitive, jurisdictions and territories, where there are few public goods provided and only minimal collective endeavours. It is typified by the prevalence of unruly 'warrior' politics and ad hoc interventions. It leads to the 'enclavization' of public and private life. This could also see the emergence of a 'leopard spot' economy – where small, isolated patches of prosperity and wealth are set among a more generalized inequality and economic failure. In many ways this strikes a chord as an image about the present international condition, though, as hinted at above, only if combined with other images such as multilateralism. The main point would be that there is no single logic to the international system that expresses an adequately homogeneous characterization. The international is made up of varying aspects existing in multiple sites of cooperation and overlapping configurations.

## Criticisms and responses

One of the main critical methodological points made in relationship to the original formulation of globalization in the previous editions of this book concerns the nature of globalization as a 'process' and globalization as a 'state of affairs'. In the discussion by Held et al. (1999) and Perraton (2001) of the approach adopted by the original edition of this book it was categorized as 'traditionalist' – which became the main way in which that approach is now understood. But these authors also suggest that it adopted a single 'end-state' conception of globalization, a single 'equilibrium outcome'. In contrast to this, it was suggested that the proper way to understand globalization was as a *process* with no single outcome, but rather with several possible trajectories dependent upon the dynamic of the various conflicts and struggles that drive the momentum of an essentially 'open system'. Indeed, this has become a defining motif for many of the claims made about globalization discussed in the previous section. But it should be recalled that, in their original analysis, Held et al. themselves plotted a much simpler possible set of outcomes (in fact four in all, so, even in its own terms, their analysis just substituted these for a single possible outcome).

What a response to this criticism requires in the first instance is a discussion of the nature of the concept 'process' as operative in social analysis, and, secondly, whether the point made by Held et al. is a valid one in respect to the discussion of 'globalization' in our own formulation. We begin with a rather general discussion of 'processes' which, it seems to us, has some wider methodological significance than just in respect to this debate about globalization. We would like to stress *five* aspects to the concept of process, which we think in a skeletal form at least are actually operating in the analysis of this book.

The first of these aspects is that processes need some idea of a *structure* that articulates them. This will involve as simple a structure as possible to express the relationships involved with the elements featured. The elements are items such as entities, agents, components, levels of analysis, relationships, and the like. Such a structure need not be a traditional 'depth structure', however, but could be a structure of affiliations operating 'all on the surface', so to speak, in the spirit of the discussion above. Secondly, all processes require some means or conception of their *periodization*. This involves such aspects as the nature of events (what is understood by the notion of an event), the ideas of turning points, break points, phases and contrasts. Thirdly, there is a problem about how *change* occurs. This involves questions of whether the process is conceived as a slow evolution or one with rapid discontinuities, the nature of disjunctures, or smooth transformations, the agency involved in change, etc.

Fourthly, it seems to us necessary to add two further aspects of processes to the more conventional and acceptable ones just outlined. Without these we do not see how the idea of a process can do much intellectual work, let alone political work. The first of these is to ask 'Where are processes going?'. This is not so much to ask a question about a necessary 'end point' but rather to pose the issue of what social order the trends are pointing towards. What *is* the direction of the trend? Thus, this conception of a process is definitely not one that favours a view of it as a completely 'open system' – one always in a state of flux and being continually 'formatted, enacted and performed'. In a way, then, this differentiates the approach of this book from those claims on globalization that precisely celebrate this analytical style, as outlined in the previous section particularly in connection to the first and fourth characterizations (see also Thompson 2004c and 2004d for a more developed critique of these kinds of open-system methodologies). Finally, and fifthly, there is a need to ask the question 'Where are we?'. Where are we in the unfolding process? And this in a way does require at least a temporary conception of something towards which the system or process is tending, as just outlined in the previous paragraph. But this aspect of processes involves the injunction to 'stop time' as it were – to interrupt the ever unfolding movement to generate some conceptual stability. And it concretely demonstrates the basic difference between evolutionary time (which does not stop, of course) and analytical time, which has to be brought to a temporary halt for any analytical work to be done in relationship to processes.

The outcome when these methodological protocols were applied to the question of globalization is shown in figure 1.1. First in Thompson (1993) and then briefly below is outlined a process involving the formation of three types of international economic mechanism: a proto-worldwide economy, an inter-national economy and a globalized economy. In this book we concentrate upon the second and third types for analytical convenience of exposition, the characteristics of which are presented in a little more detail

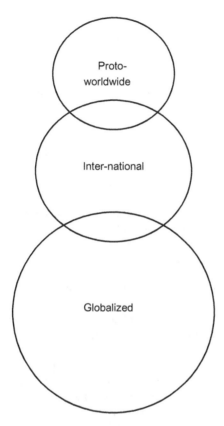

**Figure 1.1**   Three types of international economic mechanism

in a moment. So this approach periodized the international economy into (first three but here just two) different phases or forms and charts how the transformation from one form to another could be produced, which agents were involved and how, the broad time frame involved, etc. Thus our very simple schema does have an idea of what 'globalization' means in terms of a politico-economic formation, so it is 'end-stated' in this sense (which we consider a sensible and unavoidable aspect). Then we asked the key question of where we are in this process of transformation, and argued that we were somewhere in the overlapping area between the inter-national and the globalized economy. But, as will be seen later, our empirical investigation leads us to conclude strongly that the burden of evidence still remains in favour of an inter-national economy (albeit now heavily overlaid by supranational regionalization) rather than a globalized one, hence the tag of 'traditionalists' and 'sceptics' in the overall globalization debate.

In challenging some of the stronger versions of the thesis of economic globalization we might be held to be attacking a 'straw man'. But we continue to believe that these views are relatively coherent in that they at least have the merit of positing an ideal-typical conception of a globalized economic system. Without some such notion, often encompassing all of the five aspects outlined above, it is difficult to assess empirically or conceptually the claim that the world is becoming more globalized or that there are tendencies towards a global economy. In any case, as indicated above, the stronger or more extreme views continue to be influential among business and among political elites (and many academics), even if they only indicate a favoured direction of change and further liberalization. Strong versions of globalization are routinely invoked in political debate, across the spectrum, in order to add legitimacy and force to arguments that may have other bases in reality. It is, therefore, important to contest these claims at source if the case for national and regional political action to regulate the international economy is to be heard. The strong globalization thesis may have been dented by the emergence of Asian industrialization and the rise of China and India as major economic players, given the significant role of state action in these trajectories, and the welfare states of North-West Europe have proved fairly resilient at least in terms of overall levels of public expenditure. But the rhetoric of competitiveness and the injunction that ever greater areas of social activity must orient themselves to the need to compete in a global economy are still powerful statements in the political discourses of the developed countries. And while the emerging economies are rightly sceptical of the neo-liberal blandishments of organizations such as the International Monetary Fund and the World Bank, especially as they see the speed with which national states intervene to shore up crises in the developed world, there are powerful forces and mechanisms of surveillance that are designed to spread further liberalization and international market integration. The tide may be turning – it is too early to tell – but the myths of globalization still need challenging if social stability and economic performance are to be protected.

Some less extreme and more nuanced analyses that employ the term 'globalization' are well established in the academic community and concentrate on the relative internationalization of major financial markets, of technology and of certain important sectors of manufacturing and services, particularly since the 1970s. Emphasis is given in many of these analyses to the increasing constraints on national-level governance preventing ambitious macroeconomic policies that diverge significantly from the norms acceptable to international financial markets. Indeed, we ourselves have over some time drawn attention to such phenomena in our own work.

Obviously, it is no part of our aim here to deny that such trends to increased internationalization have occurred or to ignore the constraints on certain types of national economic strategy.[1] Our point in assessing the significance of the internationalization that has occurred is to argue that it is well short of dissolving distinct national economies in the major advanced industrial countries, or of preventing the development of new forms of economic governance at the national, regional and international levels. There are, however, very real dangers in not distinguishing clearly between certain trends towards internationalization and the strong version of the globalization thesis. It is particularly unfortunate if the two become confused by using the same word, 'globalization', to describe both. Often we feel that evidence from more cautious arguments is then used carelessly to bolster more extreme ones, to build a community of usage when there needs to be strict differentiation of meanings. It also confuses public discussion and policy-making, reinforcing the view that political actors can accomplish less than is actually possible in a global system.

The strong version of the globalization thesis requires a new view of the international economy, as we shall shortly see – one that subsumes and subordinates national-level processes. Whereas tendencies towards internationalization can be accommodated within a modified view of the world economic system, that still gives a major role to national-level policies and economic actors. Undoubtedly this implies some greater or lesser degree of change; firms, governments and international agencies are being forced to behave differently, but in the main they can use existing institutions and practices to do so. In this way we feel it makes more sense to consider the international economic system in a longer historical perspective, to recognize that current changes, while significant and distinctive, are not unprecedented and do not necessarily involve a move towards a new type of economic system. The two long quotations at the beginning of this chapter illustrate the point. Marx and Engels provide a telling definition of globalization that has a decidedly modern ring despite the fact that it was written over a century and a half ago. The quotation from Keynes also speaks to this point, but it further illustrates how quickly things can change – written as it was at the end of the First World War, but referring to the period just before that war. Keynes's remarks force us to recognize the unexpected – indeed always to expect the unexpected – in the international system and never to think that because things have been going on for some time they will necessarily continue in that form.

Returning to the present, the strong economic versions of the globalization thesis have the advantage that they clearly and sharply pose the possibility of such a change. If they are wrong they are still of some value in enabling us to think out what is happening and why. In this sense, challenging the strong version of the thesis is not merely negative but helps us to develop our own ideas.

One can only call the political impact of 'globalization' the pathology of overdiminished expectations. Many overenthusiastic analysts and politicians have gone beyond the evidence in overstating the extent of the dominance of world markets and their ungovernability. If this is so, then we should seek to break the spell of this discomfiting myth. The old rationalist explanation for primitive myths was that they were a way of masking and compensating for humanity's helplessness in the face of the power of nature. In this case we have a myth that exaggerates the degree of our helplessness in the face of contemporary economic forces. If economic relations are more governable (at the national, the regional and the international level) than many contemporary analysts suppose, then we should explore the possible scale and scope of that governance. It is not currently the case that radical goals are attainable: full employment in the advanced countries, a fair deal for the poorer developing countries and widespread democratic control over economic affairs for the world's people. But this should not lead us to dismiss or ignore the forms of control and social improvement that could be achieved relatively rapidly with a modest change in attitudes on the part of key elites. It is thus essential to persuade reformers of the left and conservatives who care for the fabric of their societies that we are not helpless before uncontrollable global processes. If this happens, then changing attitudes and expectations might make these more radical goals acceptable.

## Models of the international economy

As we have already noted, one of the merits of the strong globalization literature is that it offers a way of conceptualizing an alternative economic structure to that of the international economy. Globalization in this strong sense refers not just to conjunctural change towards greater trade and investment integration between relatively distinct national and regional economies but to a qualitatively different kind of world order. It is important to be able to distinguish between changes that represent more extensive and intensive integration in the international economy and those that presage a fundamentally different kind of order. Ideal-typical models of an international economy and of a globalized economy allow us to do this and make it possible to identify the different logics of economic activity and public policy that might pertain to each. Too often, in our view, evidence compatible with the latter is used as though it substantiated the former. With a few honourable exceptions, the more enthusiastic (or pessimistic) analysts of globalization have failed to specify that difference, or to specify what evidence would be decisive in pointing to a structural change towards a global economy.

An extreme and one-sided ideal type of this kind enables us to differentiate degrees of internationalization, to eliminate some possibilities and to avoid confusion between claims. Given such a model, it becomes possible to assess it against evidence of international trends and thus enables us more or less plausibly to determine whether or not this phenomenon of the development of a new supranational economic system is occurring. In order to do this we have developed two basic contrasting ideal types of international economy, one that is fully globalized, and the other an open international economy that is still fundamentally characterized by exchange between relatively distinct national economies and in which many outcomes, such as the competitive performance of firms and sectors, are substantially determined by processes occurring at the national level. These ideal types are valuable in so far as they are useful in enabling us to clarify the issues conceptually, that is, in specifying the difference between a new global economy and merely extensive and intensifying international economic relations. Increasing salience of foreign trade and considerable and growing international flows of capital are not per se evidence of a new and distinct phenomenon called 'globalization'. As we shall see in chapter 2, they were features of the international economy before 1914.

### Type 1: An inter-national economy

We shall first develop a simple and extreme version of this type. An international economy is one in which the principal entities are national economies. Trade and investment produce growing interconnection between these still national economies. Such a process involves the increasing integration of more and more nations and economic actors into world market relationships. Trade relations, as a result, tend to take on the form of national specializations and the international division of labour. The importance of trade is, however, progressively replaced by the centrality of investment relations between nations, which increasingly act as the organizing principle of the system. The form of interdependence between nations remains, however, of the 'strategic' kind. That is, it implies the continued relative separation of the domestic and the international frameworks for policy-making and the management of economic affairs, and also a relative separation in terms of economic effects. International events are of the 'billiard ball' type; international events do not directly or necessarily penetrate or permeate the domestic economy but are refracted through national policies and processes. The international and the domestic policy fields either remain relatively separate as distinct levels of governance or they work 'automatically'. In the latter case adjustments are not thought to be the subject of policy by public bodies or authorities, but are a consequence of 'unorganized' or 'spontaneous' market forces. But any 'adjustment' to domestic arrangements occasioned by pressures from international economic forces happens slowly; gradual adaptations and reconfigurations ensue which are more likely to produce new divergences and perturbations than radical transformations and homogenization.

## Type 2: A globalized economy

A globalized economy is a distinct ideal type from that of the inter-national economy and can be developed by contrast with it. In an international economy, the basic processes of allocation and production, the making of markets and the formation of the prices of key variables all take place primarily in national economic spaces, even as these processes are influenced by interactions with other economies. There are typically distinct and different patterns of economic change and development, and, while there may be an increasing range of international economic interactions (financial markets and trade in manufactured goods, for example), these tend to function as opportunities or constraints for nationally located economic actors and their public regulators. In a globalized economy, national economies and their international interactions are subsumed and rearticulated by genuinely global processes and transactions into a new structure. Economic actors and activities become disembedded from national societies and domestic policies, whether of private corporations or public regulators, and must routinely take account of the potentially global determinants of their sphere of operations. As socially disembedded global processes and transactions grow, so the national space is permeated and transformed by the global, and private and, especially, public decision-makers both face increasing uncertainty as to how to orient and decide the most appropriate course of action.

The strong concept of a globalized economy outlined above acts as an ideal type which we can compare to the actual trends within the international economy. This globalized economy has been contrasted with the notion of an inter-national economy in the above analysis in order to distinguish its particular and novel features. The opposition of these two types for conceptual clarity conceals the possibly messy combination of the two in reality. This makes it difficult to determine major trends on the basis of the available evidence. These two types of economy are not inherently mutually exclusive; rather in certain conditions the globalized economy would encompass and subsume the inter-national economy. The globalized economy would rearticulate many of the features of the inter-national economy, transforming them as it reinforced them. If this phenomenon occurred there would thus be a complex combination of features of both types of economy existing within the present conjuncture. The problem in determining what is happening is to identify the dominant trends: either the growth of globalization or the continuation of the existing inter-national patterns. To those critics who have accused us of postulating a single end to history by this approach – our 'globalized economy' – and thereby neglecting the process of globalization in which there may be multiple outcomes, we repeat the point made above that all processes must have some end in view if they are to do any serious analytical work. Our approach is to postulate in abstract such a conception and then to measure how the actual process is or is not evolving in respect to it. This seems a perfectly reasonable and indeed an analytically necessary thing to do.

It is our view that such a process of hybridization is not taking place, but it would be cavalier not to consider and raise the possibility. Central in this respect is the evidence we present later (chapter 3) for the still weak development of genuine TNCs and the continued salience of MNCs and also the ongoing dominance of the advanced countries in both trade and FDI.[2] Such evidence is consistent with a continuing inter-national economy, but much less so with a rapidly globalizing hybrid system. Moreover, we should remember that an inter-national economy is one in which the major nationally based manufacturers and the major financial trading and service centres are strongly externally oriented, emphasizing international trading performance. The opposite of a globalized economy is not thus a nationally inward-looking one, but an open world market based on trading nations and regulated to a greater or lesser degree by both the public policies of nation-states and supranational agencies (chapter 7). Such an economy has existed in some form or another since the 1870s, and has continued to re-emerge despite major setbacks, the most serious being the crisis of the 1930s. The point is that it should not be confused with a global economy.

### The chapters in outline

The rest of this book is organized as follows. In chapter 2 the history of the international economy and its regimes of regulation is considered in some detail. In particular we contrast the economic integration of the Gold Standard period before 1914 with the international economy developing during the 1980s and early 1990s. The analysis looks at a wide range of measures of integration and finds that there is nothing unprecedented about the levels of integration experienced at present, in either the real or the monetary economy. The governed nature of the international system is stressed, and the relationships between domestic and international activity during different periods are explored.

Chapter 3 combines an analysis of trade and FDI with an assessment of how far modern major companies are truly transnational. FDI is key to the proposition that capital mobility is restructuring the world economy. Here we consider the distribution of FDI and the issue of its regulation, relative to but also as distinct from that of international trade. The continued dominance of the Triad economic blocs – North America, Europe and Japan/East Asia – in trade, in FDI flows and stocks, and in world income distribution is stressed. The rest of the chapter presents the evidence on the economic role of MNCs and explores the most recent available data to show that companies are not becoming footloose as global capital but in large part remain rooted in one of the three regions of the Triad. The two aspects of this chapter thus consider the nature of the international economy of real goods and services through a thorough examination of the strategies of international companies and real resource flows. The overall conclusion is that the globalization of production has been exaggerated: companies continue to be closely linked to their home bases, and for good reasons are likely to remain so.

Chapter 4 also considers two distinct but related issues: international competition and its relationship to globalization. The key issue is that of 'international competitiveness', a central plank of much modern rhetoric on economic policy. The different meanings of competition are reviewed and assessed, the differences between nations and companies are emphasized, and a sceptical eye is cast on the discussion of this issue as inspired by the management literature. The second part emphasizes the continued pertinence of relationship between the 'North' and the 'South' for understanding the international system. The North's trade with developing countries is also modest in scale and is not as yet leading either to a reduction in Triad dominance or to excessive import penetration by newly industrializing economies. This provides a backdrop to an analysis of whether competition and import penetration from low-wage NICs are substantially contributing to unemployment and deindustrialization in the developed world. After an extensive review of the literature and evidence, the verdict is 'not proven': the effects have yet to be strongly demonstrated, and 'divergence, big time' remains the order of the day (Pritchett 1997).

In chapter 5 the issue of the developing countries, their relationship to the advanced economies and globalization, are further considered. The recent industrialization of Asia, especially China, is set in a longer-term historical perspective and the implications of this for global inequality and poverty are addressed. The chapter argues that, while Asian industrialization is important, this new episode in the international economy is less a result of globalization than an example of state-led, catch-up development in what remains a profoundly unequal world economy.

Chapter 6 takes up one of the major challenges to the notion of a fully globalized world by investigating the competing claim that supranational regionalization is a more accurate description of the international economic and political system. The chapter interrogates the evidence in respect to the real economy and particularly to the financial economy (though it also questions whether this distinction remains a valid one). The burden of the argument here is that such supranational regional tendencies are indeed strong in respect to both trade and financial markets. The chapter then goes on to explore the reasons why such a pattern of activity is developing, what its consequences might be, and why this alternative course might mature in the future. In many ways the analysis expresses the fundamental alternative characterization of the international system that emerges from the book in contrast to the strong globalization thesis.

Chapter 7 examines the present structure of governance of the world economy, particularly the financial system and the global monetary imbalances centred on the international role of the US dollar. It considers the possibilities for economic regulation at international, national and regional levels and argues that, although there is plenty of scope for regulation, a lack of political will among elites as well as divisions over policy between major centres of economic power currently present barriers to better management.

Finally, chapter 8 examines the political dimensions of governance, exploring the changing role and capacities of the nation-state and the possible roles that such entities may perform in promoting and legitimating extended governance in the international system. Our argument here is that, far from the nation-state being undermined by the processes of globalization, the state's national and international role continues to play an essential part in making and regulating cross-border activity.

# 2

# Globalization and the History of the International Economy

---

The 'globalization' of economic activity and the governance issues it raises are often thought to have appeared only after the Second World War, and particularly during the 1960s. The post-1960 era saw the emergence of MNC activity on the one hand and the rapid growth of international trade on the other. Subsequently, with the collapse of the Bretton Woods semi-fixed exchange-rate regime in the 1971–3 period, the expansion of international securities investment and bank lending began in earnest as capital and particularly money markets rapidly internationalized, adding to the complexity of international economic relations and heralding what is often thought to be the genuine globalization of an integrated and interdependent world economy.

Figures 2.1 and 2.2 indicate the nature of this popular history. In figure 2.1 an index of globalization has been constructed which combines a number of economic, social and political indicators to represent a composite indicator of the overall process. This shows a more or less continuous growth of globalization over the entire period since 1970. The data on financial globalization from figure 2.2 provide a similar overall picture: the relentless increase in financial integration since 1970. Note, however, that this has been much more intense in the case of the traditional industrialized countries than for the emerging and developing economies.

We will have occasion to question this popular history later in chapters 3, 4 and 6 in particular. The exact nature of the globalization indicated by these graphs is often disguised by the level of aggregation they contain and by the lack of attention to its geographical specificity. These are issues taken up in other chapters.

In this chapter we first of all scrutinize this history by tracing the main periods of the internationalization of economic activity over

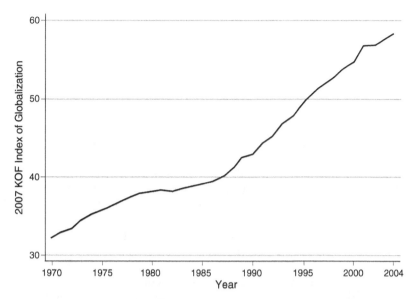

**Figure 2.1** The development of overall globalization, 1970–2004
*Source*: Swiss Federal Institute of Technology 2007, p. 1, figure 1.

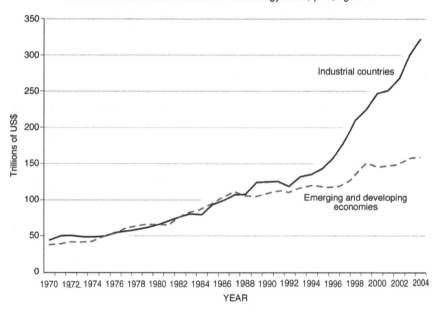

**Figure 2.2** Overall international financial integration, 1970–2004 (trillions of US dollars)
*Note*: Ratio of sum of foreign assets and liabilities to GDP, 1970–2004.
*Source*: Derived from Rose et al. 2006, p. 63, figure 1.

a much longer period than just since the 1970s. This is shown to have developed in a cyclical and uneven fashion. The key issue at stake in our assessment is the changing autonomy of national economies in the conduct of their economic activity.[1] The story in this chapter takes us up to around the mid-1990s. Later chapters develop the argument for the period since then.

## MNCs, TNCs and international business

The history of the internationalization of business enterprises is a long one, in no way confined just to the period since 1960. Trading activities, for instance, date from the earliest civilizations, but it was the Middle Ages in Europe that marked the initiation of systematic cross-border trading operations carried out by institutions of a private corporate nature (though often with strong state backing and support). During the fourteenth century, for instance, the Hanseatic League organized German merchants in the conduct of their Western European and Levantine commerce – which involved them in agricultural production, iron smelting and general manufacturing. Around the same time the Merchant Adventurers organized the sale of UK-produced wool and cloth to the Low Countries and elsewhere. In addition, Italian trading and banking houses occupied a key position in the general internationalization of business activity during the early Renaissance period. By the end of the fourteenth century it is estimated that there were as many as 150 Italian banking companies already operating multinationally (Dunning 1993, pp. 97–8).

During the seventeenth and eighteenth centuries state patronage extended as the great colonial trading companies were established: the Dutch and British East India companies, the Muscovy Company, the Royal Africa Company and the Hudson's Bay Company came into existence. These pioneered wholesale trading operations in what were to become the leading colonial areas.

However, it is the development of international manufacturing as the Industrial Revolution took hold that presents the closest precursor to the modern-day MNC. Here the early pre-eminence of British firms as multinational producers becomes apparent. Initially North and South America presented the most favourable investment opportunities, but these were soon followed by Africa and Australasia. There is some dispute as to whether 'colonial investments' should be considered a true precursor of foreign direct investment, but production abroad for the local market began in this way. Technical and organizational developments after the 1870s allowed a wider variety of similar products to be produced domestically and abroad within the boundaries of the same firm, while the exploration and development of minerals and other raw material products also attracted large amounts of FDI (Dunning 1993, chap. 5).

One of the problems with such a retrospective classification, however, is that the modern concepts of 'direct' investment on the one hand (involving some notion of managerial control from abroad) and 'portfolio' investment on the other (involving the acquisition of securities issued by foreign institutions so as to claim returns without any associated control or management participation) were drawn only in the early 1960s, at the same time as the term MNC was itself introduced. The US Department of Commerce had reported outward FDI from 1929, but this was the exception.

Despite this lack of consistently classified data, it is generally agreed that manufacturing multinationals appeared in the world economy after the mid-nineteenth century and that they were well established by the First World War. International business activity grew vigorously in the 1920s as the truly diversified and integrated MNC matured, but it slowed down during the depressed 1930s and war-torn 1940s, and began a fluctuating expansion again after 1950.

There have been two approaches to quantifying the growth of international business over time. The first involves looking at whatever statistics on international investment are available, generating additional data, and then reclassifying these on the basis of modern distinctions. The second approach focuses on the businesses themselves. It traces the history of firms and the internationalization of their activity, which involves counting multinationals and their business affiliations over time (Jones 1994).

Estimates of accumulated stock of FDI held by the leading countries in 1914 and in subsequent key years are shown in table 2.1. Clearly, the growth in importance of the 'New World' (the USA and Canada in this table) is

**Table 2.1**   Accumulated stock of FDI by country of origin, 1914–1978 (billions of current $ and percentage)

|  | 1914 | | 1938 | | 1960 | | 1971 | | 1978 | |
|---|---|---|---|---|---|---|---|---|---|---|
|  | $ | % | $ | % | $ | % | $ | % | $ | % |
| United States | 2.7 | 18.5 | 7.3 | 27.7 | 32.8 | 49.2 | 82.8 | 48.1 | 162.7 | 41.4 |
| Canada | 0.2 | 1.0 | 0.7 | 2.7 | 2.5 | 3.8 | 6.5 | 3.8 | 13.6 | 3.5 |
| United Kingdom | 6.5 | 45.5 | 10.5 | 39.8 | 10.8 | 16.2 | 23.7 | 13.8 | 50.7 | 12.9 |
| Germany | 1.5 | 10.5 | 0.4 | 1.3 | 0.8 | 1.2 | 7.3 | 4.2 | 28.6 | 7.3 |
| France | 1.8 | 12.2 | 2.5 | 9.5 | 4.1 | 6.1 | 7.3 | 4.2 | 14.9 | 3.8 |
| Belgium | – | – | – | – | 1.3 | 1.9 | 2.4 | 1.4 | 5.4 | 1.4 |
| Netherlands | – | – | – | – | 7.0 | 10.5 | 13.8 | 8.0 | 28.4 | 7.2 |
| Switzerland | – | – | – | – | 2.0 | 3.0 | 9.5 | 5.5 | 27.8 | 7.1 |
| Japan | neg. | neg. | 0.8 | 2.8 | 0.5 | 0.7 | 4.4 | 2.6 | 26.8 | 6.8 |
| Total | 27.0 | 87.7 | 22.2 | 83.8 | 61.8 | 92.6 | 157.7 | 86.65 | 358.9 | 91.4 |
| Total of all countries | 14.3 | 100 | 26.4 | 100 | 66.7 | 100 | 172.1 | 100 | 392.8 | 100 |

*Note*: neg. = negligible.
*Source*: Dunning 1983, derived from p. 87, table 5.1.

signalled up until the 1960s. As might have been expected, the traditional supplier countries such as the UK, Germany and France lost out in terms of shares. Between the 1960s and 1980s the USA's significance as a recipient of FDI faded while Germany and Japan increased in importance. And in terms of the estimated value of manufacturing exports, the UK and Germany were the leading exporters of manufactures at the outbreak of the First World War, and were over twice as important as the USA and France. Yearly export values were already less than accumulated FDI stocks by this time.

The analysis of companies and their history also shows the developed nature of international production before the First World War. The pioneer country here was the UK, but there was also a surprising extent of multi-national production organized by the smaller advanced economies. Company-based analysis reveals that a good deal of this early FDI was modest in scale, though extensive in scope, and often came from quite small foreign companies (Jones 1994).

## Trade and international integration

A better statistical base is available for exploring the trends in international trade. Again the history of this part of international economic activity goes back a long way. But good statistical evidence exists from 1830 onwards (Maddison 1962, 1987; Lewis 1981). The important period from our point of view concerns developments during the twentieth century, and particularly from the First World War. A similar pattern emerges here as in the case of FDI, though perhaps more pronounced in its features. The volume of world foreign trade expanded at about 3.4 per cent per annum between 1870 and 1913. After 1913 trade was adversely affected by the growth of tariffs, quantitative restrictions, exchange controls and then war, and it expanded by less than 1 per cent per annum on average between 1913 and 1950. After 1950, however, trade really took off, to grow at over 9 per cent per annum until 1973. Between 1973 and the mid-1980s the growth rate fell back to nearer the late nineteenth-century levels, with expansion at a rate of only 3.6 per cent.

The experience of six main economies in the development of export volumes between 1913 and 1984 is shown in table 2.2, indicating the different rates of volume growth and their fluctuations. Clearly, there was a definite fall in the volume of world trade during the 1930s. The brunt was borne first by Germany and the UK – the leading economic powers at the time – then by France, and to a lesser extent by the USA and the Netherlands. Japan suffered only as a consequence of the Second World War.

The relationship between growth in output and in trade is a central one for international economic analysis. It is not our intention to explore the theoretical links between these here (see Kitson and Michie 1995). However,

**Table 2.2**    Volume of exports, 1913–1984 (1913 = 100)

|      | France  | Germany | Japan    | Netherlands | UK    | USA     |
|------|---------|---------|----------|-------------|-------|---------|
| 1913 | 100.0   | 100.0   | 100.0    | 100.0       | 100.0 | 100.0   |
| 1929 | 147.0   | 91.8    | 257.9    | 171.2       | 81.3  | 158.2   |
| 1938 | 91.0    | 57.0    | 588.3    | 140.0       | 57.3  | 125.7   |
| 1950 | 149.2   | 34.8    | 210.1    | 171.2       | 100.0 | 224.6   |
| 1960 | 298.4   | 154.7   | 924.4    | 445.1       | 120.0 | 387.9   |
| 1973 | 922.4   | 514.3   | 5,672.7  | 1,632.1     | 241.9 | 912.0   |
| 1984 | 1,459.5 | 774.0   | 14,425.2 | 2,383.7     | 349.1 | 1,161.5 |

*Source*: Maddison 1987, p. 694, table A-21.

trade growth from 1853 to 1872 was already faster than the growth in world production, while from 1872 to 1911 it grew at about the same rate. Between 1913 and 1950 there was a devastating decline in both the rate of growth of trade (0.5 per cent per annum) and of output growth (1.9 per cent per annum). Only since 1950 has there been a consistent expansion of trade relative to production, even during the cyclical down-turn after 1973 (see also chapter 3).

## Migration and the international labour market

A third broad area of analysis in the context of the history of the international economy concerns migration and its consequences for the integration of the global labour market. It is generally agreed that migration is becoming (or has become) a 'global phenomenon' (see, for instance, Serow et al. 1990, p. 159; Segal 1993, chap. 7; Castles and Miller 1993, chap. 4). However, by 'global' these authors mean that, since the mid-1970s in particular, many more countries have been affected by migration, that there has been a growing diversity of areas of origin for migrants, and that migrants are of a wider range of socioeconomic statuses than ever before. Thus for these authors globalization registers a quantitative shift in the extent and scope of migration rather than a feature of a potentially different socioeconomic order.

There are a number of different kinds of migrants. Clearly the early slave trade was a form of 'involuntary' migration (it is estimated that 15 million slaves were moved from Africa to the Americas before 1850: Castles and Miller 1993, p. 48). Refugees and asylum seekers can also be considered as migrants. But for the purposes of our analysis we focus on 'voluntary' migration. The period considered extends from the 'mass migration' after 1815 (mainly from Europe) to the emergence and extension of labour migration of the 'guest worker' variety after the Second World War, through to the current trend for skilled voluntary migration from the emerging market economies and other developing economies to the core OECD countries of Europe and North America.

It is difficult to judge exactly how many migrants there have been since 1815, so all the following numbers should be treated with some caution. Castles and Miller (1993) report that there could have been as many as 100 million migrants of all kinds in 1992 (including some 20 million refugees and asylum seekers and 30 million overseas workers). They point out, however, that this represented only about 1.7 per cent of the world population. Thus the vast majority of the world's population remain in their country of origin.

The greatest era for recorded voluntary mass migration was the century after 1815 (figure 2.3). Around 60 million people left Europe for the Americas, Oceania, and South and East Africa. An estimated 10 million voluntarily migrated from Russia to Central Asia and Siberia. A million went from Southern Europe to North Africa. About 12 million Chinese and 6 million Japanese left their homelands and emigrated to East and South Asia. One and a half million left India for South-East Asia and South and West Africa (Segal 1993, p. 16: the statistics for Indian migration are probably severely underestimated here).

Between the two world wars international migration decreased sharply. To a large extent this was in response to the depressed economic conditions during much of the interwar period, but it was also due to restrictive immigration policies instigated in many of the traditional recipient countries, particularly the United States.

An upsurge in international migration began in the post-1945 period, particularly involving Europe and the United States once again (Livi Bacci 1993). This was the period, however, of the relative growth of migration from the developing countries to the developed ones (figure 2.4) and the introduction of the 'guest worker' phenomenon. During the 1970s and 1980s global trends favoured the controlled movements of temporary workers on a 'guest' basis, with entry for immigrants restricted to the highly skilled or those with family already in the country of destination. The emphasis on the highly skilled as 'welcomed' migrants continued late into the twentieth and early twenty-first century.

Table 2.3 reinforces these comments by showing the extent of gross migration rates relative to the home populations of various countries: the 'Old World' of Europe consistently lost migrants while the 'New World' dramatically and systematically gained them. Overall, net migration from the 'Old World' continued up until the end of the Second World War, after which this trend began to be reversed, as table 2.4 demonstrates. But the 'New World' continued to remain an attractive destination for migrants, in the case of Australia, Canada and the USA on an even greater scale.

It is generally agreed that the United States has been, and remains, the great immigrant country, as the data in table 2.4 neatly illustrate. The accumulated proportion of migrants in the USA in 1995 was 8.7 per cent

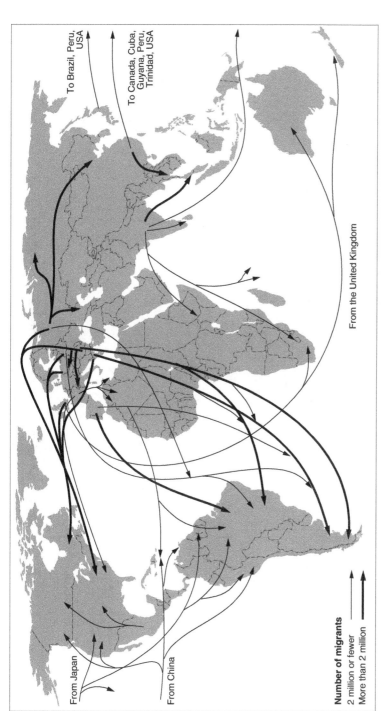

**Figure 2.3** Global voluntary migrations, 1815–1914
*Source:* Based on Segal 1993, p. 17.

To Brazil, Peru, USA

To Canada, Cuba, Guyana, Peru, Trinidad, USA

From the United Kingdom

From Japan

From China

**Number of migrants**
2 million or fewer
More than 2 million

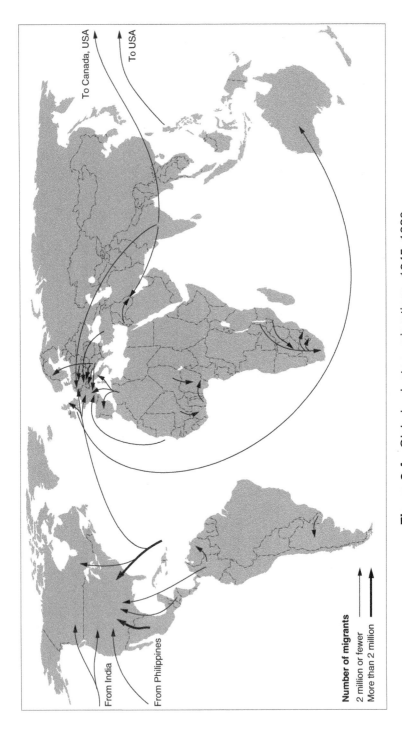

To Canada, USA

To USA

From India

From Philippines

**Number of migrants**
2 million or fewer
More than 2 million

**Figure 2.4** Global voluntary migrations, 1945–1980
*Source:* Based on Segal 1993, p. 21.

**Table 2.3**   Gross migration rates (migrants per 1,000 population), 1870–1910

| Old World | **−4.17** |
|---|---|
| Belgium | −2.12 |
| Denmark | −2.78 |
| France | −0.19 |
| Germany | −1.47 |
| Great Britain | −5.15 |
| Italy | −9.25 |
| Netherlands | −4.18 |
| Norway | −6.55 |
| Portugal | −4.35 |
| Spain | −4.54 |
| Sweden | −5.25 |
| **New World** | **12.21** |
| Australia | 14.43 |
| Canada | 14.35 |
| United States | 7.86 |

*Source*: Taylor and Williamson 1997.

**Table 2.4**   Net migration (thousands), 1870–1998

|  | 1870–1913 | 1914–49 | 1950–73 | 1974–98 |
|---|---|---|---|---|
| *Old World* | −13,996 | −3,662 | 9,381 | 10,898 |
| France | 890 | −236 | 3,630 | 1,026 |
| Germany | −2,598 | −304 | 7,070 | 5,911 |
| Italy | −4,459 | −1,771 | −2,139 | 1,617 |
| Japan | n.a. | 197 | −72 | −179 |
| United Kingdom | −6,415 | −1,405 | −605 | 737 |
| Others* | −1,414 | 54 | 1,425 | 1,607 |
| *New World* | 17,856 | 7,239 | 12,663 | 21,639 |
| Australia | 885 | 673 | 2,033 | 2,151 |
| New Zealand | 290 | 138 | 247 | 87 |
| Canada | 861 | 207 | 2,126 | 2,680 |
| United States | 15,820 | 6,221 | 8,257 | 16,721 |

*Note*: * Includes Belgium, Netherlands, Norway, Sweden and Switzerland.
*Source*: Maddison 2001.

(Papademetriou 1997–8, p. 17). For the 1980s, estimates of global flows of migrants run at approximately 25–30 million a year (Segal 1993, p. 115). Up to 4 million of these were refugees, and a good proportion of the others consisted of new temporary migrant workers (workers with the intention of returning home). But the recent period has seen this idea of 'returning home' fade in the USA, as migrants there have increasingly adopted the country as their home and have sought long-term citizenship rights.

However, the pattern of mass family migration has yet to repeat itself in the way that it operated in the period up to the First World War.

According to O'Rourke and Williamson (1998) the sustained mass migration across the Atlantic in the second half of the nineteenth century and early part of the twentieth century was one of the main mechanisms that secured the enduring prosperity of both the USA and Europe. It facilitated GDP growth in both continents as commodity prices fell and factor markets converged. Aided by a spectacular transport revolution, it enabled a 'convergence club' to form (discussed at greater length in chapter 4) which has endured in its significance as a global powerhouse for economic dominance, one that is only now being seriously challenged by the newly emerging economies of the Far East.

## The relative openness and interdependence of the international system

A key question posed by the preceding analysis is whether the integration of the international system has dramatically changed since the Second World War. Clearly, there has been considerable international economic activity ever since the 1850s, but can we compare different periods in terms of their openness and integration?

One way of doing this is to compare trade to GDP ratios. Table 2.5 provides information on these for a range of countries. Apart from the dramatic differences in the openness to trade of different economies demonstrated by these figures (compare the USA and the Netherlands), the startling feature is that trade to GDP ratios were consistently higher in 1913 than they were in 1973 (with the slight exception of Germany, where they were near enough equal).

**Table 2.5**  Ratio of merchandise trade to GDP at current prices (exports and imports combined)

|  | 1913 | 1950 | 1973 | 1995 | 2005 |
|---|---|---|---|---|---|
| France | 35.4 | 21.2 | 29.0 | 36.6 | 45.3 |
| Germany | 35.1 | 20.1 | 35.2 | 38.7 | 62.7 |
| Japan | 31.4 | 16.9 | 18.3 | 14.1 | 24.7 |
| Netherlands | 103.6 | 70.2 | 80.1 | 83.4 | 127.6 |
| UK | 44.7 | 36.0 | 39.3 | 42.6[a] | 40.1 |
| USA | 11.2 | 7.0 | 10.5 | 19.0 | 21.2 |

*Note*: [a] 1994.
*Source*: Figures from 1913 to 1973 derived from Maddison 1987, p. 695, table A-23; those for 1995 derived from *OECD National Accounts, 1997*, country tables; those for 2005 from *World Bank Data and Statistics online* (accessed 23 April 2007).

Even in 1995, Japan, the Netherlands and the UK were still less open on this measure than they were in 1913, with France and Germany only slightly more open. The USA was the only country that was considerably more open than it was in 1913. Things begin to change in the more recent period, however, as indicated by the 2005 figures. France, Germany, Japan and the Netherlands show significant increases, while the USA and the UK show a small increase and decrease respectively. But even here the differences to the 1913 figures are perhaps surprisingly small.[2] As we will see in chapter 4, concentrating on just the period after the Second World War shows a steady growth in trade openness, with a particularly dramatic entry of the East Asian economies into the international trading system.

Getting back to the longer-term trends, however, the evidence also suggests greater openness to capital flows in the pre-First World War period compared to the period up to the mid-1990s. Grassman (1980), measuring 'financial openness' in terms of current account balance to GNP ratios, finds no increase in openness between 1875 and 1975: indeed there is a decline in capital movements for his leading six countries (Great Britain, Italy, Sweden, Norway, Denmark and the USA). This is even the case for the post-Second World War period, though from the mid-1970s there is some sign of an increasing trend in financial openness. Measuring things slightly differently, the figures shown in figure 2.5 confirm the general finding of a

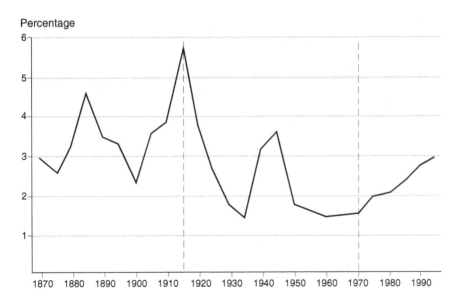

Percentage

**Figure 2.5**   International capital flows among the G7 economies, 1870–1995 (as percentage of GDP)
*Source*: Adapted from Howell 1998, fig. 7.

decrease in openness among the G7 countries from a peak in 1913, but with a steady increase after 1970.

In addition, Lewis reports that capital exports rose substantially over the thirty years before the First World War, though they were subject to wide fluctuations. But when a comparison is made with the years 1953–73, the order of magnitude of capital exports was much lower in the latter period (Lewis 1981, p. 21). Finally, in a comprehensive comparison of the pre-1914 Gold Standard period with the 1980s, Turner (1991) also concludes that current account imbalances and capital flows, measured in relation to GNP, were larger before 1914 than in the 1980s. These sentiments are confirmed by the data included in table 2.6. In terms of the foreign share of investment in GDP, the position in 1914 for these developing countries is only eclipsed by the position in 1990 in the case of Asia, reflecting the beginning of the sustained growth in FDI to the Asian area as its development took off.

Thus, using gross figures for ratios of trade and capital flows relative to output confirms that 'openness' was greater during the Gold Standard period than even in the 1990s. But these gross figures could disguise important differences between the periods. For instance, the composition of output might be important in judging the real extent of interdependence. In the case of financial flows we should also recognize the change in their character and the significance of the financial regimes under which they took place. In the high Gold Standard period long-term capital dominated international capital flows. In the recent period there has been a switch to shorter-term capital. In addition, a wider range of countries have now been included under the international capital movement umbrella.

This issue is discussed at greater length below, but at this stage it is worth pointing to the nature of the Gold Standard as a quintessential fixed exchange-rate system compared to the floating rates of the 1980s and 1990s. In a fixed exchange-rate regime, short-term capital flows are highly

**Table 2.6**  FDI in Latin America, Asia and Africa, 1900–1990 (foreign investment as a share of GDP)

| Year | 1900 | 1914 | 1929 | 1938 | 1967 | 1980 | 1990 |
|---|---|---|---|---|---|---|---|
| Latin America | 1.20 | 2.71 | 1.26 | 0.87 | 0.33 | 0.33 | 0.47 |
| Asia | 0.17 | 0.40 | 0.23 | 0.26 | 0.11 | 0.15 | 0.32 |
| Africa | 1.33 | 1.17 | 0.24 | 0.35 | 0.23 | 0.34 | 0.74 |
| Total | 0.44 | 0.89 | 0.45 | 0.41 | 0.2 | 0.24 | 0.42 |

*Note*: Total stock of foreign investment at 1900 US prices expressed as a ratio of country grouping GDP (except for Argentina the dates are 1900, 1913, 1929, 1938, 1970, 1980 and 1989, and the ratio calculation is at domestic prices).
*Source*: Twomey 2000 (compiled from various tables).

interest-rate elastic, with only small changes in interest rates causing sig-nificant capital movements (though this also means that the sensitivity of capital flow to interest rates can limit the variability of short-term interest rates as well). Some of the capital flows could thus be accounted for by the significant differences in the pattern of interest-rate variation as between the two periods, though, again, the post-war Bretton Woods system did not show any greater interest-rate variability than the Gold Standard period (Turner 1991, p. 16, table 2).

Moving away from trade and capital flows for the moment, we can now look at the implications of the trends in international migration. First, it must be emphasized that these are contained within the twin considerations of the labour market and governmental policy. A world market for labour just does not exist in the same way that it might be said to exist for goods and services. Most labour markets continue to be nationally regulated and only marginally accessible to outsiders, whether they are concerned with legal or illegal migrants or professional recruitment. Moving goods and services is infinitely easier than moving labour. Even a rapid and sustained expansion of the world economy is unlikely significantly to reduce the multiple barriers to the movement of labour. Other than in the context of regionally developing free trade agreements of the EU type, freedom of labour movement still remains heavily circumscribed. Even the NAFTA explicitly excludes freedom of movement of persons, though there is *de facto* freedom between Canada and the USA, and enormous illegal flows between Mexico and the USA. But extra-regional migration of all kinds is a small percentage of global labour movements. Most migration is of the country next door variety (see chapter 6). During the nineteenth century the mass movement of workers to the sources of capital was accepted and encouraged; now it is rejected except as a temporary expedient. The real story of migration over the recent period of globalization has been one of intra-country migration – from rural to urban areas – rather than truly global migration.

Inasmuch as there is global international migration for employment, it is concentrated on the Gulf states, on North America and between Eastern and Western Europe. A crude estimate of this category gives a figure of about 20 million in 1990 (before the Gulf War, which saw a massive return home, particularly of Third World migrant workers, from the Gulf states). This form of international labour force reached its peak in the early 1970s. The worldwide recession and later developments such as the Gulf War interrupted the growth of temporary migrant employment. A large propor-tion of these workers are illegally residing and working abroad. Legal expatriate workers tend to be in the managerial, skilled and technical employment categories.

One consequence of these levels of international migration and employ-ment is that remittances of money home now constitute an important component of international financial flows and of the national incomes of some small states. It is estimated that remittances rose from $3,133 billion in 1970 to $30,401 billion in 1988 (Segal 1993, p. 150). But this still represented less than 5 per cent of the total value of world trade, though it has been increasing at a faster pace than has the value of that trade. This suggests either that the incentives to move this kind of labour have grown relative to the movements of goods and services, or that the rewards to this kind of labour have risen independently. The latter explanation could in turn be because more of the migrants are now to be found in the higher income categories of employment. The days of the unskilled, low-income mass migration look to be numbered, though considerable scope may remain for continued temporary migration to undertake menial and domestic tasks in the richer countries.

Indeed, this is where government policy enters the picture explicitly. Policy is tightening on the growth in numbers of migrant workers, and even more so on the rights to permanent family immigration. There are differences here, particularly between Europe and the USA, with the latter still maintaining a more open and liberal regime (Livi Bacci 1993, p. 41). Indeed, *within* the EU there has been considerable migration, in recent years from the new accession countries of the East, towards Western Europe. But outside of this, as Castles and Miller suggest: 'Prospects are slim for significant increased legal migration flows to Western democracies over the short to medium term. . . . Political constraints will not permit this . . . [There is] some room for highly skilled labour, family reunification and refugees, but not for the resumption of massive recruitment of foreign labour for low level jobs' (1993, pp. 265–6). The adverse labour market conditions in the advanced countries and the difficulty of providing work for existing citizens and resident alien workers will mean the curtailment of unwanted and illegal immigration.

Two sets of more general points are worth making in the light of these remarks. The first is that there have been phases of massive international migration over many centuries, and there seems nothing unprecedented about movements in the post-Second World War period, or those in more recent decades. The second related point is that in many ways the situation between 1815 and 1914 was much more open than it is today. The supposed era of 'globalization' has not seen the rise of a new unregulated and internationalized market in labour migration. In many ways, the world's underprivileged and poor have fewer international migratory possibilities nowadays than they had in the past. At least in the period of mass migration there was the option to uproot the whole family and move in the quest for better conditions, a possibility that seems to be rapidly shrinking for equivalent sections of the world's population today. They have little choice but to remain in poverty and stick it out. The 'empty lands' available to European and other settlers in the USA and Canada, South America, southern Africa and Australia and New Zealand just do not exist today, with a concomitant loss of 'freedom' for the world's poor.

Things look different for the well off and privileged, however. Those with professional qualifications and technical skills still have greater room for manoeuvre and retain the option to move if they wish. The 'club class' with managerial expertise, though relatively few in number in terms of the global population, are the most obvious manifestation of this inequity in long-term migratory opportunities.

## Early discriminatory trade blocs

Another strong contemporary feature of the international system that is often invoked as an indicator of 'globalization' is the emergence of large discriminatory regional trading blocs such as the EU, NAFTA and ASEAN + (the Association of South-East Asian Nations plus several other large East Asian countries). We will have much to say about these institutions in later chapters, but here it is worth pointing to the historical precedents for these kinds of bodies. A marked discrimination in trade and investment patterns was produced during the colonial empire period in the nineteenth century. For the French and British empires the biases to trade between the colonial power and its colonies were between two and four times greater than would have been expected given the 'natural' economic fundamentals that determine trade, such as the size of the countries involved, GDP per capita, proximity and common borders. The biases were even higher for Belgium, Italy and Portugal and their overseas dependencies. In fact, the concentration of trade with the countries that made up the British and French empires did not peak until 1938; it declined steadily following the independence movements after the Second World War, but did not reach unity until as late as 1984 (Frankel 1997, p. 126). Trade within the Austro-Hungarian Empire, before it broke up at the end of the First World War, was also four or five times what it would have been if determined simply by the 'natural' fundamentals (ibid., p. 119). The case of Japan and its 'co-prosperity sphere' is shown in table 2.7. Note that in 1990 the simple average share of trade confined to the East Asian countries was about the same as it was in 1913, and lower than in 1938 (Pertri 1994). Intra-East Asian investment integration was higher in 1938 than it was in the early 1990s.

Thus it was in the 1930s that overt discriminatory regionalism was probably at its height. There was a definite discriminatory sterling bloc, overlapping imperfectly with the British Empire/Commonwealth. Then there was a group of countries that remained on the Gold Standard, and a subsection of Central and South-Eastern European countries that gravitated towards Germany. The USA erected trade barriers, and formed a partial dollar bloc with the Spanish-speaking countries adjacent to North America. According to Frankel, all these were heavily discriminatory – though some more than others – except for the partial dollar bloc (Frankel 1997, pp. 127–8). The differences between the blocs have, however, been

**Table 2.7**   East Asian trade as a share of total trade for different countries (exports plus imports as percentage of total trade)

|                                    | 1913 | 1925 | 1938 | 1955 | 1990 |
|------------------------------------|------|------|------|------|------|
| China                              | 65   | 46   | 70   | 43   | 59   |
| Indonesia                          | 32   | 38   | 26   | 32   | 60   |
| Taiwan                             | –    | –    | 99   | 50   | 42   |
| Japan                              | 41   | 47   | 70   | 22   | 29   |
| Korea                              | –    | –    | 100  | 35   | 40   |
| Malaysia                           | 44   | 39   | 35   | 30   | 37   |
| Philippines                        | 18   | 15   | 11   | 17   | 43   |
| Thailand                           | 62   | 71   | 65   | 52   | 51   |
| Simple average                     | 42   | 43   | 59   | 35   | 45   |
| Excluding Korea, Taiwan            | 42   | 43   | 46   | 33   | 47   |
| Excluding Korea, Taiwan and Japan  | 42   | 42   | 41   | 35   | 50   |

*Note*: Higher percentages indicate greater trade intensity.
*Source*: Adapted from Pertri 1994, p. 111, table 10.1.

emphasized by Eichengreen and Irwin (1995, 1997). Sterling bloc countries traded disproportionately among themselves, and discrimination increased during the 1930s, while those remaining on the Gold Standard were more disparate. Inasmuch as they erected barriers between themselves, this reduced trade discrimination.

There have thus been several earlier periods of regionalization, some of which were more intense than the present period (see chapter 6). What is distinctive about the present situation, however, is the formation of larger formal *de jure* free trade area blocs and the extension of their *de facto* influence over a wider range of countries and areas. For the first time there are three almost continent-wide blocs (that is, the EU, NAFTA and Japan, plus some of East Asia) either firmly established or in proto-existence. In chapter 6 the current nature of these and other trading blocs is discussed further.

As a preliminary conclusion, then, we can say that the international economy was in many ways more open in the pre-1914 period up until the late 1990s. International trade and capital flows, both between the rapidly industrializing economies themselves and between these and their various colonial territories, were more important relative to GDP levels before the First World War than they probably are today. Add to this the issue of international migration just explored and we have at the beginning of the twenty-first century an extraordinarily developed, open and integrated international economy. Thus the present position is by no means unprecedented.

## International monetary and exchange rate regimes

An issue thrown up by the previous analysis is the existence of general monetary and exchange-rate regimes under which economic activity takes place and by which the international economy is ordered and governed. In broad terms we can divide the twentieth century into a number of fairly discrete periods as far as these regimes are concerned, as indicated by table 2.8.

There are two important preliminary points to note about this table. The first is the diversity of regimes it displays. It is often thought that there were just two regimes in the twentieth century, the Gold Standard and the Bretton Woods system – the former breaking down in the interwar period and the latter in the post-1973 period. These are indeed two of the main systems characterizing the twentieth century, but they are not the exclusive ones. In addition, there are important subperiods within some of the regimes depicted. All in all a rather more complex picture of international economic orders and systems needs to be painted if we are to have an adequate analysis.

Secondly, other than the number of regimes, what is striking about table 2.8 is the short period of time over which they operated. Only the Gold Standard existed for more than thirty years, while most of the others operated for considerably less. Clearly, what is designated here as 'interwar instability' does not conform to any obvious regime, since the 'rules of the game' during this period defy a consistent characterization. Thus we have split this period into three subperiods, none of which can be said to display exclusive (or inclusive) system-like features since arrangements were very fluid and overlapping, being either in decay or in embryonic reconstruction (sometimes both at the same time).

**Table 2.8**   History of monetary and exchange-rate regimes

| Regime | Period |
|---|---|
| 1 International Gold Standard | 1879–1914 |
| 2 Interwar instability | 1918–39 |
| (a) Floating | 1918–25 |
| (b) Return to Gold Standard | 1925–31 |
| (c) Return to floating | 1931–9 |
| 3 Semi-fixed rate dollar standard | 1945–71 |
| (a) Establishing convertibility | 1945–58 |
| (b) Bretton Woods system proper | 1958–71 |
| 4 Floating rate dollar standard | 1971–84 |
| (a) Failure to agree | 1971–4 |
| (b) Return to floating | 1974–84 |
| 5 EMS and greater Deutschmark zone | 1979–93 |
| 6 Plaza–Louvre intervention accords | 1985–93 |
| 7 Drift towards renewed global floating | 1993– |
| (a) Broad multilateral surveillance | 1993–7 |
| (b) Final end of the dollar peg (except, crucially, for East Asia and the Middle East) | 1997– |

*Sources*: Compiled from Eichengreen 1990, 1994; McKinnon 1993; and authors' own assessments.

The regime emerging immediately after the Second World War is characterized as a 'semi-fixed rate dollar standard', which has two subperiods. This is really a period of significant stability in exchange rates since few and only slight adjustments were made, but they were possible and sanctioned within this regime.[3] The period in its entirety is often classified as the Bretton Woods system (BWS), after the agreement signed in 1944, but we prefer to divide it into two subperiods, since full current account convertibility of the major currencies was not established until the end of 1958 (though this was a condition of the 1944 treaty). Thus the Bretton Woods system proper operated only for some thirteen years between 1958 and 1971,[4] perhaps a surprisingly short period of time.

The following period is designated the 'floating rate dollar standard'. The tumultuous events of 1971–4 are termed here the 'failure to agree' subperiod. This was a time, after the Nixon administration unilaterally suspended convertibility of the US dollar against gold in August 1971 and subsequently devalued, during which the international community gave up any attempt to manage its exchange rates collectively. Despite various plans and schemes designed to shore up the previous system during this period, the writing for it was already on the wall. But the advent of 'flexible' rates did little to dislodge the dollar as the *de facto* standard for the conduct of official and most private international monetary transactions. Also, this subperiod, despite its designation as a 'return to floating', displayed a definite set of 'rules of the game' in the conduct of international monetary transactions, and these were closely adhered to by the industrialized countries involved (McKinnon 1993, pp. 26–9; also see below).

Although the period of floating rates lasted for ten years, an important subperiod interrupts this after the European Monetary System (EMS) was established in 1979. This is termed a 'greater Deutschmark zone', to indicate the central importance of the German currency in acting as the standard for the other European currencies in the EMS. The EMS began to unscramble after the autumn of 1992 with first the departure of a number of its key currencies and then the widening of the bands in which the remaining currencies were allowed to fluctuate. Further devaluations of the Spanish peseta and Portuguese escudo followed in early 1995. The remains of the EMS, in this modified form, functioned until 1999, however, when it was transformed with the inauguration of European Monetary Union (EMU). In January 1999 twelve EU members created the Eurozone by adopting a single currency. This remains an important subregime in the international monetary sphere. As illustrated by the data in table 2.9, the Euro is becoming a major international currency, potentially rivalling the US dollar.

The sixth regime characterized in table 2.8 follows the Plaza and Louvre accords struck in 1985 and 1987, which had as their objective the stabilization (and, indeed, initially the reduction) of the value of the US dollar

**Table 2.9**  Official holdings of foreign exchange by currencies (%, end of year)

| Currencies | 1994 | 1995 | 1996 | 1997 | 1998 | 1999 | 2000 | 2001 | 2002 |
|---|---|---|---|---|---|---|---|---|---|
| Euro | – | – | – | – | – | 12.7 | 15.9 | 16.4 | 18.7 |
| US dollar | 56.5 | 56.9 | 60.2 | 62.2 | 65.7 | 67.9 | 67.5 | 67.5 | 64.5 |
| Japanese yen | 7.9 | 6.8 | 6.0 | 5.2 | 5.4 | 5.5 | 5.2 | 4.8 | 4.5 |
| Pound sterling | 3.3 | 3.2 | 3.4 | 3.6 | 3.9 | 4.0 | 3.8 | 4.0 | 4.4 |
| Deutschmark | 14.2 | 13.7 | 13.0 | 12.8 | 12.2 | – | – | – | – |
| Unspecified currencies | 6.6 | 9.2 | 8.6 | 8.7 | 9.3 | 9.3 | 6.9 | 6.6 | 7.3 |

*Source*: Adapted from European Union 2005, p. 180, table V6.

against the two other main currency blocs: the EMS–DM zone and that of the Japanese yen. Formally these accords introduced broad 'target zones' for exchange rates between the three currency blocs (the G3), allowing 'interventions' for stabilization around these rates (with concomitant sterilization of monetary impacts), and sanctioned the adjustment of the central rates according to 'economic fundamentals' when necessary. Monitoring by the G3 continued with a successful agreement in 1995 to reverse the slide of the dollar against the yen. After that the yen began to depreciate against the US dollar. However, it is arguable whether there was ever a real commitment to managing the rates actively against market sentiment, and thereby also to managing the G3 economies more generally (see also chapter 8). This is why, when this is considered alongside the partial demise of the EMS after 1992, we suggest a final possible regime, emerging in 1993–4, that hints at a drift towards floating rates like the more obvious floating rate regime of 1974–84. Initially the period was marked by broad multilateral surveillance. Immediately after the financial turmoil in 1997 and 1998 the East Asian countries were forced to suspend their link to the dollar, but that was quickly re-established, and this, along with the consolidation of the Euro bloc, remains the most important feature of the current global financial architecture. The implications of this architecture are taken up again in chapters 5, 6 and 7.

The main point of this brief history of international monetary arrangements is, first, to demonstrate the governed nature of the system throughout much of the twentieth century (with the possible exception of the twenty interwar years). Secondly, it is to suggest that there is nothing radically unusual about the present period. In these terms, there remains at least a quasi-system of order and governance. Thirdly, given the volatile nature of the international regimes and their short-lived character, there is no reason to believe that things cannot change significantly in the future, even the near future. The length of regimes may be getting shorter. But even if they are not, thirty years looks like an absolute maximum before strains begin to pull things apart (or perhaps push things together again). With this in mind, we should remember that what is often thought to have been the key regime 'watershed' year of 1973 was already twenty-five years behind us by 1998. In chapters 5, 6 and 7 we will take up the most pressing issues that have arisen in respect to the current exchange-rate regime and character-istics of the international financial system, namely the 'global imbalances' that typify the first decade of the twenty-first century.

## Openness and integration: what is at stake?

Returning to the broad issue of integration discussed above, the actual measurement of the degree of integration in financial markets is difficult both theoretically and empirically. Economic analysis in this area tends to be driven by the idea of 'efficient (international) financial market' theory; that is, that capital markets operate competitively to allocate (interna-tional) savings and investment so as to equalize returns on capital. Thus key indicators of the degree of integration would be measures such as inter-est rates as between countries or the value of the same shares on domestic and international stock markets: the nearer these are to parity between different national financial markets, the more integrated the international economy has become. With a fully integrated capital market there would be single international rates of interest on short-term and long-term loans, and a single share or bond price, other things remaining equal.

Of course, the key constraint here is the 'other things remaining equal' one. In reality they just do not, so the task of empirical analysis from within this dominant perspective is to account, and then adjust, for these 'imper-fections' so as to arrive at a proxy measure of the degree of 'true' integra-tion.[5] As might be expected, all this requires some formidable assumptions to be made, ones that few other than the truly converted cognoscenti might either appreciate or accept. However, despite some scepticism about this underlying approach, it is worth considering its main results.[6]

The degree of international financial integration could be analysed in a number of forms and at a number of levels (Frankel 1992; Herring and Litan 1995; Harris 1995). These can be grouped under three overlapping headings: those associated with interest-rate differentials; those associated with differential prices of securities; and those associated with real resource flows and capital mobility. We deal with each of these in turn, beginning with a discussion of the relationships between interest rates and exchange rates.

One of the most straightforward indicators of financial integration con-cerns offshore markets such as that for Eurocurrencies. Formally, measures of offshore financial market integration can be established in terms of covered interest-rate parities. This implies that depositors could receive the same return on whatever Eurocurrency they held, taking into account the cost involved in protecting against possible exchange-rate changes. Such interest-rate parity seemed to hold in the Eurocurrency markets. A more developed form of integration would be when offshore and onshore markets are closely linked, but it is here that difficulties begin to arise. Banking regulations and capital controls establish a separation between these two spheres, and these have often been introduced and maintained for public policy reasons. But with the progressive harmonization of banking regulations and the abandonment of capital controls, this form of integration was effectively established between the advanced countries by 1993: thus covered interest-rate parity between national rates has now also been more or less achieved.

Deeper forms of integration would be signalled first by uncovered interest-rate parity and then real interest-rate parity between deposits in different currencies. If the first condition holds, expected returns on investments in different currencies are the same when measured in terms of a single currency, so that capital flows equalize expected rates of return regardless of exposure to exchange-rate risk. This introduces an unobservable variable into the calculation, the 'speculative premium' associated with changes in expectations. In the case of real interest-rate parity, differential inflation rates are already anticipated in the nominal rates, so that real exchange rates are maintained and capital flows serve to equalize real interest rates across countries. While tests to measure the presence of these latter two forms of integration are complex and controversial, real interest-rate parity seemed far from established by the mid-1990s, so that the level of international financial integration fell short of what would prevail in a truly integrated system. By contrast, the Gold Standard period was one where short-term interest rates were closely correlated, and there was a strong tendency for real rates of return to be equalized internationally (Turner 1991, pp. 16–17).

The second broad approach is to focus on asset prices in different national financial systems. Here one problem is to distinguish domestic influences on prices from international ones, but there is a *prima facie* case that stock markets are closely linked, with disruption in one being quickly transmitted to others (so-called contagion). In this context it is changes in the 'volatility' of price movements that would represent an indicator of increased globalization, not the existence of links as such, and the evidence on this score remains at best ambiguous (Harris 1995, pp. 204–6). In fact, historically based studies have reinforced the impression of greater financial integration, measured in these terms, in the pre-First World War period. From within the broad perspective of the efficient capital market approach, Neal (1985) focused on asset price movements during the main financial crises occurring between 1745 and 1907. He measured the rapidity with which financial panic spread between one financial centre and another. This analysis found that there was already a surprisingly high degree of capital market integration between European financial centres as early as the mid-eighteenth century, but suggested that the degree of financial integration did not develop much further between then and 1900. Zevin, in his survey of a wide range of the financial integration literature, reports on a number of measures supporting the highly integrated nature of the pre-First World War international economy. He sums up thus:

> All these measures of transnational-securities trading and ownership are substantially greater in the years before the First World War than they are at present. More generally, every available descriptor of financial markets in the late nineteenth and early twentieth centuries suggests that they were more fully integrated than they were before or have been since. (Zevin 1992, pp. 51–2)

The Gold Standard period was thus also the one displaying the most interdependent and integrated international economy in terms of security markets, the extent of which seems yet to have been repeated.

How did the international financial system adjust so rapidly when technological developments were so primitive? In fact, the idea that the contemporary era of communications technology is unprecedented again needs to be challenged. The coming of the electronic telegraph system after 1870 in effect established more or less instantaneous information communications between all the major international financial and business centres (Standage 1998). By the turn of the century a system of international communications had been established that linked parties together much in the way that the contemporary internet does. Although the networks were not so developed in terms of individual subscribers, corporate and institutional linkages were dense and extensive. Compared to a reliance on the sailing ship (and even steam propulsion), the telegraph marked a real qualitative leap in communications technology, in many ways more important than the shift into computer technology and telematics after 1970.

A third important related approach in trying to identify the extent of financial integration involves measuring real resource flows: can increased financial integration be implied from increased capital mobility? In this case it is the relationship between national savings and investment that becomes the object of analysis. This approach has generated the most extensive literature, but its results remain controversial.

The more integrated the capital markets, the more mobile capital will become internationally and the more likely it is that domestic savings and investment will diverge. If there were a completely integrated global financial system, domestic investment would not be fundamentally constrained by domestic savings, and the correlation between savings and investment would be broken. Thus national economies will lose their ability to 'regulate' or 'determine' domestic investment. In fact, this is just another way of pointing to the key role of interest-rate differentials as a measure of integration and as the determinant of investment. As openness increases, domestic savings become irrelevant to domestic investment, since interest rates converge and savings and investment adjust accordingly.

But national savings–investment correlations did not unambiguously decline in the 1980s and 1990s, during the period of capital market liberalization and floating exchange rates. Careful analysis by Bosworth (1993, pp. 98–102) and by Obstfeld (1993, e.g. p. 50) shows this not to be the case (despite the less than careful commentary by some others, for instance Goldstein and Mussa 1993, p. 25). The persistence of the correlation between national savings and investment, first established in 1980 (Feldstein and Horioka 1980), well into a period of financial liberalization, deregulation and supposed global integration, testifies to the continued robust relative autonomy of financial systems, and this despite the (sometimes desperate) attempts by conventional economic analysts to prove otherwise (e.g. Bayoumi 1990). Table 2.10 brings together previous OLS (ordinary least squares) estimates of a simple gross savings–investment equation and adds our own estimates for the period 1991–5.

The $\beta$ coefficient can be interpreted as the 'savings retention coefficient': the proportion of incremental savings that is invested domestically (Feldstein and Bacchetta 1991, p. 206). Thus, over the period 1991–5, for every dollar saved in the main OECD countries, 67 cents would have been invested domestically. Clearly the interwar period and that directly after the Second World War represented the high points of a 'closed' international financial system on this measure. Between 96 per cent and 89 per cent of incremental domestic savings was invested domestically. There was a decline in this ratio during the 1980s and 1990s, but the value of the $\beta$ coefficient eased up in the first half of the 1990s. (Most of this decline can probably be attributed to the lagged effects of the collapse in the savings ratio of a single country, the USA, after 1979: Frankel 1992 and chapter 7 below). These coefficients were also lower than that for the high Gold Standard period of 1900–13, which is often thought to have been the pinnacle of an 'open' international financial system as well. However, note that the R2 correlation coefficient has become stronger since 1974–80. Recent evidence shows the ß coefficient to have declined even further at the global

**Table 2.10**  Savings and investment correlations, 1900–1995

| $(I/Y)i = a + \beta(S/Y)i + ui$ | | | | | |
|---|---|---|---|---|---|
| 1900–13 | 1926–38 | 1960–74 | 1974–80 | 1981–90 | 1991–5 |
| $\beta$ | | | | | |
| 0.774 | 0.959 | 0.887 | 0.867 | 0.636 | 0.67 |
| (0.436) | (0.082) | (0.074) | (0.170) | (0.108) | (0.086) |
| $R^2$ | | | | | |
| 0.26 | 0.94 | 0.91 | 0.56 | 0.64 | 0.75 |

*Notes*:  Data from 1960 are for 22 main OECD-member developed economies.
I = investment; Y = national income; S = savings; u = error term.
Figures in brackets beneath $\beta$ coefficients are standard errors.
*Sources*: 1960–74, Feldstein and Horioka 1980, p. 231, table 2; 1991–5, authors' own estimates; all other years, Obstfeld 1993.

level (from 0.92 in 1987–91 to 0.25 in 2001–6 for emerging market econo-mies only) (Garcia-Herrero and Wooldridge 2007, p. 61, graph 1). All in all, this analysis does not as yet indicate any dramatic change in the rela-tionship between domestic saving and investment during the period of 'globalization'.[7]

So long as governments continue to target their current accounts, retain some sovereignty within their borders (so that at least the threat of govern-ment intervention in cross-border capital movements remains) and differ-entially regulate their financial systems, investors cannot think about domestic and foreign assets in the same way. Different national financial systems are made up of different institutions and arrangements, with dif-ferent conceptions of the future and assessments of past experience, and thus operate with different modalities of calculation. All these features factor into a continued diversity of expectations and outlooks which cannot all be reduced to a single global marketplace or logic. What is more, even the most committed of the integrationists who have looked at national savings–investment correlations tend to conclude that the less developed countries (LDCs) and most NICs remain largely out of the frame as far as this form of financial integration is concerned. Thus, even for the integra-tion enthusiasts, there are limits to the extent of the 'globalization' of financial markets.[8]

However, the basic Feldstein–Horioka findings, while proving very robust and reproducible, have attracted heavy criticism, mainly because they seem so counter-intuitive. Against the conclusion that the high correla-tion between national savings and investment is the result of a lack of financial integration are arguments that (a) it might reflect net flows, which disguise much larger gross flows; (b) if the data are disaggregated into private and public sector flows, lower correlations appear for solely private sector behaviour, so that it is government policy that accounts for the strong overall relationship (Bayoumi 1990); (c) floating exchange rates and associ-ated uncertainties have lowered capital mobility (Bayoumi and Rose 1993); (d) the close correlations may be because of exogenously determined pro-ductivity shocks and the way they are handled domestically (Ghosh 1995); and, finally (e), although the original findings are robust, they have been fatally undermined by the emergence of the large US balance of payments deficits since the mid-1980s, and this has yet to be properly picked up by econometric analyses (Frankel 1992).

Clearly, there are a number of possible reasons for the high correlation between aggregate savings and investment. Most of the points just made do not so much undermine this relationship as serve to explain it in the context of a range of contemporary conditions. One problem is to distin-guish those points that pertain to the determinants of real capital invest-ment flows as opposed to overall financial ones. With the exception of the final point, they do not undermine the result of a continued separation of capital markets: they provide reasons for the findings which are compatible with a continued relatively unintegrated international financial system – one that continues to allow for more national autonomy than might be generally appreciated. In a longer-term perspective, Zevin compares the post-1960 findings with a similar type of analysis for the 1890s onwards. This only confirms his other results showing that the Gold Standard period was an era of more effective capital mobility and financial openness than that from the 1960s onwards. Investment–savings autarky was much less between 1870 and 1910 (Zevin 1992, p. 57, table 3.2). Below and in chapter 5 we return to point (e) above – concerning the significant change in the post-1985 period vis-à-vis the USA – but this pertains to general financial flows between the USA and East Asia and not just real resource flows.

One further possible explanation for these results, particularly over the recent period, has to do with the rate of return on financial investments in different economies. If there is no significant difference in the return on financial investment, then we would not expect a large redistribution of capital relative to savings compared to a situation where there was extreme variation in returns. Thus the current situation of low financial asset mobility could be accounted for by a general convergence of returns as between different economies. In fact there was considerable convergence of underlying productivity between the main industrial economies over the period from 1962 to 1993, though with a striking general decline in productivity levels (which had yet to be reversed by the late 1990s). Of course, this does not preclude intense short-term movements of funds between financial centres in search of small arbitrage gains on currency transactions, which is something that has characterized contemporary currency markets (indeed, underlying convergence may encourage this very activity). We discuss this further below and in chapter 6.

However, with respect to convergence – which itself could constitute a measure of the integration between economies – indications of this emerged for the major economies as their real economic business cycles synchronized in the mid-1970s and early 1980s. But this was reversed during the upturn of the late 1980s to early 1990s, when a general desynchronization set in (OECD 1994a, pp. 37–43; see also table 6.2, p. 164 below). Thus it is inappropriate to read too much into any measure of 'convergence' as an indicator of integration which does not have a long-term empirical provenance or carry robust explanatory significance.[9]

Of particular importance in this context was the growing asymmetric relationship between the G3 countries over the 1970s and 1980s in terms of financial flows, even though the close relationships between their domestic savings and investment levels did not alter much (Bosworth 1993, chap. 3). While there was a decline in the savings ratios in most advanced countries, so that investment ratios also fell, there was a stronger fall in both of these in the USA than in other countries. The USA in effect imported capital to make up for a decline in its domestic saving, and not to sustain higher levels of investment. This happened along with the emergence there of a persistent current account deficit. This led to financing problems in the context of the so-called twin deficits. However, how far these international financing problems were the result of the twin deficits rather than the abandonment of fixed exchange rates and of capital controls and financial market deregulation remains a point of dispute. In chapter 7 we discuss this issue further.

The importance of this assessment of openness and integration is obvious. It has to do with the ability of distinct national economies to devise and regulate their own economic policies. The fact that the degree of constraint on national economies in the Gold Standard period seems to have been consistently greater than at any time since should not blind us to the problems and issues facing economies because of the level of integration at the present time. It is certainly the case that, on the basis of some of the measures discussed above, the level of economic integration has increased since 1960 – though this is not obvious on just the savings–investment measure, except perhaps for the most recent period. In addition, it would be difficult to accept that the qualitative dimension has been constant over the entire period since 1870. The number and range of financial instruments has changed dramatically since 1960, for instance, and with them new problems of management and regulation have arisen (Turner 1991; Cosh et al. 1992). Before we examine the internationalization of money and short-term capital markets, however, we need to look to the more mundane areas of financial integration to see whether the underlying framework for the operation of capital markets has radically changed in the recent period. Money markets are probably more highly integrated than are capital markets. But it is capital markets that most immediately affect the economic prospects for the long-term growth of national economies.

## Developments in international financial market activity up to the late 1990s

This section investigates financial market developments up until the mid- to late 1990s. More recent changes and their implications are assessed in chapters 5 and 6 in particular. The key issues can be posed by first investigating the cross-border transactions and holdings of bonds and equities between countries and in various domestic financial institutions. As a percentage of GDP, the cross-border *transactions* in bonds and equities have escalated since the mid-1970s, as shown in table 2.11. But if this is looked at from a slightly different angle, changes may not appear quite so dramatic.

For instance, table 2.12 shows the actual *holdings* of foreign bonds and equities in the accounts of institutional investors (not just transactions between countries), expressed as a percentage of their total holdings. This reveals a general trend in the growth of importance of foreign securities

**Table 2.11** Cross-border transactions in bonds and equities (as a percentage of GDP)

| | 1975 | 1980 | 1985 | 1989 | 1990 | 1991 | 1992 | 1993 | 1994 | 1995 | 1996 |
|---|---|---|---|---|---|---|---|---|---|---|---|
| **USA** | 4 | 9 | 35 | 101 | 89 | 96 | 107 | 129 | 131 | 135 | 164 |
| **Japan** | 2 | 8 | 62 | 156 | 119 | 92 | 72 | 78 | 60 | 65 | 84[a] |
| **Germany** | 5 | 7 | 33 | 66 | 57 | 55 | 85 | 171 | 159 | 172 | 200 |
| **France** | – | 5 | 21 | 52 | 54 | 79 | 122 | 187 | 201 | 180 | 227[b] |
| **Italy** | 1 | 1 | 4 | 18 | 27 | 60 | 92 | 192 | 207 | 253 | 468 |
| **Canada** | 3 | 10 | 27 | 55 | 64 | 81 | 113 | 153 | 212 | 194 | 258 |

*Notes*: Transactions are gross purchases and sales of securities between residents and non-residents.
[a] Based on settlement data.
[b] January–September at an annual rate.
*Source*: BIS 1996–7, p. 79, table V.1.

**Table 2.12** Institutional investors' holdings of foreign securities, 1980–1993 (percentage of total securities holdings)

| | 1980 | 1985 | 1990 | 1993 |
|---|---|---|---|---|
| **USA**[a] | | | | |
| Private pension funds[b] | 1.0 | 3.0 | 4.1 | 7.1 |
| Mutual funds | – | – | 4.0[c] | 8.0 |
| **Japan** | | | | |
| Postal life insurance | 0.0 | 6.7 | 11.6 | 12.3 |
| Private insurance companies | 8.1 | 23.2 | 29.9 | 22.3 |
| **Canada** | | | | |
| Life insurance companies | 2.2 | 2.3 | 2.4 | 3.1 |
| Pension funds | 6.1 | 6.6 | 7.0 | 10.6 |
| **Italy** | | | | |
| Insurance companies | – | – | 13.6 | 12.2 |
| **United Kingdom** | | | | |
| Insurance companies[d] | 6.3 | 14.1 | 14.6 | – |
| Pension funds[e] | 10.8 | 17.3 | 23.2 | – |
| **Australia** | | | | |
| Life insurance companies | – | – | 14.0 | 18.8 |
| **Austria** | | | | |
| Insurance companies | 14.1 | 11.6 | 10.1 | 9.9 |
| Investment funds | 27.0 | 13.2 | 18.7 | 25.1 |
| **Belgium** | | | | |
| Insurance companies | 5.5 | 8.6 | 5.2 | – |
| **Netherlands** | | | | |
| Insurance companies | 6.9 | 22.9 | 20.2 | 26.0 |
| Private pension funds | 26.6 | 28.1 | 36.6 | 36.9 |
| Public pension funds | 14.7 | 9.9 | 16.6 | 20.2 |
| **Sweden** | | | | |
| Insurance companies | – | 1.5[f] | 10.5 | 12.3 |

*Notes*: [a] Per cent of total assets held by these funds.
[b] Tax exempt funded schemes (excluding individual retirement accounts).
[c] 1991.
[d] Long-term funds.
[e] Pension funds exclude central government sector but include other public sector funds.
[f] 1987.
*Source*: Edey and Hviding 1995, p. 33, table 10.

since 1980 (except for Austria). For most countries the foreign securities holdings by their institutional investors were in the 10 to 30 per cent range, with only the Netherlands, Ireland and New Zealand having a stake over 30 per cent. What the figures for 1993 in table 2.12 demonstrate, however, is the enormous variation between countries in terms of the importance of foreign holdings. Some financial systems were clearly much more 'open' than others on this measure. For instance, of the G5 large countries, the UK and Japan were much more 'open' than the USA, Germany and France. And this issue of the variation in financial systems is confirmed by the data collected in table 2.13, where the domestic and international breakdown of corporate equity holdings is shown for 1996.

From all these figures, what is clear is that there is no obvious convergence of all the advanced countries to a common openness position. By and large the differences between them seem to have been maintained, indicating continued variation in the characteristics and structures of their domestic financial systems. Thus, up to the mid-1990s at least, the operation of 'globalization' did not seem to have forced the domestic financial institutions of the advanced countries to have fundamentally broken with the historical variation in their character, though there had been some increase in their overall internationalization.

Similar comments could be made about the operation of commercial banks. An increase in the importance of foreign assets and liabilities in their balance sheets is evident from table 2.14, attributable mainly to a growth between 1960 and 1980, since when the positions have tended to stabilize.

**Table 2.13**  Distribution of outstanding listed corporate equity among different categories of shareholders in selected OECD countries (percentage at year-end 1996)

|  | USA | Japan | Germany | France | UK[a] | Sweden | Australia |
|---|---|---|---|---|---|---|---|
| Financial sector | 46 | 42 | 30 | 30 | 68 | 30 | 37 |
| Banks | 6 | 15 | 10 | 7 | 1 | 1 | 3 |
| Insurance companies and pension funds | 28 | 12 | 12 | 9 | 50 | 14 | 25 |
| Investment funds | 12 |  | 8 | 11 | 8 | 15 | – |
| Other financial institutions | 1 | 15[b] | – | 3 | 9 | – | 9[c] |
| Non-financial enterprises | – | 27 | 42 | 19 | 1 | 11 | 11 |
| Public authorities | – | 1 | 4 | 2 | 1 | 8 | – |
| Households | 49 | 20 | 15 | 23 | 21 | 19 | 20 |
| **Rest of the world** | **5** | **11** | **9** | **25** | **9** | **32** | **32** |
| Total | 100 | 100 | 100 | 100 | 100 | 100 | 100 |

*Notes*: [a] United Kingdom figures are for end 1994.
[b] For Japan, pension and investment funds are included in 'other financial institutions'.
[c] Australian figures are for end September 1996; investment funds are included in 'other financial institutions'.
*Source*: OECD 1998, table 1.

**Table 2.14**   Foreign assets and liabilities as a percentage of assets of commercial banks for selected countries, 1960–1996

|  | 1960 | 1970 | 1980 | 1990 | 1996 |
|---|---|---|---|---|---|
| **France** | | | | | |
| Assets | – | 16.0 | 30.0 | 24.9 | 30.9 |
| Liabilities | – | 17.0 | 22.0 | 28.6 | 30.2 |
| **Germany** | | | | | |
| Assets | 2.4 | 8.7 | 9.7 | 16.3 | 16.0 |
| Liabilities | 4.7 | 9.0 | 12.2 | 13.1 | 12.9 |
| **Japan** | | | | | |
| Assets | 2.6 | 3.7 | 4.2 | 13.9 | 13.8 |
| Liabilities | 3.6 | 3.1 | 7.3 | 19.4 | 10.6 |
| **Netherlands** | | | | | |
| Assets | 18.4 | 23.1 | 33.0 | 33.5 | 33.2 |
| Liabilities | 7.1 | 22.2 | 33.9 | 31.2 | 34.1 |
| **UK** | | | | | |
| Assets | 6.2 | 46.1 | 64.7 | 45.0 | 47.0 |
| Liabilities | 13.9 | 49.7 | 67.5 | 49.3 | 48.8 |
| **USA** | | | | | |
| Assets | 1.4 | 2.2 | 11.0 | 5.6 | 2.6 |
| Liabilities | 3.7 | 5.4 | 9.0 | 6.9 | 8.2 |

*Source*: IMF, *International Financial Statistics Yearbook*, 1986 and 1997.

(There are some exceptions to this, notably in the case of Sweden, which experienced a rapid growth over almost the entire period 1960 to 1996, to reach one of the highest levels in the latter year.) But there remains a great variation between the economies shown, largely based on entrenched historical differences.

What the data in these tables indicate is the continued pertinence of domestic policy choices, something rather ignored by the globalization analysis. We might presume that 'globalization' had little impact on these choices since, in the case of Hong Kong and Singapore in 1993, for instance, both had been subject to similar external pressures from globalization (with total trade to GDP ratios of 252 per cent and 279 per cent, respectively) while their institutional holdings of international bonds and equities were 60 per cent and 0 per cent, respectively. The causes were purely 'domestic', to do with policy choices determining the decision whether to invest in international or domestic assets. Similarly in the case of the advanced industrial economies: it has been policy choices (and mistakes) that have driven the move towards greater interdependence and internationalization, as displayed for instance in table 2.5, not some mysterious process of 'globalization'. For instance, take the remarks of two commentators who more or less unambiguously welcome the moves towards greater openness and integration:

> In some sense, authorities have suffered the fate of getting what they asked for. They wanted greater participation by foreign investors in their government debt markets, in part to make it easier to finance larger fiscal and external balances. They wanted a more efficient financial system that would erode the power of local monopolies and offer savers a higher rate of return and firms a lower cost of capital. They welcomed innovations that provided a wider range of hedging possibilities against volatile asset prices, and that made it more convenient to unbundle risks. They wanted to regain business that had migrated to the off-shore centres in search of a less restrictive regulatory environment, and to level the playing field against foreign competitors. Much of that has taken place. But along with it has also come the creation of an enormous pool of mobile, liquid capital whose support, or lack of it, can often be the measure of difference in the success of stabilization, reform, exchange rate, and tax policy. (Goldstein and Mussa 1993, p. 42)

Despite their complacency, these authors have a point. Though, along with them, we are not suggesting here that *everything* was just the result of either deliberate policy choices or mistakes by the authorities.

Similar remarks could be made about the other ways of measuring and assessing the degree of international financial integration discussed above: real interest-rate convergence, equity price movements, offshore and onshore yields, covered or uncovered interest-rate parity, international portfolio diversity, etc. To quote Goldstein and Mussa again:

> Even though there is by now a burgeoning literature that addresses directly the measurement of international capital market integration, it has proven difficult to reach firm and clear conclusions about the degree – if not the trend – of integration. This ambiguity reflects the fact that no single method of measuring the degree of integration is completely free of conceptual and technical difficulties that cloud its interpretation. (Goldstein and Mussa 1993, p. 14)

Caution remains the order of the day. It is still reasonable to argue, for instance, that short-term interest rates are set nationally, and that even long-term interest rates are fundamentally driven by the decisions of important state authorities, as in the USA, Japan, and Frankfurt for the Eurozone, rather than totally by the anonymous forces of global markets.

Even those alternative approaches that do not concentrate directly or indirectly on financial integration, like those that stress comparisons of consumption paths between countries, cannot reach an unambiguous conclusion that financial integration has taken place (Bayoumi and MacDonald 1995).

### The rise of short-term lending

Broadly speaking, the period since the liberalization moves of the 1970s has seen an upsurge in international financial activity associated with three developments: increased extent of international lending, financial innovation and financial agglomeration. In this section we concentrate on the latter two.

The prodigious growth of international lending over the period of the 1970s to the late 1990s is indicated in table 2.15. By 1998 total loans were over US$2,000 billion – a 2,000-fold increase on the late 1970s position. A key development is the growth of 'securitization': the displacement of conventional loan business (traditionally conducted by banks) by the issue of marketable bonds and other securities. The other significant feature is the growth of 'uncommitted facilities', particularly in the Eurobond market.

As part of these processes, financial innovation has become rife, which itself involves several features. The range of new instruments is shown in table 2.16. Since most of these are derivative of the move towards security lending – they provide borrowers and lenders with the possibility of hedging against the risk of interest-rate and exchange-rate movements – they are collectively termed 'derivatives'. A lot of these are very esoteric instruments, which are quite difficult to understand, monitor or control. In part this is because new ways of trading have emerged, in particular over-the-counter (OTC) markets in which intermediaries deal among themselves in large monetary volumes, bypassing the established exchanges which use traditional trading floors.

The importance of these OTC instruments can be seen in table 2.16. By 1991 their worth was larger than that of exchange-traded instruments and was more than 50 per cent of the total of foreign currency claims of all banks reporting to the Bank for International Settlements (BIS). They showed spectacular growth during the 1990s, and the figures for 2006 indicate their continued spectacular growth through the early 2000s. Such instruments are often traded 'off-balance sheet' – they earn a fee income rather than constituting part of a financial institution's asset or liability structure. These developments provide opportunities for intermediaries to engage in risk arbitrage in a lower-cost and less regulated environment, but

**Table 2.15** Borrowing on international capital markets, 1976–1997 (US$bn, annual averages)

|  | 1976–80 | 1981–5 | 1986–90 | 1991 | 1992 | 1997 |
|---|---|---|---|---|---|---|
| Securities[a] | 36.2 | 96.4 | 234.7 | 332.1 | 357.2 | 916.7 |
| Loans | 59.4 | 72.0 | 103.1 | 116.0 | 117.9 | 390.4 |
| Committed back-up facilities |  | 35.2 | 18.7 | 7.7 | 6.7 | 2.7 |
| Uncommitted facilities[b] |  |  | 70.9 | 80.2 | 127.7 | 459.5 |
| Total | 95.6 | 203.6 | 427.4 | 536.0 | 609.5 | 1,769.3 |
| % change on previous year |  |  |  | +23.2 | +13.7 | +50.6 |

*Notes*: [a] International and foreign bonds and, as from 1986, issues of international equities.
[b] Mainly Euro-commercial paper and medium-term note programmes.
*Sources*: OECD 1993; 1994b; 1998, p. 49.

**Table 2.16** Growth in markets for selected derivative instruments: notional principal amounts outstanding at end year, in US$bn equivalent, 1986–2006

|  | 1986 | 1990 | 1997 | 2006 |
|---|---|---|---|---|
| **Exchange-traded instruments** | 588 | 2,291 | 12,207 | 70,443 |
| Interest-rate futures | 370 | 1,454 | 7,489 | 24,476 |
| Interest-rate options | 146 | 600 | 3,640 | 38,116 |
| Currency futures | 10 | 16 | 52 | 161 |
| Currency options | 39 | 56 | 33 | 79 |
| Stock market index features | 15 | 70 | 217 | 1,045 |
| Options on stock market indices | 8 | 95 | 777 | 6,565 |
| **Over-the-counter instruments** | 500ᵉ | 3,451 | 25,453 | 414,290 |
| Interest rate swaps | 400ᵉ | 2,312 | 19,171 | 229,241 |
| Currency and cross-currency interest-rate swaps | 100ᵉ | 578 | 1,560 | 40,239 |
| Other derivative instruments | – | 561 | 4,723 | – |
| *Memorandum item: Cross-border plus local foreign currency claims of BIS reporting banks* | 4,031 | 7,578 | – | – |

*Note*: e = estimate.
*Sources*: OECD 1993, p. 26, table 3; BIS 1998, p. 155, table VIII.5. For 2006, BIS 2007, Statistical Appendix, compiled from tables 19 and 20.

they thereby raise important new problems of systemic exposure to risk. The overall growth in financial derivatives between 1986 and 1997 is shown in figure 2.6. Note that the trading of these instruments is more or less totally confined to the big three financial centres associated with the Triad. We discuss these issues again in chapter 6.

Financial innovation continues apace. The latest developments represent a resurgence of bond instruments, with so-called dragon bonds and global bonds. 'Dragon bonds' are issued and traded simultaneously just on East Asian markets, while their 'global' counterparts are issued and traded in all major international financial centres on a round-the-clock basis. After the first global bond was marketed by the World Bank in 1989, this market expanded to over US$100 billion by mid-1994, capturing 8 per cent of total external bond issue in that year (OECD 1994b, p. 57, table 1).

This latest development in bond markets testifies to the strength of the trend towards internationalization in the world's financial systems. But, as mentioned above, the penetration of foreign assets into domestic institutional investment markets is still relatively light. The United States, in particular, remains highly undiversified and autonomous on this score. Inasmuch as global trading of securities and derivatives exists, it still tends to remain within a single region (North America, Europe or Asia-Pacific).

But again there is a trend in the government bond market towards further openness. The average foreign penetration of national government bond markets in advanced countries increased from 10 per cent in 1983 to

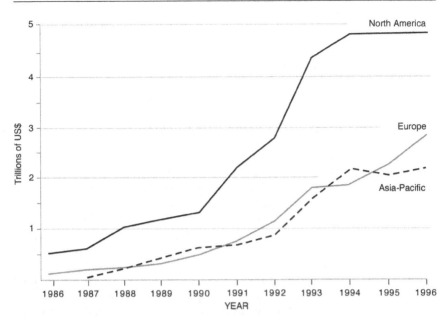

**Figure 2.6** Financial derivatives: notional amount outstanding on organized exchanges (year end)

*Source*: European Union 1997a, p. 15, chart 18.

15 per cent in 1989 (Turner 1991); for the EU countries, it increased only from 19 per cent in 1987 to 26 per cent in 1993 (European Union 1997a, p. 14, table 13).

The final issue to discuss in this section is the development of financial conglomerates. The international financial services industry is increasingly characterized by a small number of highly capitalized securities and banking houses which are global players with diversified activities. In part this is the result of the continuing trend towards predominantly institutional investment. 'Collective saving' is a strengthening feature of all OECD countries, so the institutions managing these funds could become key international players.

Broadly speaking, there is worldwide excess capacity in this industry, leading to intense competitive pressures to which cost-cutting and diversification are the strategic commercial responses. As a result, the financial conglomerates operate through very complex and often opaque corporate structures. Attempts at risk transfer between a shrinking number of players, and even between the different components of the companies themselves, are legion. Thus contagion risk, market risk and systemic risk have all increased, presenting new and important regulatory problems for governments and international bodies (see chapters 6 and 7).

An important point to note about the present era as compared with the Gold Standard period is that the recent growth of international lending has not just dramatically increased the range of financial instruments: it has changed the whole character of capital flows. As mentioned above, late nineteenth-century lending was mainly long-term in nature, going to finance investment in real assets. Even that part of total flows consisting of investment in financial assets was used mainly to finance real investment. This is no longer so. The explosion of aggregate lending had until very recently been made up almost exclusively of financial assets. Only since the mid-1980s has substantial real investment reappeared with the growth of FDI.

But financial innovation proceeds at an ever increasing rate. Just as this book was being prepared another wave of innovation was about to hit the international system, associated with sovereign wealth funds (SWF). These funds – in early 2008 estimated to total possibly US$12,000bn – are controlled by agencies closely associated with national governments. Some are highly transparent in their activities, for example, the Norwegian Fund – which only takes small positions in the companies it invests in – while others are completely opaque (for example, those from the Gulf states) and aligned with 'activist investors' or private equity groups, which have made bids for large and sometimes strategic companies in the advanced industrial countries. Because of their sheer size and connections to national governments, these SWFs are likely to become a major issue in the international financial architecture in the coming years.

### The overall picture: history, the current situation and the immediate future

In the final part of this chapter we review the changing nature of national economic management and its interaction with international mechanisms of integration so as to chart the broad contours of the present situation facing the international economy. This has as its objective an analysis of the implications of the main regimes identified in table 2.8 for economic autonomy.

To a large extent the Gold Standard must act as a benchmark in this discussion because of its pivotal position as the first integrated economic mechanism and the key features it displayed. The system carries great ideological and theoretical significance since not only was it 'voluntarily' entered into by the parties involved (there was no 'founding treaty'), it is also supposed to have embodied the principle of 'automaticity' in its operation and adjustments. In most orthodox accounts, other subsequent systems are measured against the Gold Standard – and, it must be added, often found wanting.

The basics of the system involve the fixing of an official gold price for each currency, combined with the free export and import of gold with no current or capital account restrictions. The persistent movement of gold into or out of a country is then permitted to influence the domestic money supply in each country. Thus the issue of bank notes and coinage is directly linked to the level of gold reserves. Any short-run liquidity crisis (that is, a gold drain) is met first by lending by the central bank at premium rates ('lender of last resort' facility). If the gold price ('mint parity') has to be suspended, this should only be temporary, and convertibility is restored as soon as possible – if necessary with the aid of domestic deflationary policies. Here arises the crucial link between domestic and international conditions: there must be domestic wage and price/cost flexibility to allow the nominal price level to be determined endogenously by the worldwide demand and supply of gold. Thus the Gold Standard, in so far as it actually functioned along these lines, represented the quintessential integrated economy, where 'national autonomy' was minimal.

As might be expected, the Gold Standard never worked quite in this automatic manner. Great difficulty was experienced at times in generating the deflationary domestic measures that the system implied as a condition of its operation. This led to various 'gold devices' that cushioned the domestic economy from the full rigours of gold movements, most important among these being disguised changes in the exchange rates of the domestic currency against gold to protect reserves or to maintain the level of domestic economic activity (so-called massaging of the gold points). Despite this, however, the exchange rates stayed within remarkably narrow bands between 1870 and 1914.[10] The system also required a remarkable degree of cooperation between central bankers because all manner of discretionary judgements and actions were necessary if the system was to function – there were a good many asymmetrical adjustments that needed to be made which in effect circumvented the formal rules.

Within the terms of the Gold Standard there was no single currency that provided the nominal anchor for the money supply or price level, since that was done by the system as a whole and by the supply and demand for gold. No single country took responsibility for monitoring 'the money supply' which was the supposed key to the success of the system, not even the British authorities. It was the UK's commitment to free trade (along with its ability to police this) and the depth of its financial markets in London that supported the system, however, and provided the key political anchor for its effective functioning. The economic weakness of the Gold Standard arose from the way supply and demand shocks were designed to be outside any national jurisdiction, so that volatile economic activity was magnified, a constant feature of the system. In addition, any excessive accumulation of gold stocks by a single country could also trigger a generalized deflation of the system, whether it was involuntary or not.

It is the instability of the interwar years that still haunts the international economic system, and provides the main reason for the concern and uncertainty associated with current trends in the international economy. The constant concern of the international community is to avoid a repeat of this period, when, as we have seen, international (and domestic) economic activity fell dramatically (foreign trade fell by two-thirds between 1929 and 1933, comprehensive capital controls were introduced, and devaluations and deflations took place). Even in 1938, trade volume was barely 90 per cent of its 1929 level, despite a full recovery in world production. In the wake of all this, belligerent protectionist power blocs emerged which eventually fought to challenge one another's existence.

The BWS was designed so as to avoid the external constraint imposed on national economies by the Gold Standard, which had operated so disastrously in the interwar period. What was needed was flexibility to support nationally decided policies, on the one hand, but enough stability to avoid competitive devaluations, on the other. The solution negotiated at Bretton Woods was for a fixed but adjustable system, linked to the dollar standard as numeraire (the base value for the system). Currencies were fixed in terms of the US dollar, which itself was to be convertible into gold; 'fundamental disequilibriums' were adjustable with IMF consent; national economies were given autonomy to pursue their own price level and employment objectives unconstrained by a common nominal price anchor. National capital markets were kept relatively separate by sanctioning capital controls on transactions other than current ones, and the domestic impacts of exchange-rate interventions were 'sterilized' by drawing on official exchange reserves and IMF credits, which thereby acted as the buffers between domestic and international monetary conditions, adding to domestic autonomy.

The well-known and tortuous story of how the BWS fared and its shortcomings in the post-war period will not be repeated here. Its key feature was a reliance on American 'passivity', and when this was no longer viable (because of fears of the loss of American international competitiveness) neither was the system itself. The remarks above are designed to demonstrate (a) that this was a definite regime, and (b) how the issue of (relative) national economic autonomy was built into that regime. What the BWS demonstrated, however, was that there was no autonomy, in the terms laid out so far, for the US economy if the system was to function as described. This may sound odd given the leading role that the USA played in the international economy over the period and the way it is perceived as dictating the 'rules of the game' to its own advantage. But one of the paradoxes here is that, strictly speaking, once those rules were in place, the behaviour of the US economy was just as circumscribed by them as was the conduct of the other economies in the system, if in different ways.

The USA could not 'choose' its own price and employment level independently of others. It had to remain passive in terms of its exchange rate, hold minimal reserves of foreign exchange, provide liquidity to the system by acting as its creditor, and anchor the world price of internationally tradeable goods in terms of dollars by its own domestic monetary policy. If there was to be no international inflation, then that domestic monetary policy was constrained by the dictates of a system in which partner choices were paramount – *formal* American monetary independence was just that.[11] Clearly, up to a point this also benefited the USA since, so long as it remained the strongest export economy in such a system, it required a stable exchange rate and an inflation-proof regime. However, as this position changed, and as the USA manoeuvred for some domestic economic advantage, the system collapsed.

The floating rate regime that followed the unsuccessful attempts to shore up the BWS in the period of the 'failure to agree' was one designed again to increase national economic autonomy. But the rules of this game changed surprisingly little from the previous period. As mentioned above, the US dollar remained the 'currency of choice' for the conduct of international monetary transactions – largely because of its path-dependent embeddedness. The USA also continued to remain relatively 'passive' in the face of changes in the dollar's value, though other countries conducted systematic interventions to try to stabilize their own currency dollar-equivalent rates. In the short run, other countries' national money supply policies were set so as to adjust to the relative weaknesses of their exchange rates vis-à-vis the dollar (reducing domestic money supply when currency value against the dollar weakened, increasing it as that value strengthened – that is, the non-sterilization of exchange-rate movements); while in the long run, secular adjustments in the par values were sanctioned so as to set national price level and money supply targets independently of the policy of the USA (this being the major change on the previous system). The USA, on the other hand, no longer tried to anchor a common world price level, but conducted its own monetary and exchange-rate policy independently of what other countries were doing.

One (unintended) consequence of this relative autonomy in the conduct of monetary policies was an increase in the 'world's' money supply. As the dollar weakened between 1971 and 1980 (implying a strengthening of other currencies against the dollar), the money supplies of other countries increased. The passivity of the USA, by contrast, meant that it did not offset this with a reduction of its own money supply. Inflation resulted. Then when the dollar unexpectedly strengthened after 1980, the adjustment took the form of severe deflations and world output contracted sharply. Thus, perhaps somewhat bizarrely, this period saw the closer and deeper integration of the international economy as the business cycles of all the main participants synchronized and became more pronounced. A regime designed to increase autonomy (by allowing exchange rates to float and enabling independent monetary policies) had actually led in the opposite direction. There is an important lesson to be learned here about the need to design particular rules for whatever governance mechanism is adopted.

Of course that lesson was partly learned in the case of the attempt to stabilize exchange rates associated with the period of the Plaza–Louvre accords. The USA abandoned its 'hands off' policy and initiated an attempt at more concerted action to manage exchange rates with 'discrete but clustered' interventions. The rules of this game were mentioned above. There were seventeen such concerted interventions between 1985 and 1992, most of which worked successfully in moving the exchange rates at least in the direction anticipated – and often against the prevailing trend. Thus at the level of exchange rates this cooperation between the G3 countries implied a heavier interdependence between them. But they were exercising their 'autonomy' independently of those outside the G3 framework, these other countries having to support – or not oppose – any G3 intervention (by buying or selling dollars with their national currency when the dollar was either weak or strong).

Quite whether the G3 regime remained robust is a moot point, however. The key issues were the existence or otherwise of 'target zones' and how seriously they were taken; whether the implied sterilization worked (itself leading to differences in short-term interest rates between financial centres); and the macroeconomic effects of both of these. Without direct and more continuous coordination of policies (as opposed to indirect and discrete cooperation), exchange-rate volatility is likely to remain high and international inflationary effects and output fluctuations serious. We take up some of these issues again in chapter 7.

A good many of the points made above in connection with the various international regimes could be repeated for the case of the EMS. This system in many ways paralleled the rules of the fixed rate dollar standard of the BWS, though it has had different objectives. The EMS, for instance, had as one of its objectives the successive convergence of national macroeconomic policies at an unchanging par value of the exchange rates, which can be interpreted as an eventual commitment to complete (economic and political) integration of the EU economies. This strong convergence/union theme was something missing from the BWS. The EMS also fixed the par value of exchange rates of the participants in terms of a basket of EMS currencies, weighted according to the relative country size, though the Deutschmark (DM) became the *de facto* anchor of the system much like the dollar under the BWS. Its formal rules included a commitment to keeping currency values stable within bilateral bands, though adjustments in par values were allowed to reposition price levels with the agreement of the EMS (all this before eventual convergence or full monetary union). Central bank intervention was also sanctioned if breaching of the bilateral rate bands was threatened.

The *de facto* operation of the system was to stabilize national exchange rates vis-à-vis the DM (partly because of the DM's importance in the currency basket), increasingly using the latter as the intervention currency; adjusting short-term monetary targets and interest rates so as to support exchange-rate interventions; organizing long-term money growth so that domestic inflation in tradeable goods converged to, or remained the same as, price inflation in Germany; and progressively to liberalize capital controls. Germany, much like the USA in the case of the BWS and the floating rate regime, was thus to remain 'passive' in respect to the foreign-exchange rates of other members, but to anchor the DM (and therefore the EMS) price level for tradeables by adopting an independently chosen German monetary policy.

The history of this system is well known. What it provided – indeed was explicitly designed to provide – was a reduction of autonomy, in relation to monetary policy at least, for the participants (see Thompson 1993, chap. 4, and chapters 7 and 8 below for a discussion of its implications for other aspects of macroeconomic management, particularly that of fiscal policy). The country gaining the most formal autonomy was Germany, but rather as in the case of the USA discussed above, if the system was to operate properly, German policy would also have to be heavily constrained by the 'burden' of managing the system overall, and would have had to circumscribe its own objectives at times in the interest of the other members. However, this had proved the crunch point in terms of the success or otherwise of the EMS. Partly as a consequence of constitutional issues – summed up in the so-called Emminger letter (see Kenen 1995, pp. 183–4) – and partly because of domestic political reasons, the Bundesbank was not required to support partner currencies fully in times of EMS crisis. The result was to undermine its credibility as a regime of financial governance. The fuller implications of the emergence of EMU after 1999 will be discussed in chapters 6 and 7.

The basic point to be drawn from the analysis above is that for the foreseeable future the real character of the international system will be that of one dominated by the Triad countries and their regional clusters or allies. We have entered a period when three large economic formations look to have emerged, the comparative features of which are illustrated in table 2.17. In the mid-1990s, in terms of GDP the EU and the USA were about equal, with Japan about half as big (though in terms of GDP per capita Japan leads the EU and the USA). As far as shares of world exports of goods only are concerned, while there had been some convergence, the three blocs seemed to have stabilized, with the EU at 25 per cent, the USA at 20 per cent and Japan at 19 per cent (and falling slightly).

Most of the other data in tables 2.17 and 2.18 relate to the currency role of the three big countries/blocs. This is important in terms of the way the international economic and financial system evolved as the Euro was introduced in 1999. These data indicate broadly (1) that the US dollar still remained the *lingua franca* of the international financial system in the mid-1990s; (2) that the European currencies have made some inroads into this role, particularly in terms of transactions on foreign-exchange and portfolio investments (see also table 2.9 above); and finally (3) that the yen is a relatively unimportant currency for international transactions, but has gained some advantage as a denominator of assets (largely as a consequence of

**Table 2.17** USA, Japan and the EU: relative economic size and relative use of currencies (percentages)

|  | USA | Japan | EU15 |
|---|---|---|---|
| *Relative economic size* |  |  |  |
| Shares of world GDP, 1996 | 20.7 | 8.0 | 20.4 |
| Shares of world exports, 1996[a] | 15.2 | 6.1 | 14.7 |
| *Relative use of currencies*[b] |  |  |  |
| World trade, 1992 | 48.0 | 5.0 | 31.0 |
| World debt securities, September 1996 | 37.2 | 17.0 | 34.5 |
| Developing country debt, end 1996 | 50.2 | 18.1 | 15.8 |
| Global foreign-exchange reserves, end 1995 | 56.4 | 7.1 | 25.8 |
| Foreign-exchange transactions, April 1995[c] | 41.5 | 12.0 | 35.0 |

*Notes*: [a] Goods plus services, excluding intra-EU.
[b] Shares denominated in currency (or currencies) of country (or EU).
[c] Shares adjusted for double counting that arises from the fact that each transaction involves two currencies.
*Source*: World Bank 1997, p. 71, table 12.


**Table 2.18** The international role of the main Triad currencies

**(a) Official role**
*Share of total official currency holdings (%)*

|  | End 1973 | End 1983 | End 1995 |
|---|---|---|---|
| US dollar | 76.1 | 71.1 | 61.5 |
| European currencies[a] | 14.3 | 15.8 | 20.1 |
| of which, Deutschmark | 7.1 | 11.7 | 14.2 |
| Yen | 0.1 | 4.9 | 7.4 |

*Number of currencies linked to:*

|  | 1983 | 1994 | 1994 (% of world GNP) |
|---|---|---|---|
| US dollar | 34 | 25 | 1.53 |
| European currencies (incl. the ECU) | 18 | 19 | 0.25 |

**(b) Currency use in international trade**
*Share of the main currencies as regards use in international trade*

|  | 1980 | | 1992 | |
|---|---|---|---|---|
|  | % of world exports | Internationalization ratio[b] | % of world exports | Internationalization ratio[b] |
| US dollar | 56.4 | 4.5 | 47.6 | 3.6 |
| Deutschmark | 13.6 | 1.4 | 15.5 | 1.4 |
| Yen | 2.1 | 0.3 | 4.8 | 0.6 |

**Table 2.18**   *Continued*

**(c) Transactions on foreign-exchange markets**
*Breakdown of transactions by currency[c]*

|  | April 1989 | April 1992 | April 1995 |
|---|---|---|---|
| US dollar | 90 | 82 | 83 |
| Deutschmark | 27 | 40 | 37 |
| Yen | 27 | 23 | 24 |
| Other | 56 | 55 | 56 |
| Total as %[d] | 200 | 200 | 200 |

**(d) Currency in which financial assets and liabilities are denominated**
*Share of outstanding international bonds*

|  | End 1981 | End 1992 | End 1995 |
|---|---|---|---|
| US dollar | 52.6 | 40.3 | 34.2 |
| European currencies of | 20.2 | 33.0 | 37.1 |
| which, Deutschmark | n.a | 10.0 | 12.3 |
| Yen | 6.9 | 12.4 | 15.7 |

*Share of world private portfolio*

|  | End 1981 | End 1992 | End 1995 |
|---|---|---|---|
| US dollar | 67.3 | 46.0 | 39.8 |
| European currencies of | 13.2 | 35.2 | 36.9 |
| which, Deutschmark | n.a. | 14.7 | 15.6 |
| Yen | 2.2 | 6.9 | 11.5 |

*Notes*: [a] Pound sterling, Deutschmark, French franc, Dutch guilder.
[b] Ratio of world exports denominated in currency relative to that country's exports.
[c] Gross turnover. Daily averages.
[d] Since any transaction on the foreign-exchange market involves two currencies, the total of the proportions of transactions involving a given currency is 200%.
*Sources*: European Union 1997b, p. 18, Annex 2, drawing on, for (a), IMF annual reports; for (b), European Commission; for (c), BIS, surveys of activities on foreign exchange market; for (d), BIS, international banking and financial activity, and authors' own calculations.

the appreciation of the yen against the US dollar and the DM up to 1996).

The implications of these trends are that the relationship between the USA and Europe looks to be becoming the key one for international governance, and this will be accelerated if the Euro matures to become a rival to the dollar. This will tend to reinforce the dominance of the two main blocs in the Triad. This is especially so as the Japanese economy faltered in the 1990s, and as the crisis in the Far East and Latin America matured during 1998. Without a sustained recovery in Japan, the centre of gravity of the international system could shift to the North Atlantic. But the emergence of China as a major trading nation (though as yet not a key financial player, given the fixed value of the renminbi and continued capital controls) could once again redirect the centre of gravity of the system back towards the Pacific. But whatever happens, the future for extended international governance essentially hangs not so much on global market forces as on the old-fashioned differences of interest between the USA, the EU and (to a lesser extent) Japan, and the emerging giants of China and India. This is far from comforting, but it is as well to know from whence one's problems come, and that they are still driven by the classic difficulty of the divergent interests of states, or of the political entities that are developing alongside them, such as the EU. Far from a fully integrating 'globalized world economy', we still inhabit an essentially 'internationalized' one, if one now conditioned heavily by a regionalized triadic bloc structure.

## Conclusion

We have striven to argue a number of points in this chapter. First, that the level of integration, interdependence, openness, or however one wishes to describe it, of national economies in the present era is not unprecedented. Indeed, the level of autonomy under the Gold Standard in the period up to the First World War was much lower for the advanced economies than it is today. This is not to minimize the level of integration now, or to ignore the problems of regulation and management it throws up, but merely to register a certain scepticism over whether we have entered a radically new phase in the internationalization of economic activity.

The second point has been to argue that governance mechanisms for the international economy were in place over almost the entire twentieth century, in one form or another. This is just as much the case today as it was at the start of that century. We may not like the particular mechanisms that are established now and how they work, but they are there all the same. The issue then becomes how to devise better or more appropriate ones.

Thirdly, we have argued that there are some new and different issues of economic interdependence in the present era which are particular to it. Our argument is not that things have remained unchanged: quite fundamental reorganizations are going on in the international economy to which an imaginative response is desperately needed. This is an issue we take up later in the book.

Finally, we have traced the trajectory of 'national economic autonomy' through the various regimes of governance operating over the twentieth century. This has shown that such autonomy has oscillated between periods of strong and then weak forces, and that it has operated with various degrees of effectiveness. Perhaps the overall trajectory of this assessment is to point to the impossibility of complete national economic autonomy as the twentieth century progressed. The debacle of the floating rates regime of 1974–85 seems, if nothing else, to have confirmed the demise of this form of governance as a viable long-term objective in the present era.

# 3

# Multinational Companies and the Internationalization of Business Activity

This chapter moves away from the history of the international trading and financial system. It concentrates on the major changes in the structure of the international economy since the early 1980s, particularly in terms of the internationalization of production. One of the key changes identified and explored here is the increased salience of, and rapid growth in, foreign direct investment (FDI). In the period 1945–73 the dominant factor driving the world economy was growth in international trade; from the early 1980s onwards, it is argued, it has been growth in FDI. It should be noted, however, that in this chapter we develop a critique of this particular measure of the internationalization of production. A more recent associated consequence of this internationalization of production has been the phenomenon of 'offshoring': the move of aspects of company production and service systems away from their traditional 'home' country base to foreign destinations. This phenomenon is considered in a later section.

This chapter concentrates on those international mechanisms that have an impact on the structure of and growth in the real economy: trade and FDI. International short-term financial flows, which expanded rapidly after the abandonment of semi-fixed exchange rates and capital controls in the 1970s, are analysed elsewhere (chapters 2, 6 and 7). Clearly, these short-term capital flows have some indirect impact on economic growth since they affect national exchange rates and interest rates, but we contend that they mainly redistribute success – and more often failure – around the international system, and add little to the structural capacity of economies to generate long-term aggregate growth.

It is multinational companies (MNCs) that are the agents responsible for FDI. The strategies of these organizations as they shape the role and distribution of FDI are central to the analysis that follows. As we shall see, that distribution is socially and geographically uneven on a world scale. FDI is heavily concentrated in the advanced industrial states and in a small number of rapidly developing industrial economies. This analysis is complemented later in the chapter by a detailed empirical investigation into the geographical distribution of advanced country business activity, contrasting its home and foreign concentrations.

There still remain massive and important national differences in the attractiveness of locations for investment and other business activity. Countries vary considerably in the effectiveness of their economies in delivering to multinational firms FDI advantages that cannot be ignored. Successful MNCs are those that can tap into those specific advantages. These advantages are not just ones associated with the cost of labour. Companies also need national legal and commercial policy provisions to protect their investments, constraints that prevent them being entirely extraterritorial, as we emphasize in chapters 7 and 8.

The literature on 'national systems of innovation' (Lundvall 1992; Nelson 1993; McKelvey 1991; Porter 1990), 'production regimes' (Wilkinson 1983; Rubery 1994) and 'national business systems' (Whitley 1992a, 1992b) is instructive here. These authors point to real differences in the way countries have traditionally gone about their innovative activity and established their typical business environment, and how business is conducted therein. But the role of MNCs in the development of the global economy has become of central importance in the analysis of the degree to which these national systems are thought to be in a process of fundamental transformation. Without the extensive development of MNCs, the way companies operate could be regarded as closely tied to domestic institutional structures. These domestic institutional structures were recognized as being differentially configured as between the advanced industrial countries, with, it has been argued, a profound impact on the economic performances of both the companies inhabiting those systems and the economies to which they were closely articulated (see Hollingsworth and Boyer 1996; Lazonick and O'Sullivan 1996; Soskice 1991; Whitley 1992b; Whitley and Kristensen 1996, 1997).

With the advent of 'globalization', however, and the dramatic advance of the multinational firm, this conception of the central importance of various 'national systems' (of business, innovation, labour relations, finance, production, etc.) is now often thought to be under siege as business practices rapidly internationalize. Firms are now supposed to roam the globe in search of cheap but efficient production locations that offer them the largest and most secure and profitable return on competitive success. The precise impact of these internationalizing processes on the nature of the socially and economically embedded national (or regional) business systems has become the subject of much analysis and speculation (see Chesnais 1992; Dicken et al. 1994; Mueller 1994; Tiberi-Vipraio 1996).

This chapter is concerned to do a number of things. The first is to explore the overall significance of MNC activity and the geographical concentration of traditional measures such as FDI and trade.

Secondly, in this context, we analyse whether the advance of MNC activity has been quite so rapid and widespread as is often assumed by the strong globalization thesis, and particularly so fast as to undermine seriously the continuation of a national or local business system. This will involve the examination of a range of measures of the internationalization of economic activity, not just the expansion of FDI, which is the measure most often used to bolster the strong globalization thesis. For too long, loose generalizations about the extent and nature of the internationalization of business activity have served to obscure the issue. The likelihood of a collapse of national systems of business and innovation needs to be evaluated by a serious evidential test. Until we know the true extent of such internationalization, and whether it is indeed increasing as rapidly and dramatically as is often argued, there is little point in speculating about its precise impact on the embeddedness of national systems.

One problem here is that there is no unambiguous evidence available or single statistical indicator that can point to the true position. Thus a good deal of the chapter is designed to present a range of indicators and to assess the strengths and weaknesses of each.

The chapter then moves on to look at the possible forms of the internationalization of business activity identified in the context of the review of these different measures. This is done in relation to the debate about the continued relevance of national systems of business and innovation. Finally, the implication of these trends for economic performance and the nature of the international economy are briefly examined.

### FDI and MNCs in the early 2000s

According to UNCTAD, in 2006 there were upwards of 77,000 MNCs (UNCTAD 2006, p. 10). Of these, some 57,000 were from the developed countries. In all, these MNCs involved about 770,000 foreign affiliates. Eighty per cent of MNC headquarters are in the developed world, and 80 per cent of US trade was conducted by MNCs in 2003, which is more or less the norm for advanced countries. As much as 35 per cent of total US trade was estimated to be *intra*-MNC trade – that conducted within the boundaries of the company, involving transfers across borders between different parts of the organization – which is both difficult to ascertain and to assess. Clearly, MNCs' FDI and trade are very closely linked, but important changes are occurring here and differences in the patterns between the two are emerging: we will have more to say about these in a moment.

There is great concentration in FDI. The hundred largest MNCs controlled about one-fifth of total global foreign assets, had US$2 trillion of foreign sales and employed 6 million workers in 1995. Inasmuch as these distinctions can still be made, 60 per cent of MNC stock was associated with manufacturing, 37 per cent with services and only 3 per cent with the primary sector. It is the growth in service sector FDI that has been a particular feature of the latest surge in overall investment levels.

### Character of trade and FDI

The 'long boom' after the Second World War was typified by a massive increase in world trade and domestic (and, until recently, to a lesser extent foreign) investment. The prosperity of the international economy was in large part based on these trends – it was 'export driven'. The main characteristics of this period can be seen in figure 3.1, which shows, for the years 1984 to 2000, the 'export gap' between the growth of world output and that of exports: that is, exports increasing at a much faster rate than production. This is a continuation of a trend that stretched back to the 1950s. Note, however, that it is manufacturing exports that had been driving this trend. The exports of agricultural products had been growing at a slower rate than these over the period but still faster than world production overall. Trade in manufactures, mineral products and agricultural production constitutes 'merchandise trade'. This is in distinction to 'service trade'. And it is noteworthy that merchandise trade still accounts for almost 75 per cent of world trade. What is more, trade in services has hardly increased as a proportion of total world trade since the mid-1970s.

A caveat should be entered at this point with respect to figure 3.1, however. It does not show the exact relationship between growth of exports and world

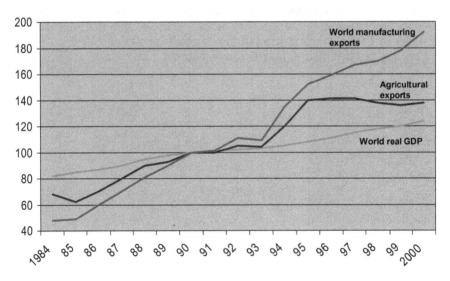

**Figure 3.1**   World merchandise exports compared to world GDP, 1984–
2000 (1990 = 100)
*Source*: Derived from WTO 2000 and WTO 2001.

income (GDP). In a multivariate context the estimated relationship between trade growth and GDP growth is actually less than 1, i.e. a 1 per cent growth in GDP leads to a less than 1 per cent growth in trade, when account is taken of other influences of trade growth, contrary to the impression given in the figure. This is because other influences on trade growth than income as such, such as changes in trade law, cultural changes, migration, etc., have had a disproportionate effect over the post-1980s period, with elasticities in respect to trade often greater than 1. Thus growth in trade has also been accounted for by these changes rather than simply as a consequence of income growth (see Thompson 2003 and chapter 6 below).

Since the early 1980s, however, a different trend has emerged, to be seen in figure 3.2. Here what is striking is the sudden increase in FDI flows from the mid-1980s, particularly to the developed countries. Export growth was eclipsed by this expansion of FDI. As indicated in figure 3.2, the flows to the developed countries fell away significantly in the recession years of the early 2000s. Several points about FDI are worth noting from this figure. First, FDI flows are very volatile: they are heavily dependent upon the general business climate, and oscillate rapidly as that climate changes. Secondly, the vast bulk of FDI has been – up until the mid-2000s at least – very much an advanced country affair. Companies from the developed countries invest in themselves. Thirdly, and as a corollary of this, FDI flows to the LDCs have been modest. But this might be about to change, as China, in particular, has entered the global trading system. The growing importance of China as a recipient of FDI relative to the EU (at that time nine countries), the USA and Japan is clear from the data plotted in figure 3.3. This also indicates that Japan has been, and remains, a very limited participant in the international *inflows* of FDI (though not to outflows), testifying to its relative protected character as a destination for foreign businesses.

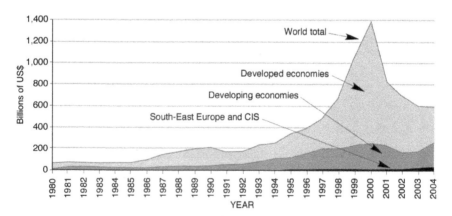

**Figure 3.2**   FDI inflows, global and by groups of economies, 1980–2004
(billions of dollars)
*Source*: UNCTAD 2005, p. 3, figure I.1.

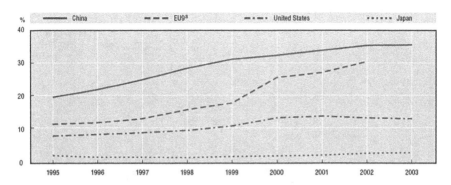

**Figure 3.3**    Inward FDI as a percentage of GDP, 1995–2003

*Note*: aIncluding Austria, Finland, France, Germany, Italy, the Netherlands, Portugal, Sweden and the UK.
*Source*: OECD 2005, p. 30, figure A.8.1.

To a large extent the growth in FDI indicated in these figures was based upon the progressive liberalization of both the developed and the less developed economies over the period since the 1980s. In particular, this stimulated a major change in the composition of FDI from its earlier character. Greenfield FDI – the establishment and operation of new businesses in foreign countries – gave way to merger and acquisition (M&A) FDI as already existing companies were acquired in those foreign countries. And this was itself associated with the privatization of previously publicly owned assets, so that newly formed enterprises were floated and made ready to be taken over as much by foreign as by domestic investors. In 2005, 78 per cent of FDI inflows was accounted for by M&A activity.

### Triad power and influence

Any discussion of the diverse strategies and tactics of firms and governments in the context of FDI should not blind us to an overarching feature of these relationships. Sixty per cent of the flows of US$ bn FDI over the period 1991–6 were between just the members of the Triad bloc, which also accounted for 75 per cent of the total accumulated stock of FDI in 1995. North America, Europe and East Asia have dominated as both the originators and the destinations for international investment (though Japan to a much lesser extent than the others in the case of inward flows, as pointed out above). These three areas have consistently accounted for between 65 and 70 per cent of all FDI flows between 1990 and 2000. In the case of investment, the flows have been particularly intense between North America and Western Europe, while Japan remained a net exporter of FDI in the mid-1990s to both the other areas (see figure 3.4 on p. 74 below).

One proviso here is that, as mentioned above, there has been a growing importance of some developing countries as the *source* of FDI on the basis

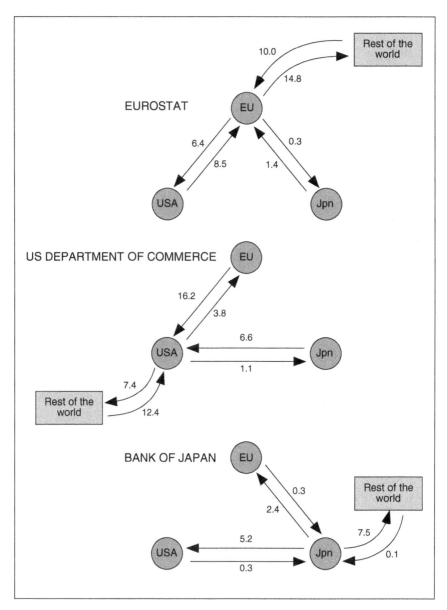

**Figure 3.4** FDI flows between the Triad countries, 1994 (ECU bn), according to three sets of calculations

*Source*: Derived from European Union 1997c, p. 22.

of their indigenous MNC activity. In particular this trend has affected the rapidly growing East Asian countries, and a few from Latin America. While important trends, these developments do not as yet threaten to undo the pattern outlined above of the continued dominance of the Triad in FDI (see also chapter 6).

But there is a range of other problems in taking FDI flows or stocks as the single most useful measure of the internationalization of productive activity. FDI has become the premier indicator because it is the most standardized international measure available. But even among the advanced industrial economies there are surprising differences in the calculations of FDI flows, as figure 3.4 reveals.

This presents estimates of the FDI flows between the Triad countries in 1994, calculated by the three main collection agencies in Europe, the USA and Japan. This is used to illustrate a basic problem with FDI as a measure of internationalization: namely that there is no common measure agreed by all. Note that there is only a single case of agreement in these figures: that between Europe and Japan calculated by Eurostat and the Bank of Japan. All the other calculations show different estimates, some very different, as in the case of EU flows to the USA (ECU 6.4 billion by Eurostat, 16.2 billion by the US Department of Commerce). Thus it is impossible to be confident of the actual flows of FDI even between the Triad countries. Perhaps we need to look at different and more appropriate indicators, which present a somewhat different picture of the extent of internationalized business activity.

Contrary to common claims, FDI is not a measure of the assets held in affiliated firms. Rather it measures what is happening on the liabilities side of companies' balance sheets. FDI flows are made up of changes in the shares, loans and retained earnings of affiliated companies that are operating abroad, though in a number of countries the reporting of FDI does not include retained earnings (hence, in part, the discrepancies shown in figure 3.4). These have become an important element in the amount of activity conducted abroad (so, in this sense, FDI might *underestimate* the extent of this activity in some countries). But in general the FDI measure is likely to *overestimate* this activity. It is not only that companies massage their liabilities for tax purposes – and this has nothing necessarily to do with their ability to produce from their assets; it is also that a major form of FDI liability management, namely the purchase of existing company shares and bonds, need have no direct relationship to changing the productive capacity of the assets so acquired.

If a foreign company acquires an already existing domestic company's liabilities through a merger or acquisition, but does not alter the asset structure of the acquired company, there is no necessary increase in the productive potential in the country where it has invested. However, this would appear as an inward flow of FDI. As mentioned above, there has been a dramatic growth in the extent of M&A activity internationally, stimulated particularly by the privatization programme embarked on by both the advanced and latterly the developing countries. At the end of the 1990s over 50 per cent of global FDI flows were made up of cross-border mergers and acquisitions (UNCTAD 1997, p. 9), and this has increased as a proportion since then, so that in 2005 it had increased to 78 per cent (UNCTAD 2006, p. 9, table 1.3).

### Measures of internationalization from national accounts data

The adjustments to measures of internationalization discussed up to now do not exhaust those needed to assess properly the popular belief that MNCs are so footloose that they are undermining the continued viability of national economies or national systems of business. They need to be supplemented by examining the extent of internationalization in relation to overall national output, and then with that derived directly from national account statistics. This gives some added insights into the true extent of internationalization.

Returning to the issues of the internationalization of production, FDI has been a feature of the international economy for more than a hundred years. There is thus an accumulated stock inherited from the past. This is shown for the years 1980 to 2005 in table 3.1, expressed as a percentage of GDP. As might be expected, there has been a growth in its importance relative to GDP since 1980: at the world level it has more than quadrupled, from 4.6 per cent in 1980 to 22.7 per cent in 2005. The absolute levels still remained modest for most countries and groupings until 1995, after which

**Table 3.1**    Inward FDI stock as a percentage of GDP, 1980–2005

|  | 1980 | 1985 | 1990 | 1995 | 2000 | 2005 |
|---|---|---|---|---|---|---|
| **World** | **4.6** | **6.5** | **8.3** | **10.1** | **18.3** | **22.7** |
| **Developed economies** | **4.8** | **6.0** | **8.3** | **9.1** | **16.2** | **21.4** |
| of which, EU | 5.5 | 8.2 | 10.9 | 13.4 | 26.3 | 33.5 |
| (UK) | 11.7 | 14.0 | 22.3 | 28.5 | 30.5 | 37.1 |
| (Germany) | 4.5 | 6.0 | 7.4 | 6.9 | 14.5 | 18.0 |
| USA | 3.1 | 4.6 | 8.0 | 14.0 | 12.9 | 13.0 |
| Japan | 0.3 | 0.4 | 0.3 | 0.3 | 1.1 | 2.1 |
| **Developing economies** | **4.3** | **8.1** | **8.7** | **15.4** | **26.3** | **27.0** |
| of which, Latin America and Caribbean | 6.4 | 10.8 | 11.6 | 18.4 | 25.8 | 36.7 |
| (Brazil) | 6.9 | 11.3 | 8.1 | 17.8 | 17.1 | 25.4 |
| Asia | 3.5 | 7.3 | 7.3 | 14.2 | 26.5 | 23.2 |
| South, East and South-East Asia | 3.8 | 6.5 | 8.7 | 15.1 | 30.5 | 25.8 |
| **Central and Eastern Europe and CIS** | – | **0.1** | **1.3** | **4.9** | **16.6** | **26.7** |

*Source*: Compiled from UNCTAD 1997, Annex, table B6; and UNCTAD 2006, Annex, pp. 307–17, table B3.

significant increases can be seen. The UK has always been a conspicuous exception among the larger advanced countries, with a much higher FDI stock to GDP ratio than most other comparable countries (Hirst and Thompson 2000). At the other end of the spectrum, Japan remained largely untouched by inward FDI (and even its outward stock, at 8.5 per cent of GDP in 2005, was modest). Clearly, a stock of foreign-owned productive activity of around 20 per cent or more of GDP for most of the advanced countries is likely to put serious pressure on any indigenously embedded national business systems, though much of this investment is designed to tap into the very strengths of those business systems, rather than to transform them. It could be argued to have been more important for a small number of rapidly developing countries that have relied on FDI as the main stimulant to their development strategies, but even this might be challenged. For China, the inward stock of FDI increased from 5.4 per cent of GDP in 1990 to 14.3 per cent in 2005, but for India from only 0.5 per cent to 5.8 per cent over the same period.

Many quite reasonable adjustments to these FDI flow and stock figures could be undertaken to make them more representative of the 'true' position that they are designed to measure. For instance, the stock figures are calculated in terms of historic costs, whereas they should perhaps be readjusted to current values, which would no doubt increase their significance somewhat (Graham 1996, pp. 10–13).

In addition, the data in table 3.2 show the relative importance of FDI inflows as a contribution to the gross domestic fixed capital formation in a

**Table 3.2**  Share of inward FDI flows in gross domestic fixed capital formation, 1985–2005 (percentages)

|  | Average | | |
|---|---|---|---|
|  | *1985–1990* | *1995* | *2005* |
| **World** | **5.1** | **5.2** | **9.4** |
| **Developed economies** | **5.5** | **4.4** | **8.0** |
| of which, EU | 9.1 | 6.8 | 16.1 |
| (UK) | 13.7 | 13.2 | 45.0 |
| (Germany) | 1.6 | 1.7 | 6.8 |
| USA | 5.3 | 5.9 | 14.6 |
| Japan | 0.2 | – | 0.3 |
| **Developing economies** | **8.0** | **8.2** | **12.8** |
| of which Latin America and Caribbean | 11.3 | 11.0 | 16.8 |
| (Brazil) | 3.1 | 4.7 | 9.5 |
| Asia | 7.6 | 7.5 | 11.2 |
| South, East and South-East Asia | 9.7 | 9.0 | 10.6 |
| Central and Eastern Europe | 1.0 | 5.2 | 17.0 |

*Source*: Compiled from UNCTAD 1997, Annex, table B.5; UNCTAD 2006, Annex, pp. 307–17, table B.3.

range of country groupings. With one or two notable exceptions (e.g. the UK again) these figures might be thought to indicate the continued relative *un*importance of FDI flows in their contribution to domestic investment (even accepting the criticisms of this measure as outlined above). The clear trend, however, is for an increase in its significance in overall investment. Nevertheless, whether economies can borrow their way to prosperity via a reliance on FDI is another matter. What remains crucial to domestic development strategies are domestic savings, which continue to be the main source of domestic investment in all advanced and developing economies. It is still the nature of domestic financial systems that is decisive for the long-run developmental success of different economies.

Another important element in the picture of increasing economic interdependency is the proportion of a country's exports that are accounted for by MNC affiliates in various countries. Although at the global level in 2005 this was estimated at about 33 per cent, the proportion varies considerably between countries, as shown in table 3.3. And there is no unambiguous trend operating here – some countries recording a declining importance between 1995 and 2000. The difference between India and China is noteworthy, indicating a very different growth strategy so far pursued by these countries.

Finally, it is worth considering other detailed attempts to assess the extent of internationalized production as derived directly from national accounts and measures of national output. For 1990, for instance, Lipsey, Blomström and Ramstetter (1995) calculated that foreign-based output amounted to only about 7 per cent of overall world output, up from 4.5 per cent in 1970 (Lipsey 1997, p. 2). Although the share was higher in 'industry' (including manufacturing, trade, construction and public utilities) at about 15 per cent in 1990 (up from 11 per cent in 1977), it was negligible in 'services', which amounted to 60 per cent of total world output in 1990. By 1995, foreign-based output was estimated to have increased to 7.5 per cent of total world output, hardly a dramatic and earth-shattering change.

**Table 3.3**  Share of exports of foreign affiliates of MNCs as a percentage of host country's total exports, selected countries, 1995 and 2000

|         | *1995* | *2000* |
|---------|--------|--------|
| China   | 31.8   | 42.7   |
| France  | 20.4   | 16.7   |
| India   | 2.4    | 3.5    |
| Ireland | 61.5   | 65.8   |
| Japan   | 5.0    | 10.1   |
| USA     | 16.6   | 15.0   |

*Source*: Derived from UNCTAD 2006, Annex, pp. 291–2, table A.V.1.

The story of US international firms is interesting in its own right. Their overseas output peaked in 1977 at about 8 per cent of US GDP, and has been declining ever since to about 5.5 per cent in 1995. In manufacturing the production by majority-owned US foreign affiliates was 15.5 per cent of US manufacturing output in 1977, reaching over 17 per cent in 1990, but settling back to 16 per cent in 1995, that is, it has remained almost stable over the past twenty years. In terms of employment the trends have been similar. There was a rapid increase in US firms' employment overseas relative to that at home from 1957 to 1977, but since then the trend has been a decreasing one. In 1994 the employment figure for foreign manufacturing affiliates of US firms remained well below its 1977 level. Most of these decreases in the overseas proportion of US firms' production and employment can be accounted for by the relative decline in the importance of the manufacturing sector in the US economy as a whole. In fact, the story of the internationalization of the US manufacturing sector has really been one confined to the inward side. Foreign MNC production in the USA as a proportion of GDP rose from almost zero in 1970 to just over 8 per cent in 1995, and in the manufacturing sector from 4 per cent in 1977 to 13 per cent in 1994 (Ramstetter 1998, p. 195, fig. 8.2).

The story of the Japanese economy is almost the reverse of the one for the USA. There has been virtually no growth in the importance of overseas production relative to GDP in Japan: indeed, in terms of directly measured output indicators, the trend has been a declining one (Ramstetter 1998, p. 194, fig. 8.2). On the other hand, Japanese multinationals have been expanding their activities abroad relative to their production at home. For all Japanese manufacturing companies, the overseas production ratio doubled from 5 per cent in 1985 to nearly 10 per cent in 1996 (for only those companies with overseas affiliates this ratio also doubled over the same period, from about 13.5 per cent to 27.5 per cent; MITI 1997). Given Japanese overall output growth rates, however, absolute levels of these ratios relative to GDP are low and changes have been modest.

Similar calculations as these for the other advanced countries are not readily available. But for the Asia-Pacific region as a whole, Ramstetter has produced a comprehensive survey along these lines, in particular comparing FDI-based indicators with those derived directly from national accounting data, the results of which are worth quoting:

> FDI-based indicators and foreign MNC shares of production often display very different trends [which] strongly suggests that FDI-related indicators are rather poor indicators of foreign MNC presence. More specifically, since foreign MNC shares of production are clearly more accurate measures of foreign MNC presence, focussing on FDI-related measures apparently leads to significant overestimation of the extent to which MNC presence has grown in the Asia Pacific region since the 1970s. (1998, p. 208)

This remains a salutary warning for all those approaches that stress the simple growth of FDI flows and stocks as indicating the necessary growth of a global business environment. It is these business-based approaches towards globalization and its supposed consequences that form the context for the next part of this chapter.

### Alternative company-based measures

What is needed are new measures of internationalization that capture more of what is going on the asset side of companies' balance sheets, or which look directly at productive activity accounted for by foreign affiliates as registered in company accounts. One consequence of the trends not quite captured so far is exactly where all the international activity for which MNCs are responsible is actually located. In fact MNCs still tend to concentrate their activities in their home territory and supranational regional location, as demonstrated in table 3.4.

**Table 3.4**   Intra-regional sales of the world's largest 500 MNCs, by country

| Country | No. of firms | Average revenues (US$bn) | Average intra-regional sales (%)* |
| --- | --- | --- | --- |
| USA | 169 | 30.3 | 77.3 |
| Japan | 66 | 28.9 | 74.7 |
| Germany | 29 | 37.3 | 68.1 |
| France | 27 | 27.2 | 64.8 |
| Britain | 27 | 25.3 | 64.5 |
| Canada | 16 | 13.5 | 74.1 |
| Switzerland | 8 | 34.7 | 49.6 |
| Italy | 5 | 38.7 | 83.4 |
| Australia | 5 | 13.6 | 71.4 |
| Sweden | 5 | 16.4 | 54.3 |
| Netherlands | 5 | 42.1 | 39.1 |
| European bi-national(*) | 3 | 73.9 | 47.9 |
| Norway | 2 | 21.6 | 83.0 |
| South Korea | 2 | 26.3 | 71.2 |
| Belgium | 2 | 18.8 | 58.4 |
| Finland | 2 | 20.0 | 55.1 |
| Spain | 2 | 29.1 | 50.3 |
| Taiwan | 1 | 11.6 | 100.0 |
| Luxembourg | 1 | 13.0 | 95.0 |
| Denmark | 1 | 10.9 | 94.3 |
| Brazil | 1 | 24.5 | 88.0 |
| Singapore | 1 | 13.1 | 22.4 |
| TOTAL | 380 | 29.2 | 71.9 |

*Notes*: Data are for 2001.
Numbers might not add up, due to rounding.
Average intra-regional sales are by the firm's size according to weighted revenues.
There are 120 firms in the world's largest 500 which report no data in regional sales.
*Source*: Derived from Rugman 2005a, chap. 4.

The final column of table 3.4 gives the proportion of *intra-regional* sales of the largest MNCs from different countries. In respect of sales, therefore, there is a determinedly regional emphasis. And while this is less pronounced in terms of assets and employment, a similar overall picture emerges with these aspects (Rugman 2005a). Only *nine* of the 500 largest MNCs were truly 'global' in Rugman's terms, with at least 20 per cent of their sales in all three parts of the Triad of North America, Europe and East Asia, but less than 50 per cent in one of these regions alone. In fact, the vast bulk of the MNCs were still 'domestically' orientated, with at least 80 per cent of their sales in their home territory or region. What is more, Rugman's analysis suggests that this supranational regionalization of MNCs is becoming stronger rather than weaker.[1] Similar sentiments are expressed by Ghemawat (2007), who argues that a genuine strategic attitude by companies towards overseas operations requires them to recognize the continued pertinence of borders and the engagement with differences between business environments in different countries. He suggests that what he calls 'semi-globalization' is the current characteristic of the international business system, leading businesses to localize their strategy and forget about any global ambitions.

This trend towards the supranational regionalization of MNC activity is confirmed for European and US companies by the data contained in figure 3.5. Although there is a slight increase in the distribution from the 'Rest of the world' category for both areas, the continued predominance of 'home country/region' is evident.

And similar evidence exists for this lack of global corporations in the case of Latin American MNCs. Minda (2008) suggests there are only two large Latin American MNCs that are anywhere near to becoming global players: CEMEX from Mexico and Embraer from Brazil. The rest can only

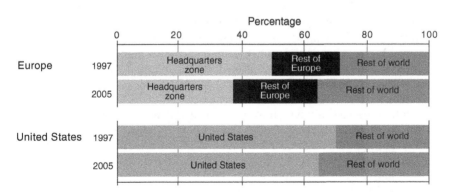

**Figure 3.5**   Average revenue distribution of European and US companies, 1997 and 2005

*Source*: Verón 2006, p. 1.

be considered supranational regional players, or with operations in one or other of the Triad locations.

What these data demonstrate is that any scrutiny of company accounts needs to recognize what companies are doing on their 'home' territory at the same time as they are investing and operating abroad. FDI flows capture only what companies are 'lending' to their affiliates abroad, not what they are at the same time investing in their home country or territory. Even where there is some assessment of MNCs according to the extent of their foreign-owned *assets*, the companies included are usually those already classified by the extent of their *foreign*-owned assets, thereby prematurely skewing the analysis in favour of the overseas orientation of company activity (e.g. UNCTAD 1997, pp. 29–31, table 1.7).

In work reported in detail elsewhere, two authors of this book developed three large-scale cross-sectional data sets designed to circumvent some of these problems (see Hirst and Thompson 1996; Allen and Thompson 1997). The first of these contains information for 1987 on the sales, assets, profits, and subsidiaries and affiliates of over 500 manufacturing and service MNCs from five countries: Canada, Germany, Japan, the UK and the USA. The second set contains information for 1990 on these aspects for just manufacturing multinationals. The third set gives data for sales and assets for 1993 of over 5,000 MNCs from six countries: France, Germany, Japan, the Netherlands, the UK and the USA.[2] The fact that these data are classified for home territory activity as well as for that conducted overseas by companies from these countries allows us to judge more accurately the extent of the internationalization of their activity. Note that these data do not indicate flows across borders but the results of such flows as expressed in terms of the ex-post economic activity they have engendered.

A way of integrating the analysis of the data sets for different years can be seen in table 3.5, which reports the geographical distribution of manufacturing subsidiaries and affiliates (S&As) of MNCs headquartered in five countries for 1987 and 1990. It shows the proportions allocated to the home country or region. Canada is the least 'home centred/regional' economy, followed by the USA and Japan. Germany remains highly concentrated in Europe. Indeed, its concentration on this area seems to have increased a little between 1987 and 1990.

Tables 3.6 and 3.7 provide added comparable results for sales and assets, integrating the 1993 analysis into the picture and also looking at the service sector position. Table 3.6 provides the relevant figures for sales activity. It compares the percentage distribution of MNC sales to the home region for the country company sets for which there were data in 1987, 1990 and 1993 (the 'home region' is common for these data, and includes the home country).[3] Clearly, although these data should be treated with some caution, they provide a reasonable guide to the magnitudes involved. The importance of the home base for manufacturing sales remained about the same for Germany, the UK and the USA between 1987 and 1993, whereas it

**Table 3.5** Percentage of manufacturing subsidiaries and affiliates located in home country/region, 1987 and 1990

|         | 1987 | 1990 |
|---------|------|------|
| Canada  | 56   | 47   |
| Germany | 76   | 78   |
| Japan   | 62   | 58   |
| UK      | 64   | 60   |
| USA     | 58   | 53   |

*Note*: Home country/region here defined as: Canada = Canada and USA; Germany = Germany and rest of Europe; Japan = Japan and South-East Asia; UK = UK and rest of Europe; USA = USA, Canada and Latin America.
*Source*: Authors' data files.

**Table 3.6** MNCs' sales to home country/region as a percentage of total sales, 1987, 1990 and 1993

|         | Manufacturing | | | Services | |
|---------|------|------|------|------|------|
|         | 1987 | 1990 | 1993 | 1987 | 1993 |
| Canada  | n.a. | 77   | n.a. | n.a. | n.a. |
| Germany | 72   | 75   | 75   | n.a. | n.a. |
| Japan   | 64   | 65   | 75   | 89   | 77   |
| UK      | 66   | 59   | 65   | 74   | 77   |
| USA     | 70   | 63   | 67   | 93   | 79   |

*Note*: n.a. = not available.
*Source*: Authors' data files.

increased for Japan. For services there was a decrease for Japan and the USA, and a slight increase for the UK.

As far as asset data are concerned, the results of a similar exercise are presented in table 3.7.[4] Overall these display slightly less bias to the home country/region than do the sales figures (which is perhaps surprising – we might have expected MNCs' sales to be more internationalized than their assets). Inasmuch as one can draw any generalizations from these figures, it seems that manufacturing asset distributions became more biased to the home country/region between the late 1980s and early 1990s, while for services US companies became less concentrated.

An interesting feature of the 'home biases' still shown by these data for the early 1990s and for a much later period by Rugman is that there is evidence that not only are profits regionally concentrated (Hirst and Thompson 1999), but profits are also higher for those companies pursuing a regional strategy than for those pursuing a global one (Rugman 2008,

**Table 3.7**   MNCs' assets in home country/region as a percentage of total, 1987, 1990 and 1993

| | Manufacturing | | | Services | |
|---|---|---|---|---|---|
| | *1987* | *1990* | *1993* | *1987* | *1993* |
| Canada | n.a. | 74 | n.a. | n.a. | n.a. |
| Japan | n.a. | n.a. | 97 | 77 | 92 |
| UK | 52 | 48 | 62 | n.a. | 69 |
| USA | 67 | 66 | 73 | 81 | 77 |

*Note*: n.a. = not available.
*Source*: Authors' data files.

pp. 110–14). After allowing for several control variables, UK companies with a European regional sales focus performed better in terms of rate of return on foreign assets than on their rest of the world assets.

These data are clearly not ideal, since for the most part the way the data are recorded in company accounts allows for the allocation of their activities as within or outside their 'home region' only by a single definition (see note 3, p. 249). However, for some of the data and countries, and for some years, it was possible to disaggregate this into a home *country* allocation which confirmed the basic home-centredness of the data as presented in these tables and the figure (see Allen and Thompson 1997, in particular).

The main conclusion to be drawn from this analysis is an obvious one. The 'home-oriented' nature of MNC activity along all the dimensions looked at remained significant, even if this could be a regionally centred one. Thus MNCs still relied on their 'home base' as the centre for their economic activities, despite all the speculation about globalization. From these results we should be reasonably confident that, in the aggregate, international companies were still predominantly MNCs (with a clear home base to their operations) and not TNCs (which represent footloose stateless companies; see chapter 1). As indicated above, there are two aspects to this home-centredness. One is the role of the 'home country' and the other that of the 'home region'. As far as the data can be disaggregated, in 1993 home-country biases were as significant as the home-region biases found in 1987. Given that for 1987 and 1990 it is possible only to specify an aggregated regional breakdown, then strictly speaking the three cross-sectional analyses can only be compared on this basis. But these confirm that as much as between two-thirds and three-quarters of MNC aggregate business activity remained centred on the home region in this sense.

However, it is worth raising a possible caveat to this conclusion, which will be additionally explored below. A strong feature of the globalization thesis is that joint ventures, partnerships, strategic alliances and liaisons are drawing firms into increasingly interdependent international networks of business activity. A potential problem, then, with the *quantitative* data presented here is that they do not capture this *qualitative* change in company business strategies. The fact that only 25 to 30 per cent of company activity is conducted abroad does not of itself tell us anything about the strategic importance of that 25 to 30 per cent to the overall business activity of firms. It might represent the key to their performative success both internationally *and* domestically. The fact that there is wider international dispersion of S&As than assets and employment could be taken as an indicator of this 'networking' trend in operation. We address this further below when discussing 'offshorization'. But there is an important caveat at this stage: as suggested above, UK company performance on regional assets is better than for all other assets.

## Business strategy and the future of national systems

Those who claim a dramatic change in the international production environment see this as heralding a new stage of MNC evolution. This involves an uncoupling of companies and networks from distinct national bases and a move towards a genuine global economy centred on truly global companies. The best example of this argument is the work of Kenichi Ohmae (1990 and 1993). The virtue of Ohmae's case is that he does at least say what he thinks the structure of a truly global, borderless economy would look like: it is summed up in the idea of an 'interlinked economy'. Ohmae argues that 'stateless' corporations are now the prime movers in an interlinked economy (ILE) centred on North America, Europe and Japan. He contends that macroeconomic and industrial policy intervention by national governments can only distort and impede the rational process of resource allocation by corporate decisions and consumer choices on a global scale. The emergence of 'electronic highways' enables anyone, in principle, to 'plug into' the global marketplace. All corporate players need to do is to shake off the burden of a nationally oriented bureaucracy, and the government intervention that goes along with it, and enter the new world of open global marketing and production. The vision is of one large interlinked network of producers and consumers plugged into an efficiently operating 'level playing field' of the open international and globalized economy. International markets provide coordinative and governance mechanisms in and of themselves: national strategies and policy interventions are likely merely to distort them. Like Robert Reich (1992), Ohmae believes that the era of effective national economies, and state policies corresponding to them, is over.

*Pace* Ohmae, the international economy looks nothing like the ILE and does not seem to be converging towards it. Current practice of international corporations is more complex, and much more akin to an MNC pattern. Strategic alliances are creating an extremely uneven international marketplace, which is being duplicated in both manufacturing and service sectors. To the extent that a globalized economy exists at all, it is organized *oligopolistically*, not according to the dictates of the perfectly competitive model as Ohmae and others wish to believe (cf. Gray 1998). The major corporate players are involved in a deadly competitive game, deploying all manner of business strategies to exclude some competing players from their networks while locking others firmly into them. For oligopolists there are massive 'first mover' advantages. If a firm can secure the originating industry standard, for instance, it has the potential to gain enormous benefits by moving down the cost curve to reap economies of scale and scope. The providers of the 'super electronic highways', for instance, compete with one another over standards and conditions of connection, precluding any open plugging in at will (Mansell 1994). They seek to attract the right kinds of customers and 'trap' them by locking them into their own particular standards and connections at the start so that sales can be guaranteed from then on. These companies seek to use market resources and public policy strongly to protect any advantages gained in this way.

## The extent of ICT-driven activity in the economy

Given the emphasis on the importance of ICT and the advent of the internet to the argument about the 'globalization of business', it is worth examining the extent of this more closely. It is very well known that ICT penetration is highly uneven (Norris 2001; United Nations 2001; Wellman and Haythornthwaite 2002; OECD 2002). Firstly, internet use is very limited worldwide – only 7 per cent of the world's population was connected in 2000 (in fact, the vast majority of the world's population has never heard the ringing tone of a telephone). Secondly, internet connections were increasingly concentrated in the USA and the high-income OECD countries in the latter part of the last century, rather than being spread more evenly between countries. But even here broadband penetration remains highly uneven – in 2006 in the EU, 30 per cent penetration in the Netherlands compared to only 5 per cent in Poland. So what is the extent of the internet-based e-economy that accompanied this?

Table 3.8 gives various estimates of the total internet business for 2001. The estimated global e-commerce turnover (section A) was between US$400 bn and 500 bn. Adding in m-commerce revenue (financial e-business) contributes a further 150 bn. Thus a reasonable estimate of total e-business would be somewhere between 550 bn and 650 bn, say 600 as an average. World GDP was estimated to be 47,000 bn in 2001. This means total e-business revenues were just about 1.28 per cent of world GDP in 2001. However, this does not compare like with like, so in part B of table 3.8 some adjustments are made. Revenue turnover figures are not comparable to GDP, which is a value-added measure. Revenues can be many

**Table 3.8**   Estimates of global internet/ICT business, 2001 (US$)

| | | |
|---|---|---|
| **A)** | e-commerce | 400–500 bn |
| | m-commerce | 150 bn |
| | TOTAL e-commerce and m-commerce | 550–650 bn, say **600 bn** |
| | World GDP | **47,000 bn** |
| | **TOTAL e- and m-commerce as % of world GDP** | **1.28%** |
| **B)** | Value-added (v-a) of business is 20%–30% of sales revenue – say 25%. Hence v-a of e- and m-commerce | **150 bn** |
| | **TOTAL v-a of e- and m-commerce as % of world GDP** | **0.3%** |
| **C)** | i) Suppose e- and m-commerce were **double** the above estimates. Then **TOTAL v-a of e- and m-commerce as % of world GDP** | **0.6%** |
| | ii) But if e- and m-commerce is only one-third of total 'e and m' business, then: **TOTAL ICT based business as % of world GDP** | **0.1–0.2%** |

*Source*: Thompson 2004c, p. 564, table 1.

times GDP. On average *company* value-added is between 20 and 30 per cent of their sales revenues (Wolf 2002). Taking 25 per cent as a reasonable estimate means that the value-added of total e- and m-commerce was only about 150 bn in 2001. Comparing this to GDP gives a figure of just 0.3 per cent of world income. Putting this another way, 99.7 per cent of the global economy was made up of 'old-economy' or 'non-e/m' economic activity. And even if total e/m-business was twice as much as this (it is very difficult to get accurate figures: Fraumeni 2001 and UNCTAD 2001 discuss the issues) it still means that e/m-business would have been just 0.6 per cent of total world output (see part Ci of table 3.8).

But total e/m-business is made up of a number of different components or 'layers'. It is the final level ('internet commerce') that attracts the attention and is the public face of the internet, but it comprises only a third of the total in terms of revenues and employment. So the real 'business' conducted over the internet as such may be even smaller than the percentages calculated so far, possibly as low as 0.1 per cent of global GDP (part Cii). However, once again some of the statistics remain a little obscure as to their true coverage, so part C of the table gives sensitivity estimates that take account of this possibility.

Whatever is made of these precise figures, the extent of the internet economy remains small, even trivial. The 'weightless economy' hardly exists.[5] In addition, B2B, B2C and m-commerce are heavily concentrated in the USA. Eighty-five per cent of total revenues in 2000 were generated in the USA (calculated from international comparative data). Thus for any real intents or purposes the internet economy – such that it is – is almost a uniquely American experience.

But do we have a new internationalized e-economy? Of course, in large part this depends upon how one defines the idea of a 'new economy'. The difficulties here are legion. Just to give two examples, the US Council of Economic Advisors (2002, pp. 58–60) restricts its analysis very much to the dominance of ICTs, whereas an analysis for the Bank of England by Wadhwani (2001, p. 495) includes a wider set of structural changes, including 'globalization', intensifying product market competition, financial market liberalization, changes in labour market flexibility and other factors. Both these argue that there is a 'new economy' in the USA and possibly the UK, but not elsewhere. In addition, McGuckin and van Ark (2002), for the US Conference Board, see a new economy appearing only in the USA, as US productivity figures soar away from those of the rest of the world. None of these analyses, then, would unequivocally support the idea of an internationalized new global economy, 'e' or otherwise.

But, as just indicated, it would be wrong to suggest it is only the internet that comprises the 'new economy'. In principle it involves much more than this: information technologies are expected to affect the entire manufacturing and service sectors. It affects the 'old economy' as well as the 'new' one. This is not the place to assess these claims in any detail, but a basic problem with the thesis has been to find convincing evidence of the productivity benefits that would be expected to have emerged across the entire economy if there had been such an ICT revolution. Again, the evidence here is at best mixed (Thompson 2004a). As of 2000 there was still no clear indication that the productivity growth in the USA was in any way historically exceptional for that economy overall. While there had been a prodigious growth in productivity in the computer manufacturing sector (between 1995 and 1999, a 42 per cent *annual growth rate* in output per hour), this sector comprised less than 1.5 per cent of total US output. Productivity in the overall manufacturing sector was increasing at about 5 per cent per annum in the late 1990s, but the record for the rest of the economy, particularly the service sector, remained modest (though see Baily and Lawrence 2001, and McKinsey and Company 2001). Subsequent estimates were more upbeat about the US position (Porter and van Opstal 2001; US Council of Economic Advisors 2002), and there is some evidence that IT-led productivity growth is developing in other OECD countries as well after significantly lagging behind the USA. However, so far there is little systematic evidence in the USA of significant spillover effects from ICT investment into the economy as a whole. Thus the reasons for the lack of a clear productivity miracle in the USA and elsewhere as a direct result of ICT investment, and whether such a miracle will emerge in the near future, still remain unclear.[6]

At the aggregate level, B2B revenues comprise 85 per cent of total e-business revenues (international comparative data). Thus what is going on in this sector is the key to the economic effects of the internet. If we examine the business strategies that it engenders these mainly involve reaping cost efficiencies from the automation of transactions between firms or parts of the same firm (e.g. Wise and Morrison 2000; Lucking-Reiley and Spulber 2001). In particular, while the establishment of intermediation agencies – such as on-line exchanges – provided a first cut at cost reduction, there is intense discussion as to whether these will themselves be eclipsed by more direct B2B trading (Wise and Morrison 2000; Kogut 2003). However, whatever one makes of these arguments, two issues are clear. First, these moves are just as likely to undermine any 'networking' relationships already established between main producers and their suppliers as to reinforce or encourage new such networking relationships (Ernst and Kim 2002). Cheaper and newer relationships found via the ICT exchanges might usurp established network suppliers, leading to a zero-sum change in networking overall. Secondly, these moves look suspiciously like a rather traditional business strategy, even as tied up with all the new imagery of an ICT-driven knowledge economy – that is, as just another move in the relentless downward pressure put on supplier cost margins in an attempt to take yet more 'fat' out of the supply chain. There is little that looks radically new here.[7]

Thus it is difficult to know what the long-term implication of e-business will be in terms of its impact on supplier networks. Leamer and Storper (2001) argue that there is a difference between those businesses that require a 'handshake' for the conduct of their activities and those that merely require a 'conversation', which can be conducted with the aid of ICTs at a distance. If new activities increase the complexity of design and production, this might increase the need for face-to-face contact. In addition, the inevitable incompleteness of contracts will always imply the necessity of handshake transactions and regular face-to-face contact to iron out difficulties. ICTs complement this; they do not displace it. Information for detailed product specifications, the organization of production schedules and the monitoring of quality standards cannot all be codified in advance. There is no quick technical fix for the monitoring of all of this activity. It requires the continuation of proximity, the clustering of activities where they can be controlled and monitored through handshake transactions (see also Porter and van Opstal (2001) and Porter and Ketels (2003) in the UK for the rationale for 'clustering' as a consequence of the continued need for close 'handshake' relationships). There is a limit to the diversification and dispersion of production. Networks continue to do their work 'locally'. Just-in-time production process technologies (which make full use of ICTs) concentrate supplier plants around assembly plants, and centralization has grown here in recent years (Klier 1999). ICT-dependent financial service industries remain tethered to a few huge cities as agglomeration economies continue to focus activities around existing centres (Venables 2002). Even ICT-based service activities, such as ISN providers, are heavily geographically concentrated (Giovannetti et al. 2003).

Finally, the advent of the widespread use of ICTs should not lead us to believe that distances and time have become unimportant (or that time is now near 'instantaneous' – as suggested by Castells 2001 and Scholte 2005). For instance, although there has been a significant reduction in the costs of conducting international trade (Baldwin and Martin 1999), there still remains an active trade-off between time and cost (Hummels 2000), and distance continues to remain a formidable barrier to trade and other economic activity (see chapter 6, table 6.8). Intriguingly, the 'distance of trade' between countries – which one might have expected to have *grown* as ICT-driven global integration increased and freight transport costs declined (thereby reducing the distance barrier to trade) – did in fact *fall* over the period 1996–2000; trading partners were drawn from those close together (Carrere and Schiff 2003). It should be recalled that 75 per cent of world trade is still merchandise trade (agricultural goods, minerals and manufactures) which requires a physical movement across space. Only 25 per cent is service trade, including financial services, which is more amenable to ICT penetration (WTO 2001, tables 1.3 and 1.4). As mentioned above, these proportions have remained more or less constant since 1975. In addition, international freight costs are increasing after several decades of decline, which may to some extent account for the finding that 'distance of trade' is also declining.

## Offshoring

These considerations of the importance of ICT to the international economy closely relate to the issue of 'offshorization' of economic activity. To some extent this has already been broached and analysed in the previous section. It refers to a general process whereby MNC supply chains are increasingly extended internationally so that economic activity and particularly employment move 'offshore' from the advanced countries and towards low-cost emerging economies and the very poor countries of the South. The important aspect of this process, however, is that it is tasks, rather than the more traditional products, that are traded in an international environment. Of course this is not exactly a new process. In principle it could be traced back to Adam Smith's discussion of specialization in his *Wealth of Nations* (1776). In 1998 the WTO described a modern-day equivalent in the case of the typical value make-up of an 'American car':

> Thirty per cent of the car's value goes to Korea for assembly, 17.5 per cent to Japan for components and advanced technology, 7.5 per cent to Germany for design, 4 per cent to Taiwan and Singapore for minor parts, 2.5 per cent to the United Kingdom for advertising and marketing services, and 1.5 per cent to Ireland and Barbados for data processing. This means that only 37 per cent of the production value ... is generated in the United States. (WTO 1998, p. 36)

But it seems to have escalated in recent years, as a new range of service tasks and jobs associated with ICT-driven call-centre, banking and software activities have migrated to offshore destinations. India, in particular, is thought to have developed a major comparative advantage in call-centre and software developments.

It is the extent of this migration of tasks that is most at issue and the consequences of it for domestic employment and wages in the traditional production and service centres. Lost jobs abroad can affect the low paid (low skilled) and the better paid (higher skilled) at home. But improvements in communications technologies that make offshoring easier and cheaper might also boost the domestic wages of those with similar skills levels as those now performing these tasks abroad. When some tasks can be more economically performed abroad, the firms that gain the most are those that use this type of labour intensively in their production processes. The augmented profitability of these firms gives them an incentive to expand relative to other firms who do not offshore these tasks, which in turn enhances their labour demand. Some of this increase in labour demand falls on local labour, who perform tasks that cannot be so easily moved abroad. The result is an all-round increase in labour productivity.

Blinder (2006, 2007) has called the process of offshorization the next industrial revolution and sees it as having a major impact on jobs in the advanced countries in the future. He suggests that between 22 per cent and 29 per cent of all US jobs are or will potentially be offshoreable in a decade or two. But both the 2007 ERM report (Ward and Storrie 2007) and the OECD (2007) are more sanguine about its impact. Figure 3.6 gives data estimates of the extent of offshorization (measured by the proportion of imported intermediate output in total output) for both the material and service sectors of OECD countries. Some growth in its importance is discernible over the five years 1995–2000, but this is perhaps less dramatic than might have been expected. There are even some falls. The USA is the least affected economy on both material and service sector counts. Although there was a doubling of the share of imported inputs in total US goods producing output between 1972 and 2000, it still amounted to only about 2 per cent in 2000 (Grossman and Rossi-Hansberg 2006, p. 68, chart 1). For Japan these figures are even lower. On the basis of a thorough investigation, the World Bank concluded in 2007 that 'contrary to some popular perceptions, offshored inputs, which accounted for about half of total imports (the rest being imports of final products), have grown somewhat more slowly than total trade. . . . Moreover, the scale of offshoring is still quite limited in the overall economy' (World Bank 2007, p. 164 – see also p. 166, figure 5.5).

In the next chapter we return to these issues in the context of country competitiveness and the debate about the decline of unskilled wages in the advanced countries.

A: Material offshoring
Percentage

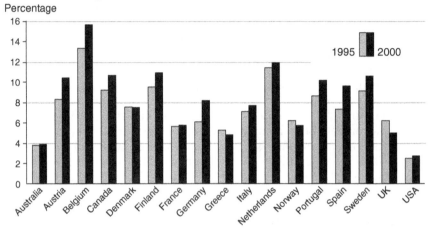

B: Services offshoring
Percentage

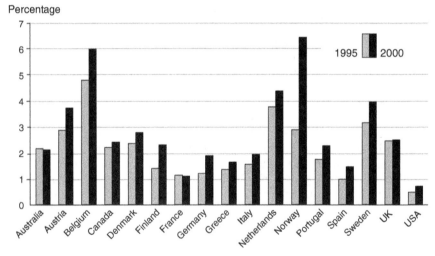

**Figure 3.6** Offshoring in selected OECD countries, 1995 and 2000[a] (percentage share of imported intermediates in total output)

Note: [a]1995 and 1999 for Greece and Portugal; 1997 and 2000 for Canada; and 1997 and 2001 for Norway.

Source: OECD 2007, p. 112, figure 3.3.

## Consequences of 'globalization' for company strategy

It is the typology by Bartlett and Goshal (1989) of different forms of international company that has struck a chord with those researchers concentrating on company form and the analysis of company strategy. Building on their suggestions, it is possible to draw a conceptual distinction between four organizational types of global business, using their labels of 'multinational', 'international', 'global' and 'transnational' respectively. The outline characteristics of these types of companies are:

1   those that build on a strong local presence through sensitivity and responsiveness to national differences ('multinational companies')
2   those that exploit parent company knowledge and capabilities through worldwide diffusion and adaptation ('international companies')
3   those that build cost advantages through centralized operations on a global scale ('global companies')
4   those that disperse their activities to relatively independent and specialized units seeking to be globally competitive through multinational flexibility and worldwide knowledge development and learning capabilities ('transnational companies').

Thus, broadly speaking, these forms proceed from a more national focus to a wider transnational one. An attempt to test empirically for these organizational types found that the most common remained the multinational type, while the least common was the transnational type (Leong and Tan 1993). This finding set the trend for further empirical work that cast doubt on the full development of the global economy and the transnational type of corporate form: the majority of 'international' firms still remain tethered to a definite national country base, confirming the analysis above.

### Technology

The issue of innovation and the role of technology is another dimension along which the process of company internationalization is often thought to be rapidly proceeding, and it is used to bolster the argument about the globalization of company activity. Again, there is little systematic company-based evidence about how much of this remains focused on the parent country rather than overseas, but what evidence is available broadly supports the conclusion that this type of activity remains far from fully globalized. For instance, in their analysis of the international distribution of R&D laboratories of 500 major firms, Casson, Pearce and Singh (1992) found some degree of interdependency, but it varied greatly according to the parent countries of firms. Firms from the Netherlands, Switzerland,

West Germany and the UK showed significant foreign orientation (the international to home ratios of laboratories for companies from these countries were all over 60 per cent), while the other nine countries or groupings studied showed considerably lower ratios (the average ratio was 39 per cent). The dominant country in terms of numbers of companies and laboratories, the USA, had a ratio of only 31 per cent, confirming it as a relatively 'closed' country on this measure. Countries such as Japan and Sweden remain very closed. In addition, papers by Cantwell (1992), Patel and Pavitt (1992) and Patel (1995) take other measures of technological activity: in patent registration, for example, no more than 10 per cent of patents granted to international firms by the US patent office originated from foreign subsidiaries, and the share of patents coming from foreign subsidiaries did not substantially increase between 1969 and 1986, or between 1986 and 1990 (based on the analysis of 686 of the world's largest manufacturing companies). The home territory remained the dominant site for the location of this form of R&D activity, reinforcing the local innovation system.

But patent registration represents an intermediate 'output' end of innovative activity. When it is supplemented by direct 'input' data associated with R&D expenditures, there is also little evidence of any systematic change as far as the advanced countries are concerned in the location or composition of this type of investment over the period from 1970 to 1990 (Archibugi and Michie 1997). Thus these national and company-based studies conclude that at most only between 10 and 30 per cent of the technological activity of multinationals is likely to be located in foreign subsidiaries. As Patel comments: 'The main conclusion of this paper is that there is no systematic evidence to suggest that widespread globalization of the production of technology has occurred in the 1980s' (1995, p. 151).

However, there is a different way in which technology can interact with the international economy, namely through the technological spillovers arising from trade and R&D expenditure. As discussed in chapter 4, R&D expenditure has traditionally been closely associated with international competitiveness. Although almost the entire world's R&D investment is concentrated in the advanced OECD countries, trade and FDI extend the benefits of this to other countries. The extent of these spillovers can look impressive (Coe and Helpman 1995; Coe et al. 1997), but they need to be set in the context of the relatively low levels of R&D expenditure conducted abroad by advanced country firms, and the relatively low levels of trade interaction between the OECD and non-OECD countries, as measured in terms of trade to GDP ratios (see chapter 4). In addition, as analysed below, a good deal of contemporary company strategy is to tap into those production locations that provide organizational advantages to their international activities but which do not necessarily involve conventional R&D expenditures.

### Behavioural characteristics

These findings about technology are reinforced by the detailed empirical analysis of Pauly and Reich (1997) into the characteristic features of US, German and Japanese MNCs. They argue that there are systematic differences between the strategies adopted by MNCs originating from each of these three countries in the areas of research and development, corporate governance and finance, and investment and intra-firm trade, arising from deeply entrenched socioeconomic institutional characteristics and cultures in the three countries. The broad but complex natures of the US, German and Japanese business systems are still intact, they argue, and they have heavily marked the MNCs originating from these countries as their activities have internationalized. In terms of technological development, Japanese firms conduct remarkably little R&D abroad, while German firms have made significant R&D commitments in the USA but little elsewhere. The bulk of the overseas R&D effort of the multinational companies from these two countries is directed either to the customization of products for local markets or to the gathering of knowledge for transfer back home. They thus organize their overseas R&D either to bolster their domestic innovation systems or to enhance their capacity to export from their domestic economies: 'trade creating' activity (this conclusion for Japan is strongly confirmed by the analysis of Fransman (1997) and Yoshitomi (1996).

US companies, by contrast, conform closely to their 'national type' in conducting much more of their R&D abroad and using this to provide substitute overseas production sites for 'trade displacing' activity. These different investment, R&D and trade strategies are reinforced, it is argued, by the domestic corporate governance systems in which the parent companies are located. The well-known nature of the links between banks and commercial enterprises, the complex cross-holding of shares in some of the countries, the differential role of the stock exchanges in each country, and the type of behaviour this engenders, are not being undermined but are being reinforced, according to this analysis. Recognizably different behavioural patterns persist in the leading MNCs' strategic orientation towards the internationalization of their activities. Table 3.9 sums up the conclusions of Pauly and Reich's analysis.

### The reorganization of production?

The analysis of Pauly and Reich (1997) provides a bridge between formal quantitative analyses of MNC activity and more qualitative approaches to the organization of the business of innovative product development and competitive success. Often the latter are based on case studies, something relatively ignored by this chapter up to now. In addition, Pauly and Reich essentially stress the effects of particular national business systems on the companies operating internationally from them. Another way of

**Table 3.9**   Multinational corporate structures and strategies of three countries

|  | USA | Germany | Japan |
|---|---|---|---|
| Direct investment | Extensive inward and outward | Selective/outward orientation | Extensive outward; limited competition from inward |
| Intra-firm trade | Moderate | High | Very high |
| Research and development | Fluctuating; diversified; innovation oriented | Narrow base/process, diffusion orientation | High, steady growth; high-technology and process orientation |
| Corporate governance | Short-term shareholding; managers highly constrained by capital markets; risk-seeking, finance-centred strategies | Managerial autonomy except during crises; no takeover risk; conservative, long-term strategies | Stable shareholders; network-constrained managers; takeover risk only within network/aggressive market share-centred strategies |
| Corporate financing | Diversified, global funding; highly price sensitive | Concentrated, regional funding; limited price sensitivity | Concentrated, national funding; low price sensitivity |

*Source*: Pauly and Reich 1997, p. 23, table 4.

approaching this issue is to look at what effects the introduction of an MNC from abroad might have on an already established business system. It is time to bring these elements into the picture.

A number of key features of contemporary business reorganization together with the role of location for competitive advantage need to be recognized here. The classic way economics tackles the analysis of technology and innovation is via the production function. Production is conceived in a 'linear' form where a series of inputs are marshalled and combined together to produce an output. Innovation is introduced into these models through the addition of another input usually measured by some variable associated with technological advance: number of patents registered, number of scientists and engineers, number and location of R&D laboratories, R&D expenditures, etc. The linear model also describes the innovation process as a sequence of stages: from research to development, then to production, and finally to marketing, with little communication or connection between these stages.

In contrast to this linear model, however, it has become increasingly clear that there is a lot more to innovation than just the application of another 'resource input' or the organization of a sequence of separated stages. Non-linear, looped and feedback models recognize the existence of many 'intangible' assets in the innovation process: those associated with incremental learning and tacit knowledge, with the locational 'milieu' in which companies operate, with the habits, conventions and routines that serve to 'socially organize' the production process, etc. One significant way of expressing these aspects is as 'untraded interdependencies' (Storper 1995). They represent an 'asset' that cannot be easily identified as a measurable input into the production process. Rather they exist as locationally specific 'externalities' which firms can only access by actually setting up operations within the location in question. This can account for the significant development of 'innovation without R&D' that is usually associated with local and regional economic districts. In part, this 'innovation without R&D' has to do with process innovation, but it also has to do with incremental product innovations based on how the innovation process is spatially organized. These issues, then, bring back into the picture the spatially and locationally specific business systems as a central element for firms' innovative activity and competitive performance.

Including these considerations enables us to make sense of the way international firms look for particular comparative and competitive strengths in locational advantages associated with national or regional production, innovation and business systems. MNCs thus seek to tap into the advantages offered by particular locations so as to strengthen their overall competitive performance and success. They often look for quite small advantages associated with a specific part of their overall production process, creating complex international divisions of labour based on locational specialization. Take the Jæren district of Norway as an example (Asheim and Isaksen 1997, pp. 317–18). This has specialized in the production of advanced industrial robots. A leading local firm (Trallfa Robot) was taken over in the late 1980s by ABB, a Swiss-Swedish MNC (creating ABB Flexible Automation). ABB produced most of its robots for the European car makers in Västerås in Sweden, but instead of restructuring by closing down the Jæren plant and moving production to Sweden, it increased capacity and employment in its Norwegian subsidiary in order to capture the specialist externalities available in the local area. In this way the presence of ABB has *strengthened* rather than undermined the local innovative and business system.

Another example of a similar process can be seen by the way that German bank multinationals have tapped into the comparative advantages of the City of London's financial system, without necessarily undermining either that system's operation or their own domestic activities (Soskice 1997, pp. 76–7). Deutsche Bank, Dresdner Bank, the Norddeutsche Landesbank and Commerzbank have all moved their international operations away from Frankfurt to London. But they have maintained their domestic operations – those that support the high skill competence and long-term relationships associated with local manufacturing – within Germany. Similarly, German chemical firms such as BASF, Bayer and Hoechst have run down their biotechnology operations in Germany and concentrated them in the USA, where there is a technical and organizational advantage.

Meanwhile their mainstream high value-added chemical research and production is still concentrated in Germany.

One way of characterizing these changes in how international business is being conducted is in terms of the introduction of sophisticated networks of specialization and value-added. In some sectors these may not even involve any direct investment overseas. The development of cross-border production networks that assemble diverse points of innovation occurs by drawing in independent indigenous suppliers who link into the commodity chain, or chains, of system assembly and standard setting (Borrus and Zysman 1997), without this requiring an explicit physical investment strategy on the part of the lead MNC firm. The MNC acts only as the 'organizer' of the independent part-contractors and subsystem assemblers that occupy the strategic positions in the network. Here we have the internationalization of production without any overseas investment being necessary. Borrus and Zysman probably exaggerate the extent of this as a new paradigm for global competition to be followed by all sectors (they call it 'Wintelism', from the combination of Windows and Intel type production technologies), but it captures elements of a number of well-recognized developments in international business.

An example of this is the way Singapore has developed a comparative advantage in hard disk drive (HDD) production and assembly, based on the technological and organizational innovativeness of its local firms (but also supplemented initially by MNC investment; Wong 1997).[8] Subsequent spin-off developments and new local investment have served to strengthen the production and innovation system. Nor is this based on any labour cost advantage, since direct and indirect labour costs amount to only 6 per cent of the total cost of an HDD (ibid., p. 199, table 7). The Singapore element in several complex transnational production networks for computer equipment is now well established. The key point to recognize from these examples is summed up by Borrus and Zysman:

> This era is ... one in which an increasingly global market coexists with enduring national foundations of distinctive economic growth trajectories and corporate strategies. Globalization has not led to the elimination of national systems of production. National systems endure; but they are evolving together in a world economy that increasingly has a regional structure. (1997, p. 143)

## Conclusion

The argument of this chapter has involved a number of points. The first is that the internationalization of production and trading activity remains extremely unequally distributed, with the domination of the Triad countries and a few favoured rapidly expanding less developed economies. The vast bulk of the world's population is heavily disadvantaged and almost ignored by these developments. Income distribution is also severely unequal, with little sign that this is changing.

Secondly, the extent of the internationalization of business activity is often exaggerated in both popular and academic accounts; and it is not increasing at a particularly dramatic rate. From the quantitative analysis reported in the first part of the chapter it is reasonable to suggest that between 65 and 70 per cent of MNC value-added continues to be produced on the home territory. This conclusion coincides with the arguments of Tyson (1991), Kapstein (1991) and Lazonick (1993) in their debate with Reich (1990, 1992) about the nature of international business (see also Hu 1992, 1995). The former authors challenged Reich on his assumption that American business had gone 'transnational', and that this did not matter. Tyson pointed out that, 'within manufacturing, US parent operations account for 78 percent of total assets, 70 percent of total sales, and 70 percent of total employment of US multinationals in 1988' (p. 38). The analysis reported here confirms this finding for a wider range of countries.

But there has obviously been some internationalization of business activity. Thus a second issue was to assess the strategies of companies originating from different business systems. Despite the home-centredness of the main findings, the remaining activity of the country groupings is quite diverse. That is, the different country MNCs operate in different areas to different extents. The MNCs are not all the same, either in terms of the geographical spread of their activity outside their home territories or in the way they have gone about internationalizing their activities. In this respect it was argued that the production and business systems of the originating countries still marked the MNCs with a particular approach and attitude.

Connected to this is the question of what effects the limited internationalization of business activity is having on national systems of business, production and innovation. Here the argument is that this has yet to develop to such an extent that national systems are being radically undermined, transformed or rendered redundant. Indeed, in many ways these systems are being reinforced and strengthened by the internationalization of business. Firms are locking themselves into the advantages offered by particular locational production configurations, which are enhancing their ability to compete. In addition, the continuation of a clear home-centredness for most MNCs also needs to be recognized as providing them with advantages that they will not easily give up.

Finally, it is worth raising the issue of the 'governance' consequences of this analysis. These are twofold. In the first place, if national systems of production, business and technology still remain relatively firmly embedded, then there is still scope for the management of these in the interests of the stability and productivity of the national economy.

Secondly, given that MNCs remain tethered to their home economies, whether these are specified nationally or regionally, the opportunity arises for national or subnational regional bodies to monitor, regulate and govern them more effectively than if they were genuinely 'footloose capital'.

Thus the overall conclusion of the chapter is that the extent of internationalization and its potential detrimental consequences for the regulation of MNC activity and for national economies is severely exaggerated. International businesses are still largely confined to their home territory in terms of their overall activity: they remain heavily 'nationally embedded'.

# 4

# Globalization and International Competitiveness

---

At the end of 2004 the UK Treasury issued a major report on the theme of globalization and the UK economy (HM Treasury 2004). Perhaps not surprisingly, this document completely accepts the conventional globalization story. It represented the high point of the then chancellor of the exchequer's uncritical endorsement of the idea that the UK economy is subject to truly global market forces and must respond with renewed vigour so as to make the economy even more 'internationally competitive'. The chancellor, Gordon Brown, went on to become prime minister in 2007, so this document signals New Labour's continuing policy commitment to the idea that international competitiveness should play the leading role in its attitude towards the international economy. Indeed, a little later the Treasury issued two further reports that repeat the basic message, one pressing 'Europe' to reform to meet the same undifferentiated global challenges (HM Treasury 2005a) and the second looking further ahead to the competitive battles emerging with China (HM Treasury 2005b).

While these examples point to the UK government's deep commitment to the idea of international competitiveness, such a commitment is not confined just to the UK. It is a trend that has become the mantra for the global system more generally. One of the most obvious examples of this is the World Economic Forum's yearly competitiveness report (World Economic Forum 2007), which develops an aggregate index of country competitiveness and ranks over 130 countries along a single scale. Many of these positionings are highly suspect, but journalists and politicians tend to ignore the methodological limitations and read only the headline figures. This kind of exercise serves to bolster the centrality to contemporary economic discussion of the notion of international competitiveness. The problem with these kinds of rankings is that they depend critically on surveying business opinion – hence they tend to magnify dissatisfaction by managers and reflect plain ignorance of real economic conditions. In its 2007 report the World Economic Forum ranked the USA as the most competitive economy (a consistent position). This was despite the well-known difficulties being experienced by the US economy in 2006 and 2007 – as documented elsewhere in this book – and it points to a certain caution that should be exercised when reading these reports. On the other hand, China was ranked 35th, India 42nd, Russia 59th and Brazil 66th. The UK was placed ninth in 2007, having fallen from second in the 2006 report. On most measures the UK is a highly internationalized economy, more so than its comparably sized 'competitors' (Hirst and Thompson 2000 – where these authors describe the UK as 'an over-internationalized economy in an under-globalized world').

## International competitiveness and globalization

As mentioned above, the issue of international competitiveness has grown alongside the concern about the effects of globalization – they are parallel developments. But there are probably five relatively separate trends that can account specifically for this growth in the discourse of competitiveness.

The first, and most obvious, has to do with the collapse of the Cold War. While the Cold War prevailed, competitiveness remained couched in fundamentally geopolitical terms: the struggle between the two main politico-ideological blocs locked all remaining world issues into a single geomilitary confrontation. Once this was over, the differences between countries came newly to the fore, and particularly the differences between them in terms of their economic performance as measured by their 'competitiveness'.

A second important development was the perceived unsuccessful nature of large-scale and grandiose 'industrial policy' initiatives. Twenty-five years ago critical economic analysis was much more concerned about different industrial policies and restructuring initiatives by states. These are now perceived to have been a failure (though we do not endorse the view that all industrial policy initiatives were in fact failures). In the wake of this, it is the emphasis on 'competitiveness' that has taken hold of both the private and the public consciousness in terms of economic matters: intervention is to be confined to making markets work better.

A third trend is the move towards policies of liberalization and privatization in terms of domestic institutional changes. Although these are often argued to be the results of internationalization and even the globalization of economic activity, we would suggest that fundamentally they have been driven by domestic decisions and policy changes (e.g. Thompson

1997). Whatever the reason, however, the result has been a reinvigorated emphasis on competition and market-driven solutions to economic problems.

A fourth issue involves the relative 'success' of those mainly inter-governmental organizations of international economic regulation and management that have governed the world economy in the post-Second World War period, such as the OECD, the GATT/WTO, the IMF and the World Bank. The activity of these organizations has resulted in a general opening up of the world economies as protectionist barriers to economic activity were eliminated or drastically reduced. In the absence of tariff barriers or capital controls, the underlying economic competitiveness of different countries has been exposed, hence the growth in concern with this aspect of their economies.

Finally, the growth of interdependencies and integrations among the world's major economies since the end of the Second World War, limited though this process is, has served to announce afresh the importance of the relative competitiveness of different countries. Thus there is a clear relationship between the growth of a concern with inter-national competitiveness and that of globalization, something we return to later.

## From 'embedded liberalism' to 'neo-liberalism'

One of the key elements in the emergence of international competitiveness as almost the defining moment of the current 'globalized era' was the move from embedded liberalism (Ruggie 1982; Steffek 2006) to neo-liberalism as the characteristic modality of international economic governance. We examine this move now and show how it impacted directly on the competi-tiveness argument.

Embedded liberalism – something argued to have characterized much of the post-Second World War period in the twentieth century – was essen-tially seen as a *political compromise*, where countries gave up the worst excesses of protectionism in exchange for the possibility of some autonomy in the conduct of domestic economic policy-making, particularly in the area of macroeconomic management. It involved *diplomatic bargaining* between countries to establish compromises on trade policy, as exemplified by the GATT mechanism. The key criterion in international trade talks was that of *non-discrimination* between partners as embodied in the 'most favoured nation' clauses of the successive GATT negotiating rounds and treaties (trading terms negotiated with a favoured trading partner should be extended to all other trading partners, i.e. there should be no discrimination between them). Difficult to uphold and police – and therefore often com-promised as it was in practice – this regime lasted roughly from the early 1950s until the late 1970s, when one of its crucial supports – the semi-fixed exchange rates and a *de facto* dollar standard – was abandoned in favour of a flexible exchange-rate regime.

This ushered in the period of neo-liberalism as market and competitive solutions were sought for economic problems. The key criterion for negotiations also changed as *obstacles* gradually displaced non-discrimination as the object of policy. This in turn opened up to international scrutiny the *domestic economic characteristics* of trading countries in the context of their *internal regulatory practices* and *the conditions for market access*. Along with this, the emphasis on the market was accompanied by moves away from political bargaining towards the resort to international public and private law as the means to settle disputes. In its wake the GATT (an 'agreement') was replaced by the establishment of the WTO (an 'institution') to oversee trade matters. The WTO mechanism is one recognized in international law, and its practices are those that have led to charges that trade law is being 'constitutionalized', particularly as its Appellate Body (AB) delivers judgements on appeals over panel rulings on trade matters (Cass 2005).

The differences between the GATT and the WTO tend to revolve around the consequences of dispute-resolution mechanisms in each case (Howse 2000). Under the GATT a consensus of member states was required in order for dispute rulings to become binding. This involved the creation of a 'positive consensus'. Dispute rulings were drafted with a 'diplomatic vagueness' often expressing an intuitive kind of law, one based on shared experiences and unspoken assumptions. It was driven by a rather cosy bureaucratic and technocratic 'club' culture, based upon shared values and a consensus that supported economic liberalism on essentially pragmatic grounds, and it met in closed session. One feature was that compliance was rather high.

With the WTO, however, dispute rulings are accepted as binding unless all the members – including the winning party – vote *against* its adoption (requiring a 'negative consensus' that is more difficult to achieve). In addition, determinations of when and how the losing party must act to implement a ruling are subject to arbitration, and, should the losing party not implement a ruling in accordance with the findings of the arbitrator, retaliation (involving the withdrawal of trade concessions to the losing party by the winning party) is automatically authorized. Moreover, as noted above, the legal determinations of any panel (known as a 'tribunal of first instance') may be appealed to the AB (which is a standing tribunal of seven jurists, three of whom sit in each case). The establishment of the AB, then, meant that the relatively 'informal' nature of the previous GATT disputes mechanism was undermined. As an adjudicative institution, separated from the bureaucratic and technical culture, the AB is open to review and scrutiny and embodies contestable legal interpretations where values can no longer be presumed to be shared. In this context, economic liberalism became much more of a dogmatic insistence (in a sharp laissez-faire style), rather than being accepted as a shared pragmatic compromise.

The results of the AB decisions then become precedents and have force of international law, though they were not formally part of the original treaty agreement, and nor are they mandated by any clear political process other than that initiated by the general WTO treaty signed in 1995 and biannual ministerial meetings (though these tend to rubber stamp things; Broude 2004). A key change is thus with the new liberal technology of rule embodied in the WTO disputes mechanism and the AB, which involves a novel way to adjudicate and enforce obligations in an international economic context (though it tends to mirror the adversarial practices of Anglo-American adjudication).

Two other elements in this transformation are also worth noting. The first of these involves the shift from what is often termed '*cooperative competition*' between states towards '*competitive cooperation*'. The key change is the move of competition to the forefront of the relationships between states in the economic field. Whereas states previously found it efficient and convenient to cooperate between themselves to foster 'limited' and 'managed' competition, or at least to 'accommodate' competition, now the issue is the perceived centrality of competition in the relationships between states, where cooperation between them – such that it is – is afforded a secondary status and seen as a complement of, or support for, competitive relationships. This means that an 'international common law' becomes necessary to adjudicate disputes between what are now considered to be competing parties: diffuse reciprocity has given way to competition between policy norms. Intergovernmental cooperation in setting up a body such as the WTO only goes to further the mechanisms of competitive relationships that it is designed to support, where 'common values' cannot any longer necessarily be presumed or shared.

While the WTO does not involve companies directly – it is an intergovernmental organization settling trade disputes only between governments – it involves them indirectly in that these lobby governments to take up grievances and are often instrumental in pressing for changes in WTO rules (in their favour).[1] But a further development is more directly associated with MNC activity. The shift from embedded liberalism to neo-liberalism arises because the integration of the international economy may itself have moved from a position of '*shallow interdependency*' to one of '*deep integration*'. Shallow interdependency involved rather straightforward trade exchanges between otherwise relatively 'closed' economies. With the growth of FDI and the operation of MNCs, however, deeper integration has occurred. FDI and MNCs 'open up' domestic economies to international economic pressures in a novel way, so that issues of domestic 'obstacles' to access and the domestic regulatory practices designed to support this become an impediment to trade openness and an object of scrutiny and policy.

## North–South divergences and differences

Another aspect of the discourse about competitiveness has to do with the differences between the 'North' and the 'South', broadly speaking. This concerns, in particular, the way that the growth of certain of the Southern economies (the 'emerging market' economies) might threaten the competitive position of the traditional developed countries of the North, which in turn involves the way in which the competitive position of the advanced countries is threatened by cheap goods and labour that emanates from those emerging economies of the South. Both of these developments – the growth of the South and its cheap goods and labour – are directly associated with globalization: they are key aspects of this process.

But we need to examine these aspects of the globalization process carefully before we can accept the clear link drawn between globalization and competitiveness that it implies. We can begin by considering the international system as traditionally divided into two different groups of countries: one set called the 'advanced' or 'developed' countries, and another called the less 'developed' or 'non-industrialized' countries.[2] The questions are what the nature of these two groups and the competitive relationship between them have been. Historically, the first group consolidated their position as high-income earners in the late nineteenth century, and there has been some considerable convergence between them over a long period of time. The other 'group', the less developed, do not have so much in common; there has been great diversity between them and they have not so obviously converged – indeed in many ways they have diverged among themselves. These countries have, on average, seen growth rates slower than have the richer countries. But they have also seen some strikingly different patterns. A few have converged on the leaders since the end of the Second World War (e.g. Korea, Singapore and, to some extent, Taiwan), others have stagnated, while still others have had a mixed record of take-offs, stalls and nosedives. In addition, a few of the original convergence group (such as Argentina and South Africa) have departed from that group to become 'troubled middle-income' countries. But what has been even more striking is that the core countries of the original convergence group, made up of the Atlantic economy states and temperate ex-colonies such as Australia and New Zealand, have consolidated its position and seen a marked stability in its membership. What is more, while this group has tended to 'converge' in terms of growth, productivity and living standards, it has in turn 'diverged' from the other group – and, as it has been described, 'diverged, big time' (Pritchett 1997). Cases where poor countries, and especially the least developed countries, actually gain significantly on the leaders are historically rare. In most poor countries there are strong forces for stagnation. Of course, the recent experiences of China and India may be about to break this pattern, but see below.

One question this raises is whether 'globalization' has made any difference to these patterns and trends (Dowrick and DeLong 2003). In fact, it seems not. If globalization is understood as the progressive liberalization and opening of economies to international trade and investment, then in the first round of globalization between 1870 and 1914, while it consolidated the original convergence club in the manner just described, it did not extend this much beyond that charmed circle (chapter 2). It brought great structural change and economic integration to the other economies, but the relative gap in income and productivity and the gap in industrial structure vis-à-vis the industrial core of the world economy both continued to widen.

During the interwar period globalization and integration were in retreat as tariff barriers were raised, autarkic economic blocs emerged, international investment shrank, the Great Depression hit and world trade collapsed. But, interestingly, there was some global convergence of 'between country' GDP per capita, and the 'convergence club' actually expanded slightly during this period (Milanović 2002, 2005; Dowrick and DeLong 2003). Thus while 'globalization' retreated, international 'convergence' grew.

The post-Second World War period was very much one in which the international system first recovered from the disintegration of the interwar period. It also brought both a slight expansion in the size and a shift in the location of the 'convergence club'. As mentioned above, a number of East Asian economies 'joined' and a number of the older members from Latin America 'retreated' from the club. But the basic core membership remained. And, as just suggested, there was no dramatic convergence in 'between country' income differences even as the second period of 'globalization' matured after the 1970s.

What this suggests is that convergence is a phenomenon somewhat independent of international economic integration or globalization. Greater trade, migration or capital flows have no discernible effect on the 'catch-up' of poorer countries. In effect, poorer countries would just as likely catch up with the subset of rich convergence club countries whether there is international economic integration and globalization or not. But why has this structural divide between the convergence club and the rest persisted for so long?

## Investment and trade

At root this has to do with the gap in productivity between the two groups, but it might be expected that this would have been eroded as capital moved to exploit the cheaper wage costs in the developing countries, or labour moved towards the developed country group to exploit the higher wages to be had there. Neither of these processes seems to have happened to the extent that might have been expected, however. The recent period of glo-balization has not seen capital resources flowing to the less developed economies of Africa, Latin America or even Asia to any great degree. There has been a massive growth of FDI in the period since 1970, but it has been *intra-developed country flows*: the convergence club has invested in itself (see chapter 3, figure 3.4).

The international inequalities in respect to capital stocks and flows have been neatly summed up as follows:

> In 1990, the richest 20 percent of world population received 92 percent of gross portfolio capital inflows, whereas the poorest 20 percent received 0.1 percent. The richest 20 percent of the world population received 79 percent of foreign direct investment, and the poorest 20 percent received 0.7 percent. Altogether, the richest 20 percent of the world population received 88 percent of gross private capital inflows, and the poorest 20 percent received 1 percent. (Easterly and Levine 2003, p. 205)

In addition, despite the growth of some developing countries, and although countries that trade more generally grew more, only a small part of world trade involves developing countries. This can be seen clearly from table 4.1, which reports on the direction of world merchandise trade for 1998. A little less than one-quarter of world merchandise exports originated in the developing countries, while just over three-quarters originated in high-income countries. Since the ability to export ultimately also determines the ability to import, these figures broadly represent the picture of world trade in general, and things have not changed much since 1998.

**Table 4.1**  World trading relations: direction of trade (percentages of world merchandise trade), 1998

| | Destination | | |
| --- | --- | --- | --- |
| Origin | High-income countries | Low- and middle-income countries | World |
| High-income countries | 58.5 | 17.3 | 75.8 |
| Low- and middle-income countries | 17.0 | 7.1 | 24.2 |
| World | 75.6 | 24.4 | 100.0 |

*Note*: These numbers may not add to totals because of the rounding of figures to one decimal place. Trade is valued at export value f.o.b. (free on board, not including insurance and freight charges). The figures are for trade in goods only; trade in services (which is less well recorded) is not included.
*Source*: Derived from World Bank (2002).

## Migration

Another element in this picture of continued divergence is that of labour migration. This has become one of the most controversial aspects of the globalization debate. In the recent period it has tended to focus around the issue of the effects of migration on the relative distribution of incomes within the advanced countries. In this case, it is the effects on unskilled migration from the South to the North that often captures the attention and the headlines. Does this added supply of unskilled labour from the South undermine the wages of the Northern unskilled workers, making them more uncompetitive, for instance, and how much is this migration responsible for the increase in wage/income inequality in the USA or Europe? Has it been responsible for the growing 'within country' inequality between wage earners in these countries?

It is important to point out that, while there has been some labour migration in the international system, most of this has been limited to skilled migration from the LDCs to the rich countries. It is skilled workers who earn relatively less rather than more in poor countries, so there is an incentive for them to migrate (Easterly and Levine 2003, p. 206). But, overall, international migration has been limited (with the partial exception of migration into the USA, though this has also favoured skilled migration). The story of migration in the twentieth century was one of *intra*-national migration, from rural to urban areas, not so much *inter*-national migration as in the nineteenth century (which helped to establish convergence in the Atlantic economy as mentioned above – see chapter 2 and O'Rourke and Williamson 1998).

And this connects to the effect of *trade* in respect to labour remuneration in various countries. As the Northern countries have imported more from the Southern ones, what is the 'skill' content of the goods and services so traded? Commodities and services 'embody' relative skill intensities. So trade and migration are to some extent substitutes in terms of the way 'within country' and 'between country' inequalities can emerge and evolve. A good deal of low-skilled manufacturing has been driven out of the advanced countries and relocated in the less developed countries, the output of which is then sold back to the advanced countries. Thus, instead of unskilled labour migrating to the Northern advanced countries to produce low-skilled goods there, it is in effect 'imported' there via the skill intensity of the products that are exported to those countries from the less advanced ones. Therefore to find out the effect of growing integration and globalization on the unskilled wages in the Northern countries requires the assessment not only of the direct effects of migration but also of the indirect effects of the skill intensity of trade.

## Technology and innovation

In addition, this emphasis on labour skill intensity raises issues about the role of technology in these international trade, migration, investment, growth and inequality relationships. The demand for different skill mixes is the response to different technologies and to the changing dynamic of technological advance. Furthermore, technological advantage is often thought to move from one country to the next – in particular as a response to the trade and investment opportunities offered by the different factor availabilities and factor price movement in different countries. In the long run, other things being equal, the convergence of the factor price of labour across countries could bring per capita incomes close together. As trade lowers the skilled wages in LDCs, and increases those in more developed countries (MDCs), this boosts the LDCs' technical progress because the cost of innovation declines here, and lowers the MDCs' technical progress as the cost of innovation has increased there, so trade leads to convergence. But, once again, this depends upon empirical factors, since we could just as easily assume that trade leads to the premium on skilled labour in developing countries to be lowered, which reduces the incentive to acquire skills there, and hence could lower their growth rate. So, under these alternative circumstances, trade leads to further divergence. It all rather depends upon the effects of trade on the skill premium and technical advance in different types of countries, which is difficult to predict *a priori*. But, as we have seen above, the net empirical result has been a trend more towards divergence than towards convergence.

An important test of some of these issues arose in the 1990s in respect to the rather sudden integration of the US economy into the international economic system as the amount of trade in the USA relative to output (the trade to GDP ratio) soared and a number of its industries were increasingly threatened by overseas competition. This happened at the same time as medium-skilled and unskilled wages in the USA fell (the skill premium increased). Migration added to these pressures. In addition, this was a time of very rapid technological advance in the US economy (the widespread introduction of ICTs), also leading to a sudden change in the demand for different skills and significant relative wage changes. So what was the relative importance of these various factors in leading to the overall result of a sharp decline in the fortunes of the less skilled US workers in particular?

There are a number of ways of looking at what various factors might contribute to the labour market and income distributional trends mentioned above. First, we could look at the *skill intensity* of the North's imports and exports: the North should export high-skill intensive products (and services) and import low-skill intensive products (and services). Second, we could concentrate on the *relative price changes* of the low-skill intensive and high-skill intensive products: the relative price of the low-skill intensive products in the North should decline, and vice versa. Third, the *wages* of low-skilled labour *relative* to those of high-skilled labour should decline in the North. Fourth, *employment* in the North should shift to the high-skill intensive output, so that *unemployment* among the low skilled will (temporarily) increase. But, fifth, Northern firms should react to the reduction in the relative wages of unskilled labour by raising the proportions of such labour in the production of *both* high-skill intensive and low-skill intensive sectors, thereby offsetting the effects in the previous point to some extent. Sixth, we could focus directly on the trends in *technological innovation*, particularly IT, which might lead to a skill-biased technical change (which is in addition to, and independent of, the trend-neutral growth of total factor productivity experienced in advanced economies for over a hundred years). Finally, we could look at the educational and skill trends of *migrants* into (and out of) the North.

This sketches a large canvas. Determining which of these features provides the most significant measure or contribution is not straightforward. Many of these potential effects and candidate influences are highly interdependent and sequentially linked. There is the added problem of constructing relevant counterfactuals. In addition, how should skill be measured – in terms of education, experience or job classification? As a consequence, estimates of the relative importance of influences vary considerably and are not easily summarized.

Gathered along one dimension are those who think that trade (and hence 'globalization') is the most important contributory factor in the decline of real wages in the USA and the plight of unskilled workers in the North as a whole. A key analysis employing the skill factor endowment approach (Wood 1994) found that a substantial proportion of the loss of market power by Northern unskilled workers was the result of the relocation of manufacturing industry and the growth of global trade. Wood argued that taking into account the low-skill intensive activities that had already been competitively driven out of the advanced countries (thus looking beyond the existing factor proportions in the remaining import-competing industries, the usual approach), and additionally taking into account the fact that a portion of the labour-saving technological change in the North arises from the need for manufacturers to compete with trade from the South, then over 20 per cent of the reduction in the demand for labour in the North was a consequence of trade alone. This claim by Wood was challenged in another influential study by Sachs and Shatz (1994), who estimated a much smaller proportion of trade-related demand influences for the US economy only, much nearer to 6 per cent.

These approaches look at factor (skill) endowments. Thus there is evidence that labour demand has shifted towards skilled workers in advanced countries both *across industries* – in that the share of output produced by low-skill intensive industries has fallen relative to that produced by more skill intensive ones – and in terms of demands *within industries* – as firms have shifted away from unskilled towards skilled workers – so that the prospects of the more skilled workers would seem to have improved even though their relative supply has increased. But, on other evidence, the skill intensity of US manufacturing has risen in both the top end and the lower end of the manufacturing sectors: this runs counter to the predictions of the traditional Heckscher–Ohlin/Stolper–Samuelson (H–O/S–S) framework[3] and points to a less than strong impact of trade effects (Krugman and Lawrence 1994, p. 47).

However, these approaches are framed in terms of factor endowments and can be criticized for not focusing on price changes. This is where the effects of any changes in factor endowments should normally work themselves out. Formally, the H–O/S–S framework operates in terms of price adjustments. There is little evidence that product prices in industrial countries have followed the expected pattern of prices of import-competing, low-skill and labour-intensive goods falling relative to the prices of high-skill embodied and capital-intensive goods. The World Bank concluded in 1997:

> For manufacturing industries in the industrial countries in the 1980s and 1990s, the prices of goods produced using relatively more skilled labour have for the most part fallen in relation to the prices of goods produced using relatively more unskilled labour. And even after taking into account the effects of technological progress on relative prices, the change in relative prices attributable to international trade has favoured goods produced by low skilled, not high skilled labour. (World Bank 1997, p. 75)

Finally these are partial equilibrium approaches, when what is really required is a general equilibrium analysis. Those attempts at providing this (such as Krugman 1995; Cline 1997; Minford et al. 1997) have produced estimates nearer the top end of the spectrum referred to above, with trade contributing about 20 per cent to the rising real wage inequality in the USA in the 1980s. In the case of Minford, Riley and Nowell (1997), estimates of these trade effects are even higher, accounting for about 40 per cent of the collapse of Northern unskilled labour employment and wages.

An alternative focus to the trade-as-cause-of-wages-decline approach is to concentrate on the movements of capital in the first instance. The outflow of FDI, with domestic jobs 'exported' to offshore sites, is often thought to be leading to the deindustrialization of the advanced economies and employment loss there. The recent growth of international outsourcing production and the development of value chains, substituting for home production, are an expression of this trend (but see chapter 3). Thus the activities of MNCs can substitute home exports to other countries by the direct output and supply from offshore production platforms. As we have seen in chapter 3, there is some evidence of this trend developing, but analysis of its importance for the US economy suggests that American firms do not seem to have substituted foreign workers for domestic workers on a large scale (e.g. Feenstra and Hanson 1996). Indeed, the number of foreign workers in US-owned firms peaked in the late 1970s. This trend may be more important for some smaller European economies and Japan, but the problem is how to demonstrate that it is this specific activity rather than other influences that has led to wage inequality.

Other than these moderate 'international' effects, the rest of the collapse in the demand for unskilled labour and wages can be attributable to 'domestic causes'. Here is the second main dimension around which an explanation lies: that of skill-enhancing technical change. From this perspective 'deindustrialization' is in part at least a consequence of the impact of unequal rates of productivity growth in manufacturing and services, which has affected the advanced economies in particular. Those economists who adopt low estimates of the trade influence think the importance of 'international competitiveness' is exaggerated. 'Domestic' influences are more important, and, given the generally accepted proportions of between 10 and 20 per cent attributable to trade, 80 to 90 per cent must still be domestic and technological in origin (Krugman and Lawrence 1994; Lawrence and Slaughter 1993). But this is not estimated directly. Technological change cannot be observed and measured with any precision. It is either proxied in equations or emerges as a 'residual' from a production function. Thus skill-biased technical change is invoked as a cause rather than being directly empirically attributable. Usually, it is the low ratios of trade to GDP between the North and the South that act as the background counterfactual here.

Clearly, this type of analysis is not entirely satisfactory. But it serves to indicate that, even with a range of sophisticated econometric and economic modelling techniques, the relative importance of global compared to domestic influences is likely to be low. One problem here is that analyses such as those of Wood (1995), which claim a larger importance for trade effects, already 'account' for some technological change in the estimates because they adjust the counterfactual to include past skill-displacing technical change indirectly induced by international trade with the South. Thus trade and technological change are interdependent and intertwined, so these estimates can be no more than educated guesses. This also leaves room for alternative explanations. Accepting for the moment that the trade influences do lie between 10 and 20 per cent, estimates of the effects of migration (another 'international' explanation) do not add much to this (Borjas et al. 1997). But conventional economic analysis ignores possible explanations other than the indirectly estimated and residual technological change variable.

What is missing from this highly aggregated level of analysis is any focus on the actual strategies of Northern firms, for instance in their dealings with labour. The period from the 1970s has seen an unprecedented attack on labour from the business interest, particularly in the USA and the UK.

Considering this also raises other structural issues, including the role of bargaining power and collective action. Not all the adjustments can be accounted for simply within the labour market (Howell and Wolff 1991). The period from the New Deal to the mid-1960s in the USA was one of a strategic accommodation between business and labour, marked by an acceptance of the legitimate interests of each in the conduct of business activity and in terms of a broad social compromise in economic policy more generally (Roe 1994, part 3; Korten 1995, pp. 1–14). But this compromise was deliberately broken in the mid-1970s in the USA and in the UK in particular, just at the time when the increases in inequality referred to above also began to emerge.

What is the possible connection between the loss of market power of unskilled workers in manufacturing and the decline in real wages in general? The break in the historical compromise mentioned above saw a renewed attack on the working conditions of American labour and a release of the constraints on managerial prerogatives and managerial salaries. David Gordon (1996) has documented the consequences of this in detail. His argument is that, despite a rhetoric of 'downsizing' in American management speak, the facts go against it. There has been an increase in the numbers and levels of supervisory and management personnel. And this analysis is supported by similar evidence from the UK (Gallie et al. 1998). In addition, the wage bill for this managerial group has expanded at the expense of those very workers who are supervised and managed. In this context a corporate strategy of deliberately undermining the wages of production workers and of cutbacks in shopfloor employment has emerged. This has simultaneously released the restraint on corporate management from rapidly increasing its own remuneration. The coincidental securitization of American savings and the stock market boom it unleashed until the late 1990s additionally fed the incomes of stockholders. The outcome was the growth in inequality in the USA, and to a lesser extent in the UK and elsewhere in Europe.

Here we have the seeds of an alternative explanation for much of the turn against the unskilled worker and the reduction of real wages in the North. This is also an explanation that is resolutely 'domestic' in origin. It provides an account for the missing 80 to 90 per cent that is complementary to that of technical advance.

But this explanation itself is not without its problems. It probably underestimates the extent of downsizing that has occurred in the USA. Other accounts testify to a genuine cut in layers of management. It also ignores the increase in high-grade jobs being driven by the growth in technical-grade workers in more sophisticated manufacturing processes, who tend to be classified in the supervisory and managerial grades.

In terms of the general debate, however, after a great deal of quite sophisticated empirical analysis and argument the consensus opinion was that about 10 per cent was due to migration, 20 per cent to trade, and the remaining 70 per cent to technical advance (see Cline 1997). But it is important to remember that many of these expectations and trends do not seem to have actually emerged in practice, since the basic long-term divergences discussed above have continued to exist. Easterly and Levine (2003) suggest that there are major external economies associated with technological spillovers that concentrate economic activity around existing areas, and indeed attract new activity to those existing locations. External economies are those economies that make it cheaper for firms to produce their own output but which are not generated internally by, say, their own increase in size, but arise because of the growing size of the whole industry or economy in which the firm operates. Thus each firm can benefit by the existence and growth of certain other firms, which help it to reduce its own costs. One source of these economies could be the development of specialized labour training facilities and a local skilled labour market that provides trained workers for a number of firms making similar products in an area. Another source could be organizational innovations (process technologies) that leak between firms so that all benefit from the innovations originally found in one firm. And similar benefits can arise from profit-motivated product technological innovations, which, as they are exploited by other firms, sets in trend an escalation of yet more innovation that further boosts output and productivity growth.

The result of all of this is that a virtuous circle of growth and innovation could be sparked off, so that the first possibly lucky accident leads to a continuing cycle for the originating group of companies or countries, who are propelled along a higher growth path while the rest are left behind. And it becomes very difficult to break into this cycle. It feeds off itself for those in the virtuous circle, which reinforces the inequalities associated with the 'divergence, big time' characterizing the international system.

## Measures and trends in international economic competitiveness

This section moves away from the analysis of the overall framework for international competitiveness to look more closely at the idea of national competitiveness. There are two main ways *national competitiveness* is discussed in the literature: in terms of 'ability to sell' and 'locational attractiveness'. Accepting for a moment the usefulness of the notion of 'national competitiveness', a country's ability to sell internationally will depend on its relative cost structure, productivity and exchange rate, so the policy areas are clear (Thompson 1987). The ability to sell approach is the traditional one. It focuses on the current account of the balance of payments, particularly the trade account. A premier measure of competitiveness is the relative unit labour cost (RULC), usually in manufacturing.

The locational attractiveness approach arises in the context of the internationalization and efficiency of financial markets, increased capital mobility, and the way in which intertemporal investment decisions are thought to follow a logic of utility maximization in an interdependent world. This approach stresses how balance of payments adjustments are secured via capital flows, and puts more emphasis on the decisions of private agents in terms of their investment choices and less emphasis on public policy, thus focusing on the capital account of the balance of payments. The premier measures of competitiveness in this approach are FDI and other investment flows. The policy areas here have to do with making a country attractive for investors, so they embrace a wider set of options than just the traditional ones associated with the ability to sell.

While these two approaches are often presented as though it is a matter of choice between them, they are in fact complementary and interdependent. It is useful to examine how the UK and other main economies have fared in relation to both ability to sell and ability to attract investment over the period from after the Second World War up until the early 1990s.

In the case of the RULC and 'ability to sell', the long-term trend until the late 1970s was for the UK economy to show an *improving* position. There was a dramatic loss of international competitiveness between 1979 and 1981, and then after 1984 a restoration of the longer-term trend of improving competitiveness, measured by RULC. The story for the US economy is much the same, though its loss of competitiveness lasted longer in the 1980s (to 1985) before the re-emergence of the older trend. The sources of improvements in the UK were mainly through exchange-rate adjustments (devaluations), while for the USA they were mainly through domestic labour cost adjustments. Comparing these experiences with those of Japan and Germany is instructive, since the trends in those countries were more or less exactly the opposite. Japan and Germany had been *losing* competitiveness in RULC terms over almost the entire period since the 1960s (Thompson 1987, 1998).

Thus the counter-intuitive paradox here, first noted by Kaldor in the 1970s (Kaldor 1978), was that, as the USA and the UK were improving their international competitiveness, they were losing on their trade accounts, and while Japan and Germany were losing their international competitiveness, they were improving or maintaining their trade account surpluses. In fact, this seeming paradox is one shared for a larger range of advanced economies, as shown by the figures in table 4.2. The relationship between the growth in market share of exports and the growth in relative unit labour cost (columns 1 and 2) is *positive and greater than 1* (slope 1.17) for the twelve countries examined. Thus as relative unit labour costs increase so does the market share, exactly the opposite to that predicted by conventional theory. Note also the positive relationship between the growth in market share for exports and the change in R&D as a share of GDP (columns 1 and 4). The very strong correlation and high value of the slope indicates the way market share is driven by technological innovation rather than by relative labour costs.

**Table 4.2**   The 'Kaldor paradox' re-examined, twelve industrialized countries, 1978–1994

|  | Growth in market share of exports[a] | Growth in relative unit labour cost[a] | Growth in GDP per capita at constant prices[a] | Change in R&D as a share of GDP[b] |
|---|---|---|---|---|
| USA | 0.08 | −1.17 | 1.36 | 0.24 |
| Japan | 0.95 | 0.82 | 2.94 | 1.10 |
| Germany | −1.03 | 1.62 | 1.65 | 0.23 |
| France | −0.98 | −0.18 | 1.36 | 0.54 |
| Italy | −0.16 | −1.13 | 2.00 | 0.59 |
| UK | −0.89 | 0.81 | 1.57 | −0.01 |
| Canada | −0.10 | −0.38 | 0.97 | 0.36 |
| Belgium-Luxembourg | −0.89[c] | −2.85[c] | 1.70 | 0.31 |
| Netherlands | −1.53 | −1.60 | 1.23 | 0.13 |
| Korea | 4.85 | 1.89 | 6.33[c] | 1.16 |
| Taiwan | 4.68 | 3.77 | 5.94[d] | 1.13 |
| Hong Kong | 8.36 | 2.58 | 5.35[c] | n.a. |
| Regression on growth in market share[e] | | | | |
| slope | | 1.17 (0.36) | 1.43 (0.21) | 4.48 (0.94) |
| $R^2$ | | 0.52 | 0.82 | 0.71 |

*Notes*: [a] Annual rate of growth.
[b] Difference between 1992 and 1979 levels of R&D as a share of GDP.
[c] 1978–92.
[d] 1978–91.
[e] Estimated by ordinary least squares with constant term (not reported), standard deviation in brackets, twelve observations except for R&D (eleven observations).
*Source*: Fagerberg 1996, p. 41.

This result is an important one in circumstances where governments insist on driving down their relative labour costs in the name of some expected beneficial effects to their current account: if historical experience is anything to go by there may be no such benefits. To a large extent it is this kind of result that led to a disillusionment with the RULC measure of international competitiveness and the rise in popularity of the locational advantage approach. We now examine this in the UK context.

A great deal is made of the record of the UK as a destination for FDI, demonstrating the success of liberalization, deregulation and policies for flexibility adopted in the UK over the past twenty years or so. However, this success should not be exaggerated. The UK has been a consistent net exporter of FDI in every year since the growth of FDI took off in the early 1980s, except for small surpluses in 1982 and 1990. In addition, the UK has been a *net exporter* of portfolio investment. During the 1980s it became the largest single outward investor in the world. The result was that in 2002, while the stock of inward FDI was £169 billion, the stock of outward investment was much larger, at £575 billion (*Economic Trends* 2004, tables 2 and 3). This would seem to point to the 'locational non-attractiveness' of the

UK economy in this regard. The only large industrial economy that displays a long-term locational advantage on this measure is the US one, which after 1983 became a consistent net importer of capital. And although this position temporarily changed in the early 1990s it has reappeared with force in the period since then. The other major European economies and Japan, however, have also been net exporters, mainly to the USA, the southern EU members, East Asia and Eastern Europe after the collapse of communism in 1989. This might seem to be expected and unexceptional – the rich countries with 'excess' capital exporting it to the poorer ones with high demands – *except* for the highly anomalous position shown by the USA. The USA proves the rule by undermining the commonly accepted approach.

The argument about the UK's unique attractiveness as a destination for foreign investment in Europe is also undermined by the fact that France had larger FDI inflows than the UK did between 1991 and 1995, despite all the talk about the supposed detrimental effects of the Social Chapter (Barrell and Pain 1997, p. 65, table 2). UK companies formed the largest category of investor in France over this period. The benefits of inward investment to the UK also tend to be exaggerated, given that a growing percentage is accounted for by service industry investments, which have not shown significant increases in productivity, and are mainly the results of takeover and acquisition activity.

An important (policy) issue arises here concerning the quality of official analysis in this area. It was claimed that inward investment had served to preserve 770,000 British jobs in the early 1990s (HMSO 1996, p. 139), but, given the net FDI exporting position, would we not expect there to be an overall *net loss* of jobs as well? British industry is being 'hollowed out' by this process. As far as can be judged there are no official UK calculations of this potential impact. By contrast, other advanced countries do make these kinds of calculations. MITI, for instance, estimates that Japanese multinationals operating abroad employed just under 2 million workers in 1993, while multinationals from overseas operating in Japan employed only 169,000 workers (MITI 1996a, p. 25; 1996b, p. 24).

Secondly, it is claimed that outward FDI added positive flows to the UK balance of payments in terms of interest, profits and dividend receipts: £24 billion in 1995. But the net position was much less, at only £6 billion. In addition, there is a possible loss of *export receipts* to the UK economy as a result of the net export of its investment capital. The MITI studies mentioned above follow up the basic statement of the net employment loss position with a discussion of the possible 'second round' impacts of the net export of FDI. Their argument is that Japanese overseas FDI has had an overall positive impact on the Japanese economy and on Japanese employment (MITI 1996a, pp. 38–42). This is because that investment has stimulated the purchase of Japanese capital goods. Such an 'export inducement effect' has outweighed the 'export substitution effect'. But this is not quantified in the report. It is only asserted, with the proviso that this net positive impact could soon wear off as the overseas investment 'matures'. An important implication of this for the advanced countries, therefore, is that they should establish a serious and ongoing 'social audit' of the full consequences of FDI flows into and out of their economies, so as to provide proper information on which to base public discussion and official decision-making.

Clearly, both the approaches indicated above suffer analytical and policy problems, so perhaps we should not expect too much from either of them. The RULC approach continues to emphasize international cost and price competition. A possible resolution of the 'Kaldor paradox' mentioned above, then, is to highlight 'quality' rather than 'quantity' as the key determinant of international success (which is itself linked to the technological inventiveness aspect, as indicated above in relation to table 4.2). In principle, this would seem extremely important and potentially fruitful. While it would be impossible to ignore prices and costs altogether, the emphasis is shifting to quality indicators. The disastrous consequences of ignoring quality can be judged by the series of agricultural and livestock crises that have hit the UK over the last fifteen years. The Anglo-American tradition tends to leave these important matters to self-regulation, to the concerns of the consumption end of economic activity (retail chains and consumer choice), or to universalized information dissemination and packaging. In the EU, and elsewhere, it is managed much more at the production level or in relation to *local* producer and municipal organizations (who do the monitoring themselves), and has a stronger institutional base. The advantage of establishing, monitoring and regulating quality is that it is not affected as much by 'globalization' as are other more overt policy initiatives. It need not implicate treaty commitments already entered into with international organizations governing trade and commerce, such as the WTO process discussed above.

### Standard-setting and benchmarking

One way this has taken hold internationally is via 'benchmarking' and quality standard-setting processes. This section lays out some issues associated with standard-setting in the international arena (Thompson 2005). Standard-setting and benchmarking have become key practices in the international competitive discussions, since meeting these is one of the mechanisms by which comparative competitiveness is judged and globalization secured (see chapter 1).

Clearly, the setting of global standards is not completely novel. These have been developing over hundreds of years. UK financial institutions set credit ratings in the late nineteenth and early twentieth centuries, Norway and the UK captured the setting of marine classification standards early in the twentieth century, and the Federal Aviation Administration in the USA effectively did the same for international air transport in the 1960s, so this cannot be used to support or explain globalization as a new process – though it does give enormous power to those institutions conducting this kind of activity.

Fundamentally all these standard-setting practices are part of the international trading system; they exist to facilitate international trade and investment yet they also confer real political power and advantage. As mentioned in chapter 1, if international activity is subject to a common standard, it is not important that it is being displaced from its domestic environment for the process of globalization to unfold. If it is subject to a genuine global standard, there is a surrogate 'internationalization' process under way such that all economic activity must conform to a common rule or rubric, which could tend to homogenize the results of that activity.

Many of the institutions establishing such standards, norms and rules are semi-private organizations that raise genuine issues about their transparency and accountability. Susan Strange (1998) was one of the first to draw attention to these practices and saw them as the most significant aspect of globalization and internationalization, one that does not show up in official statistics of the extent of international economic activity. But for her they were even more important than cross-border trade and investment. So, while these processes are obviously important, they are quite compatible with an international economy rooted in distinct national or supranational bases rather than ones centred on supranational market forces.

Global standard-setting in respect to the economy has at least four somewhat different though interlinked aspects.

First are private 'internal' company based standards, introduced by many MNCs, that are designed to act as performance benchmarking criteria against which different aspects of their businesses, or different plants located in different countries, can be compared.[3] Inasmuch as companies have been willing and able to introduce these criteria throughout their (international) supply chain, it has tended to result in a proliferation of standards that can be unique to a particular firm or sector (the latter because benchmarking is often carried out between firms in the same sector). But often these are broad enough to be compared and contrasted across firms because they are linked to, and reliant upon, the standards that arise from the second level. They have tended to implement generally accepted standards on health and safety, labour conditions, environmental sustainability, and the like, that are promoted by the external bodies that fall into our second category.

This second category involves the more formal and 'external' development of quality standards for economic activity by institutions that both claim and exercise a public power, but which are 'semi-private' in nature. Examples of these are the ISO 9000 process for production standards and

ISO 14000 process for environmental standards, or credit rating by private agencies such as Moody's and Standard & Poor for financial activity. It is at this level that most of the recent discussion of standard-setting has focused (e.g. Sinclair 2001). To this list of bodies could be added the SA8000 process and the International Labour Organization (ILO) which address working conditions explicitly. But the ILO is not a private body like some of the others mentioned in this paragraph. In fact it is more like one of the following organizations that make up a third distinct category.

This third category involves standards set by 'public' organizations that have arisen as the consequence of growing international regulation and governance of economic matters, exemplified by the activity of intergovernmental institutions such as the OECD, World Bank, IMF, WTO, and BIS and organizations such as the IOSCO. These lay down common rules and regulations for the conduct of international economic activity, enforcing them with informal pressures and official sanctions of various kinds.

Fourthly, there are common 'standards' that are brought to bear in the way in which comparisons are made between countries in terms of their different types or forms of macro socioeconomic organization and governance – Anglo-American capitalism, organized capitalism, Rhenish capitalism, corporate capitalism, 'developmental state' capitalism, etc. The issues that arise here are whether, or how far, these different systems might be 'converging' (or 'diverging') under current globalizing trends. This connects to the discussion about various 'national systems' – of production, of innovation, of business, of finance, of welfare, of labour market operation, etc. – and their fate in the face of the forces of globalization and the operation of those standards as promoted by the organizations of international economic management just mentioned.

This aspect of standard-setting could be illustrated by the way in which standards of 'good governance' have entered the vocabulary of international economic regulation, involving a particular set of institutional characteristics (openness, participation, transparency, accountability, effectiveness, coherence) modelled on those thought to typify a broadly Anglo-American operational practice. These criteria are increasingly used to judge the appropriateness of the institutional characteristics of all socioeconomic systems in the context of how the international organizations of economic management are to support or offer assistance to those countries seeking help to enter into, or adjust to, the international trading community (whether they be so-called emerging economies or more mature ones in temporary distress). A set of common operational institutionalized standards are brought to bear in this context to judge the suitability of the prospective recipient of help or to bring pressure to bear to carry out effective reform. And inasmuch as these standards are applied and work, they tend towards the production of a functional and operational convergence between different socioeconomic formations or country experiences (Best 2001). This is not necessarily, then, a convergence in terms of living standards (at least not in the first instance) – the usual way in which economics approaches the issue of convergence in the international economy[4] – but in terms of the broad institutional frameworks that shape the nature of economic activity.

A final remark here concerns how far global standards are *deliberately set* as opposed to *emerging 'spontaneously'*, as it were. Clearly, talk of any 'standard-setting process' rather implies a conscious and deliberate programme. On the other hand, in a process of economic integration and convergence, 'standards' might emerge without there being any obvious attempt to introduce them. Much of what takes place in discussions of international competitiveness uses standards in this second sense; as a *de facto ex post* outcome that may not have been deliberately planned for *de jure* or *ex ante*. It can arise, for instance, in the way that the pattern of economic activity evolves as a consequence of market forces which 'self-organize' into the supranational regional configurations that are discussed in chapter 6. Needless to say, of course, any investigation of the actual conduct of the emergence of standard-setting and its processes of development is quickly drawn to cross this divide – to oscillate between its *de facto* and *de jure* aspects.

But a problem with the emphasis on such standard-setting and benchmarking is that it often does little more than encourage a simple 'copying' of already existing products, techniques and processes, mirroring current best practice. Competitive advantage is gained by an innovative capacity to jump to a new performance plateau. Benchmarking generalizes existing best practice; it locks in the past rather than promoting radical innovation. By and large, British companies in particular are unused to institutionalized innovation and are often openly hostile to the levels of cooperation with labour and other firms that it requires. If companies refuse to cooperate, however, there is little that can be done. In general terms the UK has a smaller stock of 'world class companies' than the size of its economy would warrant. A programme of international benchmarking might serve to even up performance, but in the absence of an appropriate system of innovation it is unlikely to leap ahead of competitors on quality.

### The competitiveness of countries and the competitiveness of companies

The introduction of the nature of companies and their attitudes serves to raise a number of other issues associated with international competitiveness. The RULC and FDI measures discussed above pertain to economies rather than to companies, and it may be worthwhile trying to keep these two apart at a number of levels. To start with there is the difference between comparative advantage and competitive advantage: the one pertaining to the national economy, the other to the companies that make it up. In terms of conventional trade theory an economy always has a *comparative advantage* in some line of production, so there are always mutual gains from trade. This rather attractive outcome specified by the theory may, however, not be the case if we take seriously the notion of *competitive advantage*. It is not clear that an economy will always have a competitive advantage in some line of production if such an advantage is dependent on the success of its companies. Companies have to *organize* production, and this capacity cannot be derived from aggregate economic functions such as relative costs. Some countries' companies may be unsuccessful in internationally traded lines of production while other countries' companies are widely successful. This is especially so if we take seriously the literature on dynamic increasing returns modelling (Arthur 1996). Bandwagon effects, positive feedbacks, learning by doing, etc., can all lead to successful cumulative growth trajectories for companies or products, so that they completely outcompete others (and yet these may not necessarily lead to the most efficient or optimal outcomes overall; see also Kaldor 1981). On the other hand, those companies that are outperformed will suffer from a cumulative decline and eventually go out of business.

If one country has a critical mass of internationally competitively successful companies located on its territory, that country will demonstrate a *revealed absolute competitive advantage*, characterized by an increasing share of world trade and/or sustained appreciation of its currency. If a country is unlucky enough to have a set of companies located on its territory which lose out in the competitive struggle, then a cumulative downward spiral might result. Thus, conceptions of revealed *absolute* competitive advantage may be more important than comparative (*relative*) advantage ones. Here we must register a crucial distinction, however. Conceptions of absolute competitive advantage would apply to those sectors, usually manufacturing and services, where competitive advantage can be deliberately created and fostered (either by public policy or by the policies pursued by firms). This includes the developments associated with intra-industry trade in particular. Comparative advantage would still seem to apply to those sectors whose success remains dependent on natural comparative factor endowments, such as primary production (agriculture and mineral extraction). These formulations, then, add to the critique of the H–O/S–S approach to the skill factor endowment analysis associated with the discussion of the effects of North–South trade made earlier in this chapter.

Even perceptive commentators on these matters often fail fully to register these key conceptual distinctions about trade theory (e.g. Porter 1990; Kay 1994). Kay has argued, for instance, that the UK maintains a national *comparative* advantage in areas where the English language is important (publishing and audio-visual media; tertiary education) and also in areas such as chemicals and pharmaceuticals, aviation electronics and engines, insurance and some other financial services, and retailing. These have been British success stories, based on the competitiveness of British firms. Clearly, in our terminology, the key to a *revealed* competitive advantage for the UK economy is the competitive advantage of the companies in these fields. It is important, therefore, for both companies and governments to recognize and foster those factors that account for the present conditions of successful company performance, and to nurture those conditions that may constitute new competitive advantages in the future.

From the Kay perspective, however, there is little point in trying to enhance the existing domestic competitive configuration of sectors or branches where other countries and their firms already demonstrate current comparative advantage. Trying to emulate the current comparative success of elsewhere is unlikely to enhance the long-run strengths of the home economy, he argues. However, this can be successful at times, as is shown by the decision to foster the European civilian aircraft industry against the predominant strength of that of the USA. Again, Italy should have withdrawn from sectors such as clothing and footwear, where low-wage countries have a strong comparative advantage: yet these two sectors are major Italian export success stories. Thus, contrary to Kay's argument, a country should not totally write off the potential of a coordinated attempt to emulate or outperform already highly successful international competitor companies.

A further important consequence of stressing the differences between companies and countries is that we can draw a sharper distinction between what might be good for a company and what might be good for an economy. These two do not always coincide. For instance, what firms do to improve their international efficiency and competitiveness may have detrimental effects on the economy as a whole, as in the case of the way the labour market operates to displace problems of employment and training away from firms and on to the economy as a whole. The decisions of companies over FDI mentioned above is another potential example of this mismatch. Thus there may well be very efficient and internationally competitive firms operating in an economy while that economy overall is becoming less internationally competitive or declining relatively. Indeed, this could be the emerging pattern of the UK economy: small 'pockets' of economic efficiency, wealth and competitiveness, coalescing around successful firms, branches of industry or financial services, coexisting with a generalized poor performance of the aggregate economy characterized by stagnation, growing poverty, inequality and inefficiency. The future for the UK, therefore, could be a form of 'leopard spot' economy – patches of success against a background of increasing social degradation and poverty.

An important corollary of this is the question as to whether it is sensible to think of countries competing economically at all. While companies clearly compete – they can either grow and expand or go out of business –

countries cannot go bankrupt and disappear in the same way if they are not economically successful. They merely get relatively poorer. The only way a country can disappear is if it is conquered by another after a war, or if it agrees to merge with another. Thus the type of competition in which countries are involved *qua* countries is arrayed along quite a different dimension from that given by conventional economics. Clearly, there is some truth in this argument, and in an ultimate sense countries do not compete among themselves in quite the same way as companies do, or with the same consequences. But at another level countries clearly do compete in economic terms, even if just to attract FDI. But their competition is also wider than this, expressed in terms of such diverse characteristics as comparative living standards and military power.

Finally there is one further big difference between firms and nations in regard to their economic activity. Firms tend to 'export' the vast bulk of their output: well up to 99 per cent, one suspects. They sell it on the market 'outside' of their own institutional boundaries and they do not consume much of it themselves or allow their own workers to do so. Indeed, they do not sell much on the open market to their own workers either. However, this is not the case with nations. The bulk of their product (measured by GDP) is consumed 'internally', and by their own citizens, so that only a small percentage is exported. This varies between countries, of course. While the USA exported goods and services in 2007 of just over 12 per cent of its GDP, the UK exported much more, at nearly 30 per cent and Germany a somewhat larger proportion, at 47 per cent. But in 2007 the three Triad economic blocs as a whole (the USA, Japan and the EU) exported similar amounts – the USA 12 per cent, Japan 17 per cent and the then fifteen countries of the EU 11 per cent (the reason for the differences between individual EU countries and the EU as a whole is accounted for by intra-EU country trade).

A point made by Krugman (1994a) is that perhaps the emphasis given to trade and international competitiveness in popular economic and political discussion is misplaced if it involves only between 10 and 20 per cent of GDP. For the purposes of economic growth and living standards, the real issue then becomes one of changes in national productivity per se without worrying too much about the international dimension or international comparisons. Here we revisit the issues raised in the first part of this chapter. It means that considerations of international competitiveness should pertain to only a much smaller section of the economy – the internationally traded sector – and we should resist the 'expansion' of the concern about being 'internationally competitive' to all other aspects of economic life. There remains a large 'sheltered sector', particularly involving welfare expenditures and a large section of the privately traded service economy, that is not – and need not be – subject to all the vagaries and pressures associated with being 'internationally competitive'. Hence the perniciousness of using 'international competitiveness' as a justification for driving down wages and conditions in areas such as office cleaning and similar non-tradeable service activities. The world's janitors and cleaners do not 'compete'.

Clearly, this argument is all very well and has its place. But it could be accused of complacency. Engaging in international trade has important 'demonstration effects' for domestic economic activity overall and potential 'learning effects' for new exporters. Without it the general level of domestic productivity for those sectors not engaged in international trade could easily fall behind best practice and their activity levels could stagnate. The issue for policy is to strike a balance between competitive performance in the internationally traded sector and conditions in the rest of the economy. The rhetoric of 'competitiveness' should not be used to justify exploitation and 'sweating'. Equally the non-traded sectors must not set the cost floor so high that it damages exporters.

We can also take these arguments one step further by focusing on those countries with very high trade to GDP ratios. There may be dangers when too great a proportion of economic activity is devoted to the international market. In 2003, for instance, the following countries had trade to GDP ratios (measured as a percentage of imports plus exports/2 × GDP) of over 50 per cent: Singapore (180 per cent), Hong Kong (168 per cent), Malaysia (102 per cent), Thailand (67 per cent), Taiwan (57 per cent) and the Philippines (53 per cent). These (and others like them) are the vulnerable countries in the international economy. Without a large 'sheltered' domestic sector to fall back on, their whole prosperity has been built on exporting. The less vulnerable economies are those like the Triad, with 70 to 75 per cent of their GDP as purely domestic economic activity, able to act as a cushion in times of recession. And although several European countries also had 50+ per cent ratios (for instance, Belgium, Ireland, the Netherlands and Austria), as members of the EU they are also cushioned from the full vagaries of the international economy. These economies can more easily ride out any downturn in global economic activity that might be caused by trade policy or other economic changes. Most of the East Asian NICs,[5] by contrast, are in effect trade policy captives of the USA, Japan or the EU. Changes in domestic policy sentiment in the traditional Triad economies could have serious impacts on the East Asian NICs in the future (and potentially China). The East Asian NICs are clearly highly dependent on the continuation of a liberal and open international trading system, something that still rests largely in the hands of the Triad. Of course, if these NICs mature, they may well follow the characteristics of the older advanced economies and become less dependent on trade for their prosperity (as Korea has done). But these points should warn us against losing sight of the continued structural vulnerability of the East Asian NICs (but less so mainland China and India, with comparable ratios of 34 per cent and 16 per cent respectively in 2003).

## Borders and globalization

One question posed by the previous analysis is to ask whether national borders matter any more from the point of view of international competitiveness and globalization. It is well known that the strong globalization thesis postulates that borders are increasingly irrelevant for economic activity as trade interdependency and investment integration sweep the globe. Although not all supporters of this approach would go along with Kenichi Ohmae's rather extreme presentation of the case (Ohmae 1990, 1995), he does have the virtue of putting the issue starkly and saying what he thinks the nature of the new global 'borderless' economic system would look like. And this prefigures a lot of what more cautious observers would be forced to argue as the ultimate outcome of any commitment to a strong globalization position.

Ohmae argues that this new economy is an 'interlinked' one in which 'stateless' corporations are now the prime movers, centred on North America, Europe and Japan. He contends that macroeconomic and industrial policy intervention by national governments can only distort and impede the rational process of resource allocation by corporate decisions and consumer choices, which are now made on a global scale. The emergence of 'electronic highways' enables anyone, in principle, to 'plug into' the global marketplace. All corporate players need to do to prosper is to shake off their nationally orientated bureaucratic style of management, and the government intervention that goes along with it, and enter the new world of open global marketing and production networks. The vision is one of a large interlinked network of producers and consumers plugged into an efficiently operating 'level playing field' of open and competitive international and globalized economic relationships. International markets provide coordinative and governance mechanisms in and of themselves: national strategies and policy intervention are likely merely to distort them. The era of effective national economies, and state policies corresponding to them, is over. The market will, and should, decide. It is this basic position that provides another support for the emphasis on 'international competitiveness' among economists and policy-makers in the current era.

Ohmae's basic position is echoed by Manuel Castells (e.g. 2001), who is also persuaded that borders are becoming increasingly anachronistic, even irrelevant, though for Castells this is because of the ubiquity of the internet and the web in breaking the restraints previously provided by national borders. For Castells it is 'transnational networks' that are undermining the category of a national economy as businesses and citizens increasingly resort to a transnational framework for the conduct of their activities, interlinking globally in this case through the new ICTs.

The fact that the international economy looks nothing like that sketched by either Ohmae or Castells, and does not seem to be converging towards it, should not divert us from the power of the imagery that they offer. In fact, of course, this imagery is a familiar one. It is that of a market system of the ideal type (neo-classical perfect competition) or the inclusive technical and social networks of a social structural analysis approach (Wasserman and Faust 1994). Here we concentrate upon the more narrowly economic aspects of all of this.

In principle, the conception of a market is constructed by economics as unconstrained by space (and time, in many respects). There are no necessary 'borders' around the notion of a market in a spatial or territorial sense. Nor is there a natural 'duration' for market exchange, since it exists out of historical time; it is 'timeless'.

In effect what has just been said implies that there are no transaction costs associated with market exchange. Where there are no costs associated with the pursuit of the gains from trade, international trade (or any other trade) is limited only by the extent of the division of labour (usually expressed as 'the extent of the market'). However, with extensive property rights and transaction costs, 'the extent of the market' (and hence a 'boundary' around the market) can be established by calculating the (marginal) transaction costs and benefits of market exchange as opposed to hierarchical (or network) organization.[6] The 'externalities' of market exchange, measured in terms of transaction costs, can be 'internalized' via the activity being brought within the confines of the firm or other hierarchical (or network) form of organization. In this way, 'social costs' and 'private costs' are combined and reduced to the latter. In fact, an externality is created anywhere where social costs and private costs diverge, and externalities imply a limit or boundary within market exchange – they set up a transaction cost. Thus, in this way, property rights, transaction costs and externalities do in effect put potential boundaries around the market and create the conditions for limits on the extent of market exchange. But these limits are not territorial limits in a spatial sense – in the sense that the market is necessarily 'confined' by them to a particular location or national territory. The boundary is drawn in the first instance organizationally or institutionally, which need not coincide with a definite geographical territory.

Recently another approach to economic analysis has opened up a different way of conceiving boundaries around economic activity. The 'rediscovery of geography' among some economists has served to raise issues of the clustering of economic activity, core and periphery relations, regional specialization, and much more besides about spatial differentiation (Fujita et al. 2001). This in many ways formalizes what has long been a part of economic geography on the one hand (e.g. Storper and Salais 1997) and management strategy literature on the other (e.g. Porter 1990; Porter and van Opstal 2001). The new economic geography, however, uses formal modelling techniques associated with imperfect competition and endogenous growth theory to generate locational patterns of economic activity and city formations where increasing returns, transportation costs and factor movements serve to form agglomerations and clusters with explicit boundaries between them. Thus, as opposed to the previous discussion of a perfectly competitive world and no transport costs or increasing returns to impede economic transactions, boundaries here are 'constructed' as a consequence of these impediments to the natural division of labour and implicit absence of distance. In chapter 6 we take up this form of analysis and concentrate upon the combination of the effects of 'distance' (measured in relationship to various dimensions) and national borders and jurisdictions for the conduct of economic activity on a global scale. The implication of the analysis conducted there and the comments made in this section is that – despite what some economic fundamentalists might argue – national borders remain a fact of life from the point of view of 'international competitiveness' and cannot be ignored.

## Some final considerations

A great deal is made in policy circles of the need to improve the overall supply side of the older advanced economies, by promoting specific education and training programmes, improving R&D expenditures, creating the 'climate for enterprise', etc. (e.g. HMSO 1994). But we should be modest in our expectations about policies designed to promote international competitiveness organized around the concerns expressed earlier in this chapter. Historical reflection demonstrates that there is no systematic or robust evidence causally to link economic innovativeness, educational levels, R&D expenditures, training competencies, or any of the other worthy but specific supply-side initiatives that are often spoken about, with long-term international economic performance and success (Edgerton 1996). Much more important than these specific measures are the general institutionalized operation of the labour market (for instance, centralized versus decentralized bargaining), the forms of the 'social settlement' between the social partners or organized interest groups, the form of the financial system, the constitutional nature of company governance systems, and so on. The question is, how far are these institutionalized structural features of economies open to reform or policy initiatives? In chapters 5 and 6 we shall see some examples of policies that effectively deviate from the previous path of development. However, one must be cautious as to how effectively basic institutions and social patterns can be changed by deliberate public policy.

As a final footnote it should be emphasized that all these approaches concentrate exclusively on economic measures of international competitiveness. But it is worth making the point that the narrowly defined way in which the international competitiveness debate has been set up leads to a neglect of other important elements that go to make a nation 'competitive', many of which are non-economic. For instance, the idea that a country can be successful in the modern world without having a lively, innovative, pluralistic and open political and aesthetic culture is hardly credible. Yet these are precisely the issues neglected and dismissed by the headlong rush to redefine everything in terms of economic competence and managerial prerogatives. A country that refuses actively to foster a critical 'culture of ideas' could quickly become marginalized and isolated. This will eventually impact on its 'international competitiveness' in an adverse way.

# 5

# Emerging Markets and the Advanced Economies

## Introduction

In the light of China's continuing industrialization, economic development and structural change, the increasing attention paid to the liberalization and growth in the other potential Asian giant – India – as well as the ways in which the other Asian economies have bounced back from the crises of 1997–8, we are once again confronted with the widespread belief that a substantial proportion of the developing economies have achieved a sustained industrial take-off that will transform the international economy. Indeed, it is a staple of contemporary commentary on the world economy that rapid industrialization is creating a global economy with major implications for the relations between the older OECD economies and the dynamic emerging markets and potential powerhouses of China and India.

Between 2004 and 2008, the IMF estimates that the emerging market economies averaged an annual growth rate of 7.8 per cent while the high-income countries averaged 2.7 per cent (calculated on a purchasing power parity (PPP) basis).[1] That meant that world growth averaged 5.1 per cent a year, and around 4 per cent a year per capita. Calculated at market exchange rates, world growth was lower, but still impressive at 3.6 per cent. Never before has the gap between growth rates in the emerging markets and the high-income countries been so wide. And while much of this emerging market growth was in Asia, between 2002 and 2008 all regions of the developing world achieved rapid and sustained growth, even as recession loomed for 2008/9.

Brazil became the tenth largest economy in the world in 2005 measured at market exchange rates (the ninth largest on a purchasing power parity basis). And the investment bank Goldman Sachs predicts that, by 2040, the BRICs (the acronym coined by the bank to describe the emerging markets of Brazil, Russia, India and China) plus Mexico will be larger in dollar terms than the G7 economies, and China will be the world's largest economy measured at market exchange rates. Even the cautious and detailed work of Alan Winters and Shahid Yusuf (2006) sponsored by the World Bank estimates that China and India's share of the growth of world exports and services (18.1 per cent) will exceed that of the United States and Japan (16.2 per cent) over the period 2005–20 (see tables 5.1 and 5.2).

Assuming it were to be sustained, the implications of this economic integration and uneven 'catch-up' growth for global inequality and poverty, on the one hand, and for the future competitiveness of the North in the face of competition from the emerging South, on the other, are substantial and are, of course, hotly debated. We will review these prospects and evolving debates in what follows, but we will also take this opportunity to situate them in a longer and broader historical and geographic context, as a way

**Table 5.1** GDP in six large economies

| Economy | Share of world GNI (2004), PPP | Share of world GDP (2004), measured by exchange rates | Average real growth rates, 1995–2004 | Average contribution to world growth (measured by exchange rates), 1995–2004 |
|---|---|---|---|---|
| China | 12.9 | 4.7 | 9.1 | 12.8 |
| India | 6.0 | 1.7 | 6.1 | 3.2 |
| USA | 21.0 | 28.4 | 3.3 | 33.1 |
| Japan | 6.9 | 11.2 | 1.2 | 5.3 |
| Germany | 4.2 | 6.6 | 1.5 | 3.0 |
| Brazil | 2.6 | 1.5 | 2.4 | 1.5 |
| World | 100.0 | 100.0 | 3.0 | 100.0 |

*Source*: Winters and Yusuf 2006, table 1.1; World Bank 2006.

**Table 5.2** Trade in goods and services for six large economies

| Economy | Exports of goods and services | | | | Imports of goods and services | | | |
|---|---|---|---|---|---|---|---|---|
| | Share, 2004 | Share of growth, 1995–2004 | Projected growth rate, 2005–20 | Share of growth, 2005–20 | Share, 2003 | Share of growth, 1995–2003 | Projected growth rate, 2005–20 | Share of growth, 2005–20 |
| China | 5.7 | 8.9 | 7.8 | 15.4 | 4.8 | 7.8 | 6.6 | 11.0 |
| India | 1.2 | 1.8 | 7.5 | 2.7 | 1.1 | 1.8 | 6.3 | 2.2 |
| USA | 11.2 | 10.7 | 3.4 | 9.9 | 16.5 | 24.1 | 3.5 | 15.4 |
| Japan | 5.4 | −3.7 | 4.2 | 6.3 | 4.7 | −0.8 | 3.5 | 4.4 |
| Germany | 9.1 | 7.7 | 1.8 | 3.8 | 8.2 | 3.6 | 2.0 | 3.9 |
| Brazil | 1.0 | 0.5 | 1.7 | 0.4 | 0.7 | 0.3 | 4.3 | 0.8 |

*Source*: Winters and Yusuf 2006, table 1.3.

of gaining some purchase on the deeper aspects of international economic relations and of politics and geopolitics that lie behind the fast-moving headlines. Without seeking to minimize the continuing challenges in the path of development in what the economic historian Angus Maddison (2001) has referred to as 'resurgent Asia' as well as in the other regions of the developing world, we will argue that significant shifts in the location of industrial output and the balance of economic power in the international economy can indeed be detected and that, if sustained, these are likely to have a marked impact on the nature of the South itself as well as on the distribution of global inequality and poverty and on the nature of international economic competition. But we begin this chapter by placing contemporary trends in the context of the long run of innovation and catch-up in the international economy.

## Innovation and catch-up in the history of industrial capitalism

Viewed historically, the development of capitalist industrialization has been sequenced into a series of phases driven, firstly, by successive 'waves' of technological innovation in the leading regions that have raised labour productivity sufficiently to offset diminishing returns to capital accumulation in routine investment, and, secondly, by catch-up development in the follower regions based on more or less politically directed structural change and oriented around a redirection of social labour from lower to higher levels of productivity. These phases have been characterized by industrial 'breakthroughs' in leading centres, based on the emergence of new forms of technology and organization, management and production, followed by the generalization of these breakthroughs in the leading poles, as well as the transmission of the results of earlier development, alongside elements of the new forms, to follower regions (Freeman and Louçã 2001; Von Tunzelmann 1995). The two processes at work – that is, innovation and catch-up – have been intimately connected to one another because, for every new 'wave' of innovation, there were corresponding sets of activities, organizations and institutions that ceased to function as carriers for the most dynamic and advanced moments of capitalist development, and which were, thereby, devalued and rendered either obsolete or susceptible to transfer to (and modification by) regions where levels of labour productivity and labour costs were lower.

To be sure, all catch-up since that by which the United States and Germany overtook Britain in the late nineteenth century has been *relative*, as the leading regions of the world economy did not stay still while others converged on their levels of productivity and per capita living standards. Indeed, the pursuit of innovation has become part of the routine, competitive working of firms in the more advanced capitalist economies (Baumol 2002). Competition to innovate, rather than competition over

price, is the defining feature of advanced capitalist development, characterized by large firms operating in oligopolistic market structures with well-
developed financial systems and adequate means of protecting intellectual
property rights. In fact, throughout the period of consolidated industrial
capitalist development in the advanced centres, from the 1870s through to
the slowdown of the 1970s and beyond, the long-run rate of growth
of labour productivity in the most advanced regions of the world
economy averaged around 2 per cent per annum (typically in the range 1.5
to 2.5 per cent).

Having forged ahead of its European rivals in the first half of the twentieth century, 'American technology which was natural resource intensive,
physical capital-using and scale dependent was', says Nicholas Crafts, 'frequently not the optimal choice of technique in European conditions' (2000,
p. 24). It was only in the increasingly open, liberal international economy
of the post-war period that 'greater integration of world markets, reductions in the cost advantages of domestic natural resource endowments
combined with increased importance of intangible capital (R&D and education) subsequently reduced the obstacles to catch-up first within the
OECD and later elsewhere in East Asia' (ibid.). In 1950, the United States
accounted for three-fifths of the total output of the largest seven capitalist
economies, and 'its manufacturing industry was about twice as productive,
per person employed, as that of the UK, three times as productive as
German manufacturing and nine times as productive as Japanese manufacturing' (Glyn 2006, p. 8). Thereafter, between 1951 and 1971, US industrial
production increased 122 per cent (an annual rate of 4.0 per cent) and its
GDP rose 90.3 per cent (3.2 per cent per annum), whereas industrial production in Japan increased 1,092 per cent (12.4 per cent per annum)
and overall GDP rose by 453 per cent (an annual rate of 8.5 per cent).
The annual increase in labour productivity in manufacturing was 10.3
per cent in Japan between 1955 and 1970 and 2.3 per cent in the USA.
Western Europe's convergence started from a higher base and was less
dramatic but nonetheless substantial: for example, manufacturing labour
productivity in West Germany rose 6.7 per cent per annum between
1955 and 1970.

Of course, as relative catch-up began to close the absolute gap with the
USA, so further advances became more difficult. For example, 'growth in
Golden Age Japan was predicated on ... rapid mobilization of resources
based on low cost rather than efficient use of capital and productivity
growth concentrated on manufacturing while sheltered/non-tradable
sectors of the economy sustained employment based on low productivity.
By the 1990s, these features ... [were] obstacles to further catch-up'
(Crafts 2000, p. 37). Similarly, Glyn reports that although, by the mid-1990s,
European and Japanese manufacturing productivity had reached around
80 to 90 per cent of US levels, thereafter it fell back to around 65 to
75 per cent of the US level measured per worker (Glyn 2006, p. 79).

While the average person in the Euro area in the early part of the new century was about 30 per cent poorer than in the USA, average GDP *per hour worked* was only 5 per cent lower (cf. about 30 per cent lower thirty years before): Europeans simply translated more of their increased productivity into leisure rather than income, principally by full-time workers working shorter hours.

If we focus on the generation of productivity increases through innovation, then the USA remains at the centre of any story about the growth prospects for industrial capitalism: after the water-powered mechanization of industry and the steam-powered mechanization of industry and transport in Britain during the late eighteenth and early nineteenth centuries, virtually all the significant technological innovations of industrial capitalism, through to the current digital, IT, networked phase, have been very largely 'made in America'. Whether it is IT and the knowledge economy, or the financialization of economic activity based on the deregulation and internationalization of dollar-based finance, the USA is still firmly established at the leading edge of worldwide economic development. Of total R&D expenditure in the OECD bloc in the late 1990s, 85 per cent was in seven countries, and the US share was 43 per cent of the total – as much as the rest of the G7 countries combined. Of the top 100 firms in the new economy, as ranked by *Business Week*, seventy-five were in the USA and only six in Europe. In this respect, it remains the case that the United States has an 'innovation complex – those thousands of entrepreneurs, venture capitalists and engineers – unmatched anywhere in the world'; its universities are 'magnets for the world's talent and sources of much of its intellectual innovation' (Odom and Dujarric 2004, pp. 128, 161).

As to the dynamics of catch-up in the developing world, in those parts of the world economy operating at substantially lower levels of social and technological development, regions that were previously effectively outside the reach of world markets pursue catch-up growth in relation to those at the (intermittently advancing) leading edge of technological development. Much has been made in what is known as endogenous growth theory of the ways in which innovation is an internal aspect of capital accumulation and growth in the economy as a whole. And this is indeed an important part of the reason for the fortunes of the advanced capitalist countries. But if we consider the long-run history of industrial capitalist development, then it is not just technology but also labour supplies that have been 'endogenous' to historical capitalism as its reach into other societies, pre- and proto-capitalist and now state socialist, has expanded. When this has happened, not only have resources been reallocated from lower to higher levels of productivity but also, and more importantly, capital accumulation has enabled follower economies to adopt more advanced technologies and thereby achieve much higher rates of growth than had been possible for the technological originators.

Yet the ability to profit from this 'advantage of backwardness' has derived from an ability to combine a pre-existing pattern of development with positive interaction with world markets; and the principal vehicle by which this has been achieved – in all cases where it has been accomplished with any success – has been via the coordinated agency of the state. In an international economy characterized by innovation concentrated in the advanced regions and the potentials and pitfalls of catch-up, the principal agency for reaping the advantages of backwardness has been the state, because the fulcrum of all late industrialization is the supply of (relatively) cheap, politically quiescent labour and the ability to redeploy this to raise productivity and create international competitiveness (Amsden 1990). Understood in these terms, the current pattern of North–South relations might be interpreted as involving a generalization of catch-up from Japan, through the newly industrializing economies and South-East Asia, to China and perhaps India. The predictions of Goldman Sachs noted above assume that Brazil, Russia and Mexico at least will also be able to take advantage of this process.

At the same time, there does appear to have been a system-wide structural shift in the economic role of the state since the end of the long boom, the collapse of protectionist forms of import-substituting industrialization in the South and the dissolution of the communist model in the East, in so far as many states are seeking to maximize the gains from regional economic integration and competition on world markets while attempting to hold on to the ability to maintain internal macroeconomic balances. It is in the light of these kinds of considerations that the chief economic commentator on the *Financial Times*, Martin Wolf, in his book *Why Globalization Works*, makes the case for a global market economy in relation to developing countries as follows:

> success has not required adoption of the full range of so-called 'neo-liberal' policies – privatization, free trade and capital-account liberalization. But, in insisting on this point, critics are wilfully mistaking individual policy trees for the market-oriented forest. What the successful countries all share is a move towards the market economy, one in which private property rights, free enterprise and competition increasingly took the place of state ownership, planning and protection. They chose, however haltingly, the path of economic liberalization and international integration. This is the heart of the matter. All else is commentary. (Wolf 2004, pp. 143–4)

We do not believe that 'all else is commentary', but the shift that Wolf detects is real enough. However, Wolf is perhaps too ready to link 'economic liberalization' and 'international integration'. The two are clearly connected but their interrelations have been highly variable. And what is insufficiently recognized in the liberal case for globalization is that, in all cases where the relationship between the two has been negotiated successfully, the state has played a major role in setting the terms of their engagement as well as in managing the social and economic transformations of the societies concerned. This means that, while the technological means of catch-up may be increasingly available to all or most regions, especially given the increasing openness of world trade, what is in much shorter supply, the genuinely 'scarce' resource of late development, is the political capacity to manage the connections and trade-offs between domestic economic liberalization, on the one side, and international integration, on the other. There is, therefore, an ever-present potential for social crisis, economic regression and even political subordination in those regions where states cannot rule and order their societies in ways that are able to latch on to the privileges of backwardness or where the social and political conflicts attendant on labour mobilization from agriculture to industry, and from rural to urban locales, overrun the capacities of existing political regimes.

More specifically, many countries, accounting for what Paul Collier (2007) has termed the 'bottom billion' of the world's population, are not part of this process at all. If one averages growth rates across countries or regions on the basis of the size of the economy – as the IMF's *World Economic Outlook* does, for example – you describe what is going on 'from the perspective of the typical unit of income, not from the perspective of the typical person'. To get at the latter, Collier points out, one should average by population weights, and if we do this we find that 'developing countries that are not part of the bottom billion – the middle four billion – have experienced rapid and accelerating growth in per capita income' (2007, p. 8). By contrast, the bottom billion have seen effectively no per capita growth for a generation, and but for development aid growth rates would have fared even worse (see table 5.3).

**Table 5.3** Growth rates (percentage per capita) in the emerging South and the bottom billion

|  | Emerging South | Bottom billion |
|---|---|---|
| 1970s | 2.5 | 0.5 |
| 1980s | 4.0 | −0.4 |
| 1990s | 4.0 | −0.5 |
| Early 21st century | 4.5 | 1.7* |

*Note*: *Collier attributes this as 'likely due to the short-term effects of resource discoveries and high world prices for the natural resources that the bottom billion export' (2007, p. 10).
*Source*: Adapted from Collier 2007, pp. 8–10.

## Resurgent Asia?

Whatever the original reasons for the great divergence between the North and South in the world economy (Pomeranz 2000), the big picture for most of the nineteenth and twentieth centuries was that accurately described by Lant Pritchett as 'divergence, big time' (1997) (see chapter 2 above). For example, between 1820 and 2001, the ratio of per capita income in Western Europe to that in Asia (excluding Japan) roughly tripled. At the same time, however, the ratio of the Asian (excluding Japanese) to the European population roughly doubled. As Robert Lucas first pointed out, these economic and demographic facts are probably connected in that, despite the tendency of international trade to equalize output growth (as a result of terms of trade effects in which faster growing economies have a tendency for the terms of trade to fall), increased economic integration between North and South probably enhanced the specialization of industrial economies in high-technology, high-skill products, increased the demand for educated labour, expedited the demographic transition and stimulated innovation. In the relatively non-industrial economies, by contrast, international trade may have served to encourage specialization in low-technology, low-skill products, reduced the demand for educated labour, and delayed the demographic transition (see Lucas 2002; Galor and Mountford 2003; Galor 2005).

In the industrial core, then, growth was translated into sustained per capita increases in living standards, while a large proportion of growth in the relatively non-industrial periphery was translated into an increase in the size of the population. Once established, this process and pattern of uneven development proved to be relatively stable because increasing returns to the agglomeration of manufacturing in the North got locked in, as low wages in the South were not sufficient to attract manufacturing because of the lack of appropriate infrastructures, weak institutions and insufficient forward and backward linkages among industries. Until the mid-twentieth century, these forces of divergence were without doubt the dominant tendencies operating between North and South in the world economy (see table 5.4). However, since the 1960s and 1970s this pattern

**Table 5.4**   Distribution of world GDP by region, 1820–2001 (per cent)

|  | 1820 | 1870 | 1913 | 1950 | 2001 |
|---|---|---|---|---|---|
| **Western Europe** | 23.0 | 33.0 | 33.0 | 26.2 | 20.3 |
| **Western offshoots** | 1.9 | 10.0 | 21.3 | 30.7 | 24.6 |
| **Eastern Europe and former USSR** | 9.0 | 12.0 | 13.4 | 13.0 | 5.6 |
| **Latin America** | 2.2 | 2.5 | 4.4 | 7.8 | 8.3 |
| **Asia** | 59.4 | 38.4 | 24.9 | 18.5 | 37.9 |
| **Africa** | 4.5 | 4.1 | 3.0 | 3.8 | 3.3 |

*Source*: Calculated from Maddison 2003, table 7-1.

has begun to shift, as many countries have completed the demographic transition and as freer international trade, investment and diffusion of technology and social capabilities have allowed for significant late industrialization across the South, based on increasingly educated and skilled labour, delivering rapid advances in per capita living standards.

The downturn in the world economy since the 1970s and the ramifications of the debt crises of many developing countries in the 1980s and 1990s meant that many countries were excluded from this process. But it is likely that, for substantial parts of Asia at least, the Japanese experience was but the first in a series of interconnected developments across the region, in which successful industrialization in one country raised real wages and thus prepared the way for the spread of industry to other economies. Japan's take-off into sustained per capita growth and conditional convergence on US levels of productivity began in the mid-1950s; the newly industrializing economies (NIEs) of Hong Kong, South Korea, Singapore and Taiwan embarked on a similar trajectory in the late 1960s; the ASEAN-4 of Indonesia, Malaysia, Thailand and (more problematically) the Philippines began to follow suit in the early 1970s; China started on its new path in 1979 (see below); and India joined in during the early 1980s.

Interestingly, according to the research of the International Monetary Fund, 'later developers, including China, appear to have started their takeoff at lower income levels than Japan and the NIEs' (IMF 2006, chap. 3, p. 2). On the one hand, this may reflect the growing openness of the international economy to flows of trade and investment. On the other hand, it may be connected to the well-documented fact that, because of technological progress, even relatively income poor countries can now afford substantial levels of social development. Whatever the reasons, as table 5.5 makes clear, Asia and especially China has been the great exception to the

**Table 5.5**   Growth (annual average compound growth rates) of per capita GDP

|                     | 1950–73 | 1973–2001 |
|---------------------|---------|-----------|
| **USA**             | 2.45    | 1.86      |
| **Western Europe**  | 4.05    | 1.88      |
| **Eastern Europe**  | 3.81    | 0.68      |
| **Former USSR**     | 3.35    | −0.96     |
| **Latin America**   | 2.58    | 0.91      |
| **Japan**           | 8.06    | 2.14      |
| **Asia (excl. Japan)** | 2.91 | 3.55      |
| **China**           | 2.86    | 5.32      |
| **India**           | 1.40    | 3.01      |
| **Africa**          | 2.00    | 0.19      |
| **World**           | 2.92    | 1.41      |

*Source*: Adapted from Maddison 2003, table 8b.

worldwide slowdown in growth since the 1970s. Asia 'enjoyed both faster physical capital accumulation and faster total factor productivity (TFP) growth than other developing economies; in contrast, Asia's catch-up with advanced economies largely reflected capital accumulation' (ibid., chap. 3, p. 4). While some of the latter can be accounted for by sectoral shifts in output from lower- to higher-productivity activities, the greater part of Asia's catch-up on US levels has been the result of stronger productivity growth in both industry and services. In addition, between 1965 and 1990, East Asia's working age population grew nearly four times faster than its dependent population, and this may account for as much as one-third of its growth during this period.

The compound result of these successive waves of Asian industrialization is that the region now accounts for over 35 per cent of world output and over one-quarter of world exports and, since recovering from the 1997–8 crises, has contributed close to 50 per cent of world growth. More-over, the Asian pole of the international economy is becoming increasingly integrated on a regional basis (levels of interregional trade are comparable to those in the NAFTA, if somewhat lower than those in Europe) and there has been a rapid integration of production processes into regionally orga-nized supply chains. ASEAN signed a framework agreement on compre-hensive economic cooperation in 2002 aimed at a free trade area covering goods, services and investment by 2010. The Triad of the world economy is no longer the USA, Western Europe and Japan but NAFTA, the EU and an emerging Asia that now includes China and potentially India as well.

How long can this process continue? Many factors will impinge on this, but the basic economic mechanism is that, until it reaches levels of labour productivity associated with the (constantly advancing) technological frontier, catch-up growth is essentially demand driven. This means that, at the level of the international economy as a whole, where one country's exports are another's imports, it is capital accumulation (investment) that is the most dynamic element of aggregate demand, output and employment (Glyn 2005). As long as there are labour supplies to be mobilized in pursuit of catch-up growth, savings and investment can drive the process forward. Clearly, the entry of China and India into international markets represents a huge new incorporation of low-cost labour into the development of capi-talism as a whole, allowing investment-driven aggregate demand to play a central role in the shaping of economic activity. This opens up the *potential* for a major conjunctural shift in the balance of capital accumulation worldwide.

To the extent that much of the rural labour in China and other countries is underemployed, that is, to the extent that labour can migrate to the higher-productivity industrial sector without significantly reducing agricul-tural output, the world economy faces a source of low-cost labour supply for several decades to come. China has about half (47 per cent in 2006) of its labour force in agriculture, operating at a productivity level barely one-eighth of that in industry and one-quarter of that in services. It has a unique combination of a huge population, over 60 per cent of which still lives in the countryside (a much higher share than in Japan at a similar stage of development), and an economy that is very open to trade and investment: China's average tariffs have fallen from 41 per cent in 1992 to 6 per cent after it joined the WTO in 2001, the sum of its exports and imports as a share of GDP is around 75 per cent (cf. a figure of less than 30 per cent for the USA and a peak of 32 per cent for Japan), joint ventures with foreign firms produce over one-quarter of industrial output, and the stock of total investment owned by foreigners is 36 per cent of GDP (cf. 2 per cent in Japan). 'In 2000', Martin Wolf reports, 'inward direct investment financed 11 per cent of [China's] gross fixed capital formation, while foreign affiliates generated 31 per cent of China's manufacturing sales and, more astonishingly, 50 per cent of its exports' (Wolf 2004, p. 144). Not for nothing did *The Economist* argue that 'China's catch-up in income and its integration into the world economy could be the single biggest driver of growth over the coming decades' (2004, p. 4). Recent research at the World Bank concurs: 'even though China is not the dominant force in the world economy, the shock she is administering to it is unprecedented' (Winters and Yusuf 2006, p. 7).

In fact, China's entry into the international capitalist economy, alongside that of India and the former Soviet Union, has effectively doubled the size of the world's labour force. And while China's productive investment is similar to that of other earlier Asian growth experiences, Andrew Glyn points out that:

> it is playing out on a massive canvas and with vastly larger supplies of surplus labour than were available to its Asian predecessors in the catch-up process.... Total employment in China is estimated at around 750 million, or about one and a half times that of the whole of the OECD.... Dwarfing in significance even the rise in density, international entanglement and fragility of financial markets is the growth of China, India and other developing countries.... Since the mid 1990s the majority of world GDP has been produced outside the old OECD countries and their share is declining. The centre of capital accumulation, the driving force of the system, is shifting away from the old core countries. (Glyn 2005, pp. 15, 36)

Similarly, India's reform programme, which assumed a new urgency after the financial crisis of 1991 and in the wake of the collapse of diplomatic, strategic and trade support from the Soviet Union, is being driven forward both by pressing domestic considerations of social development and by the need to manage the strategic challenge of a rising China. India (per capita GDP ~$3,000 PPP) currently lags China's development record (per capita GDP ~$5,000 PPP) by some considerable margin: its GDP is about half the size and its exports one-sixth of China's; foreign direct investment is an order of magnitude lower and the economy is more closed; adult illiteracy is much higher; and its growth rate has been much lower. That said, since the financial crisis in 1991, India has undergone a significant liberalization of its foreign trade and investment regime. In the longer term, its opportunities for catch-up in income and its integration into the world economy are on a similar scale to those of China: a World Bank study of the potential for China and India to reshape the global industrial geography notes that India 'has the labour resources, a growing base of human capital, the domestic market potential, and the nascent industrial strength to become an industrial powerhouse comparable to China today' (Yusuf et al. 2006, p. 34).

## China: results and prospects

From 1979 onwards, China has been the fastest growing economy in the world: in the quarter century or so since the launching of the four 'modernizations' China has had 'the fastest rate of total GDP growth (9.4 per cent), of per capita GDP growth (8.1 per cent) and of per worker growth (7.7 per cent)' (Hausmann et al. 2006, p. 1). Its transition has been one of a 'take-off' into sustained and high rates of per capita growth combined with the continued dominance of the Chinese Communist Party (CCP) over the state and the broad direction of social development. Most especially, China's entry into world markets has been characterized by a fruitful embrace of foreign investment and technology alongside productive flows of domestic resources from lower to higher levels of productivity – both between agriculture and industry and between lower and higher levels of skill and technology within the industrial sector – and from plan- to market-oriented output.

Viewed in the Soviet mirror, several features serve to define the Chinese experience to date. In the first place, while the modern state is the successor to the Chinese Empire, and notwithstanding the unresolved final status of Taiwan and various 'internal' problems with national and ethnic minorities, China does not confront a legacy of modern imperial rule and control over geopolitical and political satellites of the kind that contributed to the disintegration of the Soviet Union in the 1980s. While the fragmentation of China's territory is not inconceivable, it is not on the current historical agenda and nor is it clear what the West would gain by such an outcome. Secondly, not only did China begin its reforms before the Soviet Union; it also began them from a very different starting point, developmentally speaking (Sachs and Woo 1994). When China embarked on reform, 71 per cent of employment was in agriculture and 19 per cent in industry (including construction and transport); in Russia (in 1985) the comparable figures were 14 per cent and 52 per cent, respectively. The subsidies to the state industrial sector in China were, therefore, a relatively small burden for the economy; in the context of world market prices, they were, by contrast, the central incubus of the Soviet system. In addition, whereas rural and urban living standards were broadly comparable in Russia, in China urban living standards were some two and a half times higher than rural levels, so there was a strong incentive for workers to move out of agriculture into (higher-productivity) industry.

This combination of relative political stability and difference of developmental starting point – an expression of the historical unevenness of industrialization in the state socialist world – meant that China could afford to undertake reform, first in agriculture and then in 'private' industry (joint ventures with foreign investment and township and village enterprises), while maintaining planning and output in the planned, state-owned sector. China's reforms began in the rural, agricultural sector based on decollectivization (villages retained legal ownership but contracted land out) and a two-tier output and pricing framework (1979–82); they continued with the opening to foreign trade and investment, gradually introduced in the 1980s, with currency markets emerging in the late 1980s; and the reform of urban industry began in 1984 (again using a two-tier framework). In China's case, the relative failure of market-based reform in the state-owned enterprise sector was cushioned by the scope for the growth of a capitalist sector outside the plan, so that the economy as a whole was set on a path described by Barry Naughton (1995) as 'growing out of the plan'. Thus far, China's experience has been a virtuous circle of reform, with continued absolute growth even in the state-owned sector.

And while the current Chinese experience represents an exit from a state socialist model of economic development, China's ability to combine this transition with a state-orchestrated form of catch-up capitalist industrialization is quite different from the Soviet/Russian case. This latter aspect of China's development, in fact, has much in common with the other examples of catch-up growth that have been in evidence in (capitalist) Asia from the 1950s onwards. This has meant that China has been able to become a part, perhaps now the dominant part, of a general shift in the historical geography of industrial capitalism to emerging Asia. China is also distinctive in several other respects. We noted above the degree of trade and investment openness of the economy and, while its early reform-based growth, centred on the agricultural sector, was an internal affair, 'from the mid-1980s on ... China's growth was fuelled and sustained by the opportunities that the world market offered' (Rodrik 2006, p. 1). One aspect of this is that 'China has somehow managed to latch on to advanced, high-productivity products that one would not normally expect a poor, labour abundant country like China to produce, let alone export. ... What stands out is that China sells products that are associated with a productivity level that is much higher than a country at China's level of income' (ibid., pp. 4, 23). Connected to this is the fact that, unlike the case in much of the rest of Asia, China's growth has been based not only on rapid capital accumulation but also on impressive expansion of TFP. Bosworth and Collins (2006) estimate that China's annual growth rate of TFP in the period 1993–2004 was 4 per cent (cf. 2.3 per cent for India) and its industrial TFP has grown at 6.2 per cent (cf. 1.1 per cent for India).

In this respect, while much has been made of India's service sector and IT industries and TFP in services has grown at 3.9 per cent a year since 1993, a detailed study of its prospects concluded that: 'With the exception of the business services processing and software industries, it is far from obvious that India is positioned to make a mark in the global market with its services industry at least during the next ten years' (Yusuf et al. 2006, p. 38). The clear implication is that, in order for India to realize its potential and to follow in China's wake, it will have to build a development strategy around industry. China has shown that a large country open to trade and investment, with a determined and resourceful state, can build substantial industrial capacity across a wide range of sectors in a relatively short space of time. Whether India is able to follow in this path remains to be seen. That said, India's per capita growth rate has risen from 1.5 per cent in the period 1950–80 to 3.7 per cent in the 1980s, 4.1 per cent in the 1990s and 5.3 per cent in the new century.

Perhaps the key point to grasp in all of this is that, far more important than either the imports of resources, capital and technology from international markets or the dramatic successes in exporting and amassing financial surpluses, has been the fact that what the economies of 'resurgent Asia' – China most of all – have really imported has been a 'market structure' in the sense of accepting the 'world market's requirements regarding prices and quality' as the principal mechanism of validating growth-oriented policies: it is, as Daniel Cohen rightly observes, the international economy that plays the 'fundamental role ... in the validation of the chosen strategies' (Cohen 1998, p. 26). It might be thought that the scale of Chinese development and the potential role of its vast domestic market changes this assessment. But this would be a mistake. China's economy is characterized by a fast-integrating set of nationally organized markets, with a common set of central institutions, but it is also a set of provinces whose trade with one another operates, in key respects, through the 'imported' structures of international markets. Indeed, as Alwyn Young (2000) has suggested, for some purposes it is more helpful to think of China as twenty-five economies of 50 million people all trading with one another and international markets. As we saw above, China's economy is extraordinarily open to the international economy by almost any measure.

In fact, a major question mark over the future of China's development concerns its very dependence upon access to external markets. At firm level, there is some evidence that rising industrial wage costs, shortages of managerial and technical staff, the relative lack of protection for intellectual property rights, and trade risks posed by protectionist pressures in the EU and the USA are leading many foreign firms to adopt a China +1 or 2 strategy, that is, to establish a production base in China but also another one, or others, elsewhere. And, at a macroeconomic level, China's current account surplus (around 8 per cent of GDP in 2006) and its foreign exchange reserves (around $1.3 trillion in 2007) and its unwillingness significantly to revalue its currency vis-à-vis the dollar have been a constant source of friction. These constraints are well recognized by the Chinese leadership who, in December 2004, announced an intention 'to fundamentally alter the country's growth strategy' from one based on 'investment and export-led development ... to a growth path that relied more on expanding domestic consumption' (Lardy 2006, p. 1). This stance was reiterated by Hu Jintao during his visit to Washington in April 2006 and was the subject of US–Chinese discussions when the US treasury secretary, Hank Paulson, later called for a review of bilateral relations in which each side should take a 'generational' view.

In 2005, the national savings rate, which is equal to investment as a share of GDP (42.6 per cent) plus the current account as a share of GDP (7 per cent), reached an astonishing 50 per cent of GDP and household consumption a mere 38 per cent (cf. 70 per cent in the USA, 60 per cent in the UK and 61 per cent in India). And the net exports of goods and services accounted for one-quarter of the growth in the economy in 2005 and one-fifth in 2006. This investment and export-driven growth has already produced excess capacity (for example, *excess* capacity in China's steel industry exceeds the *total* output of the next largest producer, Japan); employment growth has slowed as a result of capital-intensive production; energy demand is increasing rapidly, with severe environmental impacts (China is the second largest emitter of greenhouse gases after the USA and home to sixteen of the twenty cities with the worst air pollution in the world); falling profits as a result of excess capacity are in danger of increasing the share of non-performing loans on the balance sheets of state-owned and city commercial banks; and protectionist pressures focused on the value of the renminbi are strong in the USA. Increased consumption expenditure, by both public and private sectors, as well as currency appreciation would address many of these problems, but by the end of 2007 there had been little sign of a significant change of policy – the current account surplus was larger in 2006 than in 2005 and household consumption was marginally lower.

A second major question for China's prospects concerns its political development. There is, as yet, no sign that catch-up economic development is also bringing about convergence on US patterns of social and political development. Economic convergence does not necessarily imply social and political homogeneity: the forms of property relations through which enterprises are controlled, as well as the wider patterns of social and political development associated with these, often bear scant resemblance to the Anglo-American forms of corporate and market organization, let alone representative political systems. The fact that Asian capitalism uses world markets as the test or reference point for the success of its strategies does not indicate that its particular patterns of development, forged by means of a combination of prior historical experience and catch-up in the context of unevenness, will converge on those of the Anglo-American world.

On the contrary, thus far China's transition has been essentially social and economic, not political. It has been led throughout by the CCP and its military apparatus, the People's Liberation Army, both of which are determined to hold on to monopoly forms of control over the means of state power and to negotiate the terms of their engagements with international markets and other states on a centralized basis. Unlike the Soviet/Russian experience, in which political decentralization and party-free elections for regional government eroded central control, in China the CCP has retained the ability to reward and punish local and regional officials (Blanchard and Shleifer 2001). So whereas the collapse of the party-state in Russia produced a hypertrophy of Soviet organization of the economy (barter relations, workers' veto power over restructuring of production), where monetization and price reform with soft budget constraints led to inflation and asset diversion, resulting in a period of mafia-like contract enforcement followed by the authoritarian stabilization and recentralization imposed under President Putin, in China the party-state has remained firmly in control. The effect has been to maintain the hard budget constraints on the economy of relatively stable prices even as aspects of property relations migrate from the public to the private sector (Burawoy 1996). A rough characterization of China's transition can be seen in tables 5.6 and 5.7.

In terms of table 5.6, we can see that Russia (at least before stabilization and recentralization) and China have undertaken radically different approaches to the reform of their economic systems. And in terms of table 5.7, it is apparent that, while the CCP continues to hold a virtually complete monopoly of political power, in all other respects the Chinese system is a hybrid.

Whether China can manage the social and political stresses of economic modernization with as much facility as it has its economic development to

**Table 5.6**  Trajectories of transition

| Means of economic coordination in transition from state socialism to market capitalism | | Budget constraints | |
|---|---|---|---|
| | | Hard | Soft |
| **Property relations** | **Predominantly private** | Market capitalism | Russia before Putin |
| | **Mixed and hybrid** | China, later stages of reform | |
| | **Predominantly public** | China, early stages of reform | State socialism |

**Table 5.7**  State socialist, market capitalist and Chinese systems compared

|  | State and politics | Property relations | Means of economic coordination |
|---|---|---|---|
| **State socialism** | Monopoly of power held by the Communist Party | Dominant position of the state and quasi-state ownership | Dominance of bureaucratic planning with soft budget constraints |
| **Market capitalism** | Political power friendly to private property and the market | Dominance of private property | Dominance of market coordination with hard budget constraints |
| **China** | CCP holds monopoly of political power but the party is friendly to private property and the market | Mixed and hybrid, but growing dominance of private sector | Mixed and hybrid, but dominance of market coordination and hard budget constraints |

date remains to be seen. Russia in 1917 and Iran in 1979 are both examples of social and political upheavals – social revolutions – that were caused, in part, by the inability of authoritarian states to cope with the demands of rapidly and unevenly modernizing societies. The domestic legitimacy of the Chinese government now rests squarely on national unity and economic performance – communist ideology and mobilization no longer play a significant role. And uneven development is also as much a feature of what has been going on *within* China during its modernization as it is a feature of the fortunes of resurgent Asia.

Martin Ravallion and Shaohua Chen (2004) calculate that, between 1981 and 2001, the headcount measure of poverty fell by 45 per cent (from 53 to 8 per cent), with 33 per cent due to a decline in rural poverty, 2 per cent due to a decline in urban poverty and 10 per cent due to rural-to-urban migration. However, some two-thirds of that decline occurred in the first half of the reform period, and further reductions will require determined policies as well as continued economic growth. And while Ravi Kanbur and Xiaobo Zhang (2001) found that rural–urban inequality had not changed overly much between 1983 and 1995, interprovincial inequality increased substantially: the metropolitan provinces (Beijing, Shanghai and Tianjin), with a population of 4 billion, all had a per capita GDP in excess of 20,000 RMB in 2002; none of those in the centre and west (population 73 billion) reached 10,000 RMB, and those on the coast (40 billion) and in the north-east (11 billion) lay between these extremes (Bils 2005). At the widest, per capita income in the richest areas was an order of magnitude higher than that in the poorest provinces.

### Global inequality and poverty

The shifting historical geography of industrial capitalism defined by innovation in the high-income countries and the catch-up growth of emerging Asia is being played out in the context of another set of developments that serve to define a new distinguishing feature of the South: namely, its dissolution into a set of emerging economies, on the one side, and the fifty to sixty countries that constitute the 'bottom billion', on the other. Whereas since the 1950s emerging Asia and the other relative success stories have steadily if slowly converged towards US levels of productivity, for other regions of the developing world – including most of Africa, parts of the Middle East, and Central and Western Asia – the picture has been one of relative divergence, especially since the onset of the major downturn in the South in the early 1980s. The paradox of unprecedented growth in the world economy, with per capita GDP in the emerging economies increasing faster since 2000 than at any time since the 1970s, and widening inequality between countries is a continuing legacy of both 'divergence, big time', and the downturn from the early 1980s in the fortunes of many poor and weak developing countries.

Looking at the distribution of income between the world's citizens over the long run of industrial capitalist development, it is easy to conclude that there has been an inexorable growth of inequality worldwide (Bourguignon and Morrisson 2002). As figure 5.1 shows, worldwide, or global, inequality

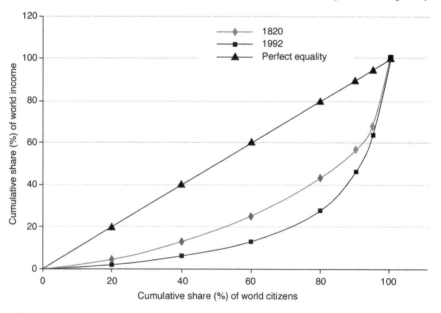

**Figure 5.1**   Lorenz curves for incomes of world citizens, 1820 and 1992
*Source*: Bourguignon and Morrisson 2002.

increased substantially between the early nineteenth and late twentieth centuries. However, a closer look suggests a more complex and interesting picture. Table 5.8 shows the Theil indices for the same years, 1820 and 1992, for which the Lorenz curves are plotted in figure 5.1. The Theil index does not have the intuitive appeal of Lorenz curves and their associated Gini coefficients but it has the important point of additive separability. With the Theil index one can decompose worldwide inequality among citizens into a component that measures inequality *within* countries and another that measures inequality *between* countries. Like the Gini coefficient, the Theil index measures the skew of a distribution away from perfect equality (0) to perfect inequality (1). The Theil index for global inequality is the sum of the Theil index for inequality between countries and (a weighted sum of) the Theil indices for inequalities within countries.

This means that the components of global inequality, in terms of the share accounted for by between-country and within-country inequality, are as in table 5.9. The overall increase in inequality is registered in the increase in the Theil (global) index from 0.522 to 0.855. Inequality within countries actually fell somewhat, from 0.461 to 0.342, while inequality between countries has increased massively, from 0.061 to 0.513. So, considering the components of inequality (within and between) as *shares* of the total, that is, global inequality, the picture is roughly as follows: in 1820, the vast bulk of global inequality was due to inequality within countries (nearly 90 per cent) and very little to that between countries. In 1992, by contrast, 60 per cent of global inequality was due to inequality between countries and 40 per cent to that within countries. That is to say, modern economic growth since the industrial revolution has been accompanied by increased global inequality overall, a modest fall in inequality within countries and a very

**Table 5.8**   Theil indices, 1820 and 1992

|  | 1820 | 1992 |
|---|---|---|
| **Theil (between country)** | 0.061 | 0.513 |
| **Theil (within country)** | 0.461 | 0.342 |
| **Theil (global)** | 0.522 | 0.855 |

*Source*: Bourguignon and Morrisson 2002, p. 734, table 2.

**Table 5.9**   Components of global inequality, 1820 and 1992 (percentages)

|  | 1820 | 1992 |
|---|---|---|
| Share of global inequality accounted for by between-country inequality | 11.7 | 60 |
| Share of global inequality accounted for by within-country inequality | 88.3 | 40 |

*Source*: Bourguignon and Morrisson 2002, p. 731, table 1.

large rise in inequality between countries, so that the relative contributions of within- and between-country inequality to global inequality have been reversed. From a world in which nearly all inequality between citizens was due to inequality within countries, there is now a much more unequal world in which inequality arises both because of inequality within countries (40 per cent of the total) and as a result of inequality between countries (60 per cent of the total). Clearly, at the level of the international economy as a whole, the major feature has been divergence in the fortunes of the developed and developing world, even as there has been a significant degree of conditional convergence in the developed world.

Since the 1970s, however, a rather different pattern appears to have been established, in which substantial parts of the developing world have started on slow processes of catch-up growth and convergence. Changes in global inequality can be attributed to within-country, pure cross-country and aggregation effects that result from the fact that countries are of different populations. Population-weighted measures, such as international inequality considered in terms of the mean incomes of countries weighted by population size, merge cross-country and aggregation effects. Looking at the most recent period since the 1970s, several studies have shown falls in this measure of inequality, probably accounted for by higher growth in large countries such as China and India, as well as increases in within-country inequality (see figure 5.2).

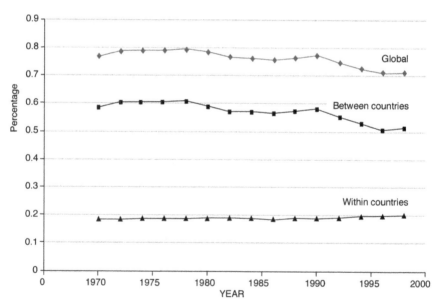

**Figure 5.2**   Components of global inequality, 1970–2000
*Source*: Sala-i-Martin 2002, p. 54, fig. 12.

How might we account for the patterns observed in the data reviewed thus far? In very broad terms one can tell the following story about this long-run evolution of growth and poverty, which is more or less consistent with the stylized facts. Weighted international inequality has fallen since the end of the long boom, largely because of growth in resurgent Asia. Global inequality – that is, the distribution of income among all of the world's citizens irrespective of statehood or nationality – rose slightly until the early 1990s and then fell back a little to below its starting point. If global inequality was roughly constant or fell only slightly, and if weighted international inequality has been falling, then inequality within countries must have been rising: in fact, this internal inequality has been rising in most countries and in all regions of the world economy.

However, even if the emerging market countries continue to grow more rapidly than the developed economies of the OECD bloc, so that relative measures of inequality (shares of world income in relation to population size) can be expected to continue to fall, absolute inequality between countries, intercountry inequality – that is, inequality between the mean incomes of all countries – is still rising and will continue to do so for a very long time. For example, Atkinson and Brandolini calculate that, 'with annual per capita growth rates of 5 per cent in China and 2 per cent in the United States, the absolute income gap between the two countries would widen for a further 41 years before starting to narrow, to finally disappear in 72 years' (World Bank 2006, p. 63).

Now, there are, of course, very significant liabilities with data on the worldwide distribution of income as well as choices to be made as to how to measure statistically the key features of that distribution (Bhagwati 2004). Perhaps more importantly, if what has been driving the long-run trends in inequalities has been the uneven spread of per capita growth, then it makes more sense to look at what has happened to poverty rather than to inequality. On this count, the *proportion* of the world's population living in absolute poverty has steadily fallen, from over 80 per cent in 1820 to about two-thirds in 1900, around one-half in 1950 and one-third in 1980. Since then, between 1981 and 2004, Shaohua Chen and Martin Ravallion (2007) estimate that the population growth rates for those living on under $1 per day, those living on between $1 and $2, and those living on over $2 were –1.4 per cent, 1.9 per cent and 3.5 per cent, respectively. Taking the developing world outside China, the respective figures were 0.1 per cent, 2.4 per cent and 2.5 per cent. Nevertheless, with a rising world population, the absolute numbers of people in poverty are still increasing.

The social correlates of these economic phenomena are closely bound up with the ongoing urbanization of the developing world. Estimates from the United Nations suggest that, while the world's rural and urban populations are currently roughly in balance, 'cities will account for *all* future world population growth' in proportional terms. And, as Mike Davis has forcefully insisted, this means that, in those cases in which urbanization 'has been radically decoupled from industrialization, even from development *per se*', the division between rural poverty and urban affluence that characterized economic development during the long boom is being overtaken by an exodus of the rural population and more or less chaotic, informal peri-urban sprawl, creating a 'planet of slums' (Davis 2004, p. 9). These vast populations – Davis suggests as many as 1 billion people may be slum-dwellers – live for the most part outside the formal economy and beyond the reach of the institutions of the state, save for its coercive apparatus during moments of open rebellion. Violence and particularistic forms of collective identity 'along lines of religion, caste, clan and tribe, or plain regional identities', as well as 'the fragmentation of labour across an enormous span of makeshift occupations and forms of casual-contractual employment', serve to divide slum-dwellers from one another, rendering their capacity for organized political agency much less than their demographic weight might suggest (Breman 2006, p. 147).

To be sure, to some extent this phenomenon characterizes all regions of the developing world, including the rising stars of emerging Asia – after all, Mumbai has some claim to be both the slum capital of the world and the home of India's dynamic, internationally competitive computer software industry. However, in those cases where this novel social and political form intersects with states that have exhausted whatever legitimacy they garnered during the long boom, the results have been particularly devastating. In states that have failed to establish the bases of national legitimacy, the result has been a general crisis of state authority, if not yet a crisis of state power, in which significant parts of the national territory are no longer governed by the formal authorities: power has devolved to local elites who have neither the incentives nor the capacities to define a coherent national interest. These territories, therefore, have become sites of instability for the regional and international order more widely.

## Emerging markets as a competitive challenge for the advanced economies?

Notwithstanding the fragmentation of the world market by multiple national currencies, there are still real and not just monetary links between countries mediated by the capital markets and the terms of trade. Analytically, we can distinguish three possible kinds of issue that might arise in relation to the competitiveness of Northern economies facing competition from the South: first, a situation in which the profitability of some areas in the traded sector declines but the average profitability of the tradeable part of the economy as a whole does not suffer – the economy has a 'sectoral competitiveness problem' in which some sectors lose and others gain; secondly, circumstances in which the average profitability in the tradeable sector as a whole declines but average profitability in the economy as a whole is maintained – the economy has a 'real appreciation problem'; and thirdly, the case where profitability in the economy as a whole has declined – in which case the economy has a 'productivity problem'. We will address these in reverse order.

The idea that faster productivity growth in the South will damage Northern living standards is false (see chapter 4 above). If real wages are flexible or if the exchange rate is adjusted appropriately, low productivity growth, whether absolute or relative to other countries, does not mean declining competitiveness. An increase in foreign productivity growth does not reduce the home country's competitiveness. The relation between the rate of productivity growth abroad and productivity growth at home is relevant only for the rate of depreciation required (with given nominal wage growth abroad and at home). The rate of growth of real wages (and real incomes) at home does not depend at all on *relative* productivity growth. It may be influenced by productivity growth abroad through terms-of-trade effects, but such effects may well be positive. If anything, there is a presumption that the terms-of-trade effects of more rapid foreign growth would actually be favourable. On the one hand, countries which grow relatively quickly, especially large ones, can be expected to face deteriorating terms of trade, which means that their trading partners benefit from improving terms of trade. By this mechanism, a rapidly growing country confers benefits on its partners. On the other hand, in so far as trade generates learning by doing, understood as a positive effect of cumulative output on total factor productivity, it can be a source of relative convergence, but this does not adversely affect the absolute performance of trading partners. Moreover, as noted above, innovation in the North is a constant source of divergence, for while 'less-developed countries benefit from R&D in industrial countries', the 'output gains of the industrial countries exceed the output gains of the less-developed countries', and so 'investment in innovation in the industrial countries leads to divergence of income between the North and the South' (Helpman 2004, p. 85).

Next, whether or not a general loss of competitiveness in the tradeable sector is a problem rests on the desirability or otherwise of the higher current account deficit which goes with the real appreciation problem. A decline in competitiveness may be the inevitable by-product of an international borrowing policy that is optimal. This is much debated in relation to the question of China's surpluses and US deficits (see chapter 7 below).

This leaves, finally, the perennial question of sectoral competitiveness. This is undoubtedly a real issue for several reasons. In the first place, whereas trade among Northern economies tends to be intra-sectoral and forces producers to innovate and align costs, North–South trade tends to be intersectoral and forces producers to abandon products. Secondly, while the net gains from trade are real, some sectors lose while others gain, and the magnitudes of these changes are typically much greater than the net benefits. If those who gain are unable or unwilling to compensate the losers, and if the assets and labour employed in sectors that lose out are not rapidly re-employed, substantial interests may be hurt. And thirdly, there are some indications that the South may be able to mount a competitive challenge to the North in the service sector.

Overall, there is little doubt that continued strong economic growth and rapid advances in productivity in China, India and elsewhere will produce strong export competition as costs fall and imports into Northern countries will become cheaper, so that real incomes will rise in both North and South. That is to say, the costs of competition are more than offset by the benefits of cheaper imports and stronger world growth. In fact, the biggest challenges will be faced not by the advanced Northern economies but by the middle-income countries elsewhere in Asia and in Latin America. For, as Winters and Yusuf point out: 'These are the countries into whose product space China in particular looks likely to expand; they are the members of production networks that may be threatened by China's move into component manufacture; and they are the recipients of foreign direct investment designed to create export platforms for the multinational corporations' (2006, p. 21).

But for Japan, North America and Western Europe, the picture is, for the most part, very different, as they:

> have little to fear over the next decade and a half from Chinese and Indian competition in the high-technology and high-skill sectors in manufacturing and services, especially when those sectors rely on highly educated and experienced workforces, accumulated tacit knowledge, and innovation supported by heavy investment in research and development. Indeed, they have much to gain from specialization in these areas. The high income countries have not been competitive in the manufacture of garments, shoes, and consumer electronics for a long time, and so they have been strong gainers from the price reductions that the Giants have engendered and will continue to engender. (Winters and Yusuf 2006, p. 22)

Glyn points out that, 'for every job in high-skill manufactures created by additional exports to the South there are as many as 6 jobs displaced by the same money value of low-tech manufactured imports from there. This disparity is just a reflection of the potential "gains from trade".' But, and this is the key point about the social sustainability of these economic shifts, 'the realisation of these gains depends on the workers concerned being re-employed' (Glyn 2005, p. 32). But if high levels of demand can be sustained in the world economy, there is nothing to suggest that this will be anything other than a major improvement in the economic fortunes of the major centres of the international economy, not least the USA.

In some respects India may also pose a challenge as far as economic adjustment in the North is concerned. China's success in export markets has been confined to the manufacturing sector; India, however, has demonstrated an ability to compete in some parts of the service sector. This is potentially significant because it opens up the possibility of international trade in sectors that have hitherto been assumed to be protected by distance. Until recently, it has been conventional to assume that, since most services are non-traded, they are immune to international competition. This may no longer be the case. One effect of ICTs has been to reduce the costs of operating supply chains within and between companies on a regional or international basis, as well as the costs of making new kinds of markets in products or services that have been previously limited by communication and coordination costs.

If we think of the shift from agriculture to industry as the 'first' industrial revolution and the shift in employment from industry to services as the 'second', we may now be at the beginning of the 'third', as impersonal services 'that are easily deliverable through a wire (or via wireless connections) with little or no diminution in quality' are now susceptible to offshore outsourcing (Blinder 2006; see also chapter 4 above). Thus far the numbers of jobs involved in this have been very small, at least as a share of total employment. But the potential significance of this can be illustrated from the US data: the share of total employment in tradeable professional services has been estimated at 13.7 per cent (cf. 12.4 per cent in tradeable manufacturing) and the share in tradeable occupations but non-tradeable industries is around another 10 per cent and much larger – typically around 25 per cent – for business and professional occupations (Jensen and Kletzer 2006). There is then some potential for changes to the boundary between the traded/non-traded sectors to open some of the service sectors of the developed world to new forms of competitive (and hence protectionist) pressures.

Finally, since the massive expansion of the labour supply was not associated with a similar increase in the capital stock, the (worldwide) ratio of capital to labour has fallen, raising the returns to capital (and hence the equilibrium level of real interest rates) and the share of national income going into profits in the capital-rich parts of the international economy. This led *The Economist* to conclude that, 'Unless a solution is found to sluggish real wages and rising inequality, there is a serious risk of a protectionist backlash' (2006, p. 17).

## Conclusions

The original (neo-classical) models of growth, due above all to Robert Solow (2000), concluded that growth rates would fall as the per capita capital stock built up to a steady state level, at which point real incomes per capita would reach a plateau. This theoretical prediction was reconciled with the empirical reality of sustained increases in per capita living standards by invoking an exogenous technological change, which Moses Abromovitz revealingly described as 'some sort of measure of our ignorance about the causes of economic growth' (cited in Coyle 2001, p. 15). The new (endogenous) growth theory, descending from Robert Lucas and, more recently, from William Baumol, aims to analyse the production of innovation as part of the endogenous workings of capitalist firms and economies. This focus on innovation puts the USA and other high-income countries at the centre of the story. The lead established by the United States and the other OECD bloc economies in the nineteenth and first half of the twentieth century represented what, following Lant Pritchett (1997), we have called 'divergence, big time'.

For much of the last century, the central story of capitalist growth was one of the USA forging ahead of its European and Japanese rivals, aided to a considerable extent by the course of the two world wars, followed by the conditional convergence of Western Europe and Japan during the long boom that followed post-war reconstruction and the construction of a high degree of political and geopolitical unity in the developed world, roughly from the late 1940s to the early 1970s. But, taking another view, we can see that *the labour force is also endogenous to the capitalist system as a whole*. Perhaps most importantly, 'capital (and capitalism) can be exported to take advantage of labour resources *in situ*'. Given this fact about historical capitalism, Stephen Marglin contends that 'over the long sweep of the history of capitalism . . . the endogeneity of the labour force has been more important than the endogeneity of technology in allowing the rich countries to sustain high rates of growth' (2000, p. 44).

Moreover, faced with ageing populations, the advanced capitalist economies may also come to rely on Asian savings. If one models the demographic and fiscal paths of the developed world – that is, the USA, the Euro area and Japan – without their interactions with China, it is highly likely that the tax increases needed to finance existing welfare commitments to ageing populations will lead to a fall in the level of capital per unit of human capital and hence a fall in real wages compared to the present. Of course real wages might continue to rise because of offsetting technical change. But if China and the other Asian labour-abundant economies are added to the model, and even if Asian savings and consumption patterns converge on those of the developed world as they get richer, Asian savings can finance capital accumulation both at home and abroad, so that the real wage per unit of human capital can continue to rise in the developed world over and above that which would follow from technical change alone (Fehr et al. 2005).

So, in the light of the developments reviewed above, the bigger picture in the future may lie elsewhere. The combination of industrialization in North-East Asia and the prospect of sustained growth in South Asia suggests that forces of convergence – due to trade, human capital formation, the provision of social overhead capital, changes of policies and institutions, the onset of diminishing returns in the North and the flows of resources, especially capital, to parts of the South – may be beginning to assert themselves in the most populous regions of the world economy. If this is so, then the long-term implications are likely to be very large indeed.

That said, the prospects for the excluded also look correspondingly bleak, for they now face an international environment in which they 'will have to wait a long time until development in Asia creates a wage gap with the bottom billion similar to the massive gap that prevailed between Asia and the rich world in 1980' (Collier 2007, p. 86). This predicament is compounded by a flight of capital and of skilled and educated labour from these countries. 'The global economy', Collier concludes, 'is now making it much harder for them to follow the path taken by the more successful majority' (ibid., p. 99). What they need is temporary protection *from* Asia and, given the current distribution of world tariffs, there is likely to be only a couple of decades before even this will become impossible.

All of these changes are fraught with danger. Rising inequalities and competitive pressures in the developed countries could provoke a backlash against ever-increasing liberalization of trade and investment. A slump in China (similar to that which befell Japan during the lost decade of the 1990s) could have damaging effects in North-East Asia and the wider world economy. The current account imbalances and the capital flows needed to finance them, in particular the US deficits and the position of the dollar, could become unsustainable. The costs of poverty and conflict among the excluded may impinge on the lives of the privileged. However, there is nothing inevitable about any of these, and the major centres of decision-making – in Washington, Brussels, Beijing and Tokyo – are not without considerable powers to manage seriously adverse developments, if they can effect a modicum of coordination among themselves (see chapter 8).

# 6

# Supranational Regionalization or Globalization?

People have been trying to create a global village. But this dream is over. Regions are drifting apart. We are also drifting apart within regions themselves.

Peter Brabeck, chairman of Nestlé, reported in *Financial Times*, 31 January 2006, p. 13

On our list of approved funds, we are currently 60 per cent US managers and 40 per cent Europe and Asia. . . . I wouldn't be surprised in five years to find us one-third America, one third Europe and one-third Asia.

Arpad Busson, founder and chairman of EIM Hedge Fund, reported in *Financial Times*, 29 March 2006, p. 12[1]

## Introduction

This chapter turns its attention to one of the most intriguing aspects of the contemporary international system. The dominant motif of the late twentieth and early twenty-first centuries has been that the international system can best be described as rapidly moving along a route towards its 'globalization'. The various aspects of such a globalization have already been discussed in chapter 1, and the possible trajectory for the international economy as it travels along this route was investigated in chapters 3, 4 and 5. However, as mentioned in chapter 1, there is another scenario that could be deployed to describe the trajectory for the international system, and that is towards its supranational regionalization rather than towards its globalization. This chapter investigates such a possibility. It does this in three registers: with respect to the real economy, with respect to the financial system, and with respect to standard-setting. First, however, we need to be clearer as to what is meant by supranational regionalization, which is discussed in the next section.

## Supranational regionalization: what is it?

The first point to make about supranational regionalization is that it remains ill-defined (though, as we have seen, this is also true of globalization). One of the main issues is to determine what is meant by a 'region' and to put some clear boundaries around this. For instance, is a region to be defined in geographical terms, in economic or political terms, or in cultural terms, and how far do these coincide or overlap? Take the European Union, for instance. Where does the boundary around Europe lie so that the extent of a possible union between 'European' countries becomes apparent and defendable? Secondly, several features of regionalism could be highlighted, for instance *de facto* and *de jure* aspects. *De facto* aspects would involve the actual mechanisms deployed and decisions made by private agents in their integration and interdependency moves – which is sometimes called 'regionalization'. *De jure* aspects refer to the way public bodies and public policy actively promote integration and interdependency between countries, often along several different dimensions – which is sometimes called 'regionalism'. Regionalization and regionalism need not always coincide or develop along similar lines. In addition, in the literature on these matters *bilateral* relationships – mainly of a *de jure* type associated with agreements to forge trade deals between countries – are often associated with, or discussed as part of, the supranational regionalization/ism process (from now on, and for convenience, we will use just the term 'regionalization' to encompass both these aspects).

But for the purposes of this chapter we take a fairly straightforward definition of supranationalization designed to by-pass many of these problems. This chapter is not about providing a rigorous definition and discussion of all the nuances of the debate and necessary caveats. Instead the following fairly non-contentious definition is suggested, which is dependent mainly upon geographical proximity:

A geographically contiguous area composed of the territories of nation-states that have either combined in an integrative economic or monetary union, or whose economies have evolved into a closely interdependent entity, or who can empirically be shown to be advancing along these routes.

Examples of this are fairly obvious and include such bodies as the European Union (EU); the North American Free Trade Area (NAFTA – comprising the USA, Canada and Mexico); Mercosur (involving Argentina, Brazil, Paraguay, Uruguay and Venezuela); the Association of East Asian

Nations (ASEAN) – and its possible offshoots: ASEAN + 3 (China, Korea and Japan) or +3 +3 (Taiwan, India and Australia) – sometimes collectively known as the East Asian region; the West African Economic and Monetary Union (WAEMU); Middle East and North Africa (MENA); the proposed FTAA (Free Trade Area of the Americas); the Gulf Cooperation Council (GCC – made up of Bahrain, Kuwait, Oman, Qatar, Saudi Arabia and the United Arab Emirates); and the like (there are several other groupings similar to these – see Lévy 2006).

The numbers and importance of these free trade agreements (FTAs) are shown in figure 6.1. Their growth between 1990 and 2002 is evident. An important point to note is that many of these FTAs are really bilateral treaties. But we concentrate here on the main multilateral ones – not all of them in the same detail – and by and large the most developed and important in terms of size and overall structure of the international economy, which comprise the so-called Triad – Europe, North America and East Asia. However, even these do not necessarily comprise coherent groups when measured along various dimensions, which will become apparent later.

The following sections lay out data and arguments designed to answer the question as to whether the international economic system is developing along paradigmatic global lines or supranational regional lines. As will become clear, drawing a sharp contrast between these two trajectories for the international economy is not altogether appropriate: they overlap and there still remains considerable distinct nation-state-based international economic activity, as we will see. Thus the case is a mixed one. But, given the overriding emphasis placed upon the ubiquity of global forces and of globalization as the main tendential features of contemporary economic relationships – something accepted as the conventional wisdom by almost

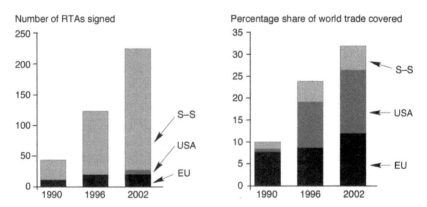

**Figure 6.1**  The growing importance of regional trade agreements

*Note*: S–S = South–South.

*Source*: World Bank 2005, p. 41.

all journalists, policy-makers, politicians, activists and most academics working in this field – the burden of the following analysis is to suggest a counter-case. It presents an argument that there are strong tendential features that might lead us to think of the international system forming into supranational regional blocs in contrast to its 'globalization', and that these moves towards such a 'regionalization' are as strong as, if not stronger than, those leading towards further globalization. As will become clear, the following sections assemble a somewhat eclectic amount of evidence to make the case, the implications of which are not altogether unambiguous even in their own terms.

### The real economy

We begin with the real economy. This comprises activity such as trade, investment, employment, R&D and the operations of companies in the production of goods and services (not all of these areas will be dealt with in detail). This is in distinction to the financial economy, which has more to do with monetary and investment matters. An early problem is whether this distinction can still be defended as the general 'financialization' of economic activity escalates (i.e. all economic activity being increasingly subject to financial calculations). As we will see, this does present problems, especially in relation to the way in which MNCs can be considered, and we will have occasion to blur this distinction as the analysis proceeds. But for the purposes of simplicity in the first instance, we hold to this distinction and proceed by keeping these two aspects apart as far as is possible.

Let us begin with trade. Figure 6.2 shows the international flows of trade between countries mapped in the form of a network diagram for the years 1980 and 2001. It shows only those flows that are above 3 per cent of world trade so as not to overcomplicate the picture (the degree of trade value interdependency is shown by the width of the lines joining countries). In addition, the main regional supranational trading blocs are considered separately so as to indicate their significance.

Close inspection of the figure reveals several things. The first is that there is a distinct regional pattern to these trade flows. Secondly, this *inter*-regional pattern intensified between 1980 and 2001. In 1980 there is a more dispersed set of relationships indicated by the lines between a wider set of countries. But by 2001, a basic Triad pattern was more firmly established, with the intensity of multilateral contacts centred on North America, Europe and Asia-Pacific (mainly East Asia). What is more, picking out the regional trade alliances separately indicates, first, more countries involved in each case (particularly for Asia-Pacific) and, second, greater *intra*-regional interdependency among those regional blocs (note that intra-EU 12 trade is treated as a single observation point in each year).

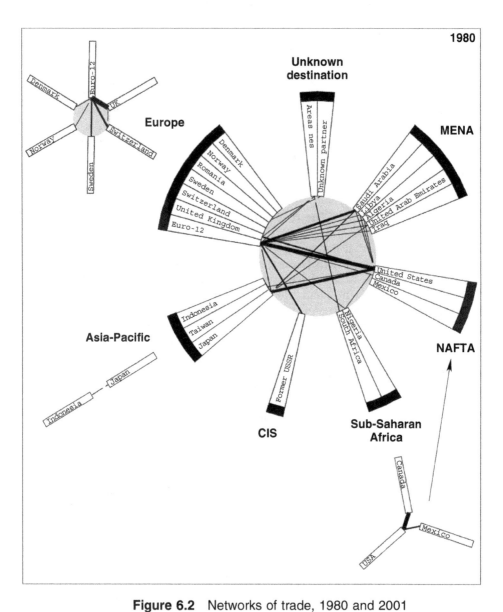

**Figure 6.2**  Networks of trade, 1980 and 2001

*Source*: Derived from Princeton Institute for International and Regional Studies (2006) *Data and Selected Images from the GKG Project.*

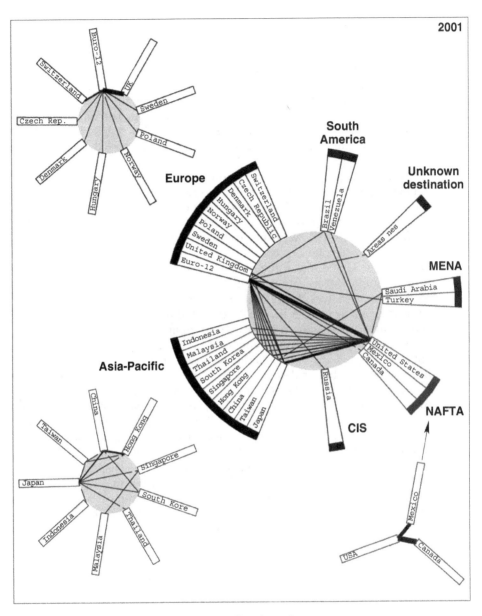

**2001**

**Figure 6.2** *Continued*

The basic message from figure 6.2 is confirmed by the data shown in table 6.1 for 2004, particularly in the cases of Europe and North America. 'Asia' is a more dispersed category than that of 'Asia-Pacific' considered in figure 6.2, but even here 50 per cent of trade was intra-Asia. In fact, this regionalized network pattern to trade has been found over a longer period.[2] For instance, on the basis of four cross-sectional analyses for the years 1928, 1938, 1960 and 2000, Tieting Su (2005) finds that trade is regionally distributed rather than global in each case, and that this regional pattern has increased in intensity over the most recent cycle (1960–2000), just as indicated in figure 6.2.

An important aspect of the regionalization of trade concerns what is happening to the USA in particular. Concentrating on the trade relationship between the USA, China and the rest of East Asia, for instance, shows the trajectory of exports to the ASEAN countries from the USA peaked in the late 1990s and went into decline in the early 2000s, while China's exports to these countries continued to rise (Thompson 2006a, figure 8.5). On the other hand, the value of Japan's imports from the USA declined while its imports from China continued to expand rapidly in the 1990s and early 2000s. For the North-East Asian economies as a whole, however, while their imports from the USA stagnated over the late 1990s and early 2000s, there was a surge in imports from Japan.

What are the overall implications of these trends? While these data are not entirely comprehensive, they do indicate two main points (which have also been noted by other analyses): first, the USA is losing ground on its exports to the East Asian region generally and, second, there seems to be growing trade integration between the North-East Asian economies (including China) and Japan and the ASEAN countries. Thus a regional trade bloc could be forming in East Asia, thereby tending to exclude imports from the USA (though *exports to* the USA from this proto-bloc continue to remain strong, leading to well-known trans-Pacific trade tensions – see chapters 5 and 7).

The increasing 'isolation' of the US economy from the rest of the international economy can be seen from the data presented in table 6.2. This shows correlations in the fluctuations of several real variables between the USA and Europe, Japan and Canada over two different time periods. In the case of USA–Europe and USA–Japan, there is a significant *reduction*

**Table 6.1** Share of interregional merchandise export flows in each region as a percentage of total merchandise exports, 2004

| Origin | Destination | | | |
| --- | --- | --- | --- | --- |
| | North America | Europe | Asia | Total |
| **North America** | 56 | 16 | 9 | 81 |
| **Europe** | 9 | 74 | 8 | 91 |
| **Asia** | 22 | 18 | 50 | 90 |

*Source*: Derived from WTO 2005, p. 40, table III.3.

**Table 6.2**  Correlations of real variable fluctuations between the USA and other economies, 1972–2000

|  |  | Output | Consumption | Investment | Employment |
|---|---|---|---|---|---|
| **Europe** | 1972–1986 | 0.71 | 0.48 | 0.61 | 0.60 |
|  | 1986–2000 | 0.31 | 0.06 | −0.03 | 0.01 |
| **Japan** | 1972–1986 | 0.61 | 0.38 | 0.59 | 0.39 |
|  | 1986–2000 | −0.05 | −0.01 | −0.17 | −0.30 |
| **Canada** | 1972–1986 | 0.76 | 0.38 | 0.01 | 0.54 |
|  | 1986–2000 | 0.84 | 0.66 | 0.43 | 0.87 |

*Source*: Adapted from Heathcote and Perri 2002, p. 7, table 6.

in the correlations for all four variables between 1972 to 1986 and 1986 to 2000, implying an increasing 'divergence' of business cycles in real global economic activity. On the other hand, between the USA and Canada the movement is in the opposite direction, with significant increases in correlations and convergence. Thus NAFTA seems to be working in these cases, with the consolidation of a North American bloc.

Another important feature of the international economy and the case for 'globalization' concerns the role of MNCs. Here the pertinent question for our purposes is 'Are MNCs genuinely globalizing their economic activity?' The conventional wisdom is that they are, but this is strongly contested by the work of Alan Rugman, which was discussed in chapter 3. In several important books and articles (Rugman 2000, 2005a, 2005b; Rugman and Verbeke 2004a and 2004b; *MIR* 2005) Rugman and his co-authors have demonstrated that the vast majority of the most important MNCs either still remain 'national' in their operating characteristics or are at best supranationally regional in their strategic outlook (see table 3.4 and figure 3.5).

## The financial economy

### Corporate loans and equity markets

A slightly different approach to Rugman's question about global or regional orientation of activities is provided by looking at the markets in corporate loans and securities. Here we move more into the financial domain of economic activity. In table 6.3 the percentages of corporate syndicated loans over the period 1992 to 2002 that were either raised in one of the Triad markets by borrowers from different countries or that appear in the market when raised by borrowers from different domiciles are shown in part A and B respectively. On both counts it is clear that the international market for syndicated loans over this period was resolutely 'regional' rather than 'global'. There is hardly any cross-borrowing by actors from one international market to another outside of their home region. However, while 80 per cent of loans raised by Canadian borrowers were from the US market, interestingly Latin American companies borrowed predominantly from

**Table 6.3**   Relationship of market region and borrower domicile

**A) Percentage of syndicated loan volume in each market due to borrowers in each domicile**

| Borrower domicile | US market | European market | Asian & SW Pacific market |
|---|---|---|---|
| United States | 97.7 | 3.2 | 2.6 |
| Europe | 0.5 | 81.8 | 1.0 |
| Latin America | 0.2 | 6.3 | 0.3 |
| Canada | 1.0 | 0.6 | 0.0 |
| Asia & SW Pacific | 0.1 | 1.9 | 94.4 |
| Other | 0.5 | 6.2 | 1.7 |
| Total | 100.0 | 100.0 | 100.0 |

**B) Percentage of syndicated loan volume issued by borrowers in each domicile appearing in each market**

| Borrower domicile | US market | European market | Asian & SW Pacific market | Total |
|---|---|---|---|---|
| United States | 98.5 | 1.2 | 0.3 | 100.0 |
| Europe | 1.7 | 98.0 | 0.3 | 100.0 |
| Latin America | 6.0 | 93.0 | 1.0 | 100.0 |
| Canada | 80.5 | 19.4 | 0.1 | 100.0 |
| Asia & SW Pacific | 0.9 | 6.9 | 92.2 | 100.0 |
| Other | 15.1 | 79.0 | 5.9 | 100.0 |

*Note*: Data are for all multi-lender loans reported in Loanware as made in the three markets during 1992–2002. Panel A examines the composition of each market in terms of borrower domicile, whereas Panel B examines the market choices of borrowers from each domicile, one at a time. *Source*: Carey and Nini 2004, p. 31, table 1.

Europe. On the other hand, Asian and South-West Pacific borrowers remain closely tethered to their home regional markets.

In part these results confirm the continued 'home biases' found in the international securities markets more generally, as reported in table 6.4. Comments by BIS economists reinforce this picture of home bias among US investors: 'Despite the disappearance of formal barriers to international investment across countries, we find that the average home bias of US investors towards the 46 countries with the largest equity markets did not fall from 1994 to 2004 when countries are equally weighted but fell when countries are weighted by market capitalisation' (Bong-Chan et al. 2006, p. 1). The reasons for this are attributed mainly to the continuation of extensive cross-holding of shares among domestic investors and corporate governance issues which militate against the diversification of portfolios internationally.

The move towards the Triadization of company activity is also indicated in the case of East Asia by examining the correlations between equity price movements across different stock exchanges. Figure 6.3 looks at the correlation of several Asia-Pacific and South Asian markets with Asia as a whole in contrast to the rest of the world. In each country case the correlation of real stock returns is greater with Asia than with the rest of the world,

**Table 6.4** Home bias: portfolio allocations of lenders in each region

| | Lender region | | | |
|---|---|---|---|---|
| Borrower region | US | Europe | Other | Global weight |
| USA | 91 | 39 | 31 | 64 |
| Europe | 6 | 51 | 12 | 22 |
| Other | 3 | 10 | 57 | 14 |
| Total | 100 | 100 | 100 | 100 |
| Memo: Lender-region share | 49% | 35% | 16% | |

*Note*: Data are for all multi-lender loans reported in Loanware as made in the three markets during 1992–2002 that include information about participating lenders' shares of the amount of the loan. If loans with missing shares are included, results are similar, except that lenders from the Other region have shares of 40, 14 and 46 per cent in loans to US, European and other borrowers, respectively (for loans without share data, we assume each lender takes an equal share).
*Source*: Carey and Nini 2004, p. 32, table 3.

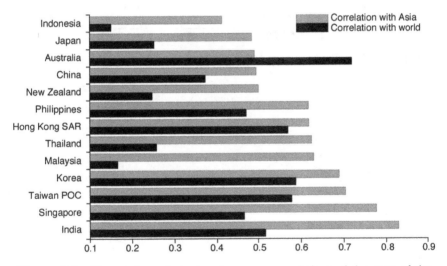

**Figure 6.3** Correlation of stock returns across Asia and the rest of the world
*Source*: Mercereau 2006, p. 13, figure 5.

indicating co-movement of stock returns across the East Asian and South Asian areas (which itself is an indication of the 'integration' of these markets).

But what about the *trends* in international securities trading? Figure 6.4 concentrates upon the shares of US and foreign equities in US and world portfolios. Figure 6.4a shows that the proportion of US equities in total world portfolios remained steady between 1990 and 2003, though there was

(a)

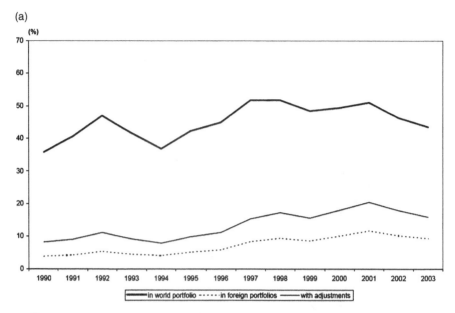

**Figure 6.4a** The share of US equities in world and foreign portfolios

(b)

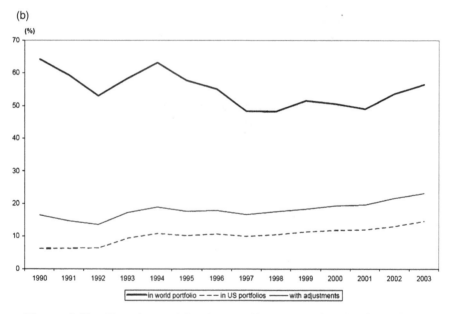

**Figure 6.4b** The share of foreign equities in world and US portfolios
*Source*: Cai and Warnock 2004, figures 1 and 2.

a slight rise of the US equity share in foreign portfolios (by about 4 to 5 per cent). In figure 6.4b the share of foreign equities in world portfolios has also remained steady, while that of the US share has risen slightly (by about 3 per cent). The general point to make in relation to these data is that there is only a slight trend growth of US equities in world portfolios, but that there is no sharp increase in foreign equity trading on the world's stock exchanges overall. Anywhere close to a truly global market for shares has yet to emerge. This also confirms the home bias argument developed in relationship to table 6.3 above.

These figures are indicative of the still limited extent of the genuine internationalization of securities trading. This is further illustrated by the data collected in table 6.5, where various measures of the internationalization of the world's major stock exchanges are shown. The table is divided between equity markets and bond markets. There are considerable variations between the exchanges, with some indicating considerable 'internationalization' (particularly in the case of bonds for Switzerland and Hong Kong on several measures). The well-known 'super-internationalization' of the London stock exchange is also apparent (Hirst and Thompson 1992). But there remain some very low percentages if the value of *trading* in equities and bonds is focused on. Thus these data give a mixed picture of the extent of these measures of financial internationalization.

Finally in this discussion of the relationship of company financial activity and its relationship to 'globalization', figure 6.5 switches to the returns on company stocks observed in the domestic and international spheres. If we were to ask what is driving any co-movement of company stock returns across national stock markets (and there is some evidence that this has happened since the mid-1980s) there are a number of possible explanations: coincidental country effects (such as macroeconomic variable shocks), international financial integration, real integration, sector or industry effects, temporary idiosyncratic effects, etc. Figure 6.5 provides evidence on these relationships based on fluctuations in the stock returns of a sample of 10,000 firms from forty-two developed and emerging market countries operating in forty industry sectors (Brooks and Del Negro 2002). The approach is to regress a value-weighted cross-section of international stock returns on a number of global, country and industry variables.

Temporary or idiosyncratic effects are not reported here. In fact these can be by far the most important in terms of coefficient value, consistently accounting for some 50 per cent of the variance in the equation formulations found in this and other studies. This alone casts some doubt on whether there is a systematic relationship between international stock returns, since half of the fluctuation is due to unidentified (non-systematic) variables. For the rest, however, the emphasis is upon country effects, industry effects and diversification effects (which is a surrogate for global financial integration). What the results show is that specific *country effects* have fallen in importance in explaining stock-market return

**Table 6.5** The internationalization of the world's stock exchanges, 2000–2005

| | Equities No. of foreign listed companies as a % of total listed companies | | | | Trading in shares of foreign companies as a % of total share trading | | Bonds No. of foreign bond issuers as a % of total bond issuers | | Value of foreign bonds as a % of total listed bonds | | Value of foreign bonds traded as a % of total bond trading |
|---|---|---|---|---|---|---|---|---|---|---|---|
| | 2000 | 2002 | 2004 | 2005 | 2004 | 2005 | 2004 | 2005 | 2004 | 2005 | 2005 |
| Nasdaq | 10.3 | 11.0 | 10.5 | 10.5 | 7.0 | 6.9 | – | – | – | – | – |
| NYSE | 17.5 | 19.2 | 20.0 | 19.9 | 8.4 | 9.6 | 21.9 | 18.5 | 6.9 | 6.5 | 1.05 |
| London SE | 18.9 | 17.5 | 12.4 | 10.8 | 43.1 | 43.9 | 37.3 | 39.4 | 36.3 | 34.9 | 1.03 |
| Deutsche Börse | 24.5 | 23.9 | 19.4 | 15.2 | 8.9 | 8.9 | 73.2 | 75.9 | – | – | 10.5 |
| Euronext | – | – | 25.1 | 23.3 | 1.9 | 4.4 | – | – | – | – | – |
| Swiss exchanges | 34.4 | 36.2 | 31.1 | 29.0 | 91.9 | 89.8 | 63.3 | 65.4 | 45.3 | 47.4 | 57.4 |
| Tokyo SE | 2.0 | 1.8 | 1.3 | 1.2 | 0.02 | 0.06 | 1.3 | 0 | 0.03 | 0 | 0 |
| Hong Kong SE | – | – | – | 0.8 | 0.08 | 0.11 | 55.8 | 41.9 | 48.3 | 41.8 | 0 |

*Sources*: Derived from Sassen 2006, p. 258, table 5.4; *World Federation of Exchanges Annual Report 2006*, p. 68, table 1.3; p. 71, table 1.5; p. 89, table 2.2; p. 88, table 2.1; p. 92, table 2.5.

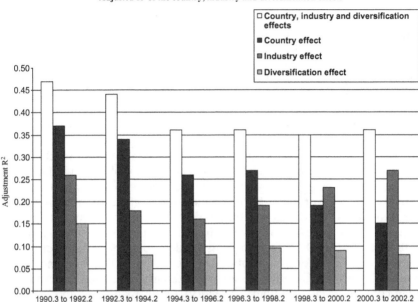

Adjusted R² of the country, industry and diversification effects

Figure 6.5   The relative importance of country, industry and diversification effects in global stock return

*Source*: Adapted from Brooks and del Negro 2002, p. 43, figure 1.

fluctuations – and this is a consistent result across a number of comparable studies. On the other hand, there is no great increase in the importance of *global financial integration* (as measured by the international diversification of balance-sheet portfolios and income statements). Overall, however, there is some indication that between 1990 and 2002 at least the international correlation between stock-market returns *decreased*. And many studies have found a similar result – a decrease in international financial integration since the late 1980s accompanied by a growing importance in explaining the actual trends of what has happened just in the USA, because of its particular relationship to other countries (see discussion and references in Brooks and Del Negro 2002, and in Klingebiel 2002).

## Long-term loans and bond markets

Let us now concentrate on another aspect of the international financial system, namely long-term lending and the bond market. In absolute terms this is huge (towards the end of 2000 outstanding accumulated government and corporate bond issues were well over US$30,000 billion). But this market was dominated by just two currencies of issue at the end of 2002 –

49.3 per cent in US dollars and 24.6 per cent in Euros (the Japanese yen total was 9.6 per cent; see Thompson 2006a, table 4) – and by 2006 Euro denomination had overtaken that of dollars. Thus there is a bifurcation of this market into just two currencies of denomination.

But where are these bonds issued and held? Table 6.6 answers this at a number of levels. Just over 93 per cent had been issued in the developed world, leaving just under 7 per cent for the emerging markets, including China and India. Local currency bonds continue to be held in their country of origin, and bonds denominated in local currencies also dominate overall country portfolios. All in all, then, there was still no serious 'global market' in bonds in 2001, despite the often cited growing extent of East Asia's holding of US Treasury bonds, which this evidence seems to challenge. Compared to the total of all bonds issued, these holdings remain small (though they may present problems in themselves for the countries concerned in such government borrowing and lending; see chapter 7 below).

Of themselves, the data in table 6.6 do not tell us from where the cross-border activity indicated originates. To some extent this is rectified by the data in table 6.7. Dealing with cross-border holdings of long-term debt expressed as a proportion of total debt securities (2001–3), the most integrated bloc is the EU, which has also invested heavily in the Eastern European countries (and in 'Others' category). Other than these, the extent of cross-regional integration looks minimal.

**Table 6.6**   World bond market portfolio[1], end 2001

| | Total bonds outstanding – % in world bond portfolio | Local currency bonds outstanding | |
|---|---|---|---|
| | | % in world bond portfolio | % of country's total bonds |
| Developed countries | 93.1 | 86.9 | 93 |
| Euro area | 22.0 | 19.5 | 89 |
| UK | 4.2 | 3.1 | 74 |
| Japan | 15.5 | 15.3 | 99 |
| USA | 46.2 | 45.3 | 98 |
| Emerging markets | 6.9 | 5.4 | 78 |
| Latin America | 1.7 | 0.8 | 48 |
| Emerging Asia | 3.8 | 3.5 | 91 |
| China | 1.3 | 1.3 | 97 |
| India | 0.4 | 0.4 | 97 |
| World total | 100 | 92 | 92 |

*Note*: Local-currency-denominated debt is the sum total of the long-term debt components ('domestic debt securities') and local currency proportions of 'international bonds and notes by country of residency' as both reported to the BIS. This is supplemented by data on other long-term debt for countries and Brady bonds. It includes $US 2.5 trillion of foreign currency, denominated primarily in US dollars, Euros and sterling.
*Source*: Calculated from Burgen and Warnock 2004, p. 29, table 1.

**Table 6.7** Average cross-border portfolio holdings of long-term debt as percentages of destination countries' total outstanding debt securities, 2001–2003

| Investment from/to | USA and Canada | Asia | EU15 | Eastern Europe | Latin America | Others |
|---|---|---|---|---|---|---|
| **USA and Canada** | 0.06 | 0.64 | 2.60 | 2.05 | 7.97 | 9.65 |
| **Asia** | 2.34 | 0.52 | 4.20 | 1.02 | 1.32 | 9.77 |
| **EU15** | 3.29 | 1.07 | 23.18 | 15.20 | 6.31 | 15.54 |
| **Eastern Europe** | 0.01 | 0.00 | 0.05 | 0.34 | 0.01 | 0.04 |
| **Latin America** | 0.08 | 0.00 | 0.02 | 0.01 | 0.86 | 0.04 |
| **Others** | 1.38 | 0.24 | 2.58 | 1.01 | 1.73 | 2.93 |
| **Total** | 7.17 | 2.48 | 32.62 | 19.62 | 18.20 | 37.98 |

*Source*: Luengnaruemilchai and Eichengreen 2006, p. 27, table 2.

Finally, much of this discussion can be summed up in terms of figure 6.6, where the aggregated global cross-border holdings and flows of financial assets are mapped for 1999 and 2004. Comparing the two years indicates that, although flows have undoubtedly increased, the pattern remains basically an interregional one between the Triad groupings. If one were to add up the *intra*-European flows, for instance (the Euro area, the UK, Western Europe, Eastern Europe), and treat this as a single bloc, then, along with the USA and Japan, these account for over 80 per cent of the total global flows in both years (as well as of domestic holdings). What we have, then, is three large, essentially supraregional 'financial blocs'. And this is important for the relative stability of the international system. It means that the key relationships are between only a few currencies and exchange rates. If there were greater differentiation, with more key players all of a relatively equal standing, then there could be greater financial risks and turmoil as countries or blocs vied between themselves. And inasmuch as this may be developing with the emergence of other key players, particularly in Asia, the future could be more uncertain on this score.

Thus, to sum up this presentation of evidence on the character of international financial activity, the approach has been to present a range of often overlapping data drawn from different sources to try to establish a robust general result. What are the implications of these data for the idea that everything economic is now global in character? They indicate that this idea is suspect on two counts. First, the bulk of economic activity still remains closely tethered to national territories and is not footloose internationally. Second, any economic activity that is resolutely 'international' in character is less globally configured than it is supranational regionally based. The question becomes, therefore, Why is this the case, and what are its implications?

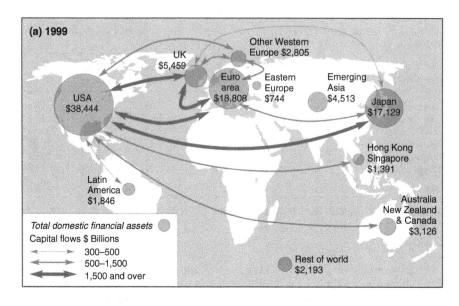

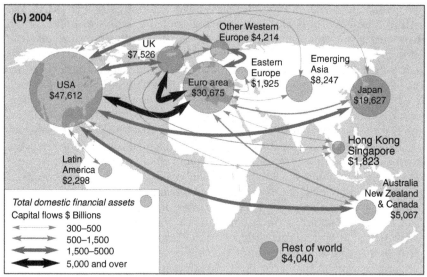

**Figure 6.6** Global capital flows and total domestic financial assets, 1999 and 2004

*Source*: McKinsey Global Institute, *Mapping Global Capital Markets*, various years.

## The empirics of international trade and investment

The usual empirics of international trade – and to an extent of investment – are modelled via the operationalization of a gravity equation. In this, trade (and investment) between two countries, i and j (Tij), is seen as a positive function of the income of the countries (GDP/P) and a negative function of the cost of trading, or the distance between the two (Dij). In addition to these two variables, a further set of 'control' variables are often introduced to account for cultural, geographical and institutional similarities or differences between countries that might also affect the amount of trade (or investment) between them (see equation below – other variables could be added here: two of the most important not considered in this short presentation would be a country size variable and one to measure factor endowments).

$$
\begin{aligned}
Tij = a + b\left(\frac{GDPi}{Pi}\right) + c\left(\frac{GDPj}{Pj}\right) - d(Dij) + e(BDRij) + f(LANij) \\
+ g(COLij) + h(BLOCij) + k(LAWij) + l(CURij) + u
\end{aligned}
$$

And it is these cultural, institutional and geographical variables that have been found to have become increasingly important in determining overall trade (and investment) flows. As income grows, by contrast, income as such becomes less important (indeed, with a coefficient of less than 1, i.e. a proportionate increase in income per capita leads to a less than proportionate increase in international trade). On the other hand, distance remains a formidable deterrent to international trade and investment activity. Typical equation coefficients with respect to (international) distances for the early 2000s are shown in table 6.8.

In addition, there is evidence that trading partners are becoming closer rather than further away, which is the opposite of what might be expected in an era of 'globalization' (Carrere and Schiff 2003). Of course, it is the relationship between cost and distance that is the major determinant of the trade coefficient in table 6.8, and the dramatic reduction in freight rates that may have fuelled any growth in long-distance trade

**Table 6.8** The effect of distance on economic interactions (international bilateral transactions); percentage reductions in the value of magnitudes relative to 1000 km

| | Trade ($\partial = -1.25$) | FDI ($\partial = -0.42$) | Equity flows ($\partial = -0.85$) | Technology (R&D stocks) |
|---|---|---|---|---|
| 1000 km | 0 | 0 | 0 | 0 |
| 2000 km | 58 | 25 | 45 | 35 |
| 4000 km | 82 | 44 | 69 | 72 |
| 8000 km | 97 | 58 | 83 | 95 |

*Note*: $\partial$ are elasticities of transactions with respect to distance.
*Source*: Calculated from Venables 2002.

since the 1970s slowed considerably towards the end of the 1990s (see Thompson 2006a, figure 8.8). Thus we might expect a slowing down of 'globalization' as a result of these trends. There is a limit to how far the physical barriers presented by distance and cost can be overcome, hence the incentive to trade (and invest) closer to home on a supranational regional basis.

And this is bolstered by the effects of some of the other 'institutional' or 'cultural' variables shown in the equation that are important in explaining the coefficients for trade and investment and the other dimensions shown in table 6.8. Legal differences (LAW) are a major factor. Language differences (LAN) are important, and past colonial ties (COL – important for migration) are another key factor. Then there are 'geographical' variables such as sharing a border (BOR) and whether the countries belong to a common trade bloc (BLOC). Finally, the sharing of a common currency (CUR) can be a major stimulant to trade and other interactions. Many of these influences favour local or regional solutions to economic relationships over global ones. The issue of currency unions is developed in a moment.

### Derivatives trading

Many aspects of the international financial system now seem to be inexorably 'global' in character, in the popular imagination none more so than the trading of financial derivatives. We all know about the dramatic rise in the extent of these (midway through 2005, outstanding exchange-traded derivatives stood at US$58.5 trillion – equivalent to US$9,000 for every person on Earth – a fourfold increase on the figures for mid-1998, and a rise from virtually zero in 1970, etc.). But there are in fact many subtle differences in the manner that such derivative instruments are treated in different financial centres and their significance for those financial systems. Significant heterogeneity can be found as between existing exchanges in Frankfurt, Stockholm, São Paulo and Singapore, and those emerging in countries such as Russia and China (MacKenzie 2007). A clear case in point is in respect to 'Islamic derivatives' and banking more generally – involving so-called Islamic permissible contracts (Maurer 2001, 2005; El Diwany 2003). So 'place' still matters. The 'cultural geographies' of economic activities remain alive and well (Thrift 2000), despite the frequent insistence that time and space have become so compressed, and the market so ubiquitous, that we are all ruled by anonymous forces displaying a singular global calculative logic imposed on any financial instrument or local financial market.

And these differences are even to be found between very similarly organized 'Anglo-American' economies such as those of the UK and the USA (let alone within the USA itself, where there are traditional differences between, say, Chicago and New York in terms of the development of derivatives trading). And this is not just a matter of the supposed 'gentlemanly' attitude thought to be the tradition among London traders as opposed to the 'single-minded pursuit of pecuniary advantage' presumed among American traders (though the London markets are now popularly thought to be inhabited more by East Enders and 'Essex boys', who have their own peculiar attitudes and cultural traits). Important sources of these differences are the tax system, the legal protection regime (e.g. of copyright on particular indexes and instruments), forms of arbitration in cases of dispute, the way clearing houses work, and attitudes towards betting (and the residual forms of the legal regulation of betting – involving the slippage between 'hedger' and 'speculator', for instance) (de Goede 2004; MacKenzie 2007). Take the tax regime for a moment. The fact that spread-betting on derivatives is rife in London but not available in the USA to the same extent has much to do with the fact that winnings are free of tax in the UK. Spread-betting firms only incur tax liabilities as bookmakers, but these are modest and absorbed into the spread between prices at which such firms buy and sell contracts. As a result, large numbers of UK residents can now use their screens, key-pads and mobile phones to enter almost instantaneously into inexpensive derivatives contracts on literally thousands of global assets, something not currently equivalently available to US residents. The point about these differences is not that they simply provide a passive 'context' into which a globally uniform derivative trading is inserted, but they are thoroughly implicated in those trading regimes themselves, helping to construct and shape their particular and unique local characteristics.

In the UK case, this has helped to 'lock in' a very wide variety of actors who now think of 'financial engineering' as an ordinary part of their everyday way of life. And, indeed, these attitudes are much wider in their significance, since they are part of a very deep trend in the UK to push welfare, pension and insurance matters away from public provision and into the personal sector. We must *all* 'learn' how to manage our financial portfolios in similar ways to this so as to secure a decent return for our future wellbeing. This is a genuinely radical 'turn' in the UK, one much further 'advanced' than elsewhere in Europe, for instance – indeed, one which is likely to continue to be rather specific to the UK in its characteristics and forms despite 'globalization'.

## The Basel II Accord

Let us now take another area of the financial system where the 'global' is rather less developed than it might appear to be, or is often thought to be. The Basel II process of establishing capital adequacy ratios for international banking business (which replaces the 1992 Basel I Accord; Thompson 2005) is a prime example of the attempted formation of a truly global standard. The emphasis of Basel II is on risk assessment and the provision of risk-adjusted capital adequacy norms, something relatively neglected by Basel I (which had the effect of encouraging investment in risky assets because these provided the highest returns – risky 'regulatory capital' was stimulated at the expense of solid 'economic capital').

But the Basel II Accord is problematic for a number of reasons, despite the faith invested in it by conventional economic opinion in terms of regulating (and thereby 'controlling') the prospect of future disruption in the global financial system (e.g. Bernanke 2004; Cornford 2005; Guttman 2006). The accord is both complicated and complex at the same time as it is weak, 'loose' and partially discretionary. Indeed, these two features go hand in hand. They are characteristic of many attempts at 'global standard-setting' (Thompson 2005). The difficulty is that the establishment of any standard at a global level requires the negotiation and agreement between often a hundred plus players. To get agreement requires many compromises and special provisions, excusals and 'derogations' (so as not to seem unfair and to cater for very diverse situations, levels of financial sophistication, sectional interests, etc.), which has the effect of complicating the final outcome. The final Basel II Accord was delayed many times as a result of this and took much longer than anticipated to be agreed. At the same time, this means that the final outcome is usually far from comprehensive and 'watertight': there are always loosely defined and policed provisions and opportunities for circumvention. This is precisely what happened in the case of Basel II (Wray 2006). And each national jurisdiction will have the task of implementing the accord in its own particular way. Indeed, the USA has more or less ignored its provisions: it has delayed its imposition until after 2009 (with a three-year transition period beginning then), and only between ten and fifteen banks will be affected (those with total assets over US$250 billion). The USA has almost taken a completely 'unilateralist' position.

Then there is a question of whether banking risk is the main source of global financial instability anyway. Smaller non-bank financial institutions, such as mortgage providers, pension funds and hedge funds, are just as likely to be the sources of instability as are big international banks, but these are not included in Basel II. Also, Basel II requires credit rating agencies to establish much of the risk profile for banks, but coverage of these is thin other than in the financially developed countries. In addition, all this prudent provision can be quickly and dramatically overwhelmed by macroeconomic developments beyond the direct control of the banking sector (as happened in the 1982–7 LDC debt crisis and the 1998–9 'Asian Tigers' financial crisis – this latter was triggered by insufficient international reserves held by nations operating with exchange-rate pegs).

Thus strictly speaking, while at one level Basel II is 'global' and a uniform 'standard', its actual applicability is far from comprehensive and its provisions are there to be adopted or virtually ignored. This is not an argument against attempts to establish prudential regulation in this area, merely one that questions whether it can be successful if it always insists on claiming a global reach and applicability. As suggested in a moment, there may be a case for less ambitious, 'subglobal' initiatives, requiring agreement between fewer players and forged at a supranational regional level, and ones which chime better with the *de facto* manner in which the international financial system is actually evolving.

## An international bankruptcy court?

Another example of the difficulty of getting truly new global standards up and running concerns the case of the 'global sovereign debt bankruptcy court'. In 2001 Anne Krueger, first deputy managing director of the IMF, suggested a new initiative to deal with sovereign financial crises (Krueger 2002). She argued for the establishment of a form of 'international bank-ruptcy court' that would act as a sovereign debt restructuring mechanism (SDRM). Major financial crises during the 1990s and early 2000s in Mexico, East Asia, Russia, Turkey, Argentina and elsewhere raised the issue of IMF 'bailouts' and the role of the private sector. What should be done to improve the international financial architecture, in part to prevent such crises reoc-curring but also to deal with them equitably should they arise again? Krueger and the IMF proposed to amend the IMF's Articles of Agreement – in the wake of a new international treaty – so as to facilitate a quasi-juridical process of debt reorganization based upon US-style bankruptcy court proceedings, but now operating internationally for sovereign debt (White 2002). Here is a case, then, of another attempt to establish a new international standard for global governance. In fact, strictly speaking, the IMF's proposal was not for a full-blown bankruptcy court but for a 'mecha-nism' akin to one to enable the easier and more timely resolution of common action problems. It was left to the NGO Jubilee 2000 actually to propose such a genuine court, which would have been far more ambitious in its intent than the one suggested by the IMF; see Jubilee Plus 2002.

The backdrop to these proposals involves a number of developments that characterized the international financial system throughout the 1990s and early 2000s. First was a move away from syndicated loans as the mecha-nism for financing country debt – which involved just a few commercial banks – to financing loans via the issue of bonds that can be traded, and which involved many more participants as a result. Second, there are the traditional differences between such bonds issued in the USA (and Germany) and those issued in the UK (as of the end of 2001, 70 per cent of bonds had been issued in the first two countries and 25 per cent in the UK; Eichengreen 2003, p. 85, table 2). For historical reasons US/German bonds were traditionally issued without 'collective action clauses', whereas those issued in the UK contained such clauses. Disputes in respect to actions over default are carried out under the jurisdiction of the issuing country. The absence of collective action clauses made it much more diffi-cult to arrange a collective response among bond-holders on default than when such clauses are part of the contract. Given the preponderance of American bonds, this has meant in practice that the bond-holders had an incentive to let the IMF arrange a bailout, thereby fully protecting those private bond-holder interests. This goes very much against the move in sentiment among supranational governance bodies to press for more equitable 'private sector burden sharing/bailing *in* of the private sector' so that private sector agents incur some losses as well as public organizations in times of default.

However, there has been no introduction of SDRM along the lines suggested by Krueger and the IMF. Several points can be made about the reasons for this. First, it has been difficult to get agreement to launch a new round of multilateral discussions to amend the IMF's Articles of Agreement. Indeed, this has been ruled out (Eichengreen 2003, p. 89). This supports the points made above about 'global' initiatives to launch new governance initiatives being hard to come by. Second, the IMF's approach – while designed to reduce the commitment of more public funds to bailouts – really spoke to an old agenda of a macro-, public sector focus of a 'court-led' approach. The main alternative to the IMF's suggestion was to encourage a 'market-led' creditor-centred solution provided by the collective action clauses found in English law and UK bonds. Such a contractual approach is 'IMF-light' and essentially non-statutory and 'voluntary' in form, placing the burden on the private sector to reform itself and seek its own self-surveillance through assessments of 'investment graded' status of bonds provided by credit agencies such as Moody's and Standard and Poor. But, as it stands, the EU has moved towards creating a common framework for the adoption of collective action agreements in bonds issued within Europe, while the US government failed to support the SDRM and confined the seeking of a solution to 'further study'. More recently, however, the 'problem' of sovereign debt restructuring has receded as the number of countries getting into difficulties declined rapidly. In addition, private sector initiatives arose among the major bond issuers and holders to reform their own house (Institute of International Finance 2006) as Wall Street moved onto the collective clause feature of bond issue, and these are gradually being introduced into the US financial system.

The purpose of the discussion in this section has merely been to establish that there are good reasons to believe that the 'global' financial system is not as developed as often thought, even in those areas where global conditions of operation seem obvious. This has been demonstrated for both the course of *de facto* economic activity and attempts at *de jure* governance. The space for local and national initiatives remains, as well as for supranational regional ones. Indeed, in the case of East Asia after the crisis of 1997, Walter (2008) found that several of the countries involved there (Indonesia, Malaysia, South Korea and Thailand), while intensely pressured by the international authorities to transform their domestic financial governance, actually engaged in only 'mock' compliance. The more enduring aspects of East Asian capitalism – family ownership, networks of cross-holdings of stocks and shares, heavy government support – militated against substantive compliance. The lack of support for radical change from local institutions, domestic politicians and firms made lasting change difficult to achieve, so things have carried on much as before.

## Pressures and reactions

Another reason for this renewed emphasis on local and regional solutions has to do with the reactions of countries when faced with the difficulties of macroeconomic management in the wake of the advent of floating exchange rates and the elimination of capital controls (the latter initially among the advanced capitalist countries but increasingly by the emerging economies as well). This creates huge new uncertainties and risks manifest in banking crises and foreign-exchange crises (de la Torre et al. 2002). Cross-border payment and transfer become less reliable because the value of a payment or transfer may vary as exchange rates vary. Money, therefore, varies in effectiveness. At one extreme, the money that is used in poorer, less developed and emergent market economies is subject to greater risk of fluctuating value because governments there find it difficult to keep their currencies convertible in a stable way against currencies issued by other governments and central banks – inflation and deflation are endemic in these countries. At the other extreme, the money of the most financially advanced countries is more or less stable in value and fluctuations are less rapid and severe. And because there is a more or less permanent demand for such currencies abroad, it is easier to keep them convertible against other currencies. The demand for the currencies of the financially sophisticated countries arises not just because they are rich and powerful but also because they have well-developed financial markets, which are deep and liquid, and in which can be traded a wide variety of financial assets. Their 'internal' domestic liquidity and convertibility makes them 'externally' internationally desirable. In the face of these developments there have been several reactions.

### Financial development in the image of 'sophisticated' financial markets

The first is for the emergent economies to try to develop financial markets in the image of those of the advanced countries. Some governments of small, usually politically stable countries manage to keep stable currencies because they in effect offer discrete, less regulated banking facilities for residents of neighbouring countries who can evade financial regulations by keeping their money in such 'offshore' financial centres. Countries such as Switzerland, Singapore and Hong Kong benefit from such a partially 'parasitic' relationship with the wealth and regulation of neighbouring countries. However, for the majority of poorer countries these options of 'offshorization' or mirroring the advanced financial systems are almost impossible to achieve, but their attempts to move down these routes (or the pressures put upon them to do so) just increase the risks and uncertainties of the international financial system further – more exchange-rate and banking crises – leading to the greater perceived need for 'global standards' to be introduced to regulate them.

## Monetary unions

A second reaction is to form a genuine 'monetary union' similar to that of the EU. This establishes a monetary unit that can be used both domestically and abroad. In January 2002 twelve members of the EU adopted a single currency (though it should be remembered that, in Europe as a whole in 2007, there had been a *net increase* of ten currencies since 1989, accounted for by the growth of new currencies in South Central and Eastern Europe). Given that the vast bulk of international economic transactions are conducted within the Union, the external use of its currency can be minimal for its residents. But this also offers the potential for concentrating financial activities in centres which can offer the range of financial assets that would create a permanent demand for its currency in international financial markets (de Ménil 1999). In addition to the EU, there are various other regional initiatives under way, or partially under way, which could result in more regionalized financial systems and monetary units. The Gulf Cooperation Council countries, for instance, have resolved to introduce a common currency by 2010 (though this deadline looks to be slipping). In addition, the Japanese floated the idea of an Asian IMF to manage the balance of payments problems of the East Asian economies. This first faltered in the face of US and Chinese opposition, but since the East Asian financial crisis of 1997–8 China has warmed to the idea, so it could be resurrected (Davies 2001, Kondo 2000 and Kuroda 2001). This was followed up by the Chiang Mai Initiative in 2000, when fourteen East Asian countries agreed to begin a process of financial support and eventual integration. To begin with, this involved currency swaps, multilateral monitoring of short-term capital movements, and bond market developments. Indeed, the current active development of an East Asian bond market represents a further indicator of a regional response, since this would allow those economies eventually to borrow in their own currencies rather than in US dollars (McCauley et al. 2002). Similarly, the Mercosur countries of Brazil, Argentina, Paraguay and Uruguay – recently joined by Venezuela – have promoted their own economic integration and the possible development of a common currency (Duina 2006; Iapadre 2004). Indeed, the prospect of borrowing from oil-rich Venezuela by the other members of Mercosur has been noted. Arguments involving similar developments in West Africa are also current (Siddiqi 2000). Indeed, sub-Saharan West Africa already has a monetary union in place – the African Financial Community (AFC) – based upon former French colonial zones (Fielding and Shields 2003). The AFC is made up of two sub-units: the West African Economic and Monetary

Union (WAEMU) and the Customs and Economic Union of Central African States (CEUCAS), both of which have a single currency and a single central bank. Their currencies are linked to the Euro. There are institutional moves to merge these, and for the regional Anglophone countries to join a newly created wider monetary and economic union (ibid.). Further, in the southern Pacific area, financial and economic integration has been suggested, organized around the Australian dollar or a new currency (de Brouwer 2000; Drew et al. 2001; Forbes 2003). Finally, the possibility of a common currency for the NAFTA countries (USA, Canada and Mexico) has also been broached, perhaps eventually to be extended to include other FTAA countries (Courchene and Harris 1999; Robson and Laidler 2002). Here, however, Canadian objections might prove impossible to overcome (Helleiner 2006). But despite this there is a growing confidence among a number of regional trading and investment groupings like these, where new institutional initiatives for governance are being floated and common regionalized standards promoted.

### Promote various forms of 'dollarization'

A third option is to go for a kind of intermediate position between the previous two, that is, to opt for various forms of 'dollarization'. This is a generic term used to describe any substitution of the domestic monetary unit for an international one, most often in the form of the exclusive use of a foreign currency as the domestic monetary unit. And there is a slightly weaker variation of this theme that establishes a 'strong currency board' for the issuance of domestic money (but we leave this out of explicit account for convenience here). In 2006 there were 189 independent countries recognized by the UN, but only about 120 different currencies operate. Many countries share a currency, and some have done so for a very long time, but in the more recent period there have been a number of countries that have experimented with abandoning their own currency in favour of the US dollar, mainly in Latin America. What are the effects of these policies on trade?

Andrew Rose (Rose 2000; Rose and van Wincoop 2001) has analysed this at length and argues that there are very large welfare gains to be made by adopting common currencies, as those countries that have done so trade with each other to a much greater extent than do those with their own currency, and this leads to positive welfare benefits. The beneficial effects have to do with the macroeconomic discipline and stability that 'dollarization' is supposed to instil in (mainly) small and wayward countries. However, as Edwards (2001; Edwards and Magenzdo 2003) has argued, on close scrutiny there is little evidence that the suggested welfare and growth benefits have actually materialized (though inflation has been lower), and he remains highly sceptical of such policy initiatives (see also Levy Yeyati 2005, 2006; and below). The case of Argentina should reinforce this very cautious attitude towards currency boards and talk of full dollarization. As the US dollar appreciated in value in the later 1990s, the Argentine peso also appreciated in value because it was linked to it via a currency board. This made Argentine exports increasingly internationally uncompetitive independently of what was actually going on in Argentina itself, which was one of the reasons undermining the stability of the Argentine economy (subsequently, Argentina abandoned its currency board). So there is dispute over the evidence about the effects of higher trade, and there is some counter-evidence to the idea that common currencies have actually led to greater trade (Persson 2001; Rose 2001).

### A single 'global' currency

However, there is a final reaction to the difficulties outlined above which is an extension to the logic of dollarization, and that is to go for a single global currency (e.g. Alesina and Barro 2001; Dornbusch 2001; Rogoff 2001). Detailed analysis of this response is not possible, but it suffers from the same basic objections as those made about dollarization just outlined. It certainly eliminates several policy variables that might be thought still to give countries some autonomy in economic policy-making, namely those associated with monetary and exchange-rate policies. In addition, there seems almost a zero possibility that this would become politically acceptable in the near future, whereas the other reactions discussed above are genuine trends. Moving away from a *de facto* trend adoption of the US dollar as the global currency is difficult, however. US dollarization may be happening by stealth, largely at the behest of the private sector. Reinhart et al. (2003) found that only twenty of the eighty-four emerging economy countries they included as dollarizers over the 1980s and 1990s had successfully resisted or reversed the domestic dollarization of their economies, though the level of dollarization is low in many of the others. And there was a group of developing countries (about a third of the total) where there was little sign of any dollarization.

Of course there are several forms of dollarization. Figure 6.7 shows the extent of *deposit* dollarization at the global level. Deposit dollarization (in this case actual dollarization – US dollars, as a percentage of total deposits) denotes the extent of financial liabilities denominated in US dollars in any financial system, so it is an 'asset'-based measure. Other measures could involve currency substitution, which is the traditional way dollarization has been understood and is largely the one discussed by the authors referred to above, or one involving an emphasis just on official reserves and their composition. Sticking to deposit dollarization for the moment (Levy Yeyati 2005, 2006), table 6.9 shows the changes in this between 1999 and 2004 expressed as a percentage of total deposits for several country groupings.

Note that there were signs of the *reduction* in the importance of this measure in Europe and Asia, and not a great deal of growth in the other

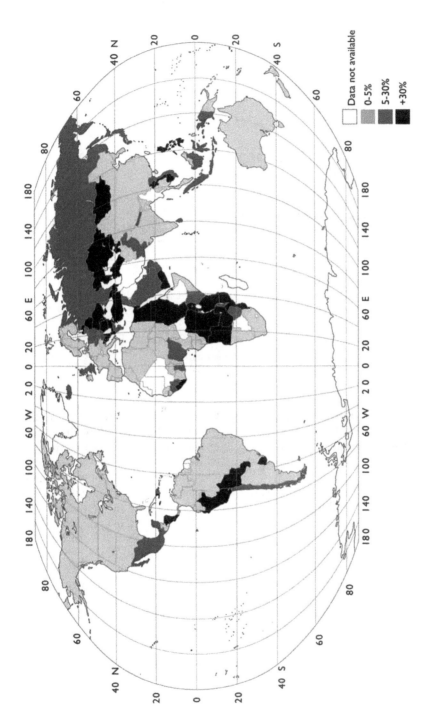

**Figure 6.7** The extent of 'global' deposit dollarization
*Source:* Levy Yeyati 2005, p. 31.

Data not available

0–5%

5–30%

+30%

**Table 6.9**   Deposit dollarization over time, 1999–2004 (percentage of total deposits)

|  |  | Latin America | Europe | Asia | Africa & Oceania |
|---|---|---|---|---|---|
| 1999 |  |  |  |  |  |
|  | Mean | 29.3 | 41.4 | 34.7 | 23.3 |
|  | *Meridian* | *20.9* | *43.7* | *26.5* | *16.9* |
| 2004 |  |  |  |  |  |
|  | Mean | 30.8 | 38.4 | 32.8 | 26.0 |
|  | *Meridian* | *27.3* | *38.0* | *29.5* | *20.1* |

*Source*: Adapted from Levy Yeyati 2005, p. 25, table 1.

**Table 6.10**   Non-industrialized countries' dollar deposit liabilities (mean) as a percentage of GDP, 1995 and 2000

|  | *1995* | *2000* |
|---|---|---|
| Full sample (59) | 54.6 | 62.8 |
| Emerging economies (17) | 43.0 | 48.2 |
| Non-emerging economies (42) | 59.3 | 68.2 |
| Latin America (18) | 51.8 | 63.0 |
| Transitional economies (19) | 28.4 | 42.9 |

*Note*: Number of observations in parentheses.
*Source*: Calculated from Levy Yeyati 2006, p. 73, table 2.

areas. In Europe there was an initial growth in the late 1990s, as the Eastern European economies converted to capitalism and formalized much of their previously informal holding to US dollars. But this gave way to Euroization after 1999 (Levy Yeyati 2006) as they diversified their portfolios into Euro assets. Thus in both Europe and Asia (where we might presume that East Asia is the most important part) there are signs of a supranational regional move away from dollarization strictly speaking. And normatively Levy Yeyati recommends this as a policy, since the presumed macroeconomic benefits of dollarization have yet to emerge, he suggests. As can be seen from table 6.10, however, deposit dollarization expressed as a percentage of GDP has increased in the non-industrialized subsection of countries, confirming the difficulty for these countries in developing their own 'autonomous' national financial systems independent of dollar dependency.

It is also important to recognize that the call for a single global currency is not a new phenomenon. In the previous period of globalization, during the second half of the nineteenth century, there was feverish discussion about the possibility of inaugurating a single 'global' currency between the developing economies of the time, originally based upon the Latin Monetary Union of 1865 (Einaudi 2001). There was a conference in Berlin in 1863, though the debate began in earnest as Napoleon III called an international monetary conference in 1867. But the vision of the 1860s was never realized (Bordo and James 2006), as the proposals foundered upon incompatible political differences as to exchange-rate conversion procedures and administrative means to 'manage' monetary policy and banking activity. The lesson of this episode should not be lost on the current debate, however. It demonstrates that money always involves matters of sovereignty – indeed, political issues are at the core of both the creation and the operation of money (Knapp 1924; Keynes 1930; Goodhart 1998; Ingham 2004, 2006). Without developing a long history or analysis, the definition, the creation, and the operation of money require a political authority for its issue and to provide for its credibility. The implications of this are that there is a need for a 'big government' with a 'strong central bank', and clear 'lender of last resort' facilities, to manage the financial cycle by constraining the boom and softening the slump. This is as necessary in an international setting as it is in a national one. Without all of these conditions, money and finance will not operate 'efficiently', let alone optimally.

And this serves to raise a very important point about the future of financial globalization and the consequences for the global financial standard-setting debate discussed above. The consequence of the remarks just made is to suggest that full economic globalization is impossible without such a single global currency, and given that such a single currency is most unlikely (indeed, we would suggest politically impossible), then there will be no full 'global' financial internationalization.

The basic argument in this respect is that, in the absence of a single global currency and a single global central bank, the introduction of global banking and creditworthiness standards are both *necessary but impossible* under a regime of financial liberalization and floating exchange rates. This is one of the great paradoxes of the international economic system. Without a single global currency and central bank the full globalization of the international financial system is impossible. While there are different currencies, not all of which are used either as international transaction currencies or as the standard of prices and asset values, uncertainty rules in financial markets, which necessitates the introduction of various creditworthiness standards (Schulmeister 2000; Basu 2002). However, these standards are inherently unstable, given the need for the less developed and emergent market countries (the vast bulk, in fact) to earn foreign currency and finance their commercial activity through the issuance of assets not denominated in their own currencies. As we have seen above, this opens up a necessary structural 'fracture' or 'separation' (a) between the 'domestic' and the 'international' financial systems of countries and (b) between those able to finance their activity in their own currency and those who cannot.

Such an inherent instability means that there are great pressures to opt for some kind of regional response. This provides for the big government, strong central bank and lender of last resort facility so necessary for some form of financial stability. The EU is the current 'home' for such a response, and not just in the case of monetary developments. This is not the place to discuss the enormous range of standard-setting initiatives being promulgated from within the EU. These not only affect intra-EU economic and other activity, but are having important effects on the wider international standard-setting environment. In many respects the EU is the main active player in developing 'international' standards, as the USA remains reluctant to initiate or participate in any standard-setting processes that do not meet its own narrow interests and advantage, and East Asia is still in the early days of forging common rules and norms. However, as has been argued above at various levels, more and more financial standard-setting looks to be becoming 'subglobal' in character even as current trends are not unambiguous.

## Conclusions

This chapter has made a number of arguments. The first is to recognize the continued robustness of national financial systems. The particular institutional arrangements associated with national economies have not all been swept aside by the forces of globalization, though they are under pressure from many quarters. The consequences of this for global measures is that these continually rub up against the domestic environment, and the resultant outcome is not necessarily one that favours an external imposition over an internal accommodation and transformation. A process of slow adaptation and accommodation takes place.

Secondly, there is increasing difficulty in getting truly multilateral and global standard-setting processes up and running. This is itself associated with the third issue, which is that the trend in the international economy, including the financial economy, is moving in a *de facto* sense towards the formation of supranational regional trading and financial blocs ('regionalization') and not necessarily towards ever more intense globalization.

However, the *political obstacles* to the formation of supranational regional blocs should also not be underestimated ('regionalism'). Although this is less a problem in the EU case, even here the system is under intense pressure. Whether the current political tensions among the East Asian countries that might form a financially united bloc (the possible ASEAN + 3 + 3 process) can be overcome, despite the economic advantages that might arise from this, remains to be seen. In several important books and articles, Christopher Dent has drawn attention to the complex FTA inter-relationships both within East Asia and across the Pacific (e.g. Dent 2005, 2006 and 2008). He describes this as 'lattice regionalism', with many cross-cutting alliances and sometimes awkward juxtapositions that are difficult to weave together. Richard Baldwin describes a similar process, which he terms 'noodle bowl regionalism' (Baldwin 2006). And a similar cautious attitude should be adopted in the case of the Free Trade Area of the Americas (FTAA) (Robson and Laidler 2002; Schott 2005; Helleiner 2006). On the other hand, the sheer force of *de facto* regionalization is difficult to deny totally, and this will produce its own pressures for an integrative political solution.

Thus finally, perhaps the best way to sum all this up is to view the contemporary conjuncture in the international economic system as one *poised between* 'globalization' and supranational 'regionalization'. If this is the case, the precise outcome in respect to the future shape of the international financial system still remains difficult to predict precisely. However, the burden of the analysis presented here is to suggest that the emergence of a supranational regional process of macro-level economic organization could be just as possible as the continuation of one centred on the global arena.

Finally, are these twin processes – supranational regionalism/regionalization and globalism/globalization – compatible or at odds with one another? Are they complementary or competitive? This remains a genuinely hard question, and it is one that at this stage is difficult to answer. We will have to see. But, from our perspective, this is not the key question. As just suggested, our primary concern in this chapter was to challenge the generally accepted notion that there is no difference between these two basic processes. We want to draw a sharper conceptual line between them, and to back this up with empirical evidence. As a result of this analysis, however, we would stress that, under current conditions, the supranational regionalism/regionalization process looks to be more robust and convincing than full globalism/globalization.

# 7

# General Governance Issues

## Introduction

This chapter aims to assess the role of the inherited framework of international or global economic governance conducted by and through national states for the future evolution of the world economy. That inheritance comprises three main elements:

1 governance through a substantial number of states operating in international, multilateral regulatory agencies designed for a specific dimension of activity, such as the WTO for trade and, increasingly, FDI; the IMF for financial and monetary matters; the World Bank for development policy; and the various bodies under the UN umbrella for issues to do with such things as labour standards (the ILO) or the environment.
2 the governance of large economic areas by regional trade and investment blocs such as the EU and NAFTA, blocs that are large enough to pursue social and other agendas in a way that many medium-sized states may be unable to do on an independent basis. These blocs – at least in the case of the EU – share sufficient common ground to elaborate forms of governance beyond the nation-state so as to make limited delegation and even pooling of national sovereignty possible in certain spheres of decision-making.
3 governance through agreement between the major political entities that represent the dominant shares of world trade, investment and monetary power – until recently the G3 of the United States, Japan and the Euro area, but now including also China (as the leading Asian surplus country) and Saudi Arabia (as the dominant oil producer) – to manage global

imbalances, to stabilize exchange-rate movements, to defuse protectionist pressures and to regulate destabilizing short-term financial
transactions.

Clearly, these elements of international economic governance overlap
and interlock with one another, and all have nation-states as their principal
political units (we return to the political and geopolitical roles of the state
in a globalizing economy in chapter 8), and many issues are addressed
through all three. For example, global monetary imbalances (discussed
below) have been addressed through discussions between the major political entities concerned, including the Euro area (a regional bloc), conducted
under the auspices of the surveillance mechanism of the IMF (a multilateral
agency). Still, for the purposes of clarity we consider them somewhat separately in what follows.

## The multilateral institutions

The core of the multilateral arrangements – namely, the Bretton Woods
trio (the IMF, the WTO and the World Bank) and the Bank for International Settlements (BIS) – have expanded to cover an ever growing number
of states and proportion of international economic activity. Thus, what
started as a set of essentially North Atlantic arrangements for post-war
reconstruction and capitalist unity in the Cold War have become genuinely
global in scope. In the course of these developments, the picture has become
more and more complex, with regional agreements playing an increasingly
important role, indeed often having provisions going further than those of
the major multilateral institutions. On the whole, however, the overall
pattern remains consistent with the broadly, if selectively applied, liberal
principles underpinning the Bretton Woods institutions. Indeed, the two
central institutions – the WTO and the IMF – increasingly set the base-line
terms for other regional arrangements, such that open regionalism has (thus
far) been the norm.

As the scope and domain of this system has expanded, so also has the
content of the governance conducted under these auspices changed. There
have been a variety of reasons for this. Firstly, governments have privatized,
liberalized and marketized a range of sectors and activities that were previously state-owned, protected and provided on a non-profit basis. This has
been described as the rise of neo-liberalism. Secondly, with the reduction
in tariffs on most manufactured goods to very low levels, further integration
of trade, especially in services, has required liberalization of the regulation
of cross-border financial flows and investment. The shallow integration
concerned with barriers to trade 'at the border' has given way to the need

for 'deep' integration that seeks to harmonize so-called behind-the-border regulations, that is, those that apply to economic activity within the economic territory concerned (see chapter 4 above). And thirdly, issues have arisen that are of collective concern to many states but which cannot be managed adequately by each state acting independently. In these circumstances, there is an incentive for states to cooperate even as they compete over the terms of that.

## A constitution for the world economy?

The first director-general of the WTO, Renato Ruggiero, spoke of it as providing a 'constitution' for the international economy, and many critics of the WTO (and the IMF and World Bank) bemoan what they see as an illegitimate encroachment on the national sovereignty of particularly the weaker and poorer developing countries. Now, the principal legal personalities in international law – that is, the agents that have legal standing and to whom the rights and obligations of that law apply – are sovereign states, such that international law and the organizations created under it serve as a 'system of rights, rules, and relationships designed to bring order into the interactions of sovereign authorities' (Young 1997, p. 7). And international *economic* law is part of the law among states, and as such one of its central principles is that of the state's economic sovereignty.[1] So although the agents that trade and invest in the international economy are, for the most part, privately owned and controlled firms operating in a market context, the rules of the WTO, for example, apply to its member *states*, for WTO rules are one important part of international economic law, and 'the Appellate Body [of the WTO] explicitly states that the WTO is part of international law' (Jackson 1998, p. 89).

However, it is nonetheless true that the purpose of international economic law is not solely or even primarily to regulate interaction between *states*, but also to facilitate and regulate the 'private' interactions of market agents and processes across national borders.[2] That is to say, its *content* covers broadly the interstate regulation of the establishment of economic activity by nationals of one state in another and of cross-border transactions in goods, services and capital. Thus whereas public international law in general 'is based on the State and the notion of sovereignty', some have argued that the core principle of international economic law:

> is based on the dictates of comparative advantage, on promoting individual cross-border exchanges and specialisation.... Accordingly, [international

economic law] (particularly International Trade Law) is defined as being concerned with those State measures that are taken at the border, or internally, that inhibit the operation of the comparative advantage (specialisation and voluntary exchange) to function effectively. International economic law is concerned with eliminating cross-border impediments. (Qureshi 1999, pp. 9–10)

This 'comparative advantage model' of international economic law certainly captures important aspects of reality. But it has not gone unchallenged. While it is undoubtedly the case that international economic law can be seen as the legal regulation of a liberal international economic order, its principal subjects and objects are states, notwithstanding the increasing legal – but still derivative – standing of international economic organizations and private agents under this law. States still retain economic sovereignty under international economic law (they are free to decide the use of their permanent resources, to choose both their economic system and how they engage with the international economy), and they are constitutionally independent and equal before the law (implying equal treatment under similar conditions). This is merely the economic parallel of their more general sovereignty under public international law.

At the same time, however, states have certain duties under international economic law to the wider international economy. So, in practice, states tend to exercise these sovereign rights collectively and reciprocally. To be sure, many states have exercised complete national autonomy over some highly limited areas of policy, but the unilateral exercise of autonomy, without regard to the actions of other states and making no attempt to coordinate and cooperate in areas of mutual benefit, is not a serious principle for the conduct of international economic governance. Put bluntly, complete national autonomy and an international economy cannot coexist. The only states that have ever taken the former idea at all seriously have either disengaged from the world economy to a considerable extent or been sufficiently powerful to impose their national decisions on their economic 'partners' via 'imperial' or 'hegemonic' harmonization. The first of these options has resulted in long-run economic stagnation and the second is less and less feasible as economic power diffuses across the system of states.

Rather, states generally retain their sovereign rights to national decision-making but choose to exercise these in common with other states, seeking reciprocal action on the basis of national treatment, mutual recognition, common standards, monitored decentralization and intergovernmental coordination (see box 7.1). In the case of the European Union, of course, this process has gone even further, to include the pooling or sharing of sovereignty in some areas.

---

**Box 7.1   Types of international economic governance**

*National treatment* is where states reciprocally open their economies to trade and investment with foreigners, but once foreign goods and services have crossed the border they are treated no less favourably than goods and services originating in the 'host' country. Rules and policies in different 'host' countries may differ and therefore there will be market competition among different national economies. *Mutual recognition*, involving agreement between two or more states on a bilateral, regional or multilateral basis, obtains where foreign standards are recognized alongside national standards and allows market competition to guide the economic process. *Common standards*, adopted on a bilateral, regional or multilateral basis, operate where states mutually agree to adopt the same set of rules and policies as each other and to implement and enforce these in their respective national jurisdictions. *Monitored decentralization* exists where states enter into macroeconomic policy undertakings with one another but are nationally responsible for the implementation of policy, subject to joint surveillance by a collective body. *Intergovernmental coordination* involves jointly designed mutual adjustments of national macroeconomic policies but still with national implementation, subject to joint surveillance by a collective body. *Quasi-federal shared, or pooled, sovereignty* involves continuous, regular bargaining and joint, centralized decision-making within a common legal order.

---

In posing the question 'How far will international economic integration go?', Dani Rodrik noted that there is a series of political dilemmas associated with national sovereignty in regard to economic policy-making, the international integration of national economies through trade and investment, and the ability of countries to choose between meaningful alternatives in the field of economic policy. What Rodrik calls the 'Bretton Woods compromise' sought to balance a degree of economic sovereignty, allowing for meaningful choices of economic policy at the national level, against a commitment to remove at-the-border barriers to trade and non-discriminatory treatment of foreign goods and services: 'The essence of the Bretton Woods–GATT regime was that countries were free to dance to their own tune as long as they removed a number of border restrictions to trade and generally did not discriminate among their trade partners' (Rodrik 2000, p. 183). This regime has also been called 'embedded liberalism' or 'shallow integration'. Under these arrangements, collective and reciprocal cooperation is intended to facilitate the competition between different national economies with their own distinctive patterns of public policy.

Clearly, the contemporary international trade agenda under the WTO has now moved well beyond its original, limited GATT framework, and the re-emergence of private international finance has undermined the effectiveness of many national controls over capital flows. Both of these developments have contributed to a more market-oriented, some would say neo-liberal, definition of international economic governance. In these circumstances, Rodrik contends that the 'price of maintaining national jurisdictional sovereignty is that politics have to be exercised over a much narrower domain' (2000, p. 182). Thomas Friedman (1999) has called this the 'golden straitjacket' because it involves constraining national policy choices within a range that is acceptable to international or global market forces. It embraces integrated international markets and national sovereignty at the price of forfeiting meaningful autonomy. If this trend were to continue, the content of international economic law would indeed increasingly come to resemble the 'comparative advantage' model.

But both in Europe and elsewhere there has been considerable concern that the agendas of the WTO and the IMF have represented a United States-inspired version of the golden straitjacket. In this scenario, states would remain formally sovereign, but their scope for meaningful choices over economic policy, the degree of national autonomy in policy-making, would be limited by ever wider and deeper international economic integration conducted under neo-liberal rules overseen by multilateral institutions. (At the same time, many critics allege, the USA selectively exempts itself from these pressures.) In part, the development of economic governance *within* the EU can be understood as an attempt to escape this golden straitjacket by resort to confederal agreements between governments, not on a global, but on a *regional* basis. For, within the economic space of the EU, economic governance has gone far beyond non-discriminatory national treatment to embrace mutual recognition and common standards and policies, organized under a confederal political and legal order. Moreover, despite the free market orientation of the single market, EU governance also serves wider social objectives relating to limited welfare and environmental concerns. The content of European economic law therefore bears the imprint of state interests as well as the dictates of comparative advantage.

Extending this kind of logic to the global level is one of the future scenarios envisaged by Rodrik – global federalism: 'Under global federalism, politics need not, and would not shrink: it would relocate to the global level' (2000, p. 183). In this scenario, states would give up national sovereignty in order to re-regulate the international economy at a higher level; autonomy in the field of policy-making would be re-established at the price of having to formulate and implement such regulations collectively with other states. Could the WTO and the IMF become the vehicles for such a development and, if so, what kinds of principles would organize decision-making? (Collectively, the member states of the EU have the largest single voice in both the IMF and the WTO.) Or does the experience of the EU demonstrate that the regional level is a more appropriate site for substantive decision-making? The trends towards supranational regionalization and the recent stresses of the multilateral institutions strongly suggest that global federalism is as distant as ever.

## Regional trade and investment blocs: the European Union and NAFTA

To the extent that it governs a liberal economic order among its member states, the EU represents a very peculiar form of political and economic organization on the international stage. So how does the EU fit into the pattern of international economic governance provided by the wider framework set by the Bretton Woods institutions? The formation of the EEC coincided more or less with the final moves towards currency convertibility among the major trading economies, at a time when conditions were ripe for a significant liberalization of world trade. Post-war reconstruction was largely completed and stable, and non-inflationary growth seemed to have been established. The major economies of Western Europe (and Japan) now had the capacity to earn sufficient US dollars on export markets to feel confident that currency and trade liberalization would advance their interests. The United States had encouraged European integration from the outset of post-war reconstruction, making Marshall Plan aid conditional on (West) European cooperation, and it looked favourably upon the creation of the EEC.

The Treaty of Rome (1957) aimed to create a customs union (a combination of internal free trade based on the four freedoms of goods, services, capital and people, and a common external tariff) as well as a range of common policies on agriculture, energy, transport and competition, together with limited fiscal transfers for regional development. Moreover, the treaties of Paris and Rome set down the pattern of governance for the EU, a combination of intergovernmental and supranational decision-making under a common legal framework. With the formation of the customs union in the EEC (substantially completed by 1968), the member states no longer had national trade policies. In their place, the Community developed a Common Commercial Policy (CCP), such that the member states acted as one in concluding trade agreements with others, whether bilateral agreements with specific countries or multilateral deals under the auspices of the GATT/WTO.

The CCP is part of the Community pillar of the EU and, as such, responsibility for its conduct is shared among the Commission, the Council of Ministers and the European Parliament. The EU is also able to enter into 'trade and cooperation' agreements, for example the 'partnership' agreements signed with countries of the former Soviet Union, and it is empowered to conclude 'association' agreements, based on Article 310 (Ex. 238), which states that: 'The Community may conclude with one or more states or international organisations agreements establishing an association involving reciprocal rights and obligations, common action and reciprocal procedure.' This partial transfer of competence over commercial policy from the member states to the Community pillar has not been unproblematic, however. There is an obvious tension between the Commission's right of initiative and its role in negotiating on the Community's behalf, on the one side, and the authorization, oversight and sanctioning of this role by the Council of Ministers, on the other.

When the CCP was originally formulated, trade policy was essentially about at-the-border tariffs and national quota restrictions on imports; trade in agriculture was largely excluded from the framework and disciplines of the GATT; there was little policy linkage between trade and investment issues; there was little trade in services; and trade was not generally seen as related to such issues as the protection of the environment or to labour standards and human rights. In short, trade policy was not high on the political agenda, and the further liberalization of trade in manufactured goods seemed to be a fairly straightforward affair, something that member states could safely delegate to the Commission. All of the above has now changed in ways that were not foreseen. Many of the most significant changes to the agenda of international trade negotiations and to the political significance of trade were highlighted by the negotiations of the Uruguay Round of the GATT (1986–94) and the establishment of the WTO in 1995. In fact, as the political salience of trade policy has increased, the member states have been careful to keep control of the new trade issues at an intergovernmental level, rather than ceding control to the more supranational elements of the EU.

### The United States and European economic integration

Almost as soon as the EEC was established, there were concerns that the formation of a customs union might be more trade diverting than trade creating, and that the EEC might abuse its strong position in world markets to rig trade in its favour. In theory, a large trading bloc can use a tariff to limit both its imports and its exports, lowering the price of the former and raising the price of the latter, thereby improving its terms of trade. If the terms of trade effect is larger than the losses that arise from the distortions to production and consumption, an 'optimal tariff' can increase overall welfare inside the bloc at the expense of outsiders. This presumes that trading partners do not retaliate with tariffs of their own, and so an optimal tariff is a potential weapon against small trading partners but not against other large trading blocs. Nevertheless, to forestall the latter eventuality the USA took the lead in pushing for two multilateral rounds of trade negotiations in the GATT, the Dillon Round (1961–2) and the Kennedy

Round (1964–7). Thereafter, tariffs served less and less as barriers to trade in manufactures, and the focus of attention shifted to non-tariff barriers created by behind-the-border measures. These were first addressed on a serious basis in the Tokyo Round of the GATT (1973–9).

Although the USA was concerned about the possibilities of trade protectionism with the formation of the EEC, on balance European integration has represented a major economic opportunity for the US economy rather than a threat. We noted above that the formation of the EEC coincided with the final moves towards the convertibility of European currencies against the dollar. One important result of this was that US MNCs increased their investment in Europe. For the US economy, overseas production by MNCs became a much more important means of penetrating overseas markets than exports. By the early 1970s, when the stock of US foreign investment still accounted for just over one-half of all foreign investment, the value of production by US affiliates abroad was some four times that of US total exports. Where the USA led, Western Europe and Japan followed, as real wages in these areas began to catch up with those in the USA, undermining their export competitiveness, and as European and Japanese firms achieved the necessary scale to contemplate an international presence.

That is to say, at least since the 1970s, the integration of the world economy has been driven as much by foreign investment as it has by trade. Indeed, already by the mid-1980s, the value produced by MNCs outside their domestic markets was greater than the value of world trade, and a significant proportion of world trade (estimates vary from around one-quarter to two-fifths) is closely linked to FDI. The growth of regional integration in the world economy, not only in the EU but also in NAFTA, as well as in various schemes for integration in the Asia-Pacific region (most notably, Asia-Pacific Economic Cooperation, APEC), is 'motivated by the desire to facilitate international investment and the operations of multinational firms as much as the desire to promote trade' (Lawrence 1996, p. 17). Writing in the late 1990s, Gerald Meier noted that: 'The stock of US direct investment in the EU has risen much more than the value of American exports to the EU. Sales of US-owned affiliates within the EU have in recent years amounted to eight to ten times the value of exports from the USA to the EU. Moreover, a third of American exports to Europe already go to US-owned affiliates' (Meier 1998, p. 252). These FDI linkages serve as a counter-balance to any tendencies towards trade rivalry between the major regions of the world economy.

For the United States, then, integration in Europe has given rise to what Gary Hufbauer (1990) called 'Opportunity Europe'. Still, there are many unresolved issues in transatlantic economic integration which relate to both trade and investment. If national and international markets function efficiently, then national treatment combined with free trade maximizes efficiency and accountability, assuming that national policies accurately reflect citizens' preferences. This 'shallow integration', together with the MFN principle, has been an important part of the framework of international governance developed since the end of the Second World War.[3] In particular, it has provided the basis for much of the expansion of trade between different national economies. However, national treatment still erects barriers to international trade (and particularly investment), since it fragments the international economy into distinct national economic spaces defined by a particular framework of rules and policies. Thus even if states agree to remove all their at-the-border restrictions, to adopt completely free trade on an MFN basis, foreign firms still have to adapt to different national rules and policies behind the border in order to do business in another state.

For this reason closer market integration for the exchange of goods, and especially of services, often requires something more than national treatment and open trade. In principle, there are two main ways of moving beyond national treatment: the first and simplest is *mutual recognition*; the second and more demanding is the development of *common standards*. Under mutual recognition, countries agree to trade and invest with one another on the basis that a good or service that can be marketed in one country can be legitimately marketed in another. Each country recognizes the other's rules and standards alongside and as equivalent to its own. This has been the basis of the completion of the internal market within the EU under the Single European Act (1987) that was designed to complete the internal market. In many instances, mutual recognition is an efficient and relatively simple way of deepening market integration. The main advantage of mutual recognition is that governments are spared the task of harmonizing previously discrepant rules and standards. The interaction of firms and consumers in the market then determines the patterns of specialization and trade. By the same token, the disadvantage of mutual recognition is that it presupposes that the states generally trust one another's standards. Where this is not the case, and where states fear that market competition might allow lower standards to drive out higher ones, then they may insist on harmonization around minimum common standards. In so far as the EU has had to develop *new* rules and standards for the single market, say in the area of environmental protection, it has generally adopted the minimum common standards approach. Common standards are particularly appropriate when there are significant externalities associated with the economic activity concerned. When common standards apply, a floor is placed under the market and the impact of regulatory competition between different national frameworks is thereby limited.

Considered in this light, the EU and its trading partners sometimes have a different understanding of 'reciprocity' in trade negotiations. The EU interprets reciprocity to mean *national treatment* plus effective access to foreign markets. But how is 'effective access' to be defined once the principal barriers to trade and investment are no longer at-the-border tariffs but behind-the-border measures? Next, the EU and its major trading partners do not have *common standards* on issues relating to health, safety and the environment, nor do they as yet operate on the basis of *mutual recognition* of each other's standards. That is to say, policy integration between the member states of the EU has gone much further than that between the EU and NAFTA or the EU and Asia. A related question concerns rules of origin and local content. For the purposes of the single market, the EU has defined what is to count as an EU product or service if it is produced by, say, a Japanese MNC operating in Europe. These rules can serve to restrict trade and discriminate between EU and foreign goods and services. And, finally, there is considerable debate on how far public procurement – government spending on goods and services – should be opened to foreign competition, especially given that this activity often has a public service component related to issues of national culture and welfare objectives.

In the industrial sector at least, the EU has not conformed to the naïve predictions of the theory of optimal tariffs. It has certainly pursued protectionist policies in relation to specific industries (for example, cars, steel and textiles) but overall it has pursued trade liberalization for manufactured goods. Moreover, and most importantly, *the provision of the four freedoms in the internal market applies as much and equally to US or Japanese firms (or indeed firms from any developed market economy) as to European business.* As John Grahl says, 'in practice economic conflicts between the US and the EU have been minimal, confined to a few sectoral issues' (2004, p. 285). In the case of agriculture, to be sure, it has been a different story. The Common Agricultural Policy (CAP) has, of course, been the largest single common policy of the EU, and before the Uruguay Round agricultural trade never came under GATT disciplines. In contrast to the EU's generally open engagement with the international trading system, Robert Lawrence says (somewhat diplomatically) that 'evidence of trade diversion is more apparent in agriculture' (1996, p. 59). Indeed, conflict between the USA and the EU over bringing agricultural trade into the GATT/WTO framework nearly sank the Uruguay Round at one point in the negotiations, and the CAP has been a continuing source of irritation to US trade officials and a cause of significant transatlantic trade tensions, as well as a major obstacle to trade liberalizing agreements with developing countries in the abortive Doha Round of negotiations.

In this context, the Uruguay Round of GATT negotiations, which led to the formation of the WTO, were especially important. The upshot of this new trade agenda has been that trade negotiations no longer focus solely or even primarily on at-the-border issues – that is, questions of tariffs and quotas – but are increasingly concerned with behind-the-border aspects of domestic policy, potentially impacting on most aspects of public policy. This means not only that questions of trade policy now go beyond national treatment to include issues of mutual recognition and common standards but also that trade policy has become a much larger political issue and something that engages the concern of consumers as well as producers. In short, trade became an important political issue.

In part because of this incipient 'constitution' for international trade and investment embodied in the WTO, EU and US economic policies have not come into significant conflict even as Europe has caught up with US levels of economic performance and weight in the world economy. Taken as a whole, however, the larger part of the reason for the absence of major EU–US economic conflict has been the dominance of the liberal view that European competitiveness requires continental solutions. As Lawrence notes, the predominant view in Europe has been 'that market forces should operate on a continental basis, that competition policy should be tough, and mutual recognition should introduce competition between regulatory regimes' (1996, p. 61). Set against this, the more interventionist strand of thinking – 'that intervention and rules should operate on a continental basis, that industrial policies should promote European competitors (rather than enforce competition), and Europe-wide regulatory, agricultural, and social policies should temper the effects of the market' (ibid.) – has been on the defensive. Thus far the former tendency has been in the ascendant: as Grahl concludes, 'European leaderships have increasingly seen Americanization as the only solution to the problems of the old continent; they have not, in recent years, envisaged divergent paths of development' (2004, p. 297).

After having caught up with America economically (to a large extent), Europe might have been expected to seek economic independence. 'But opposing forces pushing in the direction of a total integration within the American system also appeared in the last twenty years', says Emmanuel Todd: 'The liberal economic revolution ... produced at the highest European levels a new temptation' to increase integration with North America (2003, p. 172). So, while European integration began life as a project to rescue the nation-state in the aftermath of total war, to pursue economic cooperation and to strengthen the political unity of the capitalist world in the face of the Soviet challenge, it has continued to evolve despite the dissolution of its communist adversaries. And while relations between the EU and the United States have become somewhat fractious of late – not least over the war against Iraq – there is as yet no sign that the political identity and interests of Europe are being defined outside the context of ever increasing engagement with international markets and, *a fortiori*, increasing economic integration across the Atlantic.

### The United States: from NAFTA to the WTO and back?

Paradoxically, the US road to the WTO went through NAFTA in so far as the Canada–US free trade agreement, which prompted Mexico to seek the formation of a wider agreement (i.e. NAFTA), was itself a response to a failure in the early 1980s of multilateral negotiations in the GATT, problems that centred around the EC's refusal to address new trade issues. In turn, the recognition that the USA was prepared to conclude FTAs outside the wider, multilateral GATT framework was one reason for the European change of position in the mid-1980s. By the end of the 1980s, it was clear that US trade policy was essentially three-pronged: multilateral as in the GATT and its successor the WTO; regional or bilateral as in the Canada–USA agreement and NAFTA and other FTA initiatives in the Western Hemisphere; and aggressively unilateral after the fashion of the Super 301 provisions of the 1988 Omnibus Trade and Competitiveness Act, in which the USA asserted its right to define 'unreasonable' or 'unfair' trade practices on the part of others independently of whether those parties were under any treaty-defined obligations in these respects.

In the face of growing trade competition in home and overseas markets, and as the trade agenda was increasingly shaped by domestic producer interests, US strategy often involved the invitation to an FTA as an incentive and the prospect of aggressive unilateralism as a threat 'to bargain to advantage with individual, especially developing and smaller, countries', and then – in an exercise of what Jagdish Bhagwati characterized on the eve of the launch of the WTO as an instance of 'selfish hegemony' – to get these deals 'codified and enshrined eventually in the GATT on a multilateral agreement (like the Uruguay Round) with a divided, partially co-opted, and weakened opposition' (Bhagwati 1994, p. 309). That is to say, for the USA, at least in respect of smaller, poorer economies, participation in the WTO has always been a fair-weather outing. In the background, and sometimes centre-stage, there has always been the option of the fallback position of a more coercive exercise of market power. To be sure, this won't work for relations with the European Union and with the bigger Asian economies such as China and Russia, since in those cases the interdependence is for the most part mutually beneficial and significant for both sides. But for many countries in the international trading and investment system, interdependence, which is just mutual dependence, is a very asymmetrical relationship.

As we have seen in the case of the European Union, mechanisms of supranational regional governance can be intergovernmental or they can involve a pooling and/or delegation of sovereignty. Under intergovernmental arrangements, states make decisions collectively rather than individually, but on the basis of unanimity, that is, each has a veto, or at least is not bound by the decisions of others. The pooling of sovereignty involves creating decision-making procedures that do not have a built-in veto for the member states, and so a member may be bound by the decisions of others. And sovereignty is delegated 'when supranational actors are permitted to take certain autonomous decisions, without an intervening interstate vote or unilateral veto' (Moravcsik 1998, p. 67).

Posed in these terms, the governance of NAFTA is primarily of an intergovernmental kind, combined with some limited elements of delegated sovereignty. The central decision-making institutions of NAFTA are the

Free Trade Commission and the Secretariat. The Free Trade Commission, based in Mexico City, is comprised of cabinet ministers (or alternates) and operates on the basis of consensus, unless otherwise agreed. It oversees the overall functioning of the agreement, and the government representatives are 'charged with the formulation of policies affecting trade in manufactured goods, agricultural products, textiles and financial services' as well as being 'responsible for developing common rules of origin, customs procedures, transportation regulations, sanitary measures, and labelling standards' (Gruber 2000, p. 96). The Free Trade Commission does not operate as a permanent body but convenes at least once a year in regular sessions that are chaired successively by each party. The only permanent bureaucracy is the Secretariat, which has offices in Mexico City, Ottawa and Washington. Each member state appoints an individual to serve as the secretary for its section. The Secretariat is responsible for the administration of the dispute-settlement provisions of the agreement, assists the Free Trade Commission, and provides support for various non-dispute-related settlement committees and working groups.

In addition, there are separate commissions for cooperation on the environment, based in Montreal, and on labour issues, based in Dallas, Texas. These commissions were included at the beginning of the Clinton administration in order to counter opposition from environmentalists and labour unions and to secure the ratification of the agreement in the US Congress. The main obligations that NAFTA imposes on the member states arising from these two supplementary accords are to enforce their own labour and environmental legislation; not to erode further existing standards in order to attract or maintain investment; to consult with each other in the event of a complaint; and to develop transborder cooperation, particularly between Mexico and the USA. This latter was particularly directed towards the regulation of legal and illegal migration.

Finally, NAFTA includes a system of arbitration to settle trade and investment disputes in which panels of experts exercise powers of judicial review, a form of delegated sovereignty. The decisions reached by these panels of experts are binding for the member states. Moreover, it is a distinctive feature of NAFTA's dispute system that 'private' parties (that is, firms) can sue the member states if they believe that their contracts have been violated in breach of the rules of the free trade agreement. Such cases can be taken either to one of the international arbitration mechanisms provided by the agreement or to the courts of the member states.

The Doha Round of WTO talks – dubbed the 'development' round – was launched with the ambitious aims of bringing the major developing countries firmly inside the WTO framework and of completing the work of the Uruguay Round. But opposition from a range of the bigger developing countries – for example, Brazil and India – to further pressure from the developed countries, as well as continuing conflicts over agriculture between the EU, the USA and the developing countries, meant that progress was slow and difficult. As of early 2008 no agreement had been concluded, and the congressionally mandated fast-track negotiating authority of the US president had expired. This failure is unlikely to mark the end or break-up of the WTO, but the USA has made clear its intentions to push ahead with further bilateral and mini-lateral deals in the absence of a multilateral deal that meets its demands.

## Governing the world economy: the role of the major political actors

Notwithstanding the dramatic rise of China and the potential for India to follow in its wake, there is, of course, no sign that any other region of the world economy will soon amass the scale and scope of development and innovation necessary to *overtake* the United States in the way that the USA itself surpassed the British and German economies in the nineteenth century (see table 7.1).[4] Measured at PPP exchange rates, the USA still accounts for about one-fifth, and at market exchange rates slightly less than one-third, of global GDP, and these shares have been fairly stable for the last three decades.

Nevertheless, the potential long-term implications of the shifting global distribution of capital accumulation and growth are very large indeed if high levels of demand can be maintained in the world economy – that is, if China's (and then India's) growth trajectory is sustained; if the resulting changes to inequality and to labour markets and education in the North can be accommodated without large-scale social and political opposition; if the macroeconomic imbalances centred on the US deficits and Asian (and oil-producing country) surpluses can be managed in an orderly fashion; and if the more general collective management of the world economy can accommodate a genuine plurality of powers. These are all big questions, and there are no guarantees that they can be managed successfully.

These developments certainly have the potential to be of mutual economic benefit, for just as the catch-up followers benefit from the innovation of the leading poles of the world economy, so the leaders benefit from the

**Table 7.1** GDP per capita, growth projections

| Country | Based on 1960–2000 growth projections, year in which per capita GDP exceeds: | | Based on 1990–2000 growth projections, year in which per capita GDP exceeds: | |
|---|---|---|---|---|
| | USA 2000 | USA in that year | USA 2000 | USA in that year |
| China | 2052 | 2118 | 2035 | 2051 |
| India | 2116 | 7113 | 2072 | 2146 |

*Source*: Adapted from tables 11.1 and 11.3 in Brakman et al. 2006, pp. 305, 307.

falling costs, expanded markets and increased savings and investment generated by the new labour supplies of the followers. A key question, therefore, is whether the governance conducted by the major political actors can sustain more or less stable growth and accommodate to these shifts in power.

## The international monetary system

Since the end of the fixed exchange-rate regime in 1973, there has not been an equivalent set of rules governing all major currencies. It has been coordinated by a combination of the price mechanism – that is, by movements in interest rates in the capital markets of the major currencies – and the current-account policies of the major economies. On occasion some countries have set current-account targets and managed their fiscal, monetary and exchange-rate policies accordingly. Given that the USA does not intervene in its foreign-exchange market and sets its fiscal and monetary policies according to domestic considerations, the US current-account imbalance is then the residual of whatever these targets determine. Alternatively, when other countries have acted in the same way as the USA – that is, when they have not set current-account policies and have abstained from intervening in their foreign-exchange markets – all adjustment has taken place through the price mechanism and the US current account (deficit) still remains the residual variable. Despite the advent of the Euro and pegging against the dollar, no firm system-wide rules for international monetary relations have emerged.

The extent to which this absence of active governance matters remains a matter of controversy. On the one hand, there are certainly costs associated when real exchange rates are misaligned: arbitrary changes in purchasing power, adjustment costs for firms and perhaps unemployment, misleading signals for investment, inflation, and protectionist pressures. And macroeconomic simulations suggest that there are potential gains from coordinated policies to manage significant current-account imbalances. On the other hand, the correlation of supply shocks across the regions of the world economy is generally low; even quite sustained misalignments do not appear to be as damaging for cross-border trade and investment as many economists originally feared because of the limited pass through of international to domestic prices; and empirically calibrated models suggest that fixing exchange rates would *increase* the variance of other macroeconomic variables (Eichengreen 1994; Rogoff 2002).

It is true that in some previous cases of serious exchange-rate misalignment the three major trading and investment blocs (the United States, Japan and Western Europe) attempted to coordinate the management of their exchange rates. The Plaza Agreement (1985) and the Louvre Accord (1987) sought to devalue the US dollar against both the Deutschmark and the Japanese yen. (In practice, such arrangements worked by signalling policy changes, especially in relation to interest-rate movements.) And in the light of the persistent deterioration in the US trade and current account balances since the early 1990s (reaching around 6 per cent of GDP in 2006–7), international discussion of the need for coordinated exchange-rate realignments – this time between the dollar, the renminbi (and other Asian currencies) and the Euro – surfaced again in 2006. But a coordinated realignment of these currencies does not seem to be a realistic prospect in the absence of a serious breakdown of current arrangements. Rather, the key players have put their trust in the fact that high levels of liquidity and historically low levels of real interest rates, together with the scope for increased investment in the rest of the world economy outside the USA, may make reasonably stable adjustments possible. The basic reason for this absence of any enthusiasm for 'grand coordination' is that stabilizing exchange rates in a quasi-fixed regime would involve a significant compromise of domestic autonomy in monetary (and fiscal) policy, which none of the key players seems prepared to entertain.

Even the 'credit crunch' of late 2007 did not change these assessments, though the accompanying further fall in the dollar and consequent upward pressure on the Euro and other currencies (the Canadian and Australian dollars, for example) did increase the calls from the G7 for a revaluation of the renminbi. The IMF continued to maintain that the rest of the world's growth prospects, especially in the emerging markets, were sufficiently decoupled from the US economy for world growth to be only marginally affected by the likely slowdown there following the crises in the mortgage markets and the highly leveraged financial instruments associated with them.

The case for a more coordinated international response to global monetary imbalances was that the US deficits on its trade and current account, together with the fiscal deficits which developed under the Bush administrations, might prove unsustainable and lead to a sharp fall in the value of the dollar and a potential hard landing for worldwide economic growth (Obstfeld and Rogoff 2005; Krugman 2007). Added to this, growing protectionist pressure in the US Congress, which routinely turns China into a scapegoat by focusing on the bilateral US–China trade balance, means that there has been vocal concern over the alleged undervaluation of the renminbi. Thus, in the absence of exchange-rate realignment, protectionist pressures might develop. Looking to the longer term, the mismanagement of the US economy and its potential impact on the credibility of the dollar potentially threaten American monetary hegemony, given the fact that the Euro has established itself as a credible reserve currency (Chinn and Frankel 2005; Frankel 2006). The view of most commentators has been that, while these problems were very largely made in America – a result of the tax cuts and increased spending of the Bush administration and the low savings rates of the US private sector – they had a real potential to inflict damage on the rest of the world economy.

The case for the status quo, by contrast, was that the trade surpluses and reserve assets accumulated in Asia were a consequence of exchange-rate protectionism – that is, a policy-induced undervaluation of the currency to promote exports – as part of the development strategy of some emerging markets, including China. It has also been noted that world financial markets are big, even in relation to US debts, and increasingly integrated. This means that, if foreign investors continue to diversify away from 'home country bias' in their portfolios, then US current accounts might be accommodated for the foreseeable future (Cooper 2005). More generally, it has been suggested that the fact that long-term interest rates have remained low by historical standards indicates that the global monetary imbalances might be stable if growth in the United States remains higher than that in the Euro area and Japan, and if the rapidly growing emerging markets are slow to develop domestic markets in assets that foreigners might want to hold (Caballero et al. 2008). Indeed, Dooley, Folkerts-Landau and Garber (2004) went so far as to speak of a new Bretton Woods system in which China (and other emerging Asian markets) might play a functionally similar role to that of Europe for more than a decade in the first Bretton Woods regime, from 1958 to 1971/3.

In order to address these debates we need to recall that, for any given economy, the sum of domestic absorption and exports is equal to GDP plus imports, and that this implies that any excess of investment over national savings is equal to the trade deficit (that is, the excess of imports over exports). Equally, for given levels of investment and private savings, an increase in the fiscal deficit must be associated with an increase in the trade deficit. The two deficits are not 'twins' – they may move in different directions (because of other changes in investment and private saving) – but they are certainly linked. And since the world economy as a whole has a trade balance of zero, this implies, *ex post facto*, that one country's surplus of investment over savings is another country's deficit. With these points in mind, we now examine the idea of the new dollar standard, or what some commentators refer to as a second Bretton Woods.

## A new Bretton Woods?

One side of the new dollar standard is the phenomenon of what Barry Eichengreen and Ricardo Hausmann (2004) have called 'original sin'. In many developing countries, financial systems often lack fixed-interest bond markets and forward markets in foreign exchange against the dollar (and other currencies). If domestic commercial banks are unable (or not allowed) to take open positions in foreign exchange, and if there are no liquid markets in domestic bonds, then '*foreign banks are unwilling to take open positions in the domestic currency*. Thus, with a tightly regulated domestic banking system and/or capital controls, a satisfactory free float [of the domestic currency] is impossible' (McKinnon and Schnabl 2004, p. 343).

These countries cannot use the national currency to borrow abroad or even domestically for the long term. Debt-induced financial instability is, then, unavoidable, as all domestic investment will have either a currency mismatch (projects that earn the national currency are financed by dollars) or a maturity mismatch (short-term loans for long-term projects).[5] To compensate for this, governments seek to peg their currencies to the dollar, as most in Asia have done since the crises of 1997–8. Given the central role of the dollar internationally, exporters everywhere outside of the Euro area price to the world market – and not just the US market – in dollars, and so any central bank that seeks to stabilize the purchasing power of its national currency has a strong incentive to peg against the dollar, provided inflation in the USA is low and reasonably stable.

The other side of the equation is the syndrome that Ronald McKinnon has termed 'conflicted virtue'. In this case, creditor countries with similarly underdeveloped financial systems cannot *lend* internationally using the national currency; they can only lend using dollars (again the Euro area is the exception: a net creditor to the world economy that can lend using its own currency). As countries generating surpluses, these countries face a problem of potential appreciation against the dollar and are compelled to make continuous interventions to prevent this, thereby amassing expanding foreign-exchange reserves which are then switched into US Treasury bonds or similar low-risk, low-yielding instruments. One consequence of this is that 'the United States has a virtually unlimited line of dollar credit with the rest of the world'. Moreover, 'as long as the Federal Reserve Bank keeps ongoing price inflation very low, the dollar cannot be attacked in the usual sense', because dollar depreciation has no impact on the creditworthiness of US financial institutions (both their assets and their liabilities are denominated in dollars), nor does it affect the ability of the US Treasury to service its debts. The foreign exchange risk inherent in any market-based, decentralized system is 'shifted to creditor countries that, Europe aside, cannot lend to the US in their own currencies' (McKinnon 2003, pp. 3, 5, 6).

While this system is certainly open to abuse – the dollar dependence of debtors has given the US Treasury (often acting through the IMF) leverage over crisis-prone financial systems to effect premature liberalization to the benefit of US firms – it is also of benefit to both the USA and the major creditor countries. Clearly, the United States benefits from having 'a safe reserve asset, with assured international purchasing power' but it 'is also a great convenience to other countries' (McKinnon 2001, p. 11). To see why this is the case, we need to consider the development strategies of the surplus-generating creditor countries. The central point to grasp, as McKinnon says, is that 'China is merely the leading edge of a more general, albeit somewhat hidden, East Asian export expansion into the United States – which in turn reflects very high savings rates by Asians collectively and abnormally low saving by Americans' (McKinnon 2005b, p. 4).

With development strategies that are generating healthy export surpluses and, especially in China's case, with surplus labour ready to move into export industries, alongside very high savings rates because of underdeveloped financial systems, limited social protection and repressed domestic consumption, China and the five tigers – South Korea, Taiwan, Singapore, Malaysia and Thailand – have been content to pursue exchange-rate protection, even if this means building up large, low-yielding dollar reserves.

US indifference towards the deficits, especially the current-account deficit, is not just Republican politics, since there is no good economic reason to do anything until and unless the deficits produce higher inflation and/or interest rates in the United States. The steady devaluation of the dollar since President George W. Bush was elected has helped US exporters. And China is likely to move only very gradually to a full float of its currency as it has no interest in adding financial instability to its current problems. In any case, its current-account surplus is not very large – surpluses with the EU and the USA are offset by deficits with Japan, Korea and Taiwan – and the accumulation of dollar reserves is driven largely by inward capital flows rather than by (net) trade surpluses. Japan has no interest in repeating the experience of 1995 when yen revaluation choked a potential recovery. For Japan (and other Asian countries), buying dollars prevents the dollar–yen exchange rate from rising too abruptly. Equally, reinvesting those dollars in US Treasury bonds helps to keep US interest rates down and consumption up, thereby providing a market for Asian exports. Meanwhile, China worries about currency competition from other Asian economies, and these, in turn, from Japan through to India, have managed their exchange rates to match the renminbi (and the dollar) 'for fear of being "hollowed out" by China's burgeoning manufacturing prowess' (Choyleva and Dumas 2006, p. 3).

Have the resulting global imbalances helped or hindered worldwide economic growth? Overall, William Cline estimates that 'the widening of the US current account deficit after 1992 contributed to an increase in demand for the rest of the world that reached the equivalent of about 2 per cent of rest-of-world GDP annually by 2004' (Cline 2005, p. 220). Since the US call on world capital markets has not contributed to an increase in interest rates worldwide, the net effect on foreign demand and growth of the US deficits has almost certainly been positive. Moreover, while a significant devaluation of the dollar as well as a substantial correction of the US fiscal deficit would be required to restore the United States to a position of current-account balance, thus far the financing of the deficits has not been especially onerous. Not only has the real economic burden been much less than the accounting figures show, because of the valuation effects produced by a falling dollar and assets and liabilities asymmetries, but also the short-term prognosis is that 'the accumulated burden from the past remains minor and it is [the] unfavourable prospects for the future that warrant the true concern' (ibid., p. 66). Kitchen (2006) concurs on the basis of an estimate that the current real cost of servicing US net international debt is around 0.25 per cent of GDP.

Might this system persist until all the surplus labour in Asia has been redeployed into the industrial sector, and until financial systems are well enough developed and domestic inflationary pressures sufficiently dampened to allow stable floating of the major Asian currencies? Notwithstanding the benign scenario sketched thus far, there are several reasons to question the sustainability of these arrangements over the long run. In the first place, unlike the dollar standard of the Bretton Woods system, in which the USA borrowed in the short term from Europe to finance long-term investment in rebuilding the continent's war-torn capital stock, it now borrows to consume (investments in China aside). Izurieta (2005) and Godley (2003) have argued that easy access to cheap credit artificially depresses an already dangerously low US savings ratio, while McKinnon suggests that the current-account deficit also depresses domestic manufacturing output 'by the amount of the trade deficit in manufactures' (McKinnon 2005a, p. 7). These considerations may help to explain why investment in the US economy has been directed mainly to real estate and the non-traded sector and the net flow of direct investment is outwards, with inflows of shortening maturity from official, rather than private, sources. Secondly, bilateral US deficits with particular trading partners become a target for congressional efforts at protection: 'The leading indicator of American protection', says Fred Bergsten, is 'overvaluation of the dollar and its attendant external deficits' (2004, p. 82).

On the creditor side of the equation there are two main problems: first, can the countries concerned sterilize their currency interventions and, thereby, prevent excessive domestic monetary growth and inflation? And second, can they afford the reserve accumulation involved? According to the conventional wisdom – based on the Mundell–Flemming model – the answer to the first question says that a country with an open capital account cannot pursue both an exchange-rate target and monetary stability. However, there are experiences of successful sterilization over reasonably long periods, especially in 'repressed' financial systems. In any case, Godley and Lavoie (2004) have argued that the Mundell–Flemming model is not well founded and that unlimited reserve acquisition need not feed through into an increase in the domestic money supply, the latter being entirely demand-determined.

Be that as it may, there is a significant opportunity cost in holding low-yielding reserves in excess of those needed as an insurance against financial crises.[6] Dani Rodrik and, notably, Lawrence Summers (former Treasury secretary in the Clinton administration) have argued that the ten leading holders of excess reserves are incurring an opportunity cost of between 1 and 2 per cent of their combined GDP. That is to say, the answer to the second question is that, if these reserves were invested at yields similar to those gained by US institutions over the last several decades, the growth rate of GDP would increase by 1 to 2 per cent (Summers 2006). Even if this is a twofold overestimate of what more realistically might be realized, these still represent considerable losses. This may come to be too high a price to pay to maintain export competitiveness and to keep US consumption growing rapidly. And in any case, as these economies develop further they may need to focus more on domestic sources of growth in demand. Thus, Morris Goldstein notes that:

> as domestic demand, economic growth, inflationary pressures, and domestic interest rates rise in the Asian creditor countries, the benefits of using large-scale exchange market intervention to maintain undervalued exchange rates fall while the costs [including the difference between the high returns foreigners get on inward investment and the low returns Asian Central Banks get on US Treasury securities] rise. (Goldstein 2004, p. 42)

Finally, the figures do not really add up to a new Bretton Woods. As Cline (2005) points out, Japan cannot be considered a structural part of the surplus-generating periphery as it is not a labour-abundant economy. On the contrary, it is a labour-scarce economy because of an ageing population. In fact, the surpluses of the Asian periphery in total are only one half of the US current-account deficit. More recently, the rise in the price of oil has had a major impact – net oil imports account for 35 per cent of the US trade balance. In 2006, the oil exporters' current-account surpluses were $450 billion, compared with only $150 billion in 2000 (interestingly, the BIS says that it cannot trace 70 per cent of the accumulated investable funds of the oil producers since 1999). The Gulf Cooperation Council economies – Saudi Arabia, Bahrain, Kuwait, Oman, Qatar and the UAE – had a current-account surplus of $227 billion in 2006. Developing Asia, including China, had surpluses of around $150–160 billion in 2005 and 2006.

### The challenge of the Euro?

In the early 1970s, Richard Nixon's Treasury secretary, John Connally, said in response to European complaints about US policy towards the dollar: 'The dollar is our currency, but your problem'. This reflected the leverage that the USA then had over the key creditor countries, which were heavily reliant on US political and military leadership in their Cold War competition with the Soviet Union. And the European and Japanese central banks were organized in a framework in which each agreed to hold dollars on condition that the others did likewise. Today, US leverage over where creditor countries put their money is much diminished. When he was US Treasury secretary, Lawrence Summers was fond of saying that the fate of the dollar was still largely in US hands. That was and is true, but it means both that the USA can hold on to the international role of the dollar and that it can lose it. If there is a new Bretton Woods system in place, then we might be nearer to 1971 than 1958.

In the first place, it is highly unlikely that the United States can devalue its way out of difficulties even though it does benefit from valuation effects on its assets and liabilities. Cline has shown that 'US external assets tend to be more heavily in equities', which 'appreciate in nominal terms with inflation and stock market booms', whereas its external liabilities are 'more heavily in debt obligations', which are not affected by such changes. And 'the external liabilities of the United States are denominated in its own currency, whereas external assets are much more heavily denominated in foreign currency' (Cline 2005, pp. 34, 46). This means that the secular devaluation of the dollar – at around 0.25 per cent per year over the period since the move to floating exchange rates in 1973 – ameliorates the net international investment position. But once there is an alternative reserve currency – the Euro – Frankel rightly asks, 'how many times can the US fool foreign investors?' (2006, p. 11).

And secondly, the ability of the United States to finance its debts relatively cheaply is linked to the international role of the dollar and, specifically, the role of New York as the world's banker (originally pointed out by Charles Kindleberger in 1962). The US financial system has been able to garner a disproportionate share of the world's short-term, liquid deposits and to lend these on a long-term basis in riskier, higher-return assets. The large, open, deep and transparent US capital markets are a natural place for foreigners to put the low-risk (low-yield) part of their portfolios, while US investors can be expected to put their high-risk (high-yield) investments overseas. 'The result', notes Cline, 'will be a systematic excess of observed rates of return on US assets abroad over foreign assets in the United States (even though the risk-adjusted rates of return might be equal)' (2005, p. 49). Cline calculates that the interest-rate differential between what the USA earns on its investments overseas and what it has to pay on its debts has been around 1.2 per cent per year over the last several decades.

It might be argued that this is a result of the fact that the USA has a comparative advantage in supplying financial services and innovation to the rest of the world and that the rest of the world is happy to pay for this (Hausmann and Sturzenegger 2005). More likely, this interest-rate differential is simply an artefact of the dollar's international role and would not survive a serious challenge by a rival such as the Euro, as Chinn and Frankel suggest: 'Possibly this American role of the world's banker . . . would survive the loss of the dollar as the leading international currency', they note, 'but it seems possible that the loss of one would lead to the loss of the other' (2005, pp. 7–8). For whereas the post-war dollar standard was, as John Grahl has argued, an industrial phenomenon, today it is essentially financial:

The [post-war] primacy of the dollar was to a large extent an industrial phenomenon: the 'dollar shortage' represented a universal hunger for US exports.... Today, the primacy of the dollar rests on the scale and liquidity of North American financial markets ... The capitalisation of the two largest stock markets, NYSE and NASDAQ ... [is] half the world total. (Grahl 2004, p. 291)

The dollar's primacy also rests on the size and liquidity of the bond markets of the US government: the reason US Treasury bills are reckoned to be benchmark, risk-free assets is because the government owns the Federal Reserve Bank. The permissive causes of dollar primacy, as we have seen, have been the underdevelopment of such markets – private and public – elsewhere, especially in emerging Asia, and the absence of an alternative key currency. In one sense, then, the international role of the dollar has been simply what Benjamin Cohen describes as 'the revealed preference of the marketplace' (1998, p. 156) – a preference that Washington has done well to accommodate.

But it is important to see what this is a preference for. Drawing on Albert Hirschman's notions of voice, loyalty and exit, Grahl distinguishes between voice- and exit-based ways of mobilizing finance for investment. In voice-based systems, the providers of finance maintain close links with the borrower, thereby overcoming the separation of principals and agents and of creditors and debtors. As such, voice-based systems are particularistic and opaque to outsiders. Moreover, to the extent that the separations of principals and agents, creditors and debtors, are suppressed, the capital markets – that is, key institutions that drive competitive innovation – cease to function.

By contrast, the exit-based approach, Grahl explains,

controls economic relations by the threat of departure – which depends on the existence of alternatives provided by the market.... it becomes easier as the corresponding asset-markets become deeper and more liquid.... [The form of a general shift towards exit-based systems has been] the deregulation and internationalization of dollar finance.... However crude the market-based mechanisms of dollar-based global finance, they have the decisive advantage of being reproducible.... The financial regimes to which they give rise can expand without limit to obtain a truly staggering scale. This, in turn, is based on the imposition of universal standards.... market-determined finance does have decisive advantages over the voice-based mechanisms of relatively closed industrial groups. Firstly, it is able to diversify risks over a vast number of companies and investment projects. Secondly, market-based disciplines can reduce agency and information costs. (Grahl 2001, pp. 29, 30, 37)

However, in considering the *future* of the dollar-based system, it is also important to bear in mind that another key difference between the present-day dollar standard and the Bretton Woods arrangements is that there is now an alternative reserve currency: namely, the Euro. The Euro does not suffer from either original sin or conflicted virtue: there are very large private and official bond markets in Euros and well-developed forward markets in foreign exchange. 'The world already enjoys a bipolar financial market', says Bergsten, 'if not yet a bipolar international monetary system' (Bergsten 2002, p. 2). Indeed, Europe's share of gross global capital flows increased from 55 to 72 per cent between 1995 and 2005, and in 2007 the capitalization of Europe's financial markets exceeded those in the USA for the first time in over a century (Milesi-Ferretti 2007; Wade 2007).

That said, it remains the case that the official bond markets in Euros are fragmented into different national markets. And the international role of the Euro has also been hampered by the split of responsibilities between the European Central Bank and the national treasuries of the member states: the EU has no powers to tax and is legally prevented from incurring debts. Moreover, within the Euro area the presence of uncoordinated national wage-setting arrangements exercises a deflationary pressure. If one country sets national wage increases below others (as Germany has been doing since 2000) it will reap a competitive advantage; and if others retaliate in kind, then a deflationary pressure reducing consumption, investment and productivity will follow. The solution to this dilemma is either to coordinate national wage increases or to liberalize labour markets so that there are no nationally set wage levels: it is the struggle between these two models that lies behind much of the conflict over the 'social model' in the Euro area. And, finally, the private capital markets also retain pronounced national characteristics despite rapid and continuing cross-border integration and EU-level harmonization.

Nevertheless, the project of monetary integration in Europe (which gained serious momentum after the break-up of the old dollar standard) has always been, in large part, about reducing dependence on the dollar. 'The current, very determined, efforts of the European Union to integrate member state financial systems, and to build huge, liquid markets in euro-denominated securities', Grahl points out, 'should be seen in the context of this growing challenge' of the hegemony of international dollar finance (2004, p. 292). If these efforts are successful, if the design faults of the Euro can be rectified, and if the UK (and hence the City of London) were to join the Euro, then it would pose a formidable challenge to the dollar. In that eventuality, as Chinn and Frankel (2005) have shown, under reasonable assumptions about the downward trajectory of the dollar given continuing current-account deficits, the Euro could easily become the dominant international currency by 2020. In fact, UK entry into the Euro area may not be necessary; too rapid a devaluation of the dollar might by itself provide the trigger.

## Managing global imbalances

Although foreign demand for US assets must stabilize at some point – as Herb Stein (n.d.) said, 'If something cannot go on for ever, it will stop' – the rapid growth of financial globalization makes it hard to know when: gross global capital flows increased from roughly 5 to 15 per cent of world GDP between 1995 and 2005. And although thus far there has been little build-up of US net liabilities to foreigners, there is a real prospect of a significant medium-term deterioration in the US position (Milesi-Ferretti 2007). Finally, the current fiscal position in the United States is clearly unsustainable in the medium to long term: according to the US comptroller general, based on the current position, balancing the federal budget by 2040 could require actions as large as cutting total federal spending by 60 per cent or doubling federal taxes (Walker 2007).

So, in response to five years of growing imbalances and little policy adjustment to deal with them, in June 2006 the IMF launched its first multilateral consultation (MC), aimed at addressing global imbalances while maintaining growth, with the participation of China, the Euro area, Japan, Saudi Arabia and the USA. This followed the articulation in April 2004 of the so-called IMFC Strategy by the IMF Committee, which, in a communiqué in September 2006, proposed:

> steps to boost national saving in the United States, including fiscal consolidation; further progress on growth-enhancing reforms in Europe; further structural reforms, including fiscal consolidation, in Japan; reforms to boost domestic demand in emerging Asia, together with greater exchange rate flexibility in a number of surplus countries; and increased spending consistent with absorptive capacity and macroeconomic stability in oil producing countries.

According to the IMF:

> The MC – a new instrument established under the Managing Director's Medium Term Strategy – aims to bring together a small group of countries relevant to a particular problem of systemic or regional importance in order to promote strengthened dialogue and ultimately action to address it.

A central element of the medium-term strategy is the enhancement of the fund's surveillance function. The importance of this MC was underscored by the downside risks of a disorderly unwinding of global imbalances and the protectionist pressures that might accompany sustained or growing imbalances. In the MC, although each country stressed that it would take action consistent with domestically determined national priorities, and despite the fact that the consultations revealed that there was no support for 'grand policy coordination', the participants did commit to a range of policies that were consistent with the IMFC Strategy (see IMF 2007). These commitments are summarized in table 7.2.

**Table 7.2**   Country policy commitments to address global imbalances

| Country | Principal medium-term commitments |
| --- | --- |
| China | • Make reduction of external imbalance a major objective of economic and social development<br>• Boost domestic demand, particularly consumer demand, and rebalance investment and consumption<br>• Promote balanced external sector development<br>• Speed up financial reform<br>• Improve the exchange-rate regime |
| Euro area | • Reform of product markets<br>• Reform of labour markets<br>• Reform in the financial market |
| Japan | • Labour market reforms<br>• Facilitate inward FDI<br>• Strengthen competition in key sectors<br>• Advance fiscal consolidation |
| Saudi Arabia | • Increase government spending on social and infrastructure investments and on expanding oil sector capacity<br>• Maintain dollar-peg for the currency in line with the GCC agreement to establish monetary union in 2010 |
| USA | • Fiscal consolidation<br>• Reform of budget process to contain growth of expenditure<br>• Reform of entitlements to strengthen fiscal sustainability<br>• Incentives to support private saving<br>• Enhance energy efficiency (to reduce dependence on oil imports)<br>• Maintain pro-growth, open investment policies<br>• Improve capital market competitiveness |

*Source*: IMF 2007.

## Surveillance and developing country financial systems

We noted above that many developing countries face debt-induced financial instability as a result of an inability to borrow using the national currency. In a crisis, what is currency risk to firms becomes a credit risk to banks, a deposit risk to savers and, by dint of government-backed deposit insurance, government liability for losses in excess of what is typically highly leveraged bank capital. Since most bank debt is short-term debt (at least relative to the investment it finances) and payable at par, in a crisis, adjustment takes place through quantities rather than prices; and, as all debtors scramble to repay their debts simultaneously, the net result is a deep recession – what Irving Fisher (1933) called 'debt-deflation'. Central banks become borrowers (of dollars), not lenders, of last resort (Steil and Litan 2006). In the wake of the Asian crisis in 1997, and as this reverberated through to Russia and Latin America in 1998 and 1999, there was much discussion of the need for a 'new financial architecture' and much high-profile criticism of the conduct of both the IMF and the US Treasury.

Several consequences followed: many of the affected countries maintained some kind of exchange-rate peg against the dollar and accumulated large foreign-exchange reserves; the attempt to make capital account liberalization part of the IMF's articles of agreement was dropped, though financial sector reform – that is, liberalization – remains on the medium- to long-term agenda of the major creditors; and the IMF redefined its mandate and the scope of its conditionality somewhat to address the concerns of developing countries. But all the ambitious proposals for a new financial architecture – from sovereign bankruptcy rules, through international deposit insurance, to standstills on debt repayment – were stillborn (see Thirkell-White 2005).

Even though some of these proposals had high-level official support in some cases (for example, Anne Krueger, appointed as deputy director of the IMF by the first Bush administration, championed the idea of a sovereign debt restructuring mechanism; see chapter 6 above), they were widely opposed by private financial markets and actors, who were generally unwilling to accept greater international authority over their freedom of action, preferring to deal with a multiplicity of national jurisdictions. Instead, in April 1999, the Financial Stability Forum was established under the auspices of the G7 treasuries and central banks as well as the IMF, the World Bank, the BIS and private sector bodies representing financial firms. Along with the Basel II process and a series of private sector standard-setting bodies – relating to accounting, securities, etc. – this has created what Robert Wade (2007) calls a 'standards-surveillance-compliance' regime.

Whether this combination of multilateral consultation on global imbalances and market-based surveillance and standard-setting for developing countries is enough to prevent future financial crises of a regional or systemic kind remains to be seen. While the inability of policy-makers to maintain an independent position vis-à-vis the private financial markets does not augur well for the prospects for international governance, the development of the MC mechanism is a significant innovation. If this were to become a durable feature of IMF surveillance aimed at addressing regional and systemic issues, and if the major players exercise their domestic autonomy in the knowledge that they have a collective interest in, and responsibility for, global conditions for growth, then there are modest grounds for optimism. But perhaps the most that can be said is that the major participants publicly acknowledge that the governance of these issues is a shared, collective responsibility and that there is a very high level of official recognition of the potential costs of failure in regard to these issues.

## Conclusions

There are no guarantees that the mechanisms of governance we have reviewed above are up to managing a serious crisis in the world economy, such as a hard landing for the US economy, a disorderly unwinding of the global imbalances, a slump in China, and so forth. It is also true that the key poles of the international economy answer primarily to their domestic constituencies, and there are no means by which the interests of the system as a whole can be articulated and acted upon separately from the interaction of these major players. To date, the multilateral consultation has been just that – a consultation. It remains to be seen if, and when, the participants deliver on the commitments they have entered into – the stance of the USA towards the MC is at least ambiguous. It is also the case that these mechanisms of governance have not been designed to deal with some of the most pressing issues for the world economy, such as a much better deal on trade for the developing countries, especially the poorest, the problems of failing or collapsed states, and the environmental and demographic crises that confront economic development and social stability in many places.

However, it would be a mistake to conclude from this that the major players are powerless in the face of these challenges, rather than insufficiently exercised by them. The major political actors in the system retain considerable powers to manage and shape international economic events, and they have shown, in certain circumstances and on behalf of certain interests, a willingness to use them. It is not an absence of capacity as such that we need worry about so much as the social purposes for which these powers have been used. It may be difficult to change those social purposes and challenge the interests behind them, but that is not because states are powerless in the face of a global economy. We take this discussion further in chapter 8.

# 8

# Globalization, Governance and the Nation-State

## Introduction

So far we have been concerned mainly with the economic aspects of globalization, and have considered governance primarily in terms of its economic necessities and possibilities. In this chapter we consider the wider political issues raised by globalization theorists and, in particular, the role of the nation-state in the future of international and global governance.

We begin with a reminder that the modern state is a relatively recent phenomenon, and that 'sovereignty' in its modern form is a highly distinctive political claim – to exclusive control of a definite territory. We emphasize the international aspects of the development of sovereignty, that agreements between states not to interfere in each other's internal affairs were important in establishing the power of state over society. We go on to consider the development of the nation-state's capacity for governance and how these capacities are changing in the modern world, especially after the end of the Cold War, and the turn towards more liberalized and open markets both domestically and internationally.

While the capacities of states for governance have changed in some respects (especially as national macroeconomic managers), and many states have lost the ability to act independently, they remain pivotal institutions, especially in terms of creating the conditions for effective international governance. We shall make the following main points in our discussion of the possibilities of governance and the role of the state.

1   If, as we have argued in earlier chapters, the international economy does not correspond to the model of a globalized economic system, then

nation-states have a significant role to play in economic governance at the level of both national and international processes.

2  The emerging forms of governance of international markets and other economic processes involve the major national governments but in a new role: states will come to function less as all-purpose providers of governance and more as the authors and legitimators of an international 'quasi-polity'; the central functions of the nation-state will become those of providing legitimacy for and ensuring the accountability of supranational and subnational governance mechanisms which exercise various forms of 'private' authority.

3  While the state's claim to exclusive control of its territory has been reduced by international markets and new communication media, it still retains one central role that ensures a large measure of national control: the regulation of populations. People are much less mobile than money, goods or ideas, and in a sense they remain 'nationalized', dependent on passports, visas, residence and labour qualifications. The democratic state's role as the possessor of a territory is that it regulates its population, and this gives it a definite and unique legitimacy internationally in that it can speak for that population.

4  Given that the major nation-states involved in the provision of international economic governance include both broadly representative, rule-of-law states and more authoritarian models (e.g. Russia and China), that international governance does not address the huge inequalities of power and wealth between the advanced and poorest parts of the system, that supranational regional integration is assuming a greater importance, and that the shifting geopolitical alignments as a result of the end of the Cold War and the dissolution of communism and industrialization in resurgent Asia are uncertain – all of these imply that the continuation of the relative stability of the open, liberal order embodied in the major multilateral institutions is not guaranteed.

### The rise of 'national sovereignty'

Political theorists and sociologists commonly assert, following Max Weber, that the distinctive feature of the modern state is its ability to uphold a claim to a monopoly of the legitimate use of force on its territory. In seventeenth-century Europe, the modern states system was created and mutually recognized by its members. Central to that recognition was that each state was the sole political authority with exclusive possession of a defined territory. The 'state' became the dominant form of government, accepting no other agency as rival. The territoriality of European feudalism was multiple and did not depend on a singular relationship between authority and territory. Political authorities and other forms of functionally specific governance (religious communities and guilds, for example) had existed in overlapping forms that made parallel and often competing claims to the same area (Gierke 1988). And while territorial states of one form or another are as old as human civilization, the modern European state, which developed out of the early modern period, has now become 'the global state-form' (Finer 1997, p. 88).

Some would claim that the period of the domination of the nation-state as an agency of governance is now over and that we are entering into a period when governance and territory will pull apart, when different agencies will control aspects of governance and when some important activities will be ungoverned or subject to so-called private governance (Cerny 1998). This is questionable, as we shall argue, but the claims of nation-states to exclusivity in governance across such broad areas of social and economic life are historically specific and by no means preordained. What is more likely is that the content of statehood and the meanings and implications of territorial borders are changing for some purposes and some actors.

The modern state did not acquire its monopoly of governance by its own internal efforts alone. After the Peace of Westphalia in 1648, governments gradually ceased to support co-religionists abroad in conflict with their own states. The mutual recognition by states of each other's sovereignty in the most important contemporary matter, religious belief, meant that states were willing to forgo certain political objectives in return for internal control and stability (Hirst 1997). By exploiting the autonomy from external interference sanctioned by this mutual and international agreement, states were able to impose 'sovereignty' on their societies. The agreement of states changed the terms of conflict between territorial authority and confessional groups in favour of the former. Thus to a significant degree the capacity for sovereignty came from without, through agreements between states in the newly emerging society of states.

The rise of the modern state as a territorially specific and politically dominant power thus depended in part on international agreements. The doctrine of the 'sovereignty' of states in the new international law, and the mutual recognition of their internal powers and rights by European states, thus played a central part in the creation of a new relationship between power and territory, one of exclusive possession (Hinsley 1986). These international understandings made possible an 'internalization' of power and politics within the state. States were perceived as the primary political communities, with the capacity to determine the status of and to make rules for any activity that fell within contemporary understandings of the scope of legitimate authority. States were sovereign, and hence each state determined within itself the nature of its internal and external policies. States monopolized not only internal but also external violence. Only the state could make war and use force externally, pirates and private armies being gradually suppressed by interstate agreements and enforcement (Thomson 1994).

The society of states thus became a world of politically self-sufficient entities, in which each acted according to its own will, and international politics was limited by mutual recognition and the obligation to refrain from interfering in the internal affairs of other states. The anarchical society of external interactions between states, their autonomy one from another, was thus a precondition for an effective monopoly of power within. In the nineteenth and twentieth centuries liberal and democratic governments inherited from the earlier absolutist regimes these claims to sovereignty within a coherent and exclusively governed territory, and brought to them new and powerful legitimations.

So to this fundamental sovereignty postulated by seventeenth-century states could be added, without excessive contradiction, most of the other features of modern politics. States were autonomous and exclusive possessors of their territory, and this fact did not alter whether they were dynastic or national, autocratic or democratic, authoritarian or liberal. The notion of a 'nation'-state actually reinforces the conception of a sovereign power having primacy within a given territory. Nationalism is in essence a claim that political power should reflect cultural homogeneity, according to some common set of historically specific political understandings of the content of the nation.

Nationalism thus extends and depends on the scope of 'sovereignty', requiring certain kinds of cultural conformity for citizenship. In this respect the advent of nationalism did not alter our understanding of states as 'sovereign' bodies, but rather it required or presupposed it. The concept of a culturally homogeneous and therefore legitimately sovereign territory could justify both the formation and the break-up of states. The result of the various waves of nationalism from the early nineteenth century onwards has been to increase the population of the anarchical society of sovereign states, rather than change its nature. Indeed, if anything, nationalism rendered international cooperation more difficult, reinforcing the notion of the national community as the master of its fate.

Democracy had no greater effect on the fundamental characteristics of the sovereign state, a political entity created in a pre-democratic era. Democracy, in the sense of basic civil rights and representative government based on universal suffrage, has become a virtually universal ideology and aspiration in the Western world in the late twentieth and early twenty-first centuries even if powerful autocratic states still exist. The notion of a sovereign people could easily replace the 'sovereign', annexing the latter's claims to primacy in the making of political decisions within a given territory. Similarly, democracy and nationalism can, at a price, be made compatible. Democracy requires a substantial measure of cultural homogeneity (or publicly recognized cultural difference within some overarching political identity) if it is to be tolerable (Hindess 1992). Bitterly divided communities cannot accept the logic of majority rule or tolerate the rights of minorities. National self-determination is a political claim that derives its legitimacy from the notions of democracy and cultural homogeneity in equal measure, its essence being a plebiscite on independence in a territory claimed to have a degree of distinctive cultural coherence.

Modern political theory – that is, the theory of government and political obligation in a sovereign state – evolved before mass democracy but adapted relatively easily to it. This is not just because it was possible to substitute the people for the monarch. It is also because the nation-state is simply the most developed form to date of the idea of a self-governing political community, and the very possibility of a distinctive 'political' theory has been bound up with that idea (Hindess 1991, 1996). Democracy is a source of legitimacy for government and a decision procedure within an entity seen to be self-determining. From the Greek polis, through the civic republicanism of the Italian city-states, to seventeenth-century ideas of government by consent, the notion of the community that controls its social world through collective choice has been central to the Western understanding of politics. Modern liberal, representative democratic theory founded sovereignty in the rule of law rather than in a mere assertion of either *raison d'état* or in unmediated and unlimited popular will. Indeed, the constitutional sovereignty of liberal democracies is best understood, in its internal respect, as a compromise between the claims of *raison d'état* on the one hand, claims that were originally advanced on behalf of the state executive and rulers against popular and republican notions of citizen self-rule, and the claims of democratic legitimacy and unmediated popular sovereignty in relation to collectively binding decisions on the other. The compromise involved locating sovereignty in the law-based, constitutional state, a state based on the popular legitimacy accorded by a homogeneous and individuated people (Hinsley 1986). Democratic elections and the rule of law legitimated the sovereign powers of state institutions, and thus provided a better foundation for a state viewed as the organ of a self-governing territorial community than did the will of a prince. Democratic sovereignty includes citizens and binds them through a common membership that is denied to others.

The notion of the self-governing community has ancient sources, but in the form of the modern nation-state it acquired a distinctive credibility. First, in its pre-democratic guise, the state (as a distinct entity separate from society) monopolized violence, imposed uniform administration and provided a form of the rule of law. States claimed to guarantee a substantial measure of security to citizens from external enemies and internal tumults. This claim, advanced as the justification for enlightened autocracy, became fully credible only when states became representative democracies and matters of war and peace ceased to be determined by princely ambitions and dynastic considerations. Second, the modern state based on representation, and blessed with industrial means of surveillance, communication and transport, could govern its territory with a degree of completeness and comprehensiveness unavailable to previous regimes. Representative government reinforced and legitimated the state's capacities for taxation and, given this fiscal power and the removal of competing and subordinate authorities, could create a uniform national system of administration. On this basis it could extend social governance, for example, creating universal systems of national education or bringing in public health measures. Third, but only in the twentieth century, states acquired the means to manage or direct national economies, either through autarchy and state planning, as with the state-directed economies in Britain and Germany in the two world wars, or through Keynesian measures, using monetary and fiscal policy to influence the decisions of economic actors and thus alter economic outcomes.

Thus by the 1960s the state appeared to be the dominant social entity: state and society were virtually coterminous. The state governed and directed society in both the communist and the Western sphere, albeit in rather different ways. Communist states used one variety of national economic management, through permanent central planning. In the 1960s the excesses of forced socialist construction seemed to be over and reformers such as Khrushchev were promising greater prosperity and peaceful coexistence rather than open conflict with the West. In the advanced Western industrial states it was widely believed that national economic management could continue to ensure both full employment and relatively steady growth. Industrial states, in the East and in the West, were ramified public service agencies, omnicompetent to supervise and to provide for every aspect of the life of their communities. In Western societies still shaped by the industrial revolution, in which the majority of the employed population remained manual workers even into the 1960s, uniform and universal national services in health, education and welfare remained popular. Populations that had only recently escaped the crises of unregulated capitalism continued to welcome collective state social protection, even as they began to enjoy the new mass affluence created by full employment and the long boom after 1945.

This perception of the state has changed out of all recognition and with surprising rapidity. The revolutions of 1989 in Eastern Europe and their aftermath have led to a widespread perception of the modern world as one in which nation-states are losing their capacities for governance and national-level processes are ceding their primacy to global ones. What 1989 ended was a specific structure of conflict between allied groups of nation-states, the Cold War. The Cold War reinforced the need for the nation-state, for its military capacities and for the national-level forms of economic and social regulation necessary to sustain them. The states system was frozen into a pattern of rigid passive confrontation at the centre, with conflict by proxy at the margins. The state continued to be necessary, even though its powers remained in reserve in a suspended conflict. Until 1989 it was still possible, although unlikely and mutually suicidal, that the two superpowers and their allied states might go to war. This eventuality, the fear of a mobilized and immediate enemy, made nation-states necessary. If they weakened or lost their capacity to control their societies, then the enemy might overrun them and, depending on one's viewpoint, destroy the gains of socialism or impose communist tyranny. This blocked conflict preserved the saliency of the national level of government in a way that delayed or masked the changes that would subsequently weaken it.

## The political rhetoric of 'globalization'

In the interregnum of the 1990s, when neo-liberal capitalism appeared to be sweeping triumphantly across the globe, it became fashionable to assert that the era of the nation-state was over, and that national-level governance was ineffective in the face of globalized economic and social processes (Horsman and Marshall 1994). National politics and political choices had been sidelined by global market forces which were stronger than even the most powerful states. Capital was mobile and had no national attachments, locating wherever economic advantage dictated, but labour remained both nationally located and relatively static, and had to adjust its political expectations to meet the new pressures of international competitiveness. Distinct national regimes of extensive labour rights and social protection were thus seen as obsolete. So too were monetary and fiscal policies contrary to the expectations of global markets and transnational companies. The nation-state had ceased to be an effective economic manager. It could only provide those social and public services deemed essential by international capital and at the lowest possible overhead cost. Nation-states were perceived by authors such as Ohmae (1990, 1993) and Reich (1992) to have become the local authorities of the global system. They could no longer independently affect the level of economic activity or employment within their territories: rather that was dictated by the choices of internationally mobile capital. The job of nation-states was like that of municipalities within states heretofore, to provide the infrastructure and public goods that business needs at the lowest possible cost.

This new political rhetoric was based on an anti-political liberalism, and it has by no means vacated the contemporary political scene. Set free from politics, the new globalized economy allows companies and markets to allocate the factors of production to their greatest advantage, and without the distortions of state intervention. Free trade, transnational companies and world capital markets have liberated business from the constraints of politics, enabling it to provide the world's consumers with the cheapest and most efficient products. Globalization realizes the ideals of mid-nineteenth-century free trade liberals such as Cobden and Bright; that is, a demilitarized world in which business activity is primary and political power has no other task than the protection of the world free trading system.

For the political right in the advanced industrial countries, the rhetoric of globalization is a godsend. It provides a new lease of life after the disastrous failure of their monetarist and radical individualist policy experiments in the 1980s. It has argued that labour rights and social welfare of the kind practised in the era of national economic management will render Western societies uncompetitive in relation to the newly industrializing economies of Asia and must be drastically reduced.

For the radical left the concept of globalization also provides release from a different kind of political impasse. Confronted with the collapse of state socialism and of Third World anti-imperialist struggles, the left can see in globalization evidence of the continued reality of the world capitalist system. It can also see the futility of national social democratic reformist strategies. The revolutionary left may be weakened, but the reformists can no longer claim to possess a pragmatic and effective politics. Both right and left are thus able to celebrate the end of the 'Keynesian' era.

Once national politics is held to become more like municipal politics, a matter of providing mundane services, energy drains out of conventional politics, away from established parties, and first-rate people cease to be attracted by a political career. The decline in the centrality of national-level politics, of war, of class conflict and revolution, of effective economic management and social reform, frees political forces from the need to cooperate against enemies without or to collaborate within to maintain national prosperity. Subnationalities and regions can assert their autonomy with less fear: being, for example, an active advocate of Breton culture and interests will no longer have the effect of weakening France in its life or death conflicts with Germany. Equally, cultural homogeneity at the 'national' level is less central in advanced states linked to world markets, since the nation-state as a political entity can offer less. Hence religious, ethnic and lifestyle pluralism can expand within such states, and groups within national states grow in significance as alternative focuses of allegiance for their members.

These arguments have some force. There is no doubt that both the salience and the role of nation-states have changed markedly since the Keynesian era. States are less autonomous, they have less exclusive control over the economic and social processes within their territories, and they are less able to maintain national distinctiveness and cultural homogeneity. But it is increasingly clear that the breathless enthusiasm for the novel in the

1990s overlooked some obvious continuities and did not foresee some not so obvious developments.

## The changing capacities of the nation-state

There are certain areas in which the role of the state has changed radically, and its capacities to control its people and domestic social processes have declined as a consequence. The first of these is in relation to questions of war. The state acquired a monopoly of the means of violence within, the better to be able to mobilize the resources of a territory for external conflict. From the sixteenth century to the present, the primary defining capacity of the modern state has been the power to make war, and to draw on the lives and property of its citizens in order to do so. As we noted, the Cold War kept this power alive. Mutual enmity between East and West reinforced the need for permanent mobilization against an ever-present threat of war. The development of nuclear weapons, however, has had the effect of making war impossible, in the traditional sense of the use of force to attain some objective, at least between the major nuclear powers.

Classically war was seen as a means of decision, victory settling an issue between states that could be resolved in no other way. Clausewitzian war was purposive, and to that degree rational, the continuation of policy by other means. Nuclear war between roughly equal combatants could end only in mutual destruction and the negation of any rational policy pursued by the officials of the participating states. As Bernard Brodie perceptively observed (immediately after Hiroshima), the principal function of nuclear weapons was deterrence: 'Thus far the chief purpose of our military establishment has been to win wars. From now on its chief purpose must be to avert them' (1965, p. 31). War between nuclear states had become, if not impossible, then irrational, whether they were liberal or illiberal, provided their leaders were possessed of minimal rationality. Non-nuclear conflicts could only occur in peripheral regions, conflicts by proxy where the defeat of one side would not lead to the threat of nuclear war. The possession of nuclear weapons thus also ended the possibility of conventional war between nuclear states. Nuclear weapons drove war out of international relations between advanced states, being no longer an alternative means of decision but the threat of a terrible mutual disaster that needed to be negotiated away.

Armed forces will not cease to exist, but they cannot decide matters between advanced states. And the disparity of forces between the great powers and major states in the South is so great that, when the great powers perceive their vital interests to be at stake, the latter cannot rearrange matters to their advantage by conventional armed force, as the Gulf War of 1991 proved. On the other hand, the great powers cannot easily install new states more to their liking in the aftermath of military victories over militarily weak rivals or enemies, as the continuing wars in Afghanistan and Iraq have demonstrated. Empire without imperialists on the ground, what Michael Ignatieff (1997) has termed empire-lite, simply doesn't work against mobilized populations with ready access to lethal, if low-technology, force.

This does not mean we shall live in a peaceful world. Outside relations among the main powers, the post-war picture was very different, and this may continue. Despite the UN Charter's prohibition on the use of force except in self-defence, 'Between 1945 and 1999, two-thirds of the members of the United Nations – 126 states out of 189 – fought 291 inter-state conflicts in which over 22 million people were killed' (Michael Glennon, cited in Freedman 2004, p. 107). Lesser states will fight one another. Advanced states, specifically the USA, may continue to fight preventive wars and will likely continue to be threatened by terrorism. Revolutionary movements will continue to arise on the impoverished periphery, new but local 'beggars' armies' such as the Zapatistas in Chiapas, Mexico. Revolutionary movements will articulate specific local antagonisms, but they will no longer seem to be detachments in a single struggle united by a common anti-capitalist and anti-imperialist ideology. But it does mean, in the advanced states at least, that governments are unlikely to have the occasion to call on the lives and property of their citizens for war. They will no longer be able to mobilize their societies and demand and create the solidarity and common identification with authority necessary to the effective pursuit of total war. It is no accident that, among the European members of NATO, states – for example, Germany – with conscript armed forces are extremely reluctant to fight even in NATO-sanctioned operations such as Afghanistan, while those with all-volunteer forces – such as the United Kingdom – face fewer constraints. War presupposes a degree of domestic social consent.

War, the presence of a genuine enemy, reinforced national solidarity and made credible the claim to national cultural homogeneity. Without war, without enemies, the state becomes less significant to the citizen. When peoples really faced enemies, invaders and conquerors, they needed their state and their fellow citizens. The liberal state, claiming to live peacefully with its neighbours and to make limited demands on its own people, could claim great legitimacy if attacked, thereby rousing its people to a degree of commitment and common effort that authoritarian states could seldom match. These legitimations are gone, and with them whole classes of provision for 'national' needs justified by the possible contingency of war: 'national' industries, health and welfare to promote 'national efficiency', and social solidarity to unite rich and poor in a common struggle. European social democracy profited from industrialized conventional war: it could deliver organized labour to the all-out war effort at the price of economic and social reforms. The European society of states has passed from an anarchical condition to a quasi-civil one and, especially in relation to economic and social matters, the vast majority of states are bound together in numerous ways in what amounts to an international political society – in the case of the major advanced states of the G8 and OECD, a virtual standing association of states with its own rules and decision procedures. This does not mean that national states are irrelevant, but it does mean that their claim to a monopoly of the means of legitimate violence within a given territory is no longer so defining of their political existence.

That said, the world is not moving beyond a situation where military power continues to play a very important indirect political role. Brodie was substantially correct, but he could not be expected to have foreseen the complexity in the evolution of doctrines of deterrence. In practice, deterrence, especially extended deterrence – that is, its use to protect allies and to signal political intentions in conflict involving proxies – was never simple and straightforward; rather deterrence was unstable and nuclear stalemate was bought at ever higher cost, and it took half a century of extreme risk and the danger of extinction before the bipolar order of the Cold War superpowers came to an end. Even then, the Cold War ended only as a result of the political dissolution of one of the contending parties; it was not negotiated away as a matter of military logic, notwithstanding the elaborate treaty and mutual inspection regimes that developed under détente and after. Moreover, the continuing evolution of nuclear weapons policy in the USA since the end of the Cold War – the Revolution in Military Affairs, the development of new missile and bomb technologies, the withdrawal from the Anti-Ballistic Missile Treaty and the development of missile defence systems, and the space-based technologies – has involved 'the reliance on new technology, both nuclear and non-nuclear, to provide new "options"; the restatement that nuclear weapons remain "fundamental"; and the expressed desire and willingness to effect this transition from present to future force posture without negotiation with, or possibly even reference to, other states' parties' (Prins 2002, p. 255). Whether the modernization of Russian nuclear forces under President Medvedev and Prime Minister Putin and the ongoing modernization of China's nuclear capacity and strategy will alter this posture and produce a new kind of détente remains to be seen.

The continued reliance of the major powers on nuclear weapons for some kind of deterrence (as well as the possibilities of further nuclear proliferation beyond Israel, Pakistan and India to Iran and beyond) has implications for the geopolitical integration of the North Atlantic Treaty Organization (NATO). Perhaps the central question facing US policy towards this region is how, if at all, to develop further the forms and levels of cooperation achieved thus far. At the core of this is the question of American attitudes towards the European Union and NATO. Although the reproduction of mass production, mass consumption

capitalism in Europe provided an economic basis for transatlantic cooperation, there can be little doubt that the Cold War rivalry between the superpowers, and the competition for global influence between capitalism and
communism, also served to cement political and military relations across
the Atlantic.

It was NATO's guarantee of the post-war division of Europe, defining
the westward limit of Soviet power and settling decisively the German
problem, which stabilized the states system in Western Europe. The American military presence in Western Europe, as well as the extension of the
US nuclear guarantee to its NATO allies – that is, extended deterrence –
may have been a form of informal empire, or hegemony, but it was also an
'empire by invitation', and it provided the framework within which the EU
could develop as a 'civilian' power. European integration has, in effect,
been the enemy of European military power on a wider international
stage.

One implication of this massive disparity in military power, as Robert
Kagan has pointed out, is that the USA and Europe see questions of power
and international order in radically different ways. This is also a consequence of the fact that the EU is more a regional than a global power,
whereas the converse is the case for the United States. The EU has developed as a civilian power. Indeed, European integration has, thus far, gone
hand in hand with a *decline* in Europe's relative military power, while that
of the USA has increased. This leaves the EU no option, for the present,
but to conduct its foreign policy through diplomacy and economic statecraft. Simply put, it has no serious military options. Yet, it aspires to a global
role in a world that is far from dispensing with military power. 'Today's
transatlantic problem', writes Kagan:

> is a [military] power problem. America's power, and its willingness to exercise
> that power – unilaterally if necessary – represents a threat to Europe's new
> sense of mission.... American [military] power made it possible for Euro-
> peans to believe that power was no longer important. (2002, p. 23)

This is an oversimplification, since much of the transatlantic debate – as
in the dispute over how to deal with Iraq – turns on different assessments
of the long-term costs and benefits of using military power (it also overlooks
the fierce divisions *within* both Europe and America, as evidenced by the
run-up to the war in Iraq in 2003), but it does capture an important reason
why politicians across the Atlantic often appear to talk past one another.
Nevertheless, the only distributive power possessed by the EU is economic.
The USA, by contrast, has military power as well. Consequently, the assessment of how far to pursue some goals collectively is bound to differ from
one side of the Atlantic to the other.

Just as nuclear weapons have transformed the conditions of war, weakening the central rationale for the state's ability to mobilize its citizens in

the process, so too the new communications and information technologies have loosened the state's exclusiveness of control of its territory, reducing its capacities for cultural control and homogenization. It is a commonplace that digitalized communications, satellites, fax machines and computer networks have rendered the licensing and control of information media by the state all but impossible, not merely undermining ideological dictatorships but also subverting all attempts to preserve cultural homogeneity by state force.

Modern communications form the basis for an international civil society, people who share interests and associations across borders. The international media also make possible a set of cosmopolitan cultures, elite and popular, scientific and artistic, linked through the medium of English as a universal rather than a national language. Such cultures, from children watching Tom and Jerry cartoons on TV to physicists gossiping on e-mail, are inevitably international. Cultural homogeneity becomes increasingly problematic, since 'national' cultures are merely one of several cultures in which people participate for different purposes. Cosmopolitan and national cultures interact. Complete cultural homogeneity and exclusiveness are less and less possible. 'National' cultures that aim to be dominant over the individuals who belong to them are increasingly projects of resistance to and retreat from the world. Inward-looking nationalism and cultural fundamentalism are, to put it bluntly, the politics of losers. It is virtually impossible to continue to operate in the various world markets and still ignore the internationalized cultures that go along with them. Such inward-looking nationalisms do exist and will continue to develop, but, to the degree that their political projects are successful, they have the effect of marginalizing their societies. Although they are responses to economic backwardness, such nationalisms act to reinforce it. The same is true of social groups within advanced states that claim an all-pervasive identity, be that ethnic, religious or whatever: they condemn their members to social marginality.

The existence of different languages and religions, as Kant pointed out, virtually guarantees cultural diversity. Distinct local cultural traditions will continue to coexist with cosmopolitan cultural practices. What is threatened, however, is the idea of an exclusive and virtually self-sufficient 'national' culture, of which individuals are simply exemplars, sharing a common language, beliefs and activities. States strenuously attempted to create such cultures through common systems of national education, military service, etc. (Anderson 1991). That such projects are no longer possible for advanced states means that they have to seek bases of citizen loyalty outside of basic cultural homogeneity. In the major cities of most advanced states dozens of languages and almost every conceivable religion are commonly used and observed. As we shall see, the state will probably find a new rationale in managing this very diversity, acting as the public power that enables such communities to coexist and to resolve conflicts. Space and culture have no definite relation to one another. In the great cities of the advanced countries at least, the cultures of the world are more or less randomly mixed. The state in the era of 'nation building' tried to turn its people into artefacts of itself, representative specimens of the 'national' culture. In the interest of individual liberty and the values of cosmopolitanism and cultural diversity, we should be grateful that states can make fewer and less credible claims on our imaginations and beliefs.

The state may have less control over ideas, but it remains a controller of its borders and the movement of people across them. As we have seen, apart from a 'club class' of internationally mobile, highly skilled professionals, and the desperate, poor migrants and refugees who will suffer almost any hardship to leave intolerable conditions, the bulk of the world's population now cannot easily move. Workers in advanced countries have no 'frontier' societies to which to migrate as they did in huge numbers to countries such as the United States, Australia or Argentina in the nineteenth century and in lesser numbers in the 1970s. In the absence of substantial, routine labour mobility, states will retain powers over their peoples. They define who is and who is not a citizen, who may and who may not receive welfare. In this respect, despite the rhetoric of globalization, the bulk of the world's population lives in closed worlds, trapped by the lottery of birth. For the average worker or farmer with a family, one's nation-state is a community of fate. Wealth and income are not global, they are nationally and regionally distributed between poorer and richer states and localities. For the vast majority of people, nation-states cannot be regarded as just municipalities or local authorities, providing services that one chooses according to their relative quality and cost.

Nationally rooted labour has to seek local strategies and local benefits if it is to improve its lot. The question is whether business is similarly constrained, or whether it can simply choose new and more optimal locations. Internationally open cultures and rooted populations present an explosive contradiction. The impoverished can see the consumption and lifestyles of the affluent. They know another world is possible, whether they are watching it in a slum apartment in an advanced country or a shanty town in the South. The ideology of socialist revolution may have few takers, but one should not imagine that the world's poor will remain cowed or passively accept their poverty. Their responses, whether through street crime or guerrilla struggles as in Chiapas, will be far harder to cope with than old-style revolts in the name of communism. Such responses will be local, and less aggregated in ideological terms with other conflicts. Hence these struggles will be left in the main to local states and local elites to contain. The advanced world currently does not think its frontier begins in the jungle of Yucatan in the way it once thought it did in the jungles of Vietnam or Bolivia.

As the advanced countries seek to police the movement of the world's poor and exclude them, the capriciousness of the notions of citizenship and of political community will become ever more evident. Advanced states will not be able to make effective use of the claim to cultural homogeneity as a principle of exclusion – for they are already ethnically and culturally pluralistic. Exclusion will be a mere fact, with no other logic or legitimacy than that states are fearful of the consequences of large-scale migration. A world of wealth and poverty, with appalling and widening differences in living standards between the richest and the poorest nations, is unlikely to be secure or stable. Industrial workers in the advanced countries fear the cheap labour of well-educated and skilled workers in the upper tier of developing countries such as Taiwan or Malaysia or even China and India. The poor of the South see themselves as abandoned by a rich world that trades more and more with itself and with the emerging South. Both groups are stuck within the borders of states, forced to regard their countries as communities of fate and to seek solutions within the limits of their enforced residence.

However, as we have argued above, mere nationalism as such will provide no solution to these problems. The assertion of ethnic, cultural or religious homogeneity may serve as a cultural compensation for poverty, as an opium of the economically backward, but it will not cure it. Such localizing ideologies will continue to be politically successful in areas where significant numbers of people see they have not benefited at all from the world free trade order. But such ideologies will not alter the fact of poverty.

National revolutions in the South may have been successful in political terms, in overthrowing colonial domination, but, as projects of economic and social modernization, too many have proved to be failures. They required autarchic withdrawal from world markets, the socialization of agriculture and forced-march industrialization. Everywhere – save for North Korea – such strategies have been abandoned. Unfortunately for the world's poor, they cannot exit the free trade system and transform their societies by their own efforts within their own borders. The problem is that, without a transformation in the international economic order, without new strategies and priorities in the advanced countries towards the bottom billion in the South, and without large-scale foreign capital investment and trade protection against resurgent Asia, poor countries are unlikely to benefit much from turning away from autarchy either.

## Governance and the world economy

There can be no doubt that politics is becoming more polycentric, with states as merely one level in a complex system of overlapping and often competing agencies of governance. But this complexity and multiplicity of levels and types of governance implies a world quite different from that of the rhetoric of 'globalization', and one in which there is a distinct, significant and continuing place for the nation-state. We should make it clear again at this point that the issue of control of economic activity in a more integrated internationalized economy is one of govern*ance* and not just of the continuing roles of govern*ments*. Sovereign nation-states claimed as their distinctive feature the right to determine how any activity within their territory was governed, either performing that function themselves or setting the limits for other agencies. That is, they claimed, though never fully achieved, a monopoly of the function of governance. Hence the tendency in common usage to identify the term 'government' with those institutions of state that control and regulate the life of a territorial community. But governance – that is, the purposive control of an activity by some means such that a range of desired outcomes is attained – is not just the province of the state. Rather it is a function that can be performed by a wide variety of public and private, state and non-state, national, transnational and international institutions and practices. The comparison or analogy of present-day governance with the Middle Ages simply helps us to grasp this by thinking back to a period before the attempt at the monopolization of governance functions by sovereign nation-states. That is its only and strictly limited purpose.

Some authors, such as Cerny (1998) and Minc (1993), press the analogy with the Middle Ages much too far. The reference is at best metaphoric and in many ways is far from apt. We are not returning to a world like the Middle Ages and before the development of national 'sovereignty'. This is not just because national states and the 'sovereign' control of peoples persist but also because the scope and role of forms of governance are radically different today. In the Middle Ages, the coexistence of parallel, competing and overlapping authorities was possible, if conflictual, because economies and societies were far less integrated. The degree of division of labour and hence economic interdependence was relatively low, whereas today communities depend for their very existence on the meshing and coordination of distinct and often remote activities. Markets alone cannot provide such interconnection and coordination – or rather they can do so only if they are appropriately governed and if the rights and expectations of distant participants are secured and sustained (Durkheim 1964).

Hence governing powers cannot simply proliferate and compete. The different levels and functions of governance need to be tied together in a division of control that sustains the division of labour. If this does not happen, then the unscrupulous can exploit and the unlucky can fall into the 'gaps' between different agencies and dimensions of governance. The governing powers need to be 'sutured' together into a relatively integrated system. If this is not the case, then these gaps will lead to the corrosion of governance at every level. The issue at stake is whether such a coherent system will develop, and it takes priority over the question of whether international governance can be democratic or cosmopolitan. The answer to this former question remains moot. But simplistic versions of the globalization thesis do not help to resolve it, because they induce fatalism about the capacity of the key agencies in promoting coherent national, regional and international strategies.

The nation-state is central to this process of 'suturing': the policies and practices of states in distributing power upwards to the international level and downwards to subnational agencies are the ties that will hold the system of governance together. Without such explicit policies to close gaps in governance and elaborate a division of control in regulation, then vital capacities will be lost. Authority may now be plural within and between states rather than nationally centralized, but to be effective it must be structured by an element of design into a relatively coherent architecture of institutions. This the more simplistic 'globalization' theorists deny, either because they believe the world economy is ungovernable, given volatile markets and divergent interests, and therefore that no element of design is possible, or because they see the market as a mechanism of coordination in and of itself that makes any attempt at an institutional architecture to govern it unnecessary.

The evidence we have considered so far on the key aspects of this question – the character of the world financial markets, the pattern of world trade and FDI, the number and role of MNCs, the prospects for growth in the developing world and the key aspects of international economic governance – all confirms that there is no strong tendency towards a globalized economy and that the major advanced nations and regions and the emerging powers of the South continue to play key political roles.

The main reason why such international governance is provided by nations and regions is that most players in the international economy have an interest in financial stability, including the major companies, for whom a reduction in uncertainty is of obvious advantage in their planning of investment and in their production and marketing strategies. It has become obvious that derivatives, once turned into speculative investment, no longer offer adequate means of containing risk: they show the advantages of stabilization of the international financial system by public regulation. The idea, common among extreme globalization theorists, that major companies will benefit from an unregulated international environment remains a strange one. Calculable trade rules, settled and internationally consistent property rights, the containment of excessive volatility in security markets, and exchange-rate stability add up to a level of elementary security that companies need to plan ahead, and therefore a condition of continued investment and growth. Companies cannot create such conditions for themselves, even if they are 'transnational'. Stability in the international economy can be had only if states combine to regulate it and to agree on common objectives and standards of governance. Companies may want free trade and common regimes of trade standards, but they can only have them if states work together to achieve common international regulation.

Equally, the notion that companies should wish to be 'transnational' in the sense of extraterritorial is also a strange one. The national economic bases from which most companies operate actually contribute to their economic efficiency, and not just in the sense of providing low-cost infrastructure. Most firms are embedded in a distinct national culture of business that provides them with intangible but very real advantages. Managers and core staff have common understandings that go beyond formal training or company policies. Genuinely transnational companies, with no primary location and a multinational workforce, would have to try to create within the firm the cultural advantages and forms of identification that other firms get almost free from national institutions. They would have to get core workers to put the company first as a source of identification and build a cohesive non-national managerial elite that can communicate implicitly one with another. This transnationality has traditionally been achieved only by non-economic organizations with a strong ideological mission providing a focus of loyalty alternative to countries and states, such as the Society of Jesus. This would be difficult for companies to match. After all, the Jesuits are culturally distinct, even if multinational, products of a distinctive Latin Catholic environment and education. It is difficult to make the firm the exclusive cultural focus of an individual's life, and for individuals to make an ongoing commitment to one company, entirely removed from national connections. Those Japanese managers and core workers who see the firm as a primary and ongoing social community do this in a *national* context where this makes sense.

Companies benefit not just from national business cultures, but from nation-states and national communities as social organizations. This is emphasized by the literature on national systems of innovation and on national business systems (Athreye and Simonetti 2004). These national business systems are quite distinct from the forms of homogeneity preached by cultural nationalists, but they remain tenaciously distinctive in a way that many other forms of national culture do not. Companies benefit from being enmeshed in networks of relations with central and local governments, with trade associations, with organized labour, with specifically national financial institutions oriented towards local companies and with national systems of skill formation and labour motivation. These networks provide information, they are a means to cooperation and coordination between firms to secure common objectives, and they help to make the business environment less uncertain and more stable. A national or supranational regional economic system provides forms of reassurance to firms against the shocks and risks of the international economy. As we have argued, such national business-oriented systems have been most evident in the developed world in Germany and Japan, both of which have had strongly solidaristic relationships between industry, labour and the state, and in the developing world in such countries as South Korea and Taiwan. To varied extents, these national systems are being reconfigured in more regional terms, especially within Europe and in the Euro area.

But national advantages are not confined to those societies whose institutions promote solidarity in order to balance cooperation and competition between firms and between the major social interests. The USA has a national business culture that emphasizes competition and the autonomy of the individual corporation. But, contra fashionable arguments such as those of Reich (1992), US firms find that there are very real benefits in remaining distinctly American that stem from the power and functions of the national state (Kapstein 1991; Tyson 1991; Doremus et al. 1998): for example, that the US dollar still largely remains a key medium of international trade, that regulatory and standard-setting bodies such as the Federal Aviation Administration and the Food and Drug Administration are world leaders and work closely with US industry, that the US courts are a major means of defence of commercial and property rights throughout the world, and that the federal government is a massive subsidizer of R&D and also a strong protector of the interests of US firms abroad.

The advantages provided by public power to companies and markets are not confined to the national level. Indeed, for many vital services to business and forms of cooperation between firms, national-level institutions are too remote for adequate local knowledge and effective governance. We argued earlier that regional governments are providers of vital collective services to industry throughout the advanced industrial world. In particular, regional governments are the public articulation of industrial districts composed of small and medium-sized firms, and are a major reason why such firms can be internationally competitive and enjoy advantages comparable to the economies of scale of larger firms. The existence of regional economic governance, of thriving industrial districts and of an effective partnership and division of labour between national states and regional governments is a central component of the success of national economies in world markets.

The general point is that markets and companies cannot exist without a public power to protect them, including in the international arena, where the world's trading order ultimately requires military force to back it, to keep markets relatively open and to guard access to key resources, and this is something that, for the OECD world at least, only NATO and Japan, and specifically the United States, can provide.

If the foregoing arguments have any merit, then the majority of companies, large and small, that are active in international markets have a strong interest in continued public governance, national and international, of the world economy. Internationally they seek a measure of security and stability in financial markets, a secure framework of free trade, and the protection of commercial rights. Nationally they seek to profit from the distinct advantages conferred by the cultural and institutional frameworks of the successful industrial states. If companies have such interests, then it is highly unlikely that an ungoverned global economy composed of unregulated markets will come into existence.

In this and previous chapters we have demonstrated that there are good economic and political grounds for arguing that the international economy is by no means ungovernable. In chapter 7 we discussed three levels of international economic governance:

1   governance through a substantial number of states operating in international, multilateral regulatory agencies designed for a specific dimension of activity, such as the WTO for trade and, increasingly, FDI; the IMF for financial and monetary matters; the World Bank for development policy; and the various bodies under the UN umbrella for issues to do with such things as labour standards (the ILO) or the environment.
2   the governance of large economic areas by regional trade and investment blocs such as the EU and NAFTA, blocs that are large enough to pursue social and other agendas in a way that many medium-sized states may be unable to do on an independent basis. These blocs – at least in the case of the EU – share sufficient common ground to elaborate forms of governance beyond the nation-state so as to make limited delegation and even pooling of national sovereignty possible in certain spheres of decision-making.
3   governance through agreement between the major political entities that represent the dominant shares of world trade, investment and monetary power – until recently the G3 of the United States, Japan and the Euro area, but now including also China (as the leading Asian surplus country) and Saudi Arabia (as the dominant oil producer) – to manage global imbalances, to stabilize exchange-rate movements, to defuse protectionist pressures and to regulate destabilizing short-term financial transactions.

In the light of what has just been discussed, to this list we should add two more:

4   national-level policies or, as in the case of some aspects of European governance, supranational regional policies that balance cooperation and competition between firms and the major social interests.
5   regional (subnational) policies of providing collective services to industrial districts.

Taken together, such institutional arrangements and strategies can assure some minimal level of international economic governance, to the benefit of at least the major advanced industrial nations and perhaps now substantial parts of resurgent Asia. Such governance cannot alter the extreme inequalities between those nations and the rest in terms of trade and investment, income and wealth. Unfortunately, that is not really the problem raised by the concept of globalization. The issue is not whether the world's economy is governable towards ambitious goals such as promoting social justice, equality between countries and greater democratic control for the bulk of the world's people, but whether it is governable at all.

## The 'new' sovereignty

If such mechanisms of international governance and re-regulation are to be developed further, then the role of nation-states will be pivotal. Nation-states should no longer be seen as 'governing' powers, able to impose outcomes on all dimensions of policy within a given territory by their own authority, but as loci from which forms of governance can be proposed, legitimated and monitored. Nation-states are now simply one class of power and political agency in a complex system of power from world to local level, but they have a centrality because of their relationship to territory and population.

Populations remain territorial and subject to the citizenship of a national state. States remain 'sovereign', not in the sense that they are all-powerful or omnicompetent within their territories, but because they police the borders of a territory and, to the degree that they are credibly democratic, are representative of the citizens within those borders. Regulatory regimes, international agencies, common policies sanctioned by treaty, all come into existence because major nation-states have agreed to create them and to confer legitimacy on them by exercising their sovereignty collectively in and through them. The capacity for decision-making is alienable – states cede power to suprastate agencies – but it is not a fixed quantum.

Authority is, in effect, alienable and divisible, but states acquire new roles even as they cede some power, and in particular they come to have the function of legitimating and supporting the authorities they have created by such grants of rightful decision-making. If 'sovereignty' is of decisive significance now as a distinguishing feature of the nation-state, it is because the state has the role of a source of legitimacy in transferring power or sanctioning new powers both 'above' it and 'below' it: above – through agreements between states to establish and abide by forms of international governance; below – through the state's constitutional ordering within its own territory of the relationship of power and authority between central, regional and local governments and also the publicly recognized 'private' governments in civil society. Nation-states are still of central significance because they are the key practitioners of the art of government as the process of distributing power, ordering other governments by giving them shape and legitimacy. Nation-states can do this in a way no other agency can; they are pivots between international agencies and subnational activities because they provide legitimacy as the exclusive voice of a territorially bounded population. They can practise the art of government as a process of distributing power only if they can credibly present their decisions as having the legitimacy of popular support.

In a system of governance in which international agencies and regulatory bodies are already significant and are growing in scope, nation-states are crucial agencies of representation. Such a system of governance amounts to a global polity, and in it the major nation-states are the global 'electors'. States ensure that, in a very mediated degree, international bodies are answerable to the world's key publics, and that decisions backed by the major states can be enforced by international agencies because they will be reinforced by domestic laws and local state power.

Such representation is very indirect, but it is the closest to democracy and accountability that international governance is likely to get. The key publics in advanced democracies have some influence on their states, and these states can affect international policies. Such influence is likely to be increased if the populations of major states are informed and roused on an issue by the world 'civil society' of transnational non-governmental organizations. Such NGOs, for example Greenpeace or the Red Cross, are more credible candidates to be genuine transnational actors than are companies. It is easier to create a cosmopolitan agency for common world causes such as the environment or human rights than it is to build a rootless business whose staff are asked to identify with its mundane activities above all else in the world.

Moreover, the category of non-governmental organization is a misnomer. These are not governments, but many of them play crucial roles of governance, especially in the interstices between states and international regulatory regimes. Thus Greenpeace effectively helps to police international agreements on whaling. Equally, where nation-states are indeed as weak and ineffective as the globalization theorists suppose all states to be, as in parts of Africa, NGOs such as Oxfam provide some of the elementary functions of government such as education, as well as famine relief.

An internationally governed economic system in which certain key policy dimensions are controlled by world agencies, trade blocs, major treaties between nation-states ensuring common policies, and elements of coordination in the management of the major currencies will thus continue to give the nation-state a key role. This role stresses the specific feature of nation-states that other agencies lack, their ability to make bargains stick: upwards because they are representative of territories, and downwards because they are constitutionally legitimate powers. Paradoxically, then, the degree to which the world economy has internationalized (but not globalized) reinstates the need for the nation-state, not in its traditional guise as a body that attempts to monopolize all governance within its territory, but as a crucial relay between the international levels of governance and the articulate publics of the developed and emerging developing worlds.

## Nation-states and the rule of law

So far we have discussed the persistence of the nation-state primarily in terms of its role within a system of international governance. There is, however, another reason to argue that the 'nation'-state will persist as an important form of political organization, a reason closely connected with one of the central traditional claims to 'sovereignty', that is, to be the primary source of binding rules – law – within a given territory. This role of the state as monopoly lawmaker was closely connected with the development of a monopoly of the means of violence and with the development of a coherent system of administration providing the principal means of governance within a territory. Today, however, this role of upholding the rule of law is relatively independent of those other elements in the historical process of the formation of the modern state.

To sum up the argument in advance: nation-states as sources of the rule of law are essential prerequisites for regulation through international law, and as overarching public powers they are essential to the survival of pluralistic 'national' societies with diversified forms of administration and community standards. States may be the key source of the rule of law without being 'sovereign' in the traditional sense, that is, standing against all external entities as the sole means of government in a territory, or standing above subnational governments and associations as the body from which they derive their powers by recognition and concession. Omnicompetence, exclusivity and omnipotence of the state are not necessary to the rule of law: indeed, historically they have been the attributes of states, deriving from the portmanteau theory of sovereignty, that have served to undermine it.

States have been Janus-faced: embodying substantive decision-making and administrative powers, on one hand, and sources of rules enabling and limiting their own actions and those of their citizens, on the other. These two aspects may be pulling apart, and in large measure for the good. The power of nation-states as administrative and policy-making agencies has declined. We have seen that the decline in the salience of war and the restriction of the scope of national economic management have lessened the claims that states as governing agencies can make on their societies. This does not mean that the lawmaking and constitutional ordering functions of states will decline in the same measure. One aspect of the state is substantive and outcome oriented, a matter of political decision and the implementation of such decisions through administration; the other aspect is procedural and concerns the state's role as regulator of social action in the widest sense, of rules as guides to action and of constitutional ordering as adjudicating between the competing claims of corporate entities and citizens.

The state as a source of constitutional ordering, enabling and limiting its own and others' powers and guiding action through rights and rules, is central to the rule of law (Hirst 1994). Commercial societies require that minimum of certainty and constancy in the action of administrators and economic actors that the rule of law implies. Western societies have been economically successful and reactively civilized in their treatment of their members when they have provided the security and the certainty of the rule of law, limiting the harms that citizens, companies and governments could do. Politics, ideology and state policy have frequently undermined the rule of law, governments abandoning the civilized limits of state action in the pursuit of overarching political goals, especially in circumstances of military conflict.

If we are moving into a more complex and pluralistic social and political system, then the rule of law will become more rather than less important. Even more so than in the sphere of administrative regulation, 'gaps' between jurisdictions are fatal to the certainty and security necessary for actors in a commercial society, for they allow the unscrupulous to evade their own obligations and to violate others' rights. For example, tax havens, flags of convenience, dumping grounds for pollution, etc., all allow advanced world economic actors to avoid First World obligations. A world composed of diverse political forces, governing agencies, and organizations at both international and national level will need an interlocking network of public powers that regulate and guide action in a relatively consistent way, providing minimum standards of conduct and relief from harms. In this sense we are considering constitutional ordering and the rule of law in their aspect as a *pouvoir neutre*, not as part of issue-oriented politics or administrative regulation. Our model for such a power remains the *Rechtsstaat*, and national states are its primary embodiment in so far as they correspond to that conception of authority as a source of law that is itself lawful and limited in its action by rules.

Within states, the role of such an independent public power that arbitrates between other powers, that is neutral between plural and competing social communities with different standards, and that provides highly individuated citizens with a common procedural basis on which to regulate their interactions will become more rather than less important. A pluralistic system of authority and pluralistic communities require a public power as the medium through which they may contain their conflicts. As Figgis (1913) argued at the beginning of the twentieth century, the decline of the excessive claims of state 'sovereignty' does not mean the end of a lawmaking public power. The state may no longer be 'sovereign' in this old sense, it may share authority with subnational governments whose specific autonomous powers are guaranteed, and it may no longer view associations and corporate bodies as legal fictions that have been granted what powers they have by its own revocable fiat, but it will define the scope of legitimate authority and legitimate action in its roles as constitutional arbitrator and lawmaker.

In an individualistic and pluralistic society, where there are few common standards, where strong binding collectivities have declined and been replaced by communities of choice, and where informal social sanctions have weakened, then the rule of law is more rather than less necessary. This does not mean that states will be able to cope fully with the multiple problems and conflicts that arise from the growing pluralism of modern societies; rather we are claiming that, without a public power that mediates between these plural groups through the rule of law, such conflicts will become intolerable (Hirst 1993, chap. 3). In a sense the decline of war as a source of national cohesion and the lessening role of the state as an economic manager reduce the powers and claims that states can exert over society as administrative agencies and focuses of political identification. They have less capacity to impose external cohesion on groups. The other consequence of this is that they are becoming less Janus-faced, less encumbered with the need to balance their roles as primary administrator and neutral public power in a way that makes it easier for them credibly to give primacy to the latter role. A cooling of national politics gives states the space to expand their role as arbiters between conflicting interests, something that the excessive and overcharged claims to 'sovereignty' as omnicompetence made problematic.

Externally, the role of states as sources of the rule of law will also become more central. If international economic, environmental and social governance expands, so the role of international law will increase. International agencies, international regimes based on treaties and interstate agreements, international 'civil' agencies performing world public functions in the defence of human rights and environmental standards, all imply an extension of the scope of international law. However, international law cannot function without national states, not merely as its material supports and the agents to whom it is addressed, but as *Rechtsstaats*, agencies that create and abide by law. International law without a significant population of states that are sources of the rule of law is a contradictory enterprise. An international society as an association of states cannot rely on supranational bodies to make and enforce laws but requires states that accept constitutional limitations above and below them. In this sense the move from an anarchical society of states to a world in which states are part of a common association requires that the member states of that association accept international legal obligations and also govern internally according to the requirements of the rule of law. In this sense the state as the source and the respecter of binding rules remains central to an internationalized economy and society, for there is simply no other repository of political authority and power that bears such an integral relation to law as the broadly representative rule-of-law state. Without law states (i.e. a territorially organized people whose political system is constitutionalized under the rule of law) as the primary subjects of interstate law, there would be nothing for multilateral or supranational rules of adjudication and change to latch on to, and hence the legal order would unravel for want of valid recognition, legitimation and enforcement.

To this extent, while we agree with Saskia Sassen (2006) that instantiations of the global inside the national do not need to run through supra- or international arrangements, or through more 'globalized' domains such as financial markets, that they can be assembled by new assemblages of actors, rights and institutions within the nation-state, we do not think that this heralds a system-wide shift to a global assemblage of territory, authority and rights. However, Sassen is surely right to suggest that, by contrast with earlier world scales, which were 'constituted through the projection of emerging national territorial states onto the world', 'today's world scale . . . is constituted in good part through the insertion of global into a growing number of nation-states with the purpose of forming global systems' (Sassen 2006, p. 16). Does this also imply that, although the growth of that older world scale was imperial and led to heightened international rivalry, today the production of global integration by virtue of its instantiation inside the national means that world scale and international rivalry are 'inversely related'? Perhaps, but not only or even primarily for the reasons addressed by Sassen.

## Conclusions: cooperation or conflict?

We have argued that forms of international economic governance are possible and that states that are representative of their population and operating under the rule of law can coordinate elements of a quasi-constitutional order for the world economy. Among the states involved in these arrangements there will be considerable competition and occasional conflict over the distribution of the benefits, but the overall picture is one in which the major players gain and do not worry overly about their relative positions. This is because there are few circumstances in which a position of relative advantage, used as a means of power in situations of conflict with other states, can be used to gain more than can be achieved from cooperation. In general, the costs of exercising such power are too high and the benefits too elusive to make conflict a rational policy. Collective empowerment, followed by bargaining over the distribution of the benefits, is the default option. It is above all this basic economic logic, as well as the insertions of the global into the national emphasized by Sassen, that glues the system together.

That said, there are states that are partly integrated into this order – Russia and China to mention two important ones – that are not representative rule-of-law states. And there are still geopolitical divisions among the major powers of the system, even if the bipolar confrontation of the Cold War has gone. We have also argued that much of the *de facto* and *de jure* integration of this governance is supranational or regional in form rather than fully global. For instance, the instantiation of the *European* inside the national within the nation-states of the EU has a much greater solidity in the relevant political and legal systems than more global insertions. It is, for example, the *European* Convention on Human Rights to which citizens of the EU appeal, whether in the European Court of Justice or in their national legal systems, not the general UN one. To be sure, the one derives from the other, just as, say, European commercial policy and law seeks to be WTO compatible, but the point still stands that global standards, rules and the like are often inserted into the national via the mediation of the supranational regional order.

Yet, not only are the major regions of the world economy – the EU, NAFTA and APEC – quite differently placed in terms of their economic integration internally and with one another, but also the major states in these regional agglomerations have complicated geopolitical alignments with one another. It is thus an open question as to how far supranational regional integration and economic governance will interact with the wider multilateral order, on the one side, and with the arrangements between the major political entities that represent the dominant shares of world trade, investment and monetary power, on the other. And it is also an open question as to how the governance of international economic matters will interact with the changing geopolitical alignments consequent upon the collapse of communism and the revival of industrialization in resurgent Asia. There is little in the economic logic of globalization that guarantees that these political and geopolitical challenges will be stably managed.

Previous conjunctures of integration in the world economy, from the 1870s until 1914 and after 1945, rested on specific conjunctions of political support within key states and geopolitical alignments between them. But social and political conflict within states and geopolitical rivalries between them rapidly undid this order in the First World War and during the interwar years. Thus far, the period of liberalization since the fall of communism has been accompanied by relative social peace within the major players and relatively benign geopolitical alignments among them. There are no immediate reasons to think that this is about to change in major ways, but it would be premature, even foolish, to think that the future will simply be an extrapolation of the recent past.

# Notes

## Chapter 1  Introduction: The Contours of Globalization

1  Obviously, conjunctural changes *could* result in a change of the international economic system: the question is whether they have. Our point here is to caution against citing phenomena generated by such changes as if they were part and evidence of a process of structural transformation driven by deep-seated causes, called 'globalization'.

2  This distinction between MNCs and TNCs is not usual. MNCs in this book are those international companies that are still tethered to a national economy, despite the fact that they may operate in a supranational regional context. By contrast TNCs are those international companies which have a genuine global strategy, and have severed their contact to any particular national economy. There is a tendency to use the terms interchangeably, with TNC increasingly adopted as a generally accepted term for both types. Where we use the term TNC it should be clear that we are referring to *true* TNCs in the context of discussing the strong globalizer's view.

## Chapter 2  Globalization and the History of the International Economy

1  By the term 'autonomy' we mean the ability of the authorities in a national economy to determine their own economic policy and implement that policy. This is obviously a matter of degree. Autonomy is closely linked to 'openness', 'interdependence' and 'integration', three other categories used in this and subsequent chapters. Openness implies the degree to which national economies are subject to the actions of economic agents located outside their borders and the extent to which their own economic agents are orientated towards external economic activity. This is in turn linked to the degree of interdependence of the economic system in which these agents operate. Thus

interdependence expresses the systemic links between all economic activity within a system or regime. Integration is the process by which interdependence is established.

2   There have been several objections to these figures. In Hirst and Thompson (1999) chapter 2, appendix, this dispute is addressed in the context of the general argument presented here.

3   France devalued twice, in 1957 and 1958, Germany in 1961, Britain in 1967 and Germany and France again in 1969 – all against the US dollar, hence the designation of this period as a dollar standard.

4   This refers to the exchange-rate element of the BWS only. The total BWS package comprised not just its exchange-rate part but also the activity of the International Monetary Fund and the World Bank. In so far as these two institutions still exist and function much as planned at the Bretton Woods conference, these elements of the BWS still operate.

5   Take possibly the simplest case of short-term interest-rate differentials. These rates will be affected by local regulations, by the riskiness and precise duration of the loans, by local structural conditions, by the possibilities of generating monopoly rents, and so on. Thus differences between rates in financial centres could be due to these conditions rather than to the integration or separation of markets as such.

6   This scepticism is registered in the careful analyses contained in Banuri and Schor 1992.

7   An analysis using the Feldstein–Horioka framework for the EU countries' savings and investment ratios over two subperiods, 1971–89 and 1990–5, found an ambiguous change in the value of the $\beta$ coefficient, but concluded that this indicated 'weak, but positive evidence that the EU as a whole has been more open to the rest of the world as regards capital movements' (European Union 1997a, p. 5, box 1). Recent evidence puts the $\beta$ coefficient for emerging EU economies at 0.4 (Garcia-Herrero and Wooldridge 2007, p. 60).

8   Of course this emphasis on the relationship between domestic savings and domestic investment might seem to reinforce the neoclassical view of investment determination. The critique of this from an essentially post-Keynesian perspective is that the constraint on investment is not savings but the ability to raise finance for investment. In an advanced industrial economy with a developed financial system, credit creation is the key to investment; it is the access to 'liquidity' that determines economic activity, and this is endogenously created.

Formally we would agree with this analysis for mature advanced economies with a developed banking system operating efficiently in an essentially stable financial environment. However, we would emphasize that there are two exceptions to this image. The first is for those societies that remain less developed, that have an *underdeveloped* banking system in particular. The second is for those economies that have an *overdeveloped* financial system typified by speculation and instability. In both these cases, the 'normal' financing system for investment either simply does not exist, or breaks down in the face of speculative pressures. In addition, we would argue that it is this second case that increasingly typifies the position faced in the advanced industrial countries. In both of these cases, however, we are thrown back on to a more 'primitive' conception of what determines investment, namely the brute force of national savings.

9   Of itself convergence is not an adequate indicator of integration. In systems theory and evolutionary biology, for instance, there is a tendency for elements and species to converge despite there being no necessary *relationship* between them. Thus the key to integration is to specify a relationship, which convergence does not of itself provide.

10   Before 1870 the British suspended convertibility three times, in 1847, 1857 and 1866, but each time restored it quickly again at the previous parity. It should be noted, however, that there were a large number of suspensions of, withdrawals from and readmissions to the system among the peripheral economies.

11   This is a somewhat controversial position: the general sentiment is that the US Federal Reserve Board was unique among central banks in being able unilaterally to stabilize its own price level – inclusive of tradeable goods.

## Chapter 3   Multinational Companies and the Internationalization of Business Activity

1   Rugman concentrates on sales in his analysis to the (relative) neglect of assets, employment and sourcing. There is some strong support that assets are also supranationally regionally distributed (Rugman 2008), but sourcing is completely neglected. Some companies, for instance, may sell most of their output 'nationally' but source their raw materials, components and intermediate or retail products 'internationally'. This has yet to be systematically investigated (though see the discussion of outsourcing later in this chapter).

2   In 1993 the six most important country investors abroad were the USA ($50,244 million), the UK ($25,332 million), Japan ($13,600 million), France ($12,166 million), Germany ($11,673 million) and the Netherlands ($10,404 million) (OECD 1994, p. l6, table 1). Thus this analysis covers the main externally investing countries in the late 1980s and early 1990s.

3   Thus the 'home region' for German companies in all years comprises Germany itself, the rest of Europe, the Middle East and Africa (although these latter two areas account for a very low proportion of overall sales); 'home region' for Japanese companies comprises Japan and South-East Asia; for the UK it comprises the UK itself, the rest of Europe, the Middle East and Africa (here, too, the latter two areas were not very important for sales); and for US companies it includes the USA and Canada. These aggregations are dictated by the way it was possible to code the 1987 data.

4   Assets are measured as total assets for these calculations (total assets include financial assets and inventories as well as fixed assets). A better indicator would be either net fixed assets or operating assets, which relate more closely to the real capital stock. These were not extractable from the company accounts. Thus these data probably overestimate the value of real capital assets involved. These problems become more acute for some of the financial institutions included in the 'service' category of companies.

5   There exist many wild 'estimates' forecasting a spectacular growth of IT business in the future, particularly B2B (see, for instance, comments in Fraumeni 2001 and Lucking-Reiley and Spulber 2001). Since most of these forecasts were produced by management consultants who have a vested interest in 'boosting' the importance of the sector, these need to be taken with extreme caution. In

addition, most of these estimates were made before the crash of the IT sector stock values, before the downturn in the US economy, and before the events of September 2001. Comparing these to later OECD figures indicates no dramatic increases in ICT commercial activity, though these figures do suggest that total global ICT *spending* (on hardware, software, telecommunications, and other ITC services) was US$2.1 trillion in 2001, boosting the total ICT sector to world GDP ratio to 4.5 per cent (OECD 2002, p. 6). However, once again, this does not compare like with like. Expressing this in comparable value-added terms reduces the estimate to 1.1 per cent, similar to the other figures quoted above.

6   As well as significant differences *between* the EU and the USA as a whole, there are major differences *within* Europe. Some European countries have displayed ICT-driven productivity growth rates much higher than those found in the USA; see Timmer et al. 2003.

7   Some would challenge this as a *future* model for all new businesses, however. For instance, in respect to a particular business sector, the US and UK advertising industry, Grabher has argued these are adopting a completely new business organizational type – the 'project model' – that is emblematic of wider changes in networking structures that will infect all business relationships as a result of the emergence of ICTs (Grabher 2001). While such a 'project model' of time-limited collaborative relationships between parties to complete a specific task may be all very well for 'creative' enterprises in the advertising sector, it does not look an attractive or viable option for the production of complex manufacturing goods, for instance, which requires the establishment of enduring and long-term relationships. For a review of the impact of ICTs on global production networks, see the papers collected in the special issue of *Industry and Innovation* (Ernst and Kim 2002).

8   The analysis conducted here refers mainly to manufacturing, banking and new information technologies. But the traditional service sectors are also internationalizing, as indicated by the quantitative analysis reported above. In fact, the case of accounting and law firms largely confirms the points already made. The strategic management of these firms and the way they 'fit' into the business systems where they are newly locating is evolving in a similar way to that analysed in the case of manufacturing firms (see Barrett et al. 1997; and Spar 1997).

## Chapter 4  Globalization and International Competitiveness

1   In fact, companies are absolutely central to the way the WTO functions and has evolved. See, for instance, Sell (2003) for a fascinating account of how the WTO was influenced by American companies in particular over the TRIPS Agreement and the copyrighting of intellectual property.

2   Whether this is still an appropriate division in a 'globalized' world is challenged by Payne (2005), who argues that the pattern is now much more diverse and multilayered. In part, the analysis in the main text supports this view. But given that there remains such a vast difference between the incomes of the very poor and those of the very rich, with not much in between (an absent 'global middle-class' – Milanovic 2005), a division along these lines still seems worthwhile.

3   A model of trade suggesting that countries will export products that utilize their abundant factor(s) of production and import products that utilize their scarce factor, i.e. that comparative advantage operates, and furthermore that commodity price convergence leads to factor price convergence.

4   The economics approach is well illustrated by Pritchett (1997), Milanovic (2002) and Dowrick and DeLong (2003).

5   NICs included here are Hong Kong, Taiwan, Singapore, Thailand, Indonesia, Malaysia and the Philippines in East Asia and Argentina, Brazil and Mexico elsewhere. India and China might be added to this group, but they are such large economies that they are less vulnerable, as indicated in the main text.

6   'In a zero transaction cost world, infinite exchange would allow perfectly efficient allocation. In a positive transaction cost world – the world as it is – a decision-maker might accept some transaction costs in order to enhance gains from trade, or accept reduced gains from trade in order to reduce transaction costs even more. The actual decision depends on the magnitude of each.' (Trachtman 1996, pp. 501–2)

## Chapter 5  Emerging Markets and the Advanced Economies

1   PPP calculations, which take into account the local prices of goods and services, increase the weight of large and poor countries in such measures, but give a better picture of the rises in economic welfare – at least in so far as that is registered in income data. But if we are interested in the overall size and growth rates of markets around the world, then exchange-rate calculations are more relevant. A firm selling in a foreign market, for example, does not care about the PPP measure of GDP but about what its sales are worth in a convertible currency. Similarly, a domestic firm engaged in international trade wants to know international prices converted into its currency at the official exchange rate.

## Chapter 6  Supranational Regionalization or Globalization?

1   In 2006, the EIM hedge fund had assets of US$8 bn. That same year all hedge funds had a total of US$1,500 bn in assets.

2   For accessible aggregate level evidence, see Thompson (2002) and Hirst and Thompson (1999). For the case of trade, see Su (2002, 2005), Chortareas and Pelaglidis (2004) and Iapadre 2004. On the basis of various different approaches, these demonstrate that supranational regional trade is expanding at a faster rate than overall global trade, or that regional networks of trade are a strong feature of the international system. In the case of the EU alone, see Fligstein and Menard (2002), and, for overall East Asian integration, Sakakibara and Yamakawa (2004). For disaggregated evidence in the context of two industries that are often thought to be among the most highly globalized, see Rugman and Girod (2003) and in the case of retailing and for the financial aspects of the motor industry, see Dupuy and Lung (2002). See also Thompson (2004a).

## Chapter 7 General Governance Issues

1   International economic law is not to be confused either with international commercial law, which deals with relations between private parties in the international business environment, or with international commercial arbitration or private international law, which directs national courts when to exercise jurisdiction in cases with a foreign element, when to apply foreign laws and when to recognize and enforce the judgements of foreign courts. (There are in principle as many systems of private international law as there are states, even if states sometimes conclude treaties to unify their systems and thus regulate their content by public international law.)

2   We put the word 'private' in quotes because the public/private distinction is itself one that is founded, in part, in public law and because there exists – at least in liberal capitalist societies – a condition of mutual subjection between the public and private spheres.

3   The MFN (most favoured nation) principle states that, at the border, a good or service coming from a given economic partner is treated no less favourably than the same good or service coming from any other country. Within the GATT/WTO, unconditional MFN is the norm.

4   At least not in the foreseeable future. But the possibility cannot be ruled out in the very long run. Given the scale of economic development in emerging Asia and the efforts that the Chinese and Indian states are putting into technological transfer and education, there is no reason, in principle, why the future development of financial markets and innovation complexes in Asia could not come to rival those in the USA.

5   Note that the problem is not the *indebtedness* as such. Given the stage of development these countries are at, it is probably appropriate that they take on debt to finance the necessary investment and cover the external balance. The problem is that they cannot use their own currencies to do this.

6   Of course, if the countries concerned experience real appreciation of their currencies, then the returns may fall to zero or even turn negative.

# References

Agamben, G. (1998) *Homo sacer: Sovereign Power and Bare Life*. Stanford, CA: Stanford University Press.

Agamben, G. (2005) *State of Exception*. Chicago: University of Chicago Press.

Albert, M., and Hilkermeier, L. (eds) (2004) *Observing International Relations: Niklas Luhmann and World Politics*. London: Taylor & Francis.

Albert, M., Jacobson, D., and Lapid, Y. (eds) (2001) *Identities, Borders, Orders: Rethinking International Relations Theory*. Minneapolis: University of Minnesota Press.

Alesina, A., and Barro, R. J. (2001) 'Dollarization', *American Economic Review*, 91 (May), pp. 381–5.

Allen, J., and Thompson, G. F. (1997) 'Think global, and then think again: economic globalization in context', *Area*, 29(3), pp. 213–27.

Amsden, A. (1990) 'Third World industrialization', *New Left Review*, no. 182.

Anderson, B. (1991) *Imagined Communities*. London: Verso.

Archibugi, D., and Michie, J. (1997) 'The globalization of technology: a new taxonomy', in D. Archibugi and J. Michie (eds), *Technology, Globalization and Economic Performance*. Cambridge: Cambridge University Press.

Arrighi, G., and Silver, B. J. (1999) *Chaos and Governance in the Modern World System*. Minneapolis: University of Minnesota Press.

Arthur, W. B. (1996) 'Increasing returns and the new world of business', *Harvard Business Review*, July–August, pp. 100–9.

Asheim, B. T., and Isaksen, A. (1997) 'Location, agglomeration and innovation: towards regional innovation systems in Norway?', *European Planning Studies*, 5(3), pp. 299–330.

Athreye, S., and Simonetti, R. (2004) 'Technology, investment and economic growth', in W. Brown, S. Bromley and S. Athreye (eds), *Ordering the International*. London: Pluto Press.

Baily, M. N., and Lawrence, R. Z. (2001) 'Do we have a new e-economy?', *American Economic Review*, 91 (May), pp. 308–12.

Baldwin, R. E. (2006) *Managing the Noodle Bowl: The Fragility of East Asian Regionalism*. London: Centre for Economic Policy Research.

Baldwin, R. E., and Martin, P. (1999) 'Two waves of globalization: superficial similarity and fundamental differences', in H. Siebert (ed.), *Globalization and Labor*. Tübingen: Mohr Siebeck.

Banuri, T., and Schor, J. B. (eds) (1992) *Financial Openness and National Autonomy*. Oxford: Clarendon Press.

Barrell, R., and Pain, N. (1997) 'The growth of foreign direct investment in Europe', *National Institute Economic Review*, no. 160 (April), pp. 63–75.

Barrett, M., Cooper, D. J., and Jamal, K. (1997) '"That's pretty close" and the "friction of space": managing a global audit', in H. K. Rasmussen (ed.), *Accounting Time and Space, Proceedings*. Copenhagen: Copenhagen Business School.

Bartlett, C. A., and Goshal, S. (1989) *Managing across Borders: The Transnational Solution*. Boston: Harvard Business School Press.

Basu, S. (2002) *Financial Liberalization and Intervention: A New Analysis of Credit Rationing*. Cheltenham: Edward Elgar.

Baumol, W. (2002) *The Free-Market Innovation Machine*. Princeton, NJ: Princeton University Press.

Bayoumi, T. (1990) 'Saving–investment correlations: immobile capital, government policy or endogenous behaviour?', *IMF Staff Papers*, 37(2), pp. 360–87.

Bayoumi, T., and MacDonald, R. (1995) 'Consumption, income and international capital integration', *IMF Staff Papers*, 43(3), pp. 552–76.

Bayoumi, T. A., and Rose, A. K. (1993) 'Domestic savings and intra-national capital flows', *European Economic Review*, 37, pp. 1197–202.

Bergsten, C. F. (2002) 'The Euro versus the dollar', paper presented at the annual meeting of the American Economic Association, Atlanta, 4 January.

Bergsten, C. F. (2004) 'The risks ahead for the world economy', *The Economist*, 11 September.

Bernanke, B. S. (2004) 'The implementation of Basel II: some issues for cross-border banking', http://www.federalreserve.gov/boarddocs/speeches/2004/20041004/default.htm.

Best, M. (2001) *The New Competitive Advantage: The Renewal of American Industry*. Oxford: Oxford University Press.

Bhagwati, J. (1994) 'Threats to the world trading system: income distribution and the selfish hegemon', *Journal of International Affairs*, 48.

Bhagwati, J. (2004) *In Defense of Globalization*. New York and Oxford: Oxford University Press.

Bils, B. (2005) 'What determines regional inequality in China?', Bank of Finland Online no. 4; http://www.bof.fi/bofit.

BIS (1996–7) *Annual Report*. Geneva: Bank for International Settlements.

BIS (1998) *68th Annual Report*. Basel: Bank for International Settlements.

BIS (2007) *Annual Report*. Basel: Bank for International Settlements.

Blanchard, O., and Shleifer, A. (2001) 'Federalism with and without political centralization: China versus Russia', *IMF Staff Papers*, 48 [special issue].

Blinder, A. (2006) 'Offshoring: the next industrial revolution?', *Foreign Affairs*, 85(2).

Blinder, A. S. (2007) *How Many US Jobs Might be Offshorable?*, CEPS Working Paper no. 142, March. Brussels: Centre for European Policy Studies.

Bong-Chan, K., Stulz, R.-M., and Warnock, F. E. (2006) *Financial Globalization, Governance and the Evolution of the Home Bias*, BIS Working Paper no. 220, December. Basel: Bank for International Settlements.

Bordo, M., and James, H. (2006) 'One world money, then and now', *International Economics and Economic Policy*, 3(3–4), pp. 395–407.

Borjas, G. J., Freeman, R. B., and Katz, L. F. (1997) 'How much do immigration and trade affect labor market outcomes?', *Brookings Papers on Economic Activity*, no. 1, pp. 1–90.

Borrus, M., and Zysman, J. (1997) 'Globalization with borders: the rise of Wintelism as the future of global competition', *Industry and Innovation*, 4(2), pp. 141–66.

Bosworth, B. P. (1993) *Saving and Investment in a Global Economy*. Washington, DC: Brookings Institution.

Bosworth, B. P., and Collins, S. (2006) 'Accounting for growth', http://www.tcf.or.jp/data/2006120607_B_Bosworth-S_Collins.pdf.

Bourguignon, F., and Morrisson, C. (2002) 'Inequality among world citizens: 1820–1992', *American Economic Review*, 92(4), pp. 727–44.

Brakman, S., Garretsen, H., van Marrewijk, C., and van Witteloostuijn, A. (2006) *Nations and Firms in the Global Economy*. Cambridge: Cambridge University Press.

Breman, J. (2006) 'Slumlands', *New Left Review*, 2nd series, no. 40, July/August.

Brodie, B. (1965) *Strategy in the Missile Age*. Princeton, NJ: Princeton University Press.

Brooks, R., and Del Negro, M. (2002) *Firm-Level Evidence on Globalization*. Washington, DC: Financial Studies Division, IMF, April.

Broude, T. (2004) *International Governance in the WTO: Judicial Boundaries and Political Capitulation*. London: Cameron May.

de Brouwer, G. (2000) 'Should Pacific island nations adopt the Australian dollar?', *Pacific Economic Bulletin*, 15(2), pp. 161–9.

Burawoy, M. (1996) 'The state and economic involution: Russia through a China lens', *World Development*, 24(6).

Burgen, J. D., and Warnock, F. E. (2004) *Foreign Participation in Local Bond Markets*, International Finance Discussion Paper 2004-794. Washington, DC: Federal Reserve Board.

Caballero, R., Farhi, E., and Gourinchas, P.-O. (2008) 'An equilibrium model of "global imbalances" and low interest rates', *American Economic Review*, 97, pp. 358–93.

Cai, F., and Warnock, F. E. (2004) *International Diversification at Home and Abroad*, International Finance Discussion Paper 2004-793. Washington, DC: Federal Reserve Board.

Cantwell, J. (1992) 'The internationalisation of technological activity and its implications for competitiveness', in O. Granstand, L. Hakanson and S. Sjolander (eds), *Technology Management and International Business*. Chichester: Wiley.

Carey, M., and Nini, G. (2004) *Is the Corporate Loan Market Globally Integrated? A Pricing Puzzle*, International Finance Discussion Paper 2004-813. Washington, DC: Federal Reserve Board.

Carrere, C., and Schiff, M. (2003) *On the Geography of Trade: Distance is Alive and Well*. Washington, DC: World Bank; http://www.econ.worldbank.org/view.php?_type=5&id=33022.

Cass, D. Z. (2005) *The Constitutionalization of the World Trade Organization: Legitimacy, Democracy, and Community in the International Trading System*. Cambridge: Cambridge University Press.

Casson, M., Pearce, R. D., and Singh, S. (1992) 'Global integration through the decentralisation of R & D', in M. Casson (ed.), *International Business and Global Integration*. Basingstoke: Macmillan.

Castles, S., and Miller, M. J. (1993) *The Age of Migration*. Basingstoke: Macmillan.

Castells, M. (2000) *The Internet Galaxy*. Oxford: Oxford University Press.

Cerny, P. (1998) 'Neomedievalism, civil war and the new security dilemma: globalization as a durable disorder', *Civil Wars*, 1(1), pp. 36–64.

Chen, S., and Ravallion, M. (2007) *Absolute Poverty Measures for the Developing World, 1981–2004*. Policy Research Working Paper no. WPS4211. Washington, DC: World Bank.

Chesnais, F. (1992) 'National systems of innovation, foreign direct investment and the operations of multinational enterprises', in B.-A. Lundvall (ed.), *National Systems of Innovation: Towards a Theory of Innovations and Interactive Learning*. London: Pinter.

Chinn, M. D., and Frankel, J. A. (2005) *Will the Euro Eventually Surpass the Dollar as Leading International Reserve Currency?*, Harvard University Working Paper no. RWP05-064; http://ssrn.com/abstract=806288.

Chortareas, G. E., and Pelaglidis, T. (2004) 'Trade flows: a facet of regionalism or globalization?', *Cambridge Journal of Economics*, 28, pp. 253–71.

Choyleva, D., and Dumas, C. (2006) *The Bill from the China Shop*. London: Profile Books.

Cline, W. R. (1997) *Trade and Income Distribution*. Washington, DC: Institute for International Economics.

Cline, W. R. (2005) *The United States as a Debtor Nation*. Washington, DC: Institute for International Economics.

Coe, D. T., and Helpman, E. (1995) 'International R & D spillovers', *European Economic Review*, 39 (May), pp. 859–87.

Coe, D. T., Helpman, E., and Hoffmaister, A. (1997) 'North–South R & D spillovers', *Economic Journal*, 109, pp. 134–49.

Cohen, B. (1998) *The Geography of Money*. Ithaca, NY: Cornell University Press.

Cohen, D. (1998) *The Wealth of the World and the Poverty of Nations*. Cambridge, MA: MIT Press.

Collier, P. (2007) *The Bottom Billion*. Oxford: Oxford University Press.

Cooper, A. F., Hughes, C. W., and de Lombaerde, P. (eds) (2008) *Regionalisation and Global Governance: The Taming of Globalisation?* London: Routledge.

Cooper, R. (2005) *Living with Global Imbalances: A Contrarian View*, Policy Brief no. 05-3. Washington, DC: Institute for International Economics.

Cornford, A. (2005) *Basel II: The Revised Framework of June 2004*, Discussion Paper no. 178. Geneva: United Nations Conference on Trade and Development; http://www.unctad.org/en/docs/osgdp20052_en.pdf.

Cosh, A. D., Hughes, A., and Singh, A. (1992) 'Openness, financial innovation, changing patterns of ownership, and the structure of financial markets', in T. Banuri and J. B. Schor (eds), *Financial Openness and National Autonomy*. Oxford: Clarendon Press.

Courchene, T. J., and Harris, R. G. (1999) *From Fixing to Monetary Union: Options for North American Currency Integration*. Toronto: C. D. Howe Institute.

Coyle, D. (2001) *Paradoxes of Prosperity: Why the New Capitalism Benefits All*. London: Texere.

Crafts, N. (2000) *Globalization and Growth in the Twentieth Century*, IMF Working Paper no. WP/00/44. Washington, DC: International Monetary Fund.

Cutler, A. C. (2003) *Private Power and Global Authority: Transnational Merchant Law in the Global Political Economy*. Cambridge: Cambridge University Press.

Cutler, A. C., Haufler, V., and Porter, T. (eds) (1999) *Private Authority and International Affairs*. Albany, NY: State University of New York Press.

Davies, K. (2001) 'From EMU to AMU?', *Business Asia*, 33(10), pp. 1–4.

Davis, M. (2004) 'Planet of slums', *New Left Review*, 2nd series, no. 26 (March/April).

Dent, C. (2005) 'Bilateral free trade agreements: boon or bane for regional co-operation in East Asia', *European Journal of East Asian Studies*, 4(2), pp. 287–314.

Dent, C. (2006) *New Free Trade Agreements in the Asia Pacific*. Basingstoke: Macmillan.

Dent, C. (2008) *East Asian Regionalism*. London: Routledge.

Dicken, P., Forsgren, M., and Malmberg, A. (1994) 'The local embeddedness of transnational corporations', in A. Amin and N. Thrift (eds), *Globalization, Institutions, and Regional Development in Europe*. Oxford: Oxford University Press.

Dooley, M., Folkerts-Landau, D., and Garber, P. (2004) 'The revived Bretton Woods system', *International Journal of Finance and Economics*, 9(4).

Doremus, P., Keller, W., Pauly, L., and Reich, S. (1998) *The Myth of the Global Corporation*. Princeton, NJ: Princeton University Press.

Dornbusch, R. (2001) 'Fewer monies, better monies', *American Economic Review*, 91 (May), pp. 238–42.

Dowrick, S., and DeLong, J. B. (2003) 'Globalization and convergence', in Michael D. Bordo, Alan M. Taylor and Jeffrey G. Williamson (eds), *Globalization in Historical Perspective*. Cambridge, MA: National Bureau of Economic Research.

Drew, A., Hall, V. B., McDermott, J., and St Clair, R. (2001) *Would Adopting the Australian Dollar Provide a Superior Monetary Policy in New Zealand?*, Reserve Bank of New Zealand Discussion Paper, DP 2001/03, http://www.rbnz.govt.nz/research/search/article.asp?id=3842.

Duina, F. (2006) *The Social Construction of Free Trade: The European Union, NAFTA, and MERCOSUR*. Princeton, NJ: Princeton University Press.

Dunning, J. (1983) 'Changes in the level and structure of international production: the last one hundred years', in M. Casson (ed.), *The Growth of International Business*. London: Allen & Unwin.

Dunning, J. H. (1993) *Multinational Enterprises and the Global Economy*. Wokingham: Addison-Wesley.

Dupuy, C., and Lung, Y. (2002) 'Institutional investors and the car industry: geographic focalism and industrial strategies', *Competition and Change*, 6, pp. 43–60.

Durkheim, E. ([1893] 1964) *The Division of Labor in Society*. New York: Free Press.

Easterly, W., and Levine, R. (2003) 'It's not factor accumulation: stylized facts and growth models', *World Bank Economic Review*, 15(2), pp. 177–219.

*Economic Trends* (2004) 'Geographical breakdown of UK international investment position', no. 607, June.

*The Economist* (2004) 'The dragon and the eagle', 2 October.

*The Economist* (2006) 'The new titans', 16 September.

Edey, M., and Hviding, K. (1995) *An Assessment of Financial Reform in OECD Countries*, Economics Department Working Paper no. 154. Paris: OECD.

Edgerton, D. (1996) *Science, Technology and the British Industrial 'Decline', 1870–1970*. Cambridge: Cambridge University Press.

Edwards, S. (2001) *Dollarization and Economic Performance: An Empirical Investigation*, NBER Working Paper no. 8274. Cambridge, MA: National Bureau of Economic Research.

Edwards, S., and Magendzo, I. (2003) *A Currency of One's Own? An Empirical Investigation on Dollarization and Independent Currency Unions*, NBER Working Paper no. 9514. Cambridge, MA: National Bureau of Economic Research.

Eichengreen, B. (1990) *Elusive Stability*. Cambridge: Cambridge University Press.

Eichengreen, B. (1994) *International Monetary Arrangements for the Twenty-First Century*. Washington, DC: Brookings Institution.

Eichengreen, B. (2003) 'Restructuring sovereign debt', *Journal of Economic Perspectives*, 17(4), pp. 75–98.

Eichengreen, B., and Hausmann, R. (2004) *Other People's Money*. Chicago: University of Chicago Press.

Eichengreen, B., and Irwin, D. A. (1995) 'Trade blocs, currency blocs and the reorientation of world trade in the 1930s', *Journal of International Economics*, 38, pp. 1–24.

Eichengreen, B., and Irwin, D. A. (1997) 'The role of history in bilateral trade flows', in J. A. Frankel (ed.), *The Regionalization of the World Economy*. Chicago: University of Chicago Press.

Einaudi, L. (2001) *Money and Politics: European Monetary Unification and the International Gold Standard (1865–1873)*. Oxford: Oxford University Press.

El Diwany, T. (2003) *The Problem with Interest*. 2nd edn, London: Kreatoc.

Ernst, D., and Kim, L. (2002) 'Introduction: global production networks, information technology and knowledge diffusion', *Industry and Innovation*, 9(3), pp. 147–53.

European Union (1997a) 'Advancing financial integration', *European Economy, Supplement A: Economic Trends*, 12 (December). Brussels: European Union.

European Union (1997b) *External Aspects of Economic and Monetary Union*, Euro-Paper 1. Commission Services, July.

European Union (1997c) *European Union Direct Investment Yearbook 1996*. Luxembourg: European Union.

European Union (2005) *EMU after Five Years*, European Economy Special Report no. 1, February.

Fagerberg, J. (1996) 'Technology and competitiveness', *Oxford Review of Economic Policy*, 12(3), pp. 39–51.

Feenstra, R. C., and Hanson, G. H. (1996) 'Globalization, outsourcing, and wage inequality', *American Economic Review*, 86(2), pp. 240–5.

Fehr, H., Jokisch, S., and Kotlikoff, L. J. (2005) *Will China Eat our Lunch or Take Us Out to Dinner? Simulating the Transition Paths of the U.S., E.U., Japan, and*

*China*, NBER Working Paper no. 11668. Cambridge, MA: National Bureau of Economic Research.

Feldstein, M., and Bacchetta, P. (1991) 'National savings and national investment', in B. D. Bernstein and J. B. Shoven (eds), *National Savings and Economic Performance*. Chicago: University of Chicago Press.

Feldstein, M., and Horioka, C. (1980) 'Domestic savings and international capital flows', *Economic Journal*, 90 (June), pp. 314–29.

Fielding, D., and Shields, K. (2003) *Economic Integration in West Africa: Does the CFA Make a Difference?*, UNU-CRIS e-Working Papers W-2003/4; http://unpan1.un.org/intradoc/groups/public/documents/NISPAcee/UNPAN015232.pdf.

Figgis, J. N. (1913) *Churches in the Modern State*. London: Longmans Green.

Finer, S. (1997) *The History of Government*, Vol. 1. Oxford: Oxford University Press.

Fisher, I. (1933) 'The debt-deflation theory of great depressions', *Econometrica*, 1(5), pp. 337–57.

Fligstein, N., and Menard, F. (2002) 'Globalization or Europeanization? Evidence on the European economy since 1980', *Acta Sociologica*, 45, pp. 7–22.

Forbes, M. (2003) 'Howard push for Pacific union', *The Age*, 18 August.

Frank, A. G., and Gills, B. K. (eds) (1996) *The World System: Five Hundred Years or Five Thousand?* London: Routledge.

Frankel, J. A. (1992) 'Measuring international capital mobility: a review', *American Economic Review*, 82(2), pp. 197–202.

Frankel, J. A. (1997) *Regional Trading Blocs in the World Economic System*. Washington, DC: Institute for International Economics.

Frankel, J. A. (2006) *Global Imbalances and Low Interest Rates*, Harvard University Working Paper RWP06-035; http://ssrn.com/abstract=902385.

Fransman, M. (1997) 'Is technology policy obsolete in a globalised world? The Japanese response', in D. Archibugi and J. Michie (eds), *Technology, Globalization and Economic Performance*. Cambridge: Cambridge University Press.

Fraumeni, B. M. (2001) 'E-commerce: measurement and measurement issues', *American Economic Review*, 91 (May), pp. 318–22.

Freedman, L. (2004) *Deterrence*. Cambridge: Polity.

Freeman, C., and Louçã, F. (2001) *As Time Goes By*. Oxford: Oxford University Press.

Friedman, T. (1999) *The Lexus and the Olive Tree*. London: HarperCollins.

Fujita, M., Krugman, P. R., and Venables, A. J. (2001) *The Spatial Economy: Cities, Regions and International Trade*. Cambridge, MA: MIT Press.

Gallie, D., White, M., Chang, Y., and Tomlinson, M. (1998) *Restructuring the Employment Relationship*. Oxford: Oxford University Press.

Galor, O. (2005) 'The demographic transition and the emergence of sustained economic growth', *Journal of the European Economic Association*, 3(2–3).

Galor, O., and Mountford, A. (2003) *Trading Population for Productivity*, Brown University Working Paper no. 2004-16; http://www.brown.edu/Departments/Economics/Papers/2004/2004-16_paper.pdf.

Garcia-Herrero, A., and Wooldridge, P. (2007) 'Global and regional financial integration: progress in emerging markets', *BIS Quarterly Review*, September, pp. 57–70.

Gerber, D. J. (1994) 'Constitutionalizing the economy: German neo-liberalism, competition law and the "new" Europe', *American Journal of Comparative Law*, 42(1), pp. 25–84.

Ghemawat, P. (2007) *Redefining Global Strategy: Crossing Borders in a World where Differences Still Matter*. Cambridge, MA: Harvard Business School Press.

Ghosh, A. R. (1995) 'International capital mobility amongst the major industrialised countries: too little or too much?', *Economic Journal*, 105 (January), pp. 107–28.

Gibbon, P., Bair, J., and Ponte, S. (2008) 'Governing global value chains: an introduction', *Economy and Society*, 37(3), pp. 315–38.

Gierke, O. von ([1900] 1988) *Political Theories of the Middle Ages*, ed. and trans. F. W. Maitland. Cambridge: Cambridge University Press.

Giovannetti, E., Neuhoff, K., and Spagnolo, G. (2003) 'Agglomeration in the Internet: does space still matter?', paper given at the conference 'Economics for the Future', Cambridge, 17–19 September.

Glyn, A. (2005) 'Global imbalances', *New Left Review*, 2nd series, no. 34 (July/August).

Glyn, A. (2006) *Capitalism Unleashed*. Oxford: Oxford University Press.

Godley, W. (2003) *The U.S. Economy: A Changing Strategic Predicament*. Annandale-on-Hudson, NY: Levy Economics Institute, Bard College.

Godley, W., and Lavoie, M. (2004) *Simple Open Economy Macro with Comprehensive Accounting: A Radical Alternative to the Mundell Fleming Model*, Working Paper no. 15. Cambridge: Cambridge Endowment for Research in Finance.

de Goede, M. (2004) 'Repoliticizing financial risk', *Economy and Society*, 33 (May), pp. 197–217.

Goldstein, M. (2004) 'Adjusting China's exchange rate policies', paper presented at the IMF seminar on China's foreign exchange system, Dalian, China, 26–7 May.

Goldstein, M., and Mussa, M. (1993) *The Integration of World Capital Markets*, Research Department Working Paper WP/93/95. Washington, DC: International Monetary Fund.

Goodhart, C. A. E. (1998) 'Two concepts of money: implications for the analysis of optimal currency areas', *European Journal of Political Economy*, 14, pp. 407–32.

Gordon, D. M. (1996) *Fat and Mean: The Corporate Squeeze of Working Americans and the Myth of Managerial 'Downsizing'*. New York: Free Press.

Grabher, G. (2001) 'Ecologies of creativity: the village, the group, and the hierarchic organization of the British advertising industry', *Environment and Planning*, A 33, pp. 351–74.

Graham, E. M. (1996) *Global Corporations and National Governments*. Washington, DC: Institute for International Economics.

Grahl, J. (2001) 'Globalized finance', *New Left Review*, 2nd series, no. 8 (March/April).

Grahl, J. (2004) 'The European Union and American power', *Socialist Register 2005*. London: Merlin Press.

Grassman, S. (1980) 'Long-term trends in openness of national economies', *Oxford Economic Papers*, 32(1), pp. 123–33.

Gray, J. (1998) *False Dawn: The Delusions of Global Capitalism*. London: Granta Books.

Grossman, G. M., and Rossi-Hansberg, E. (2006) 'The rise of offshoring: it's not wine for cloth anymore', paper given at the symposium 'The New Economic Geography: Effects and Policy Implications', Federal Reserve Bank of Kansas

City, 24–6 August; http://www.kansascityfed.org/publicat/sympos/2006/sym06prg. htm.

Gruber, L. (2000) *Ruling the World*. Princeton, NJ: Princeton University Press.

Guttman, R. (2006) 'Basel II: A new regulatory framework for global banking', Institute of Economics, University of Campinas, Brazil, March.

Harris, L. (1995) 'International financial markets and national transmission mechanisms', in J. Michie and J. Grieve Smith (eds), *Managing the Global Economy*. Oxford: Oxford University Press.

Hausmann, R., and Sturzenegger, F. (2005) *Global Imbalances or Bad Accounting?*, Working Paper no. 124. Cambridge, MA: Harvard University, Centre for International Development.

Hausmann, R., Lim, E., and Spence, M. (2006) *China and the Global Economy*, KSG Working Paper no. RWP06-029. Cambridge, MA: Harvard University.

Heathcote, J., and Perri, F. (2002) *Financial Globalization and Real Globalization*, NBER Working Paper no. 9292. Cambridge, MA: National Bureau of Economic Research.

Held, D. (2004) *Global Covenant: The Social Democratic Alternative to the Washington Consensus*. Cambridge: Polity.

Held, D., and McGrew, A. (2002) *Globalization and Anti-Globalization*. Cambridge: Polity.

Held, D., McGrew, A., Goldblatt, D., and Perraton, J. (1999) *Global Transformations: Politics, Economics and Culture*. Cambridge: Polity.

Helleiner, E. (2006) *Towards North American Monetary Union? The Politics and History of Canada's Exchange Rate Regime*. Montreal and London: McGill–Queen's University Press.

Helpman, E. (2004) *The Mystery of Economic Growth*. Cambridge, MA: Harvard University Press.

Herring, R. J., and Litan, R. E. (1995) *Financial Regulation in the Global Economy*. Washington, DC: Brookings Institution.

Hindess, B. (1991) 'Imaginary presuppositions of democracy', *Economy and Society*, 20(2), pp. 173–95.

Hindess, B. (1992) 'Power and rationality: the Western concept of political community', *Alternatives*, 17(2), pp. 149–63.

Hindess, B. (1996) *Discourses of Power: From Hobbes to Foucault*. Oxford: Blackwell.

Hinsley, F. H. (1986) *Sovereignty*. 2nd edn, Cambridge: Cambridge University Press.

Hirst, P. Q. (1993) *Associative Democracy*. Cambridge: Polity.

Hirst, P. Q. (1994) 'Why the national still matters', *Renewal*, 2(4), pp. 12–20.

Hirst, P. Q. (1997) 'The international origins of national sovereignty', in Hirst, *From Statism to Pluralism*. London: UCL Press.

Hirst, P. Q., and Thompson, G. F. (1996) *Globalization in Question*. Cambridge: Polity.

Hirst, P. Q., and Thompson, G. F. (1999) *Globalization in Question*. 2nd edn, Cambridge: Polity.

Hirst, P. Q., and Thompson, G. F. (2000) 'Globalization in one country? The peculiarities of the British', *Economy and Society*, 29(3), pp. 335–56.

HMSO (1994) *Competitiveness of UK Manufacturing Industry*, Trade and Industry Committee, 2nd Report, 20 April, HCP 41-I. London: HMSO.

HMSO (1996) *Competitiveness: Creating the Enterprise Centre of Europe*, Cm 3300. London: HMSO.

HM Treasury (2004) *Long-Term Global Economic Challenges and Opportunities for the UK*. London: HM Treasury.

HM Treasury (2005a) *Global Europe: Full Employment Europe*. London: HM Treasury.

HM Treasury (2005b) *Responding to Global Economic Challenges: UK and China*. London: HM Treasury.

Hollingsworth, J. R., and Boyer, R. (eds) (1996) *Contemporary Capitalism: The Embeddedness of Institutions*. Cambridge: Cambridge University Press.

Horsman, M., and Marshall, A. (1994) *After the Nation-State*. London: HarperCollins.

Howell, D. R., and Wolff, E. N. (1991) 'Skills, bargaining power and rising interindustry wage inequality since 1970', *Review of Radical Political Economics*, 23(1–2), pp. 30–7.

Howell, M. (1998) 'Asia's Victorian financial crisis', paper presented at the conference on the East Asian economic crisis, Institute for Development Studies, University of Sussex, 13–14 July.

Howse, R. (2000) 'Adjudicative legitimacy and treaty interpretation in international trade law: the early years of WTO jurisprudence', in J. H. H. Weiler (ed.), *The EU, the WTO, and the NAFTA: Towards a Common Law of International Trade?* Oxford: Oxford University Press.

Hu, Y.-S. (1992) 'Global or stateless firms are national corporations with international operations', *California Management Review*, 34(2), pp. 107–26.

Hu, Y.-S. (1995) 'The international transferability of the firm's advantage', *California Management Review*, 37(4), pp. 73–88.

Hufbauer, G. (ed.) (1990) *Europe 1992: An American Perspective*. Washington, DC: Brookings Institution.

Hummels, D. (2000) 'Time as a trade barrier', Purdue University, October, hummelsd@purdue.edu.

Huntington, S. P. (1996) *The Clash of Civilizations and the Remaking of World Order*. New York: Simon & Schuster.

Iapadre, L. (2004) *Regional Integration Agreements and the Geography of World Trade: Measurement Problems and Empirical Evidence*, UNU-CRIS e-Working Papers W-2004/3; http://www.cris.unu.edu/admin/documents/IapadreWorkingPaper2004.pdf.

Ignatieff, M. (1997) *The Warrior's Honor: Ethnic War and the Modern Conscience*. New York: Metropolitan Books.

IMF (2006) *World Economic Outlook*, September. Washington, DC: International Monetary Fund.

IMF (2007) *Staff Report on the Multilateral Consultation on Global Imbalances with China, the Euro Area, Japan, Saudi Arabia, and the United States*, 29 June. Washington, DC: International Monetary Fund.

Ingham, G. (2004) *The Nature of Money*. Cambridge: Polity.

Ingham, G. (2006) 'Further reflections on the ontology of money', *Economy and Society*, 35(2), pp. 259–78.

Institute of International Finance (2006) *Principles for Stable Capital Flows and Fair Debt Restructuring in Emerging Markets: Report on Implementation by the Principles Consultative Group*, September. Washington, DC: IFC.

Izurieta, A. (2005) *Can the Growth Patterns of the US Economy be Sustained by the Rest of the World?*, May. Cambridge: Cambridge Endowment for Research in Finance.

Jackson, J. H. (1998) *The World Trade Organization*. London: RIIA/Pinter.

Jayasuriya, K. (2001) 'Globalization, sovereignty, and the rule of law: from political to economic constitutionalism?', *Constellations*, 8(4), pp. 442–60.

Jensen, J. B., and Kletzer, L. G. (2006) 'Tradable services', http://www.iie.com/publications/papers/paper.cfm?ResearchID=638.

Joerges, C., Sand, I.-J., and Teubner, G. (2004) *Transnational Governance and Constitutionalism*. Oxford: Hart.

Jones, G. (1994) 'The making of global enterprise', *Business History*, 36(1), pp. 1–17.

Jubilee Plus (2002) *Chapter 9/11? Resolving International Debt Crises: The Jubilee Framework for International Insolvency*. London: Jubilee Plus; http://www.jubilee2000uk.org/analysis/reports/jubilee_framework.pdf.

Kagan, R. (2002) 'The power divide', *Prospect*, August.

Kaldor, N. (1978) 'The effect of devaluations on trade in manufactures', in Kaldor, *Further Essays in Applied Economics*. London: Duckworth.

Kaldor, N. (1981) 'The role of increasing returns, technical progress and cumulative causation in the theory of international trade and economic growth', *Economie Appliquée*, 34(4), pp. 593–617.

Kanbur, R., and Zhang, X. (2001) *Fifty Years of Regional Inequality in China*. London: Centre for Economic Policy Research.

Kant, I. ([1919] 1990) *Perpetual Peace*, in *Political Writings*, ed. H. Reiss. 2nd edn, Cambridge: Cambridge University Press.

Kapstein, E. B. (1991) 'We are us: the myth of the multi-national', *The National Interest*, Winter, pp. 55–62.

Kay, J. (1994) *The Foundations of National Competitive Advantage*. Swindon: Economic and Social Research Council.

Kenen, P. B. (1995) 'Capital controls, the EMS and EMU', *Economic Journal*, 105 (January), pp. 181–92.

Keynes, J. M. (1930) *A Treatise on Money*. London: Macmillan.

Kindleberger, C. P. (1962) *Europe and the Dollar*. Cambridge, MA: MIT Press.

Kitchen, J. (2006) 'Sharecroppers or shrewd capitalists', http://users.starpower.net/jkitch/ShareShrewd.pdf.

Kitson, M., and Michie, J. (1995) 'Trade and growth: a historical perspective', in J. Michie and J. Grieve Smith (eds), *Managing the Global Economy*. Oxford: Oxford University Press.

Klier, T. H. (1999) 'Agglomeration in the US auto supply industry', *Economic Perspectives*. Chicago: Federal Reserve Bank of Chicago.

Klingebiel, D. (2002) 'Capital markets and financial integration in Europe: discussion of firm level evidence on globalization', mimeograph. Washington, DC: World Bank.

Knapp, G. (1924) *The State Theory of Money*. New York: Augustus M. Kelley.

Knox, P. L., and Taylor, P. J. (eds) (1995) *World Cities in a World-System*. Cambridge: Cambridge University Press.

Kogut, B. (ed.) (2003) *The Global Internet Economy*. Cambridge, MA: MIT Press.

Kondo, T. (2000) 'A common currency for the Asia-Pacific', *Focus Japan*, July–August, pp. 12–13.

Korten, D. C. (1995) *When Corporations Rule the World*. West Hartford, CT: Kumarian Press.

Krueger, A. (2002) *A New Approach to Sovereign Debt Restructuring*. Washington, DC: International Monetary Fund.

Krugman, P. (1994) 'Competitiveness: a dangerous obsession', *Foreign Affairs*, 73(2), pp. 28–44.

Krugman, P. (1995) 'Growing world trade: causes and consequences', *Brookings Papers on Economic Activity*, no. 1, pp. 327–77.

Krugman, P. (2007) 'Will there be a dollar crisis', *Economic Policy*, 22(51).

Krugman, P., and Lawrence, R. Z. (1994) 'Trade, jobs and wages', *Scientific American*, April, pp. 44–9.

Kuroda, H. (2001) 'The quest for regional financial and monetary co-operation in Asia', paper given at the conference 'Regional Economic Co-operation in Asia: Challenges for Europe', WIIW, Vienna, 4–5 October.

Lardy, N. (2006) *China: Toward a Consumption-Driven Growth Path*, Policy Brief no. 06-6. Washington, DC: Institute for International Economics.

Latour, B. (2004) 'Whose cosmos, which cosmopolitics? *Common Knowledge*, 10(3), pp. 450–62.

Lawrence, R. (1996) *Regionalism, Multilateralism and Deeper Integration*. Washington, DC: Brookings Institution.

Lawrence, R. Z., and Slaughter, M. J. (1993) 'International trade and American wages in the 1980s: giant sucking sound or small hiccup?', *Brookings Papers on Economic Activity*, no. 2, pp. 161–226.

Lazonick, W. (1993) 'Industry clusters versus global webs: organizational capabilities in the American economy', *Industrial and Corporate Change*, 2(2), pp. 1–21.

Lazonick, W., and O'Sullivan, M. (1996) 'Organization, finance and international competition', *Industrial and Corporate Change*, 5(1), pp. 1–49.

Leamer, E., and Storper, M. (2001) 'The economic geography of the Internet age', *Journal of International Business*, 32(4), pp. 641–65.

Leong, S. M., and Tan, C. T. (1993) 'Managing across borders: an empirical test of the Bartlett and Ghoshal [1989] organizational typology', *Journal of International Business Studies*, 24(3), pp. 449–64.

Lévy, B. (2006) 'Emerging countries, world trade and regionalization', *Global Economy Journal*, 6(4), pp. 1–29.

Levy Yeyati, E. (2005) 'Liquidity insurance in financially dollarized economies', mimeograph, November.

Levy Yeyati, E. (2006) 'Financial dollarization', *Economic Policy*, January, pp. 61–118.

Lewis, A. (1981) 'The rate of growth of world trade, 1830–1973', in S. Grassman and E. Lundberg (eds), *The World Economic Order: Past and Prospects*. Basingstoke: Macmillan.

Lipsey, R. E. (1997) 'Global production systems and local labour conditions', paper given at the conference on international solidarity and globalization, Stockholm, 27–8 October.

Lipsey, R. E., Blomström, M., and Ramstetter, E. (1995) *Internationalized Production in World Output*, NBER Working Paper no. 5385. Cambridge, MA: National Bureau of Economic Research.

Livi Bacci, M. (1993) 'South–North migration: a comparative approach to North American and European experiences', in *The Changing Course of Migration*. Paris: OECD.

de Lombaerde, P. (2007) *Multilateralism, Regionalism and Bilateralism in Trade and Investment*. Dordrecht: Springer.

Lucas, R. (2002) *Lectures on Economic Growth*. Cambridge, MA: Harvard University Press.

Lucking-Reiley, D., and Spulber, D. F. (2001) 'Business-to-business electronic commerce', *Journal of Economic Perspectives*, 15(1), pp. 55–68.

Luengnaruemitchai, P., and Eichengreen, B. J. (2006) *Bond Markets for Conduits of Capital Flows: How Does Asia Compare?* IMF Working Paper no. WP/06/238. Washington, DC: International Monetary Fund.

Lundvall, B.-A. (ed.) (1992) *National Systems of Innovation: Towards a Theory of Innovation and Interactive Learning*. London: Pinter.

McCauley, R. N., Fung, S.-S., and Gadanecz, B. (2002) 'Integrating the finances of East Asia', *BIS Quarterly Review*, December, pp. 83–95.

McGuckin, R. H., and van Ark, B. (2002) *Performance 2001: Productivity, Employment, and Income in the World's Economies*, Report no. 13, January. New York: Conference Board.

McKelvey, M. (1991) 'How do national systems of innovation differ? A critical analysis of Porter, Freeman, Ludvall and Nelson', in G. Hodgson and E. Screpanti (eds), *Rethinking Economics*. Cheltenham: Edward Elgar.

MacKenzie, D. (2007) 'The material production of virtuality: innovation, cultural geography, and facticity in derivatives markets', *Economy and Society*, 36.

McKinnon, R. (1993) 'The rules of the game: international money in historical perspective', *Journal of Economic Literature*, 31 (March), pp. 1–44.

McKinnon, R. (2001) 'The international dollar standard and sustainability of the U.S. current account deficit', http://www.stanford.edu/~mckinnon/.

McKinnon, R. (2003) 'The world dollar standard and globalization', http://www.stanford.edu/~mckinnon/.

McKinnon, R. (2005a) 'Trapped by the international dollar standard', http://www.stanford.edu/~mckinnon/.

McKinnon, R. (2005b) 'China's new exchange rate policy', http://www.stanford.edu/~mckinnon/.

McKinnon, R., and Schnabl, G. (2004) 'The East Asian dollar standard, fear of floating, and original sin', *Review of Development Economics*, 8(3).

McKinsey and Company (2001) *US Productivity Growth: 1995–2000*. New York: McKinsey & Co.

Maddison, A. (1962) 'Growth and fluctuation in the world economy, 1870–1960', *Banca Nazionale del Lavaro Quarterly Review*, no. 61 (June), pp. 127–95.

Maddison, A. (1987) 'Growth and slowdown in advanced capitalist economies: techniques of quantitative assessments', *Journal of Economic Literature*, 25(2), pp. 649–98.

Maddison, A. (2001) *The World Economy*, Vol. 1: *A Millennial Perspective*. Paris: OECD.

Maddison, A. (2003) *The World Economy*, Vol. 2: *Historical Statistics*. Paris: OECD.

Mansell, R. (1994) *The New Telecommunications: A Political Economy of Network Organizations*. London: Sage.

Marglin, S. (2000) *Keynes without Nominal Rigidities*, Discussion Paper no. 1907. Cambridge, MA: Harvard Institute of Economic Research; http://www.economics.harvard.edu/pub/hier/2000/HIER1907.pdf.

Maurer, B. (2001) 'Engineering an Islamic future: speculations on Islamic financial alternatives', *Anthropology Today*, 17(1), pp. 8–11.

Maurer, B. (2005) *Mutual Life, Limited: Islamic Banking, Alternative Currencies, Lateral Reason*. Princeton, NJ: Princeton University Press.

Meier, G. (1998) *The International Environment of Business*. Oxford: Oxford University Press.

de Ménil, G. (1999) 'Real capital market integration in the EU: how far has it gone? What will the effect of the euro be?', *Economic Policy*, 14(28), pp. 165–201.

Mercereau, B. (2006) *Financial Integration in Asia: Estimating the Risk-Sharing Gains for Australia and Other Nations*, IMF Working Paper no. WP/06/267. Washington, DC: International Monetary Fund.

Milanović, B. (2002) *Income Convergence during the Disintegration of the World Economy, 1919–39*. Washington, DC: World Bank.

Milanović, B. (2005) *Worlds Apart: Measuring International and Global Inequality*. Princeton, NJ: Princeton University Press.

Milesi-Ferretti, G. M. (2007) 'IMF offers compromise path on imbalances', *IMF Survey*, 7 August.

Minc, A. (1993) *Le Nouveau Moyen Âge*. Paris: Gallimard.

Minda, A. (2008) 'The strategies of multilatinas: from the quest for regional leadership to the myth of the global corporation', *GRES Cahier no. 208-08*, Groupement de Recherches Économiques et Sociales; http://ideas.repec.org/d/gressfr.html#a.

Minford, P., Riley, J., and Nowell, E. (1997) 'Trade, technology and labour markets in the world economy, 1970–90: a computable general equilibrium analysis', *Journal of Development Studies*, 34(2), pp. 1–34.

*MIR* (2005) Special issue on regional multinationals, *Management International Review*, 45(1), pp. 5–166.

MITI (1996a) *Summary of 'The Survey of Trends in Overseas Business Activities of Japanese Companies'*, International Business Affairs Division, January (N-96-2). Tokyo: Ministry of International Trade and Industry.

MITI (1996b) *The 28th Survey of Trends in Business Activities of Foreign Affiliates*. International Business Affairs Division, January (N-96-3). Tokyo: Ministry of International Trade and Industry.

MITI (1997) *The Sixth Basic Survey of Overseas Business Activities*. Tokyo: Ministry of International Trade and Industry.

Moravcsik, A. (1998) *The Choice for Europe*. London: UCL Press.

Mueller, F. (1994) 'Societal effect, organizational effect and globalization', *Organization Studies*, 15(3), pp. 407–28.

Naughton, B. (1995) *Growing out of the Plan*. Cambridge: Cambridge University Press.

Neal, L. (1985) 'Integration of international capital markets: quantitative evidence from the eighteenth to twentieth centuries', *Journal of Economic History*, 45(2), pp. 219–26.

Nelson, R. (ed.) (1993) *National Innovation Systems*. Oxford: Blackwell.

Norris, P. (2001) *Digital Divide?: Civic Engagement, Information Poverty, and the Internet Worldwide*. Cambridge: Cambridge University Press.

Obstfeld, M. (1993) *International Capital Mobility in the 1990s*, NBER Working Paper no. 4534. Cambridge, MA: National Bureau of Economic Research.

Obstfeld, M., and Rogoff, K. (2005) *The Unsustainable US Current Account Position Revisited*, NBER Working Paper no. 10864. Cambridge, MA: National Bureau of Economic Research.

Odom, W., and Dujarric, R. (2004) *America's Inadvertent Empire*. New Haven, CT: Yale University Press.

OECD (1993) *Financial Market Trends*, no. 55 (June). Paris: OECD.

OECD (1994a) 'Desynchronization of OECD business cycles', *Economic Outlook*, no. 55 (June). Paris: OECD.

OECD (1994b) *Financial Market Trends*, no. 58 (June). Paris: OECD.

OECD (1998) *Financial Market Trends*, no. 69 (February). Paris: OECD.

OECD (2002) *Information Technology Outlook 2002*. Paris: OECD.

OECD (2005) *Economic Globalization Indicators*. Paris: OECD.

OECD (2007) *Employment Outlook 2007*. Paris: OECD.

Ohmae, K. (1990) *The Borderless World*. London and New York: Collins.

Ohmae, K. (1993) 'The rise of the region state', *Foreign Affairs*, Spring, pp. 78–87.

Ohmae, K. (1995) *The End of the Nation State*. London: HarperCollins.

Ong, A., and Collier, S. J. (2004) *Global Assemblages: Technology, Politics, and Ethics as Anthropological Problems*. Oxford: Wiley-Blackwell.

O'Rourke, K. H., and Williamson, J. G. (1998) *Globalization and History: The Evolution of a Nineteenth-Century Atlantic Economy*. Cambridge, MA: MIT Press.

Papademetriou, D. G. (1997–8) 'Migration', *Foreign Policy*, no. 109 (Winter), pp. 15–31.

Patel, P. (1995) 'Localised production of technology for global markets', *Cambridge Journal of Economics*, 19, pp. 141–53.

Patel, P., and Pavitt, K. (1992) 'Large firms in the production of the world's technology: an important case of "non-globalization"', in O. Granstrand, L. Hakanson and S. Sjolander (eds), *Technology Management and International Business*. Chichester: Wiley [also in *Journal of International Business Studies*, 22(1), 1991, pp. 1–21].

Pauly, L. W., and Reich, S. (1997) 'National structures and multinational behaviour: enduring differences in the age of globalization', *International Organization*, 51(1), pp. 1–30.

Payne, A. (2005) *The Global Politics of Unequal Development*. Basingstoke: Palgrave Macmillan.

Perraton, J. (2001) 'Global economy: myths and realities', *Cambridge Journal of Economics*, 25, pp. 669–84.

Persson, T. (2001) 'Currency unions and trade: how large is the treatment effect?', *Economic Policy*, no. 33, pp. 435–48.

Pertri, P. A. (1994) 'The East Asian trading bloc: an analytical history', in R. Garnaut and P. Drysdale (eds), *Asia Pacific Regionalism*. Sydney: Harper Education.

Pomeranz, K. (2000) *The Great Divergence*. Princeton, NJ: Princeton University Press.

Porter, M. E. (1990) *The Competitive Advantage of Nations*. London: Macmillan.

Porter, M. E., and Ketels, C. H. M. (2003) *UK Competitiveness: Moving to the Next Stage*, DTI Economics Paper no. 3. London: Department of Trade and Industry.

Porter, M. E., and van Opstal, D. (2001) *U.S. Competitiveness 2001: Strengths, Vulnerabilities and Long-Term Policies*. Washington, DC: Council on Competitiveness.

Prins, G. (2002) *The Heart of War*. London: Routledge.

Pritchett, L. (1997) 'Divergence, big time', *Journal of Economic Perspectives*, 11(3), pp. 3–17.

Qureshi, A. (1999) *International Economic Law*. London: Sweet & Maxwell.

Ramstetter, E. (1998) 'Measuring the size of foreign multinationals in the Asia-Pacific', in G. F. Thompson (ed.), *Economic Dynamism in the Asia-Pacific*. London: Routledge, pp. 185–212.

Ravallion, M., and Chen, S. (2004) *China's (Uneven) Progress Against Poverty*, World Bank Policy Research Working Paper no. 3408, September; http://econ.worldbank.org.

Reich, R. B. (1990) 'Who is us?', *Harvard Business Review*, January–February, pp. 53–64.

Reich, R. B. (1992) *The Work of Nations*. New York: Vintage.

Reinhart, C. M., Rogoff, K. S., and Savastano, M. A. (2003) *Addicted to Dollars*, NBER Working Paper no. 10015. Cambridge, MA: National Bureau of Economic Research.

Robson, W. B. P., and Laidler, D. (2002) *No Small Change: The Awkward Economics and Politics of North American Monetary Integration*, C. D. Howe Institute Commentary no. 167, July.

Rodrik, D. (2000) 'How far will economic integration go?', *Journal of Economic Perspectives*, 14(1).

Rodrik, D. (2006) *What's So Special about China's Exports?*, Harvard University Faculty Research Working Paper no. RWP06-001; http://ksgnotes1.harvard.edu/Research/wpaper.nsf/rwp/RWP06-001.

Roe, M. J. (1994) *Strong Managers, Weak Owners: The Political Roots of American Corporate Finance*. Princeton, NJ: Princeton University Press.

Rogoff, K. (2001) 'Why not a global currency?', *American Economic Review*, 91 (May), pp. 243–7.

Rogoff, K. (2002) 'Why are G-3 exchange rates so fickle?', *Finance and Development*, 39(2).

Rose, A. K. (2000) 'One money, one market: estimating the effect of common currencies on trade', *Economic Policy*, no. 30, pp. 7–73.

Rose, A. K. (2001) 'Currency unions and trade: the effect is large', *Economic Policy*, no. 33, pp. 449–61.

Rose, A. K., and van Wincoop, E. (2001) 'National money as a barrier to international trade: the real case of currency union', *American Economic Review*, 91 (May), pp. 386–90.

Rose, M. A., Prasard, E., Rogoff, K., and Wei, S.-J. (2006) *Financial Globalization: A Reappraisal*, IMF Working Paper no. WP/06/189. Washington, DC: International Monetary Fund.

Rubery, J. (1994) 'The British production regime: a societal-specific system?', *Economy and Society*, 23(3), pp. 355–73.

Ruggie, J. (1982) 'International regimes, transactions, and change: embedded liberalism in the postwar economic order', *International Organization*, 36(2).

Rugman, A. M. (2000) *The End of Globalization*. London: Random House.

Rugman, A. M. (2005a) *The Regional Multinationals*. Cambridge: Cambridge University Press.

Rugman, A. M. (2005b) 'Regional multinationals and the myth of globalization', paper given at the CSGR annual conference, Warwick University, 26–8 October.

Rugman, A. M. (2008) 'Regional multinationals and the myth of globalization', in A. W. Cooper, C. W. Hughes and P. de Lombaerde (eds), *Regionalisation and Global Governance: The Taming of Globalisation?* London: Routledge.

Rugman, A. M., and Girod, S. (2003) 'Retail multinationals and globalization: the evidence is regional', *European Journal of Management*, 21(1), pp. 24–37.

Rugman, A. M., and Verbeke, A. (2004a) 'A perspective on regional and global strategies of multinational enterprises', *Journal of International Business Studies*, 35, pp. 3–18.

Rugman, A. M., and Verbeke, A. (2004b) 'Regional transnationals and triad strategy', *Transnational Corporations*, 14(3), pp. 1–20.

Sachs, J., and Woo, W. T. (1994) 'Structural factors in the economic reforms of China, Eastern Europe, and the Former Soviet Union', *Economic Policy*, no. 18.

Sachs, J. D., and Shatz, H. J. (1994) 'Trade and jobs in US manufacturing', *Brookings Papers on Economic Activity*, no. 1, pp. 1–84.

Sakakibara, E., and Yamakawa, S. (2004) *Regional Integration in East Asia: Challenges and Opportunities, Parts I and II*. Washington, DC: World Bank.

Sala-i-Martin, X. (2002) *The Disturbing 'Rise' of Global Income Inequality*, NBER Working Paper no. 8904. Cambridge, MA: National Bureau of Economic Research.

Sassen, S. (ed.) (2002) *Global Networks, Linked Cities*. London: Routledge.

Sassen, S. (2006) *Territory, Rights and Authority*. Princeton, NJ: Princeton University Press.

Scholte, J. A. (2005) *Globalization: A Critical Introduction*. 2nd edn, Basingstoke: Macmillan.

Schott, J. J. (2005) *Does the FTAA Have a Future?* Washington, DC: Institute for International Economics; http://www.petersoninstitute.org/publications/papers/schott1105/pdf.

Schulmeister, S. (2000) 'Globalization without global money: the double role of the dollar as national currency and world currency', *Journal of Post Keynesian Economics*, 22(3), pp. 365–95.

Segal, A. (1993) *An Atlas of International Migration*. London: Hans Zell.

Sell, S. K. (2003) *Private Power, Public Law: The Globalization of Intellectual Property Rights*. Cambridge: Cambridge University Press.

Serow, W. J. et al. (eds) (1990) *Handbook on International Migration*. New York: Greenwood Press.

Siddiqi, M. (2000) 'A single currency for West Africa?', *African Business*, no. 257 (September), pp. 16–17.

Sinclair, T. J. (2001) 'The infrastructure of global governance: quasi-regulatory mechanisms and the new global finance', *Global Governance*, 7, pp. 441–51.

Slaughter, A.-M. (2004) *A New World Order*. Princeton, NJ: Princeton University Press.

Solow, R. M. (2000) *Growth Theory: An Exposition*. Oxford: Oxford University Press.

Soskice, D. (1991) 'The institutional infrastructure for international competitiveness: a comparative analysis of the UK and Germany', in A. B. Atkinson and R. Brunetta (eds), *Economics for the New Europe*. New York: Macmillan.

Soskice, D. (1997) 'German technology policy, innovation, and national institutional frameworks', *Industry and Innovation*, 4(1), pp. 75–96.

Spar, D. L. (1997) 'Lawyers abroad: the internationalization of legal practice', *California Management Review*, 37(3), pp. 8–28.

Spivak, G. C. (2003) *Death of a Discipline*. New York: Columbia University Press.

Standage, T. (1998) *The Victorian Internet: The Remarkable Story of the Telegraph and the Nineteenth Century's Online Pioneers*. London: Weidenfeld & Nicolson.

Steffek, J. (2006) *Embedded Liberalism and its Critics*. London: Palgrave Macmillan.

Steil, B., and Litan, R. (2006) *Financial Statecraft*. New Haven, CT: Yale University Press.

Stein, H. (2008) 'Balance of payments', *The Concise Encyclopaedia of Economics*, http://www.econlib.org/library/Enc/BalanceofPayments.html.

Storper, M. (1995) 'The resurgence of regional economies, ten years later: the region as a nexus of untraded interdependencies', *European Urban and Regional Studies*, 2(3), pp. 191–221.

Storper, M., and Salais, R. (1997) *Worlds of Production: The Action Frameworks of the Economy*. Cambridge, MA: Harvard University Press.

Strange, S. (1998) *States and Markets*. London: Pinter.

Su, T. (2002) 'Myth and mystery of globalization: world trade networks in 1928, 1938, 1960 and 1999', *Fernand Braudel Center Review*, 25, pp. 351–92.

Su, T. (2005) *Globalization and Trade: World Trade Networks 1900–2000*. London: Routledge.

Summers, L. (2006) 'Reflections on global account imbalances and emerging markets reserve accumulation', http://president.harvard.edu/speeches/2006/0324_rbi.html.

Swiss Federal Institute of Technology (2007) *KOF Index of Globalization*. Zurich.

Taylor, A. M., and Williamson, J. G. (1997) 'Convergence in the age of mass migration', *European Review of Economic History*, 1, pp. 27–63.

Taylor, P. J. (2003) *World City Network: A Global Urban Analysis*. London: Routledge.

Teubner, G. (ed.) (1997) *Global Law without a State*. Aldershot: Dartmouth.

Thirkell-White, B. (2005) *The IMF and the Politics of Financial Globalization*. London: Palgrave.

Thompson, G. F. (1987) 'The supply side and industrial policy', in G. Thompson, V. Brown and R. Levacic (eds), *Managing the UK Economy*. Cambridge: Polity.

Thompson, G. F. (1992) 'Economic autonomy and the advanced industrial state', in T. McGrew and P. Lewis (eds), *Global Politics*. Cambridge: Polity.

Thompson, G. F. (1993) *The Economic Emergence of a New Europe? The Political Economy of Cooperation and Competition in the 1990s.* Cheltenham: Edward Elgar.

Thompson, G. F. (1997) 'What kinds of national policies? "Globalization" and the possibilities for domestic economic policy', *Internationale Politik und Gesellschaft*, no. 2, pp. 161–72.

Thompson, G. F. (1998) *Economic Dynamism in the Asia-Pacific.* London: Routledge.

Thompson, G. F. (2002) 'Perspectives on governing globalization', in A. H. Qureshi (ed.), *Perspectives in International Law.* The Hague: Kluwer Law International, pp. 31–43.

Thompson, G. F. (2003) *Between Hierarchies and Markets: The Logic and Limits of Network Forms of Organisation.* Oxford: Oxford University Press.

Thompson, G. F. (2004a) 'The US economy in the 1990s: the "new economy" assessed', in J. Perraton and B. Clift (eds), *Where Are National Capitalisms Now?* Basingstoke: Macmillan.

Thompson, G. F. (2004b) 'Is all the world a complex network?', *Economy and Society*, 33(3).

Thompson, G. F. (2004c) 'Getting to know the knowledge economy: ICTs, networks and governance', *Economy and Society*, 33(4), pp. 562–8.

Thompson, G. F. (2005) 'Is the future "regional" for global standards?', *Environment and Planning A*, 37(11), pp. 2053–71.

Thompson, G. F. (2006) 'Global inequality, the "great divergence" and regional growth', in D. Held (ed.), *Global Inequality Today.* Cambridge: Polity.

Thompson, G. F. (2007) 'Religious fundamentalisms, territories and globalization', *Economy and Society*, 36(1), pp. 19–50.

Thomson, J. E. (1994) *Mercenaries, Pirates, and Sovereigns: State-Building and Extraterritorial Violence in Early Modern Europe.* Princeton, NJ: Princeton University Press.

Thrift, N. (2000) 'Pandora's box? Cultural geographies of economics', in G. L. Clark, M. S. Gertler and M. P. Feldman (eds), *Oxford Handbook of Economic Geography.* Oxford: Oxford University Press, pp. 689–704.

Tiberi-Vipraio, P. (1996) 'From local to global networking: the restructuring of Italian industrial districts', *Journal of Industry Studies*, 3(2), pp. 135–51.

Timmer, M., Ypma, G., and van Ark, B. (2003) *IT in the European Union: Driving Productivity Divergence?*, Research Memorandum GD-67, Groningen Growth and Development Centre, University of Groningen.

Todd, E. (2003) *After the Empire.* New York: Columbia University Press.

de la Torre, A., Yeyati, E. L., and Schmukler, S. L. (2002) *Financial Globalization: Unequal Blessings*, Policy Research Working Paper no. 2903. Washington, DC: World Bank.

Trachtman, J. P. (1996) 'The theory of the firm and the theory of international economic organization: towards comparative institutional analysis', *Northwestern Journal of International Law and Business*, 17, pp. 470–510.

Tsing, A. L. (2005) *Friction: An Ethnography of Global Connections.* Princeton, NJ: Princeton University Press.

Turner, P. (1991) *Capital Flows in the 1980s: A Survey of Major Trends*, BIS Economic Papers no. 30. Geneva: Bank for International Settlements.

Twomey, M. J. (2000) *A Century of Foreign Investment in the Third World*. London: Routledge.

Tyson, L. (1991) 'They are not us: why American ownership still matters', *American Prospect*, Winter, pp. 37–49.

UNCTAD (1997) *World Investment Report 1997: Transnational Corporations, Market Structure and Competition Policy*. New York: United Nations.

UNCTAD (2001) *E-Commerce and Development Report 2001*. New York: United Nations Conference on Trade and Development.

UNCTAD (2005) *World Investment Report 2005: TNCs and the Internationalization of R&D*. Geneva and New York: United Nations Conference on Trade and Development.

UNCTAD (2006) *World Investment Report 2006: FDI from Developing and Transition Economies: Implications for Development*. New York: United Nations.

United Nations (2001) *Human Development Report 2001: Making Technologies Work for Human Development*. New York: United Nations.

US Council of Economic Advisors (2002) *Economic Report to the President 2002*. Washington, DC: US Government Printing Office.

Venables, A. J. (2002) 'Geography and international inequalities: the impact of new technologies', *Journal of Industry, Competition and Trade*, 1(2), pp. 135–59.

Verón, N. (2006) 'Farewell national champions', *Bruegel Policy Brief*, no. 4; www.bruegel.org/Public/Publication_detail.php?ID=1169&publicationID=1260.

Von Tunzelmann, G. N. (1995) *Technology and Industrial Progress*. Cheltenham: Edward Elgar.

Wade, R. (2007) 'A new global financial architecture?', *New Left Review*, 2nd series, no. 46 (July/August).

Wadhwani, S. B. (2001) 'Do we have a new economy?', *Bank of England Quarterly Bulletin*, 41 (Winter), pp. 485–510.

Walker, D. M. (2007) 'US financial condition and fiscal future briefing', paper given to the American Accounting Association, Chicago, 7 August, GAO-06-1189CG.

Wallerstein, I. (2004) *World-Systems Analysis: An Introduction*. Durham, NC: Duke University Press.

Walter, A. (2008) *Governing Finance: East Asia's Adoption of International Standards*. Ithaca, NY: Cornell University Press.

Ward, T., and Storrie, D. (2007) *ERM Report 2007 – Restructuring and Employment in the EU: The Impact of Globalisation*. Luxembourg: European Foundation for the Improvement of Working and Living Conditions; www.eurofound.europa.eu/publications/htmlfiles/ef0768.htm.

Wasserman, S., and Faust, K. (1994) *Social Network Analysis: Methods and Applications*. Cambridge: Cambridge University Press.

Wellman, B., and Haythornthwaite, C. (eds) (2002) *The Internet in Everyday Life*. Oxford: Blackwell.

White, M. J. (2002) 'Sovereigns in distress: do they need bankruptcy?', *Brookings Papers on Economic Activity*, no. 1, pp. 287–319.

Whitley, R. (1992a) *Business Systems in East Asia: Firms, Markets and Societies*. London: Sage.

Whitley, R. (ed.) (1992b) *European Business Systems: Firms and Markets in their National Contexts*. London: Sage.

Whitley, R., and Kristensen, P. H. (eds) (1996) *The Changing European Firm: Limits to Convergence*. London: Routledge.

Whitley, R., and Kristensen, P. H. (eds) (1997) *Governance at Work: The Social Regulation of Economic Relations*. Oxford: Oxford University Press.

Wilkinson, F. (1983) 'Productive systems', *Cambridge Journal of Economics*, 7(3–4), pp. 413–30.

Winters, A., and Yusuf, S. (2006) 'Introduction', in A. Winters and S. Yusuf (eds), *Dancing with Giants: China, India, and the Global Economy*. Washington, DC: World Bank, Institute of Policy Studies.

Wise, R., and Morrison, D. (2000) 'Beyond the exchange: the future of B2B', *Harvard Business Review*, November–December, pp. 88–96.

Wolf, M. (2002) 'Countries still rule the world', *Financial Times*, 6 February.

Wolf, M. (2004) *Why Globalization Works*. New Haven, CT: Yale University Press.

Wong, P.-K. (1997) 'Creation of a regional hub for flexible production: the case of the hard disk drive industry in Singapore', *Industry and Innovation*, 4(2), pp. 183–205.

Wood, A. (1994) *North–South Trade, Employment and Inequality: Changing Fortunes in a Skill-Driven World*. Oxford: Oxford University Press.

Wood, A. (1995) 'How trade hurt unskilled workers', *Journal of Economic Perspectives*, 9(3), pp. 57–80.

World Bank (1997) 'Globalization and international adjustment', *World Economic Outlook* (May).

World Bank (2002) *World Development Indicators 2002*. Washington, DC: World Bank.

World Bank (2005) *Global Economic Prospects: Trade, Regionalism and Development*. Washington, DC: World Bank.

World Bank (2006) *World Development Report*. Oxford: Oxford University Press.

World Bank (2007) *World Development Report 2007: Development and the Next Generation*. Washington, DC: World Bank.

World Economic Forum (2007) *The Global Competitiveness Report 2007–2008*. Geneva: World Economic Forum.

Wray, L. R. (2006) *Can Basel II Enhance Financial Stability? A Pessimistic View*, Public Policy Brief no. 84. Annandale-on-Hudson, NY: Levy Economics Institute, Bard College.

WTO (1998) *Annual Report 1998*. Geneva: World Trade Organization.

WTO (2000) *Annual Report 2000*, Vol. 2. Geneva: World Trade Organization.

WTO (2001) *International Trade Statistics*. Geneva: World Trade Organization.

WTO (2005) *International Trade Statistics*. Geneva: World Trade Organization.

Yoshitomi, M. (1996) 'On the changing international competitiveness of Japanese manufacturing since 1985', *Oxford Review of Economic Policy*, 12(3), pp. 61–73.

Young, A. (2000) *The Razor's Edge: Distortions and Incremental Reform in the People's Republic of China*, NBER Discussion Paper no. 7828. Cambridge, MA: National Bureau of Economic Research.

Young, O. (1997) 'Rights, rules and resources in world affairs', in Young (ed.), *Global Governance*. Cambridge, MA: MIT Press.

Yusuf, S., Nabeshima, K., and Perkins, D. (2006) 'China and India reshape global industrial geography', in A. Winters and S. Yusuf (eds), *Dancing with Giants*. Washington, DC: World Bank, Institute of Policy Studies.

Zevin, R. (1992) 'Are world financial markets more open? If so, why and with what effects?', in T. Banuri and J. B. Schor (eds), *Financial Openness and National Autonomy*. Oxford: Clarendon Press.

# Index

Page numbers followed by 't' refer to a table; those followed by 'f' refer to a figure.